THE PSALMS AS CHRISTIAN PRAISE

The Psalms as Christian Praise

A Historical Commentary

Bruce K. Waltke and James M. Houston

WILLIAM B. EERDMANS PUBLISHING COMPANY

GRAND RAPIDS, MICHIGAN

Wm. B. Eerdmans Publishing Co.
4035 Park East Court SE, Grand Rapids, Michigan 49546
www.eerdmans.com

25 24 23 22 21 20 19   1 2 3 4 5 6 7

ISBN 978-0-8028-7702-4

Library of Congress Cataloging-in-Publication Data

Names: Waltke, Bruce K., author.
Title: The Psalms as Christian praise : a historical commentary / Bruce K. Waltke and
    James M. Houston.
Description: Grand Rapids : Eerdmans Publishing Co., 2019. | Includes bibliographi-
    cal references and index. |
Summary: "Completes a trilogy of exegetical volumes on the Psalms, following up on
    The Psalms as Christian Worship and The Psalms as Christian Lament. Examines
    twelve praise psalms, each including a translation, commentary, and how the
    psalm was interpreted in the Christian tradition. Intended especially for preach-
    ers and students of Psalms"—Provided by publisher.
Identifiers: LCCN 2019022635 | ISBN 9780802877024 (trade paperback)
Subjects: LCSH: Praise—Biblical teaching. | Bible. Psalms—Criticism,
    interpretation, etc.
Classification: LCC BS1199.P67 W38 2019 | DDC 223/.206—dc23
LC record available at https://lccn.loc.gov/2019022635

CONTENTS

Contents

Contents

PREFACE

The Psalms are part of the hymnbook of the Lord Jesus Christ. As a child, brought up in a Jewish home, he recited and learned the Book of Psalms. But as an adult, he uniquely makes the sevenfold claim "*I AM*" which is recorded in John's gospel. His use of "*I AM*" for himself makes him the object of praise in the Psalms for Christians. So with reference to Christ, Christians read the psalms in two ways. They join him as the son of David in petitioning and praising God, and they petition and praise him as the Son of God.

In our first commentary, we focused on Christian worship, then in our second commentary on Christian lament, and now, thirdly, we are exploring the depths of Christian praise. The most profound level of praise is that creation itself was brought into being to give praise to the Creator. Anyone familiar with art and engineering marvels at the Creator of heavens and earth. More than that, the Creator brought the earth-disc into existence by triumphing over the inexplicable chaotic abyss, and gave it to humankind as a breathtaking gift, a place to live and have their being. The creation of the earth-disc was the first of *I AM*'s many saving acts. He created humankind to reflect upon his triumph and his gift to them, and to praise him.

Like a temple built for worship and praise, the earth-disc is an amphitheater for praise. And the earth-disc is the stage in unfathomable space where God through Christ and his church triumphs over Satan, sin, and death, and so gives meaning to humankind's existence. God gave his people the voice of the psalmist as a vehicle to express their praise of him as Creator and Lord of history.

Praise is the essence of the Psalter, but since so many psalms are entirely songs of praise, we have mostly narrowed the focus to a subspecies of praise psalms: those that proclaim "*I AM* reigns." This proclamation is heard in Psalms 47:8[9] ("God reigns"); 93:1; 96:10; 97:1; and 99:1. Aside from Psalm 47, that proclamation is heard in the context of Book IV of the Psalter (Psalms 90–106). The theme of God's kingship is clearly heard also in other psalms of Book IV.

The pivot and nutshell of Psalm 92, "You are on high forever, *I AM*" (v. 8[9]) sounds the theme's first note. Psalm 95:3 entitles *I AM* as "the great King," and Psalm 98 celebrates him as the Divine Warrior. Psalm 100, which, according to David Howard, functions as an inclusio with Psalm 95, calls upon all the earth to praise him.[1] The theme is picked up in the climax of Psalm 103:19: "*I AM* has set up his throne in heaven, and his kingdom rules over the whole [universe]." The most famous psalm acclaiming him as Creator is the exquisite Psalm 104, and Psalm 103 is one of the most cherished psalms that praise him as Savior. So our focus is on Book IV of the Psalter (Psalms 90–106); namely, Psalms 90–100—aside from the lament Psalm 94—and Psalms 103–104.

Before hearing the inspired Voice of the Psalmist and the believing Voice of the Church in response, we introduce the selected corpus by reflecting on praise, attempting to answer such as questions as "Why praise God?" and "How to praise him?" In light of his untarnished holiness, we are deeply conscious of our unclean lips, yet fully persuaded that the death of Christ and purging Spirit are the double cure to save from wrath and make us pure.

Our aim in all three commentaries on the Psalms is to edify the Church by hearing both the Voice of the Psalmist through the careful exegesis of the selected corpus and by hearing the Voice of the Church in response. By "edify" we mean to add substance to faith, ardor to virtue, conviction to confession; and that the Church be nerved to fidelity, especially in this time of persecution in many parts of the world and of apostasy in the West.

We introduced ourselves in the Prologue to *The Psalms as Christian Worship*. Bruce Waltke (Professor Emeritus of Biblical Studies, Regent College) contributes "The Voice of the Psalmist" and the "Conclusions." James Houston (Professor Emeritus of Spiritual Theology, Regent College) contributes "The Voice of the Church in Response." In the first two volumes we first presented the Voice of the Church and then the Voice of the Psalmist. We did so because in the history of interpretation Bruce's exegesis is informed by the latest advances in biblical hermeneutics. Here we reversed the order to a more natural chronological sequence, hearing first the inspired Voice of the Psalmist and then the believing Voice of the Church in response. For a fuller understanding of these two voices, see the Prologue to *The Psalms as Christian Worship*.

We thank Eerdmans Publishing for giving us a voice, and we are especially grateful to Samuel Kelly and Andrew Knapp for their superb editing to help us speak more clearly.

1. David M. Howard, Jr., *The Structure of Psalms 93–100*, BJSUCSD 5 (Winona Lake, IN: Eisenbrauns, 1997), 176.

CHAPTER 1

The Psalms as Christian Praise

In the Preface we explain why we selected the psalms in Book IV of the Psalter to hear the voices of the inspired psalmist and of the church in response. To help us introduce this corpus, we rather flippantly employ Rudyard Kipling's six honest serving-men: "I keep six honest serving-men/ (They taught me all I knew);/ Their names are What and Why and When/ And How and Where and Who."

I. What: The Object of Praise, *I AM*

The Psalter petitions and praises Israel's living God, YHWH—traditionally "the LORD" and in this volume rendered "*I AM*." Psalm 99 has *I AM* as its first and last word, the alpha and the omega. God's name occurs seven times in that psalm, and independent pronouns (not required in Hebrew) for *I AM* also occur seven times. In Scripture, the number seven symbolizes divine attributes and works (cf. Josh. 6:4).

A. Reflections on the Progressive Revelation of God

God progressively reveals himself to Israel, his adopted family, today identified as the church. When God called Moses to lead his people out of Egypt to the land that he promised the patriarchs, he patiently revealed his name. Names in the Bible commonly involve wordplay (association of a proper name with a similar-sounding word). Wordplay in the Pentateuch, according to Austin Surls, has four possible functions: commemoration (e.g. Cain, Gen. 4:1), anticipation (e.g., Noah, Gen. 5:29), description (e.g., Eve, Gen. 3:20) and renaming (e.g., Abraham, Gen. 17:5).[1] The parallelism of Exodus 3:14 and 3:15 implies that

---

1. Austin Surls, *Making Sense of the Divine Name in Exodus*, BBRSup 17 (Winona Lake, IN: Eisenbrauns, 2017), 28. "Pentateuchal naming wordplay" means "the utter-

God explains his personal name YHWH (Exod. 3:15) by his sentence name: "I AM WHO I AM" or "I WILL BE WHO I WILL BE" (Exod. 3:13–14). Presumably, then, his name is descriptive ("He is") or anticipatory ("He will be"). Janet Soskice has pointed out the Septuagint translated the sentence name by "I am the Being," understanding "the metaphysical ultimacy of the Tetragrammaton of God as 'Being Itself.' "[2] Her interpretation partially supports the traditional meaning "I AM WHO I AM." Thus his name speaks of his eternal, unchanging Being. Israel's God is an aseity; he is not a derivative of someone or something.

Austin Surls recently argued on the basis of Hebrew syntax that the sentence name means "I WILL BE WHO I WILL BE," signifying anticipation—the progressive revelation of himself, not a description of his being.[3] Thus Israel learned for the first time through *I AM*'s plagues on Pharaoh that the name signified his awesome power (see Exod. 6:1–4); and Israel learned through the Golden Calf incident of his amazing grace (Exod. 34:6; see Ps. 103:6–7). The more traditional interpretation, however, in addition to communicating his unchanging Being, also provokes the notion that he will progressively reveal who he is. Climactically, *I AM* revealed himself in his Son, the Lord Jesus Christ, and the Holy Spirit, who convinces the world of Truth (John 4:24).

In the New Testament, *I AM* fully reveals himself as a Trinity: an ontological Trinity of three persons—Father, Son, and Holy Spirit—and an economic Trinity with each person having a unique function.[4] Today, the Father wants to be known by the name of his Son, the Lord Jesus Christ. And so his church prays in the Son's name to bring glory to the Father (John 14:13) and the apostles preached in his name (Acts 16:31). Paul taught, "Everyone who calls on the name of the Lord [Jesus] will be saved" (Rom. 10:13, cf. v. 9), a quotation from Joel 2:32[3:5]: "Everyone who calls on the name of *I AM* will be saved." The apostle admonished the church: "Let *the message of Christ* dwell among you richly as you teach and admonish one another with all wisdom through

---

ance of a character (or a comment by the narrator) who names a person or place and explains *immediately* and *explicitly* why he or she chose such a name."

2. Janet Martin Soskice, "The Gift of the Name: Moses and the Burning Bush," in *Silence and the Word: Negative Theology and Theamation*, ed. Oliver Davies and Denys Turner (Cambridge: Cambridge University Press, 2007), 70ff.

3. Surls, *Making Sense of the Divine Name in Exodus*, 53, 57, 61.

4. The Trinity is like a C-major triadic chord: It consists of three notes of the same substance, which function differently and together are one, a unity necessary to exist. Some of God's attributes, such as love, demand more than one person to be meaningful.

psalms, hymns, and songs from the Spirit, singing to God with gratitude in your hearts" (Col. 3:16, emphasis mine).

Providentially, the rabbis in the period of the Second Temple considered the Tetragrammaton too sacred to be pronounced and used synonyms for it, such as *Adonai* ("Lord") and *HaShem* ("The Name"). As a result, the original pronunciation of YHWH was lost. We say "providentially," because the change from worshiping with the personal name of YHWH to worshiping with the personal name of Jesus Christ would otherwise have been too abrupt. The title, "the Lord," however, could readily be applied to both the Father and the Son.

In his scholarly history of the Tetragrammaton, Robert J. Williamson has shown how the understanding of Jesus as "*I AM*" is first expressed by Justin Martyr and then the Alexandrines, and so to Augustine of Hippo.[5] Augustine as a worldly rhetorician had profoundly misused the name of God. But after his radical conversion, as he narrates in his *Confessions* and later develops in his commentaries on the Psalms, the praise of God's name continued to change him for the rest of his life. His opening lines of the *Confessions* voice all our need of praise to *I AM*: "Man, a little piece of your creations, desires to praise you, a human being 'bearing his mortality with him' (2 Cor. 4:10), carrying with him the witness of his sin and the witness that you 'resist the proud' (1 Pet. 5:5). Nevertheless, to praise you is the desire of man, a little piece of your creation. . . . Have mercy so that I may find words."[6]

"Finding words" was no problem for a rhetorician, but finding "the right words" of divine praise was an epistemological quandary for Augustine. For how could he search for God if he did not yet know who or what he was searching for? How could he praise God if he did not know how to call upon him? How could he praise God if God is beyond all knowing, or name him without misnaming him? Like Moses, Augustine realized that it must first be God who called him, even though he was enjoined to call upon God—"speak to me so that I may hear."[7] But such a prayer is already a gift of God, a gift of faith, a gift of speech. We too, as we take up this gifted task of praise, join in Augustine's prayer: "My faith, Lord, calls upon you. It is your gift to me. You breathed it into me by the humanity of your Son, by the ministry of your

5. Robert J. Williamson, *Tetragrammaton: Western Christians and the Hebrew Name of God* (Leiden: Brill, 2015) 136–38.

6. Augustine, *Confessions* 1.1, 5, trans. by Henry Chadwick (Oxford: Oxford University Press, 1992), 1, 5.

7. Augustine, *Confessions* 1.5 (Chadwick, 5).

preachers."[8] As Janet Martin Soskice so beautifully concludes: "This speaking of God, made possible because God first speaks to us, opens for us not only the possibility of praise but of our true sociality, our true and truthful use of the shared possession that is speech."[9]

B. Reflections on Kingship

It is fitting that a commentary focusing on the theme "*I AM* is King" elucidate the notion of kingship.

A king is a male ruler, usually among competitors, of a major territorial unit such as a city or a nation. In the biblical world, kings were invested with supreme authority by virtue of their ability to lead, especially in *war* and in *the administration of justice*.[10] Also, the king is *a builder*: of temples (1 Kings 6–8),[11] palaces (7:1–8) and even cities (12:25).[12] Psalm 93 praises the divine King as a warrior, judge, and builder, but it intersects and magnifies these qualities. Indeed, as a warrior he is mightier even than the wild fury of raging seas (vv. 3–4); as a judge, he even decrees laws (v. 5); and as a builder, he established the earth-disc so firmly that it cannot be toppled (v. 1). Indeed, as will be argued in our chapter on Psalm 98, the psalms that proclaim "*I AM* is King" or praise him as such are "Divine Warrior victory songs" (see pp. 216–17).

A king's ability to lead depends on his noble qualities: strength, justice, majesty, and longevity (cf. Isa. 11:2–5; Ps. 45:3[4]).[13] *I AM* possesses these virtues in an incomparable way. He may be compared to a human king, but no human king compares to him (cf. Jer. 10:6). Psalm 93 lauds both his majesty, which is redefined as strength (vv. 1, 3–4) and justice (v. 5). As for longevity, he is from the "eternal" past (v. 2) to "endless days" (v. 5).

---

8. Augustine, *Confessions* 1.1 (Chadwick, 1).

9. Soskice, "The Gift of the Name," 75.

10. Marc Zvi Brettler, *God Is King: Understanding an Israelite Metaphor*, JSOTSup 76 (Sheffield: JSOT Press, 1989), 31, 109–16.

11. Arvid Kapelrud, "Temple Building: A Task of Gods and Kings," *Or* 32 (1963): 56–62.

12. Brettler, *God Is King*, 117–22.

13. Brettler, *God Is King*, 51–75.

C. General Praise and Grateful Praise

Praise is the essential gift of worship. Daniel Block declares: "True worship involves reverential acts of human submission and homage before the divine Sovereign in response to his gracious revelation of himself and in accord with his will."[14] Praise involves enthusiastic and joyful acclaim to God for his sublime characteristics and his saving deeds.

The Chronicler speaks in terms of two kinds of praising: "to praise" (*hallēl*) and "to give grateful praise" (*hôdôt*) (1 Chr. 16:4). The former, whose nominal derivative is *tᵉhillâ* ("praise"), is a joyful response to God's sublime essence and/or to the *magnalia Dei*—his might acts—such as the creation and the exodus. It is often called a hymn. The latter, whose nominal derivative is *tôdâ* ("grateful praise"), is the joyful response to God's saving act in particular, such as to his answering a petition. Westermann notes, "The profane use of the two verbs indicates . . . that [*hallēl*, "praise"] is the reaction to an essence, [*hôdôt*, "give grateful praise"] the response to an action or a behavior."[15] "Thanksgiving" is the impoverished traditional gloss of Hebrew *hōdâ*. Indeed, all words are "clumsy bricks." The derivative *tôdâ*, unlike English "thanksgiving," always occurs in a group, never in private, and it finds fulfillment in expressing what God has done, not in the saying of "thank you."[16] The two terms for praise, however, overlap, because God's nature expresses itself in saving acts. Moreover, "grateful praise" may also refer to the so-called peace sacrifice/offering that accompanied the words. Of the noun's thirty-two occurrences, it refers to the sacrifice thirteen times (cf. *zᵉbaḥ tôdâ*, "the sacrifice of grateful praise," Pss. 107:22; 116:17; or simply *tôdâ*, Ps. 56:12[13]; 2 Chr. 29:31).[17] So grateful praise psalms function as a libretto to accompany the grateful praise sacrifice. This interpretation finds support in Jeremiah 33:11, which speaks of "the rejoicing voices of those who bring grateful praise offerings to the house of *I AM*."

---

14. Daniel I. Block, *For the Glory of God: Recovering a Biblical Theology of Worship* (Grand Rapids: Baker Academic, 2014), 23–24.

15. C. Westermann, *TLOT*, 2:503, *ydh* Hiphil.

16. C. Westermann, *TLOT*, 2:506, *ydh* Hiphil.

17. F. Delitzsch, *Psalms*, trans. Francis Bolton, Keil and Delitzsch Commentary on the Old Testament 5 (London: T&T Clark, 1866–91; repr., Peabody, MA: Hendrickson, 1996), 635.

II. Why Praise

We are not expecting the answer "because he is good." We will come to that later. Rather, we are asking: "Why praise God at all?" Several answers come to mind and are given here without regard to their relative importance.

A. Praise Is Right and Fitting

The Christian liturgy historically prepares for the celebration of the Eucharist with this preface (or a variation thereof):

> Priest: "Let us give thanks to *I AM*, our God."
> People: "It is right to give him thanks and praise."
> Priest: "It is right, and a good and joyful thing."

The psalmist agrees: "How pleasant and fitting to praise him" (147:1).

C. S. Lewis confesses that for some years, as a young Christian, the command to praise God caused him to stumble. "We all despise the man who demands continued assurance of his own virtue," he observes. Lewis was troubled until he asked what we mean when we say an inanimate object, such as a painting, is admirable. He answered that we mean "that admiration is the correct, adequate or appropriate, response to it . . . and that if we do not admire we shall be stupid, insensible, and great losers, we shall have missed something." He likens a person who does not admire God to "the crippled lives of those who are tone deaf, have never been in love, never known true friendship, never cared for a good book, never enjoyed the feel of the morning air on the cheeks."[18]

B. Praise Is Intuitive to Humankind

Praise is what psychologically healthy humans do, just as a dog behaves in the way dogs do. C. S. Lewis also noticed, "The world rings with praise—lovers praising their mistresses, readers their favorite poet, walkers praising the countryside. . . . Just as men spontaneously praise whatever they value, so they

---

18. C. S. Lewis, *Reflections on the Psalms* (Glasgow: Fount, 1967), 77–79.

spontaneously urge us to join them in praising it."[19] Human beings are political animals and want to persuade others that what they praise is admirable and worthy of praise; and when others join them, it makes their joy even better. Lewis continued: "I think we delight to praise what we enjoy because the praise not merely expresses but completes the enjoyment. It is not out of compliment that lovers keep on telling one another how beautiful they are; the delight is incomplete till it is expressed."[20]

Lewis also notes that people differ in what they value, and what they praise tells us a lot about them. Musicians, not the deaf, praise composers; readers, not the illiterate, celebrate writers; and sports fans, which many wives are not, rave about their heroes. So also the spiritually alive, not the spiritually dead, praise God. As a person without a pulse is clinically dead, so a person without praise to God is spiritually dead. William Romaine (1714–1795), an Anglican pastor and scholar, rightly said, "Our dignity as human creatures is to glorify God." If we do not praise the One truly worthy of praise, we are, to use Lewis's words, "a faint image" of what it means to be human.[21]

But even though alive, we are prone to sleep. So the psalmist constantly stirs us up and calls us to praise. Hymns typically consist of *calls* for praise and *cause* for praise, as in: "Declare his glory among the nations . . . / For great is *I AM* and most worthy of praise" (Ps. 96:3-4). Hermann Gunkel (1864–1932), the founder of form criticism, questionably labels the call to praise "the introduction"[22] and the reason for praise "the main part."[23] But when about 70 percent of Psalm 96 is dedicated to the call to praise and 30 percent to reasons for praise, those labels seem inappropriate. The Psalter—its title in the Hebrew Bible is *Tehillim* ("Praises")—is brought to its climactic conclusion in Psalm 150 with ten versets (i.e., half-verses) that are introduced by the imperative "praise God." To these is added, "Let everything that has breath praise *I AM*" (v. 6). And the whole of the psalm is framed by *halǝlûyâh* ("Praise *I AM*"). Only verse 2 gives reasons: "his acts of power" and "his greatness." The call to praise is more than an appetizer; it is part of the entré. The repeated imperative call to praise may imply our praise is lacking or insufficient and must be stirred up.

---

19. Lewis, *Reflections on the Psalms*, 80.

20. Lewis, *Reflections on the Psalms*, 81.

21. Lewis, *Reflections on the Psalms*, 78–79.

22. H. Gunkel and J. Begrich, *Introduction to the Psalms: The Genres of the Religious Lyric of Israel*, trans. James D. Nogalski (Macon, GA: Mercer University Press, 1998), 23.

23. Gunkel and Begrich, *Introduction to the Psalms*, 29.

C. Praise Makes Us More Fully Alive

When we praise *I AM*, we become more fully alive. And so the psalmist wakes us up to be fully alive. C. S. Lewis said: "In commanding us to glorify him, God is inviting us to enjoy him."[24] Praise pours an oil of gladness on our heads, and joy lifts us to a higher level of being alive. Complaint and worries take us down a notch. "The joy of *I AM* is your strength," said the postexilic reformer Nehemiah (Neh. 8:10). Spurgeon put it this way: "To dance, like David, before the LORD, is to quicken the blood in the veins and make the pulse beat at a healthier rate."[25]

D. God's Existence Depends on Praise

We can infer the importance of praise by reflecting that if everybody ceased to praise God, God would die. If a large tree falls in a forest and nobody knows it, so far as mankind is concerned, the tree doesn't exist. To put it philosophically, the tree exists ontologically (i.e., as God knows, absolutely), but not epistemologically (i.e., as human beings know, relatively). If one generation knew of the tree but never praised or talked about it so that their children grew up ignorant of it, it could figuratively, but truthfully, be said that the tree died. The same is true of God. And of what value is anything to people if they do not know of it? But does God's epistemological existence depend on mortals' praise? Well, obviously the answer is yes in the theoretical sense as just argued, but in a practical sense the answer is no: God will not let that happen. God *chooses* Israel as his son to sing his praises, and Jesus *irresistibly calls out* his church to praise the Trinity. Peter explains: "You are a chosen people . . . that you may declare the praises of him who called you out of darkness into his wonderful light" (1 Pet. 2:9). If Jesus's disciples kept quiet, Jesus said, "the stones would cry out" his praises (Luke 19:40). The Trinity will not die epistemologically any more than the Eternal can die ontologically.

---

24. Lewis, *Reflections on the Psalms*, 82.
25. Charles Spurgeon, "The Power and Pleasure of Praise," in *The Power of Prayer in a Believer's Life*, ed. Robert Hall (Lynwood, WA: Emerald Books, 1993), 99.

E. Praise Benefits Others

When God delivered David from Abimelek, David sang: "I will glory in *I AM*; let the afflicted hear and rejoice . . . / I sought *I AM*, and he answered me; he delivered me from all my fears . . . / Taste and see that *I AM* is good; blessed is the one who takes refuge in him" (Ps. 34:2–9). Indeed, through the power of the Holy Spirit, God may use our praise to wake up the dead. In the present dispensation, no one has ever come alive to God through Jesus Christ without the agency of Christians in one way or another, and their praise is a potent enticement to conviction.

F. Praise Imposes God's Eternal Kingdom into the World

Praise, the verbal expression of sincere and deep approval and admiration of Israel's God, "dethrones and nullifies every other claimant," notes Brueggemann.[26] By exalting God's glory, worshipers align themselves with God's ways: his character and his purpose of establishing his kingdom. Brueggemann reflects: "When a community praises, it submits and reorders life. It is not only a moment of worship but it also embraces a doxological life, which is organized differently [than a self-grounded life]." By "self-grounded" Brueggemann means a "life of autonomy and self-invention, which imagines that one is self-made, need answer no one and rely on no other."[27] Praise of God separates the church from the world, is a polemic against the world, and by confessing that the Trinity alone is worthy of praise is not politically correct.

God's temple—today that is the church collectively (1 Cor. 3:16) and Christians individually (1 Cor. 6:19)—is, to use N. T. Wright's figure, "a bridgehead for God's own presence within a world that has very determinedly gone its own way." Through that temple, the Creator aims "to recreate the world from within, to set up a place within his creation where his glory will be revealed and his powerful judgements unveiled."[28] Singing the psalms creates an alternative, eternal reality that transforms this messed-up world mankind has made for itself.

26. Walter Brueggemann, "Psalm 100," *Int* 39 (1985): 66.

27. Brueggemann, "Psalm 100," 65.

28. N. T. Wright, *The Case for the Psalms: Why They Are Essential* (New York: HarperCollins, 2013), 91.

G. Praise Pleases God

Praise is a sweet savor to God: "Through Jesus, therefore, let us continually offer to God a *sacrifice of praise*—the fruit of lips that openly profess his name" (Heb. 13:15). In Noah's first recorded act after the flood, "he built an altar to *I AM* and . . . sacrificed burnt offerings on it. *I AM* smelled the pleasing aroma and said in his heart: 'Never again will I curse the ground' " (Gen. 8:20–21). Our praise, like Noah's sacrifice, is pleasing to God (Ps. 69:30–31[31–32]).

H. Praise Honors I AM

"Those who sacrifice grateful praise offerings honor me" (Ps. 50:23). There is a growing awareness among sociologists of the importance of honor and shame in all societies, however subtly they may be communicated. By honor is meant both "the assertion of worth and the acknowledgment of a person's claim to worth."[29] "Honor," says Daniel Wu, "forms a sort of social rating system that guides in the reactions with others based on one's relative place within social groupings."[30] For God's incomparable virtues and deeds, he deserves the highest place of honor in society: "He is the great King above all gods" (Ps. 95:3).

I. Praise Makes Us More like God

When a host asked me (Bruce) to lecture on a non-Christian campus, he instructed me that the first lecture must be "Why I am the way I am." As I reflected upon who I was, I realized that, aside from the physical data on my birth certificate and my genetic disposition, to a large extent I am who I am because of people I admired and praised—at least in my self-talk. We humans are imaging beings; that is to say we all imitate somebody. Children and young people admire and imitate role models whom they aspire to be like. In my case, I admired and praised my Greek professor; he shaped the way I read the Bible and inspired me to become a teacher. Gregory Beale argues in *We Become*

29. Bruce J. Malina, *The New Testament World: Insights from Cultural Anthropology* (Louisville: Westminster John Knox, 1993), 12.

30. Daniel Y. Wu, *Honor, Shame, and Guilt: Social-Scientific Approaches to the Book of Ezekiel*, BBRSup 14 (Winona Lake, IN: Eisenbrauns, 2016), 9.

What We Worship: A Biblical Theology of Idolatry that the Israel described in Isaiah 6:9–13 became incapable of hearing, seeing or understanding what was spoken to them by God or the prophets because they had become like their idols, who likewise do not hear, see or understand their own cultic worship. Beale may be over-reading that text, but he rightly says, "We resemble what we revere, either for ruin or for restoration."[31] Paul put it best: "And we all, who with unveiled faces contemplate the Lord's glory, are being transformed into his image with ever-increasing glory, which comes from the Lord, who is the Spirit" (2 Cor. 3:18).

J. Praise Fortifies the Christian's Worldview

Praise also perfects the spectacles through which Christians view the world. The lenses of those spectacles are ground by what they believe about their origins, purpose, and destiny. Many "moderns" (i.e., secularists) think their worldview is new. It is not. It is as old as the Epicureans (ca 300 BCE): they too did not fear God. Secular people *believe* that the cosmos evolved by chance; that there are no absolute truths or certain values, only relative evaluations; that the highest good is pleasure; and that the undertaker's shovel of dirt in their face or his cremating torch has the last word, with no final judgment after death. Secularism puts more faith in unintelligent chance than Christians can muster.

By contrast, the prescription for the spectacles of God's covenant people has always been "the fear of *I AM* is his due." God's people believe God created and sustains the cosmos; that he revealed how humankind should live and holds each person accountable; and that after clinical death there is a final judgment, when God sentences the guilty to eternal condemnation and rewards those who are righteous through their faith in Jesus Christ with eternal bliss with him. By singing the psalms, Christians add substance to faith, ardor to virtue, conviction to confession; they are nerved to fidelity to God in testing, and God will reward that faith.

31. G. K. Beale, *We Become What We Worship: A Biblical Theology of Idolatry* (Downers Grove, IL: InterVarsity, 2008), 16, 22.

K. God's Presence and God's Praise Enjoy a Reciprocal Relationship

We also praise God because God's presence and his people's praise enjoy a re-ciprocal relationship. Gabriele G. Braun documents this in both the Old and New Testaments.[32] On the one hand, she notes, the people's praise followed the manifestation of God's presence, as when Solomon built the First Temple (1 Kgs. 8:6–12) and when the Holy Spirit came upon the new believers in Jesus Christ: first the Jews (Acts 2:1–4) and then the Gentiles (10:44–46). On the other hand, Is-rael's praise prompted God's presence on the battlefield (2 Chr. 20) and instigated the refilling of the new believers in Jesus Christ with the Holy Spirit and other manifestations of divine presence (Acts 4:23–32). In the Chronicler's account of Solomon's dedication of the temple and *I AM*'s consecration of it, the praise of the Levites instigated the manifestations of God's presence, and his presence prompted the people's praise (2 Chr. 5–7). Psalm 22:3[4] also correlates God's presence with the people's praise. David sings, albeit in a lament: "You are holy, enthroned on the praises of Israel" (Ps. 22:3). Delitzsch explains, "The songs of praise, which resounded in Israel as the memorials of His deeds of deliverance, are like the wings of the cherubim, upon which His presence hovered in Israel."[33]

L. Praise Is a Matter of Life and Death

Finally, praise of God is not only right and fitting; it is a matter of life and death. Psalm 95 warns that God so loathed the wilderness generation for their murmuring against him and for their not praising him by faith that he silenced them in death in that harsh landscape and barred them from the promised land, the symbol of eternal peace and rest. The writer of Hebrews drives home that warning to the church (Heb. 4:12).

III. Who, Where, and When

The questions of who sang the psalms and where and when they sang them are so intertwined that the three questions are better answered together. The

---

32. Gabriele G. Braun, "The Connection Between God's Praise and God's Pres-ence" (PhD diss., The North-West University in cooperation with Greenwich School of Theology, 2017).
33. Delitzsch, *Psalms*, 196.

Psalter calls upon three assemblies to praise *I AM*: Israel (i.e., the people whom God adopted as his family), the nations, and the whole creation.

A. Israel

The default antecedent of "we/our/us" in the Psalter is the people of God who sing the Psalms. But they find themselves in four chronological temples: David and his tent, the First Temple, the Second Temple, and the church, a spiritual temple. These changing settings enrich a psalm's meaning.

1. The Question of Davidic Authorship

The superscripts of the Septuagint (LXX), the Greek translation of the Old Testament by Jewish scholars in Egypt roughly 200 years before Jesus Christ, which was used and possibly re-edited by early Christians,[34] attributes the compositions of many of the psalms in Book IV of the Psalter (91, 93–99, 101, 103, 104) to King David (c. 1040–970 BCE). But the venerable Masoretic Text (MT)—which is behind most English versions and reaches back to the time of the Babylonian exile—lacks superscripts for these psalms aside from "a psalm" in Psalm 98 and "by David" in 103, so in that tradition these psalms are mostly anonymous. Because the superscripts in the LXX differ from one another,[35] they don't seem to be merely boilerplate additions. Their origins are uncertain. Most academics do not give historical credence even to the superscripts in the MT—wrongly in our view[36]—much less to the superscripts of the LXX. But there is good external and internal textual evidence to think otherwise.[37] The collective evidence that the superscripts in the LXX are historically accurate is stronger than the isolated evidence of one superscript. However, the liturgical notice in the LXX superscript of Psalm 96, "when the house was built after the captivity," is obviously a later addition than "a song by David"; the psalm may have been used for the dedication of the Second Temple (516 BCE).

---

34. Melvin K. H. Peters, "Septuagint," *ABD* 5:1094, 1098–1100.

35. "The praise of a song, by David" (91, 93, 95); "a psalm by David" (94, 95, 98, 99, 101;); "a song by David" (96); and "by David" (97, 103, 104).

36. Bruce K. Waltke and James M. Houston with Erika Moore, *The Psalms as Christian Worship: A Historical Commentary* (Grand Rapids: Eerdmans, 2010), 86–91.

37. External textual evidence refers to the testimony of sources outside the text; internal evidence refers to indications within the text itself.

The Chronicler (c. 400 BCE) attributes Psalm 96 to David (1 Chr. 16:7–36), and that psalm has such striking similarities to Psalm 98 that David Howard suggests, "They may even have come from the same hand."[38] Many commentators, however, date these two psalms to the Second Temple period because of intertextualities with Second Isaiah (ca 550 BCE).[39] But as A. Anderson rightly comments, "This similarity could be explained in many different ways."[40] For example, is it not plausible that exilic Isaiah depends on a First Temple tradition? John Eaton rightly comments: "The question of priority was misconceived. The psalms and the lyrical prophecies [of Second Isaiah] should be seen as witnesses to different roles in the use of the poetic tradition of worship."[41] The writer of Hebrews draws on the LXX and so attributes Psalm 95 to David (Heb. 4:7). G. Henton Davies and others think Psalm 95 is preexilic (see p. 146).[42] Davies gives no reason to discredit Davidic authorship. The imagery of Psalm 93 depends on a Canaanite myth (c. 1400 BCE). Psalm 99:1 says: "*I AM* sits enthroned between the cherubim." Assuming with most scholars that cherubim are winged sphinxes (see pp. 237–38n66), cherubim images are attested in Canaan and as parts of thrones at the time of David. In the Old Testament, these composite figures are last encountered in Ezekiel (9:3; 10:1–22; 11:22).[43] They are not heard of again either in the Bible (Jer. 3:16; cf. Jer. 52:17–23 [= 2 Kgs. 25:13–17]) or in Babylonian records. Mowinckel thinks the speaker in Psalm 94 is most likely the king[44]; Israel had no king after 586

38. Howard, *The Structure of Psalms 93–100*, 178.

39. H. C. Leupold (*Exposition of the Psalms* [Columbus: Wartburg, 1959], 691) compares: 98:1b with Isa. 59:16 and 63:5, but "arm of *I AM*" is not unique to these texts; v. 2 with Isa. 52:10, but the direction of dependence is unclear; v. 3 with Isa. 63:7, but the conjunction of "remember" and "kindness" is not unique (cf. Ps. 25:6; 2 Chr. 24:22); v. 6 with Isa. 6:5, which is not Second Isaiah; and v. 8 with Isa. 55:12, but in v. 8 the currents, not the trees, clap their hands, and the question of dependence comes into play.

40. A. A. Anderson, *The Book of Psalms 73-150*, New Century Bible Commentary (Grand Rapids: Eerdmans, 1972), 691.

41. J. H. Eaton, *Psalms of the Way and the Kingdom: A Conference with the Commentators*, JSOTSup 199 (Sheffield: Sheffield Academic, 1995), 119.

42. G. Henton Davies, "Psalm 95," *ZAW* 85 (1973): 195.

43. The cherubim and God's glory vacated the temple, assuring the doom of Jerusalem, and stopped over the mountain east of the city. Their departure prefigures the glorious Son of God leaving the temple and going to the Mount of Olives, east of Jerusalem, where he laments Jerusalem's impending doom (Matt. 24:1–22).

44. Sigmund Mowinckel, *The Psalms in Israel's Worship*, trans. D. R. Ap-Thomas, vol. 1 (Nashville: Abingdon, 1967), 227.

BCE. So, if Mowinckel is right, the psalm was sung in the temple designed by David, Israel's poet laureate. Moreover, that psalm's presumed scenario neatly matches David's struggle against Saul.

If the external or internal evidence supports the LXX's historical credibility regarding authorship for Psalms 93, 94, 95, 96, 98 and 99, then its other superscripts also seem credible.

2. David's Tent and the Levites

King David pitched a tent for the ark of God, *I AM*'s throne, south of the walls of Jerusalem's old city.[45] This royal and talented poet and musician (1 Sam. 16:18) handed over his psalms to the Levites for musical accompaniment (1 Chr. 15:16). As the Levites had the technical education to offer sacrificial gifts, so also they had the musical expertise to perform the psalms as a libretto to the sacrifices. They also sang hymns and made music daily for the whole congregation; the people praised *I AM* through the Levites (1 Chr. 16).

3. The First Temple

Solomon built the First Temple on Mount Zion, north of the southern walls of Jerusalem's old city, in accordance with David's inspiration for its construction: "All this," he said to Solomon, referring to the plans for the temple, "I have in writing as a result of *I AM*'s hand on me" (1 Chr. 28:19; see vv. 10–18). Here the Levites praised *I AM* day and night (1 Chr. 9:33).

4. Exile and Second Temple: Praise in Book IV of the Psalter

The First Temple was destroyed in 587/6 BCE and the Second Temple was built in 516 BCE. Israel's historical circumstances differed radically between the First Temple period, when the psalms were composed, and the Second Temple period, when they were compiled in Book IV of the Psalter (Pss. 90–106). This book, according to the widely accepted thesis of Gerald E. Wilson, wrestles with the fall of the House of David and with the exile, lamented in Psalm 89.[46] The editor(s) of Book IV reprised Psalm 90 as its appropriate introductory psalm—"the prayer of Moses," who composed it as a psalm of hope for a

---

45. There are only three psalms that reference that tent (15:1; 27:5–6; 61:4), and they are all attributed to David.

46. Gerald Wilson, *The Editing of the Hebrew Psalter* (Chico, CA: Scholars, 1985).

blessed future after the nightmarish wilderness wanderings (see pp. 53–54). The change of temple settings from when the House of David ruled to when Persia ruled over kingless Israel radically reshapes our understanding of "*I AM* reigns." In David's day, the proclamation celebrated what was seen (see 1 Chr. 14:17; Ps. 96:3); in Book IV of the Psalter, the proclamation "*I AM* reigns" celebrates what is not seen. In the context of Book IV, *I AM* does not reign even on his own mountain. Amid rampant evil, such as the exile in Babylon and hardships under Persian rule (see Neh. 9:32), God's people unequivocally and enthusiastically confess through these psalms their confidence that God, who today wants to be known through God the Son, Jesus Christ (see p. 2), is *Pantokrator*, "Ruler of All." To praise *I AM* as Pantokrator when the Persians rule Judah demands faith "amid circumstances that would seem otherwise."[47] The extant Psalter is the songbook for the Second Temple, for the synagogues of the diaspora, and for other situations, such as the Last Supper (Matt. 26:30).[48] When Jesus sang these hymns, Rome ruled Jerusalem politically.

5. New Testament: A Prosopological, a Messianic, and a Prolepsis Reading of the Psalms

a) A Prosopological Reading

The advent of Jesus Christ occasioned an even more radical rereading of the Psalter, a prosopological hermeneutic—to wit, reading the Psalms as two voices, from two perspectives. Christians read the Psalms both as the voice of Christ and his church to the Father and as the words of the Lord and Savior, Jesus Christ, to the church. In the former perspective, David and Israel are types of Christ and his church.

47. Jerome F. D. Creach, "The Righteous and the Wicked," in *The Oxford Handbook of the Psalms*, ed. William P. Brown (Oxford: Oxford University Press, 2014), 535.

48. According to the Mishnah, the Levitical choir chanted a psalm each day of the week; they were successively Pss. 24, 48, 82, 94, 81, 93, and 92. Ps. 92 was sung at the libation of wine offering that accompanied the sacrifice of the first lamb of the Sabbath burnt offering (Num. 28:9). The origin of this custom cannot be dated with certainty. The superscript of Ps. 96 ("When the house was built after the captivity, a song by David") suggests "a song by David" may be original or added during the First Temple period, and that "when the house . . . captivity" is a later addition of the Second Temple period.

b) Jesus as Messiah

The psalmists believed that *I AM*, at the end of salvation history, will set things right. They also anticipated a Messiah (the "anointed one") who would bring it about. To the puzzled and downcast disciples on the Emmaus road, who had hoped Jesus would redeem Israel, Jesus said: " 'Everything must be fulfilled that is written about me in the Law of Moses, the Prophets, and the Psalms.' Then he opened their minds so they could understand the Scriptures. He told them, 'This is what is written: The Messiah will suffer and rise from the dead on the third day' " (Luke 24:44-46). Christians read the Psalms with unveiled hearts and see Jesus. They understand that his reign began at Pentecost and will be fully realized at his parousia (the apostles' way of referring to his second appearance).

The editors of Book IV positioned the messianic psalms 91 and 92 before the psalms that proclaim God as King (93, 95-99), probably to imply that the Messiah gives *I AM* the human face through whom he judges the world.

c) A Prolepsis Reading

Since the psalms proclaiming "*I AM* is King" represent his rule as presently universal, over all the earth (cf. 96:7; 97:7–9; 98:4–9; 99:2; 100:1), they are a prolepsis (i.e., as though already fulfilled).[49] Even at the height of David and Solomon's reigns, *I AM*'s kingship was not recognized universally. How much less so when Book IV was arranged?

In light of the inaugurated eschatology of the New Testament, these representations of *I AM*'s reign are no longer a prolepsis. Jesus began to put the pieces together for his puzzled disciples on the Emmaus road: the Messiah's suffering precedes his glory. That sequence is a cameo of church history. The Messiah, God the Son, has two advents. In the first, he came as a sacrificial Lamb; at the second, he will come as a roaring Lion. At his first advent, he refused to avenge himself or his church; at his parousia, he will take vengeance on his malefactors. This distinction can be seen clearly in our Lord's reading (Luke 4:17–21) of Isaiah 61:1–2, which says: "The Spirit of the Sovereign *I AM* is on me, because *I AM* has anointed me . . . to proclaim the year of *I AM*'s favor and the day of vengeance of our God." Our Lord identified himself as the anointed one "to proclaim the year of *I AM*'s favor" but omitted "the day

---

49. Here is an example of a prolepsis: "He was a dead man when he walked into the room."

of vengeance" (Luke 4:19). The New Testament projects his day of vengeance to the parousia.

But it must not be thought that the Lamb is not presently ruling the nations. Theologians refer to Christ's reign as "inaugurated eschatology." By "inaugurated" they refer to his present, expanding reign among nations; by "eschatology" they mean the consummation of his universal reign, when he will eliminate all evil.

B. The Nations: Why They Praise I AM

In our psalms, God's family calls upon all nations to join them in praise to their God (e.g., 100:1–2). But why should the nations praise *I AM* for saving Israel, their nemesis? God's deliverance of Israel is a double-edged sword: It looks at both victorious Israel and the defeated nations (98:1–2). Three reasons suggest themselves. First, his victory for Israel shows that he is righteous and faithful. He does what is right by his worshipers and shows unfailing love to them (98:3). Here is a God the nations can trust. Second, *I AM*'s victory for Israel shows he is greater than the nations' gods, and so *I AM* alone is worthy of their praise (96:3–4). Third, Israel's salvation fulfills the divine purpose. *I AM* chose and blessed the true Israel, who keeps faith with *I AM*, to bring his blessings on the nations—not to exclude them from his blessings. The nations bring blessings upon themselves by blessing Israel (Gen. 12:1–3). Blessing Israel entails forsaking their worthless gods and praising the living God who blesses Israel. So when the nations praise the Lord Jesus Christ, they are blessing themselves.

C. The Whole Creation

J. Clinton McCann, commenting on Psalm 96, says, "Because God rules the world, it is not sufficient to gather a congregation less than 'all the earth.' "[50] Psalm 98 calls for the praise of God in expanding horizons: from Israel (vv. 1–3) to the nations (vv. 4–6) to the whole creation (vv. 7–9). But how do the land and its animals and the sea and all that is in it shout God's praises? Though animals have a larynx, their mouths are incapable of forming words; birds have a syrinx; vegetables and minerals are mute. Additionally, only humankind, not animals, displays the image of God, and only human beings have the intellect,

50. J. Clinton McCann, Jr., *Psalms*, NIB 4 (Nashville: Abingdon, 1996), 1065.

sensibility and will to praise God. So the poet personifies the rest of creation as praising him. The whole creation, each part in its particular and peculiar being, declares his glory: the butterfly on a daisy, the triggerfish in a coral reef, the emerald in a cave, the fiery lightning, the crashing thunder, and the immense galaxies in incomprehensible space. All depend on the Creator for their existence and sustenance. He fills them, saturates them, and drenches them in his glory. The saint and poet looks at it all and hears God's glory declared through them as a shout of praise to God.

D. The Question of an Enthronement Festival

One cannot read very far in the scholarship on hymnic literature written after 1925 without encountering the notion that the songs that proclaim "*I AM* is King" were sung at a fall festival in which God was enthroned annually.[51] Hermann Gunkel identified as a distinct form "songs about YHWH's enthronement" (47, 93, 96, 97, and 99). He did so because this small collection of psalms is characterized by the words *yhwh mālāk*, which according to him means, "YHWH *has become* king."[52] (We need not waste time critiquing Gunkel's thesis that these originally royal psalms of the First Temple period were reprised as eschatological YHWH psalms in the Second Temple period because in this regard he has no significant following.) Sigmund Mowinckel, Gunkel's student, agreed with his mentor's translation, but he identified their setting as part of a creative cultic, dramatic fall festival that rehearsed Yahweh's annual accession to his throne (the ark) in the First Temple. He wrote:

> The feast is a 'holy drama', where the contents of the festal myths are presented, and thus are embodied and re-experienced as something which is actually creating what is then coming into existence. . . . It is just possible that most of the things 'taking place' were presented by means of suggestive symbols. . . . The fundamental idea itself, the epiphany of Yahweh as a victorious king, was suggested by carrying the ark in the festal procession.[53]

51. Marvin E. Tate, *Psalms 51–100*, WBC 20 (Dallas: Word, 1990), 482.

52. Gunkel and Begrich, *Introduction to the Psalms*, 66. Brettler (*God Is King*, 144) proposes: "The pausal form *mālāk* [*mālāk*, not *mālak*] . . . might have served as a self-sufficient cultic exclamation."

53. Mowinckel, *The Psalms in Israel's Worship*, 1:169–70.

With this imagined setting in hand, Mowinckel, against Gunkel's objections, thought many other psalms—about a third of the Psalter—could be fitted into the ritual enthronement of *I AM* in a New Year festival.[54] Mowinckel's imagined enthronement festival still commands a significant following.

However, almost all English versions translate *yhwh mālāk* with either "*I AM* reigns" or "*I AM* is king," not by "*I AM* has become king." Faith for Christians is living in imagination that is informed by Scripture. It makes a difference in reading the Psalter whether the believer imagines God as being annually renewed as King in an enthronement ritual or as a God who was king from the beginning, is now, and will be evermore, apart from any ritual. So let us critically appraise Mowinckel's alleged setting to rightly inform our imagination.

First, whether *yhwh mālāk* means "*I AM* has become king" or "*I AM* is king/reigns" cannot be decided philologically. A verb like *mālak* can mean either one (cf. 1 Sam. 12:14; 2 Sam. 15:10; 2 Kgs. 9:13)[55]; it can signify "a general state or a new fact."[56]

Second, it is alleged that "say among the nations, *yhwh mālāk*" (Ps. 96:10) corresponds to the proclamations *mālak 'abšālôm* ("Absalom has become [or is] king," 2 Sam. 15:10) and *mālak yēhû'* ("Jehu has become [or is] king," 2 Kgs. 9:13). But Brettler notes: "one cannot determine if 2 Sam. 15:10 definitely describes a coronation ritual."[57] More importantly, it is at the least hazardous to reconstruct an annual coronation ritual for the eternal God from the coronation of a mortal. And even more importantly, the proclamation occurs only with Absalom and Jehu, each of whom is a usurper to the throne, making it appear to be an ad hoc proclamation, not part of an enthronement ritual. Apart from the questionable interpretation of these texts, no other text that describes a coronation mentions the proclamation (1 Sam. 9:20–23; 10:1–9, 24–25; 11:15; 16:13; 2 Sam. 2:4; 5:1–3; 1 Kgs. 1:9–25, 33–45; 2 Kgs. 11:11–20; 23:30, 34; 24:17).[58]

54. Mowinckel, *The Psalms in Israel's Worship*, 1:106–92.

55. *IBHS*, §§30.2.3a; 30.5.3.

56. Brettler, *God Is King*, 144. Hans-Joachim Kraus (*Theology of the Psalms*, trans. Keith Crim [Minneapolis: Augsburg, 1979], 87) argued subjectively that the placement of the subject distinguished the two options, citing 1 Kgs. 1:11 and 18 as a textbook example. NRSV and NIV, however, translate both *mālak 'ădōniyyāhû* (1 Kgs. 1:11) and *'ădōniyyâ mālāk* (1 Kgs. 1:18) as "Adonijah has become king." More probably, placement of the subject first signifies that *I AM*, and no other, is king; so W. H. Schmidt, *Königtum Gottes in Ugarit und Israel*, 2nd ed., BZAW 80 (1966), 76.

57. Brettler, *God Is King*, 128.

58. See chart in Brettler, *God Is King*, 131.

Third, Mowinckel says: "Everything contained in the enthronement psalms . . . gives the strongest impression of belonging to the actual present."[59] He cites, "Yahweh 'comes' (98:9), 'makes himself known' (98:2), 'goes up' (47:6) in solemn procession to his palace, seats himself on his throne (93:2; 97:2; 99:1) and receives his people's acclamation as king (47:2)."[60] But his somewhat exaggerated representations may be literary fictions that are based on the historic event of bringing the ark to the temple in Jerusalem (2 Sam. 6; 1 Kgs. 8; 1 Chr. 16).[61] Christmas carols dramatically represent the birth of Christ as a present experience: "O come all ye faithful . . . to Bethlehem"; "We three kings of orient are"; "O little town of Bethlehem, how still we see thee lie." Everyone knows these carols are poetic fictions, not part of a ritual reenactment of Christ's birth. The same may be true of the representations of bringing the ark into Jerusalem.

Fourth, Mowinckel reconstructed his imagined festival from various sources: "the Babylonian Akitu Festival, the Osirus-Horus complex in Egypt, late Jewish sources, and various materials scattered throughout the Old Testament (over 40 psalms; II Sam. 6, I Kgs. 8; I Chr. 16; Neh. 8:10-12; Zech, 14[:16]; and Hos. 7:5)."[62] But the intractable fact remains, as Kidner notes, that the non-figurative literature of the Old Testament "looks back to no event that invested YHWH, like the Babylonian Marduk, with sovereignty, and makes no provision in the calendar of feasts (Leviticus 23) for an enthronement festival."[63] No mention is made of an annual enthronement festival in Samuel, Kings, Chronicles, Ezra-Nehemiah, or Esther, nor in Exodus, Leviticus, Numbers, or Deuteronomy. Second Samuel 6, 1 Kings 8, and 1 Chronicles 16 record historic events, not an annual ritual. Nehemiah 8 and Zechariah 14 also refer to historic, not annual cultic, events. Hosea alludes to the "festival of our king" but makes no reference to the enthronement of *I AM*. As for the poetic literature, even Mowinckel acknowledges, "The poets never *describe* [italics his]

59. Mowinckel, *The Psalms in Israel's Worship*, 1:111.

60. Mowinckel, *The Psalms in Israel's Worship*, 1:107.

61. Most scholars presuppose a festival procession in which Yahweh, enthroned upon the Ark of the Covenant, is brought into the sanctuary. But P. Sumpter (*The Substance of Psalm 24: An Attempt to Read Scripture after Brevard Childs* [London: Bloomsbury T&T Clark, 2015], 133), following Kraus, argues that the ritual is based on the historical event of bringing up the ark to Jerusalem, not on myth.

62. Leo Perdue, "Yahweh Is King over All the Earth," *ResQ* 17 (1974): 87.

63. Derek Kidner, *Psalms 73–150*, TOTC (Downers Grove, IL: IVP Academic, 2009), 170.

the alleged ritual."[64] Because there is no substantial evidence for the existence of such a rite in ancient Israel, Robert Alter refers to the massive literature about it as "a scholarly exercise in historical fiction."[65] Moreover, it is methodologically and theologically wrong to import what smacks of voodoo magic of pagan myths and rituals into the ethical monotheism of the Old Testament.

Fifth, and finally, in Psalm 97 *yhwh mālāk* is proclaimed in connection with *I AM*'s descent on the wings of a black, flashing cloud. Such a setting cannot be harnessed into the scholarly invention of an annual ritual of God's enthronement, though some vainly try.[66]

We conclude that believers ought not to imagine God as being annually enthroned as king. Nevertheless, pitting "*I AM* has become king" against "*I AM* is king" creates false alternatives. The Eternal is unchanging and so always has the noble qualities of a king and has never been less than Lord of all. But he first asserted his royal sovereignty when he firmly established the earth-disc on the primordial watery deep (*tᵉhôm*, Gen. 1:2). Goldingay rightly comments: "Creation involved an assertion of sovereign authority over any other powers."[67] His reign is "permanent, uninterrupted, and never in question."[68] Similarly, God had the personal name YHWH before the exodus, but he demonstrated its meaning when he destroyed Egypt (Exod. 6:2-4; 15:1, 21), compelling the mightiest political power in Israel's world to recognize him as Lord. The proclamation "*I AM* is King" dethrones all pretenders to ultimate sovereignty.

IV. How to Praise

A. Mood: Enthusiasm and Joy

After his detailed study of the Psalms, Gunkel found its "*basic mood is awe and enthusiasm*" (italics his). He confesses, however, "This mood, particularly the enthusiasm toward God, is foreign to the perception of later times, including ours." This is so, he thinks, because "all the huge predicates of divinity, which

---

64. Mowinckel, *The Psalms in Israel's Worship*, 1:111.

65. Robert Alter, *The Book of Psalms: A Translation with Commentary* (New York: Norton, 2007), 328.

66. Tate, *Psalms 51-100*, 520-21.

67. Goldingay, *Psalms*, vol. 3, BCOTWP (Grand Rapids: Baker Academic, 2008), 67.

68. Frank-Lothar Hossfeld and Erich Zenger, *Commentary on Psalms 51-100*, trans. Linda M. Maloney, Hermeneia (Minneapolis: Fortress, 2005), 449.

appear as self-evident to us. . . , were then something relatively new in Israel."[69] More probably, it is due to his dispassionate, scientific method. We too confess that our enthusiasm in praise pales in comparison to the psalmists, but our lack of enthusiasm is due to what the monks call "acedia" (i.e., spiritual sloth). Thomas Aquinas (following Gregory the Great) numbers our languor or torpor as one of the seven deadly sins: a source of many others.

Based on his study of Psalm 97:4, Claus Westermann regards the mood of joy as an essential element of praise.[70] The moods of enthusiasm and joy kiss in the verb "shout for joy" (*hārî'û*; see 100:1; 95:1, 2; 98:4–6; 100:1).

B. Poetry

The psalmist concentrates his enthusiasm, joy and thoughts in artful poetry, "a sustained rhythm . . . formally structured according to a continuously operating principle of organization."[71] Hebrew poetry has three benchmarks: terseness, concrete and imaginative images, and parallelism.

Like all poetry, Hebrew poetry is terse. Its terseness becomes visible when a poem is written on a page. Its "sharply chiseled"[72] lines leave a lot more space on a line than run-on prose. Prose is like a motion picture; poetry is like a snap-shot; its style is more like a telegraph than a news report.

Additionally, like all poetry, the Psalms are filled with vivid and evocative imagery. To contrast the transience of the wicked with the endurance of the righteous, Psalm 92 says: "the wicked flourished like plants" (v. 7) and "the righteous flourish like a palm tree" (v. 12). Poems turn ink on a page into blood, deflate windiness, replace "ho-hum" with "ah-ha," and transport us into eternity.

Hilary of Poitiers (c. 315–367) describes these Hebrew poems:

Preserved in the inner parts
Inscribed on the heart
Stamped on the memory
Treasure of this brevity to be bought by us day and night.

69. Gunkel and Begrich, *Introduction to the Psalms*, 49.

70. C. Westermann, *TLOT*, 1:372, s.v. *hll* Piel.

71. Barbara Herrnstein Smith, *Poetic Closure: A Study of How Poems End* (Chicago: University of Chicago Press, 1968), 23.

72. Leupold, *Exposition of the Psalms*, 665.

Biblical poetry, however, distinguishes itself from English poetry by parallelism. Apart from the optional prose superscription, which grounds a psalm in historical data, every verse in the Psalter has this essential characteristic. English poetry is developed from Greek and Latin poetry, which is primarily sound-based. But Hebrew poetry derives from old Canaanite poetry, which is based on semantics and philology. A verse is divided into two balanced versets[73] of thought and grammar, and this balance is called "parallelism."[74] (Unlike the semantic component, the philological component cannot be translated.) Our understanding of the relationship of these balanced/parallel versets has changed in the last half-century. From Bishop Robert Lowth's groundbreaking book, *Lectures on the Sacred Poetry of the Hebrews* (1753) to James Kugel's *The Idea of Biblical Hebrew Poetry* (1981) and Robert Alter's *The Art of Biblical Poetry* (1985), the *emphasis* was on the correspondence of the two versets; the second verset was thought to *restate* the first. T. H. Robinson wrote: "So the poet goes back to the beginning again and says the same thing once more, though he may partly or completely change the actual words to avoid monotony." This emphasis can be likened to Wordsworth's:

> The Swan on still St. Mary's Lake
> Float double, Swan and Shadow.

Since Kugel and Alter's works, however, the emphasis has been on how the second line *intensifies* the first: it supports it, backs it up, carries it further, completes it, and/or goes beyond it.[75] The new emphasis can be likened to:

> The Swan on still St. Mary's Lake
> Float double, Goose and Gander.

The contrast between prose and poetry can be readily seen in the prose and poetic accounts of Jael's killing of Sisera. The prose account records: "And

---

73. Surprisingly, no consensus has been reached regarding the nomenclature for the parts of the line or stich. They are commonly referred to as a hemi-stich, colon (pl. cola)—with the two together making a bicolon—or verset.

74. The two versets of a bicolon are symbolized by "a" and "b." Sometimes verset "a" or "b" has a parallel verset within it, making a tricolon, symbolized by "α" or "β" (e.g., vv. 7aα, 7aβ, and 7b; or vv. 7a, 7bα, and 7bβ). Occasionally both "a" and "b" contain parallels within them, making a quatrain.

75. James Kugel, *The Idea of Biblical Poetry* (New Haven: Yale University Press, 1981), 51–52.

he [Sisera] said to her [Jael], 'Please give me a little water to drink because I am thirsty.' And she opened a milk skin and gave him some to drink and she covered him" (Judg. 4:19). The poetic account records:

> "Water," he [Sisera] asked,
> > Milk she [Jael] gave;
> > In a princely bowl she offered curds (Judg. 5:25).

Note the terseness of the poetry: "And . . . thirsty" (thirteen words, seven in Hebrew) versus "Water, he asked" (three words, two in Hebrew). Note the focus and escalation from "water" to "milk" to "curds." And note the vivid and evocative imagery: "in a princely bowl."

C. Music

The verbal root of the Hebrew word *mizmôr*, traditionally glossed by "psalm," is *zmr* (Piel), "to make music." So a "psalm" is a song with musical accompaniment. The Psalms refer to a variety of musical instruments.[76] Gunkel says that the imperatives to rejoice and sing occur some 200 times in the Psalter.[77]

David was the Mozart of ancient Israel: He transformed the Mosaic ritual into opera. He designed Solomon's magnificent temple for its staging; he wrote the Psalter's songs of grateful praise as a libretto to accompany the sacrifices and its hymns to fill the temple with music day and night. Music affects our emotions (e.g., joy), it causes us to empathize with the composer, and it inspires us to action. Praise psalms unite fervency with dignity, joy with seriousness, exultation with humility, conviction with confession and ardor with virtue. They are aesthetically pleasing, emotionally stirring and motivationally powerful. "Science all but confirms that humans are hard-wired to respond to music."[78]

---

76. According to Dennis McCorkle (*The Davidic Cipher: Unlocking the Hidden Music of the Psalms* [Denver: Outskirts, 2010], xvn2), the twelve instruments mentioned in the biblical texts are "the lyre, harp [lute], melodic cymbals, *shofar* (typically made of a ram's horn), the two silver trumpets, reed-pipe, *ugav*, wooden clappers, rhythm bones, cymbal clappers, finger cymbals, and shakers."

77. Gunkel and Begrich, *Introduction to the Psalms,* 23.

78. " 'The Power of Music' to Affect the Brain," NPR, June 1, 2011, http://www.npr.org/2011/06/01/136859090/the-power-of-music-to-affect-the-brain.

In the MT, every word has, above and/or below it, an "accent" mark that adds dignity, solemnity, beauty, and clarity to the readings. These accent marks may have symbolized hand signals or musical notes.[79] The Chronicler says that various Levitical musical guilds were led "under the hands of" directors, perhaps meaning by chironomy (1 Chr. 25:2, KJV, ASV). As pictured in Egyptian iconography from as early as the third millennium BCE, directors stand in front of the musicians giving hand signals for the notes. Dennis McCorkle thinks that what we have in the MT are the score sheets for the conductor.[80]

Let us now hear the voice of the psalmist and of the church in its response.

79. Suzanne Haïk-Vantoura, *The Music of the Bible Revealed*, trans. Dennis Weber, ed. John Wheeler (North Richland Hills, TX: Bibal, 1991); J. Wheeler, "Music of the Temple" in *Archaeology and Biblical Research*, 2 (1989).

80. McCorkle, *The Davidic Cipher*, 47.

CHAPTER 2

Psalm 90: The Voice of Chastened Wisdom

PART I. VOICE OF THE PSALMIST: TRANSLATION

1 A prayer by Moses, the man of God.
   O Lord, you have been a dwelling place[1] for us
        throughout generations.
2 Before the mountains were born,
        and you brought to birth the earth and the world,
        from eternity to eternity you are God.[2]
3 You return[3] the mortal to dust;
        you say: "Return humankind."
4 Surely, a thousand years in your estimation
        is like yesterday when it is over,
        and like a watch in the night.
5 You make an end of their lives;[4] they fall into deep sleep[5];

1. LXX and a few Heb. MSS read *mʿwz* ("place of safety"/ "refuge").

2. LXX reads *ʾal* instead of *ʾēl* in v. 2 in combination with *tāšēb* in v. 3, read as a jussive = "From eternity to eternity you are. Do not turn back."

3. The short prefix conjugation (*IBHS*, §31.1h) may be due to its being as far as possible from the *athnaḥ* (GKC, 109k).

4. Or, "you sweep them away as in a flood." *Zrm* may be a homonym. According to G. R. Driver ("Some Hebrew Medical Expressions," *ZAW* 65 [1953], 259), *zrm* is cognate to an Arabic root meaning "to interrupt, to stop." *HALOT* glosses it: "to make an end of life." In this verse, however, it has traditionally been interpreted as *zrm* II Polel "to unload clouds of water accompanied by thunder" (cf. Ps. 77:17[18]).

5. Lit. "they are sleep." The predication of an abstract noun to a person signifies that the subject is totally characterized by the abstraction: e.g., "I am peace" = "I am wholly given to peace" (Ps. 120:7); "I am prayer" = "I am totally given to prayer" (Ps. 109:4).

in the morning they are like grass that is renewed.[6]

6 In the morning it blossoms and is renewed;
   in the evening, it withers and dries up.

7 Surely, we perish in your anger;
   we are terrified by your wrath.

8 You set our iniquities before you,
   our hidden sins in the light of your face.

9 All our days pass away in your fierce anger;
   we finish our years like a sigh.

10 As for the days of our years, with them are seventy years;
   or if with strength,[7] eighty years.
   And their proud achievements[8] are toilsome and futile,[9]
   for they pass away[10] quickly,[11] and we fly away.

11 Who knows the vehemence of your anger,
   and, according to the fear due you,[12] your fierce anger?

6. *HALOT* glosses *yaḥălōp* by "to fly along, to pass over, away," but BDB glosses it "to sprout anew." The sense of "change" informs all the uses of the lexeme *ḥālap*. LXX and Vulg. invest it with sense of "pass away." But since the grass of the morning is contrasted with the withered grass of the evening, the more suitable sense is with respect to the beginning of the movement, and so with grass it means "to come anew, be renewed."

7. GKC (124e) classifies *gəbûrôt* in Job 41:4, and presumably so *gəbûrōt* in Ps. 90:10, as an intensive plural—"(exceptional) strength"—but it could be an abstract plural (*IBHS*, §7.4.2a).

8. Both the text and meaning of *rohbām* are uncertain. Many emend the text to *rᵉḥābām* ("their span," so NRSV and NIV 1984) or read with help of versions *rubbām* ("multitude of them"). LXX reads "the greater part of them" (see NAB: "most of them"); Vulg., "and what is more of them"; Tg., "most of them." But MT cannot be explained away, whereas *rᵉḥābām* or *rubbām* can be readily explained as facilitating readings. The noun *rōhab* occurs only here, and its verbal equivalent occurs twice in Qal, meaning "to storm"/"to behave violently"/"to act insolently": of youth against the elder (Isa. 3:5); of the debtor against the creditor (Prov. 6:3). (The noun *rahab* refers to a mythical monster, "Surger," and "plays upon the restlessness and crashing of the sea.") The singular *rōhab* is collective.

9. K. H. Bernhardt (*TDOT*, 1:145, s.v. *ʾāwen*) comments: "Psalm 90:10 sees in *ʾaven* the ultimately vain toil of life, determined by God for man in general." This is consistent with the following clause: "for they pass away quickly."

10. The subject of masc. sg. *gāz* is *rōhab*.

11. The gloss of unique *ḥîš* as "quickly" is based on the root *ḥûš*: "to hasten, make haste."

12. *Yirʾātəkā* is usually construed as an objective genitive ("the fear of you"), an assertion of a fact; but the rhetorical question suggests it would be better glossed as a genitive of advantage ("the fear due to you," *IBHS*, §9.5.2e).

12   In numbering our days, so[13] cause [us] to know [your anger]
        that[14] we may gain wise hearts.
13   Turn back,[15] *I AM*! How long?
        And take pity[16] on[17] your servants.

13. BDB (p. 485, s.v. *kēn*) glosses *kēn* by "*so*" (usu., as has been described or commanded, with ref. to what has preceded), mostly of manner." Accordingly, the meaning is "in numbering our days, in this way teach us to know." Moreover, according to the syntax of the Masoretic accents, *kēn* ("so, thus") modifies *hôdaʿ* ("cause to know"), not *limnôt* ("to count"). In sum, the Hebrew text rules out the translation "so to number our days teach [us]" (*pace* KJV, ASV, JPS, NRSV, ESV). Also, *kēn* does not signify purpose, disqualifying the translation "teach us so that we may know" (*pace* NAB, NIV, NJB, CSB, NET). *HALOT* (1:482, s.v. *kēn* I) interprets *kēn* as an adjective (= "to know [what is] correct/right/accurate"?), but in the cited parallels, *kēn* follows the verb it modifies and is not medial (see Judg. 12:6; 21:14; 1 Sam. 23:17; cf. Amos 5:14). No English translation, to my knowledge, accurately represents the Hebrew text. The object of "to know" must be supplied from v. 11, namely "*I AM*'s anger" (see commentary).

14. Semantically, a logical consequence (so also BDB, p. 99, s.v. *bôʾ* Hiphil, §1g).

15. "Turn back from judgment" (see BDB, p. 997, s.v. *šûb*, §6f). Traditionally, "return" suggests that *I AM* has abandoned his people, but that notion does not comport well with the confession that *I AM* is the penitents' dwelling place forever. This difference in interpretation is as old as the rabbis. Avrohom Chaim Feuer (*Tehillim: A New Translation with a Commentary Anthologized from Talmudic, Midrashic and Rabbinic Sources*, trans. Avrohom Chaim Feuer in collaboration with Nosson Scherman [Brooklyn: Mesorah, 1982], 1.129) notes the difference in the rabbinic literature: "Turn back Your anger (Rashi) . . . *How long* will You abandon us? (Radak)."

16. Elsewhere *nḥm* Niphal with *ʿl* governing a personal noun means "to be consoled/comforted" (see 2 Sam. 13:39; Jer. 31:15; Ezek. 32:31), but that sense is inappropriate in Psalm 90:13. Most English versions agree with BDB (p. 637, s.v. *nḥm*, §1: "be moved to pity, have compassion") and gloss the collocation "have pity on" or the like (see "Exegesis"). Marvin E. Tate (*Psalms 51–100*, WBC 20 [Dallas: Word, 1990], 436n13b) rejects "have pity/compassion" because, following Dale Patrick ("The Translation of Job 42:6," *VT* 26 [1976]: 324–27), "when it [the verb] is used with *ʿl*, it regularly means 'to change one's mind about something planned' " (i.e., "relent"/"regret"; cf. Jer. 18:8; 26:3, 13, 19; Joel 2:13; Jonah 3:10; 4:2; Deut. 32:36). But, as noted by H.-J. Stoebe (*TLOT*, 2:738, s.v. *nḥm* Piel) that is true only when the preposition *ʿl* governs an impersonal object, usually *rāʿâ* ("Yahweh regretted/relented from the threatened disaster"). This may also be true in Ezek. 14:22, but most English versions gloss it there as "be consoled/comforted." If the object is personal, a further distinction, not noted by Stoebe, must be made: to wit, "to feel pain for oneself or for others."

17. The gloss "on" obfuscates the meaning of the Hebrew, for it appears to be a necessary addition to introduce the object of "take pity/pity someone." *HALOT* invests

14 Satisfy us in the morning with your unfailing love
    that[18] we may shout for joy and rejoice in all our days.
15 Make us rejoice according to the days you afflicted us,
    [according to] the years we saw disaster.
16 Let your deeds[19] appear[20] to your servants
    and your splendor[21] to[22] their children.
17 Let the beauty of the Lord our God rest upon us,[23]

'al with the meaning "because," but more probably it means "for the sake of" (BDB, p. 754, s.v. '*l*, §1.f.[c]; cf. Ps. 44:22[23]).

18. *Waw* with the cohortative after the imperative signifies purpose (see GKC, 108d; *IBHS*, §34.5.2b).

19. *Pō'al* is construed as a collective singular.

20. In the petition stanza and in conjunction with the initial jussive *wîhî* ("and let be," v. 17), *yērā'eh* is best construed as a non-apocopated jussive (cf. Gen. 1:9).

21. The LXX mistakenly repoints text as *hadrēk* "direct," a facilitating reading for a figure of speech. The meaning "vision/revelation/apparition" for *hādār* is widely adopted on the basis of an Ugaritic cognate. But *hādār* in numerous instances in the Hebrew Bible consistently means "splendor" and here forms an excellent parallel to "works" (see Ps. 96:9; p. 166n2).

22. *'Al* may have the same dative sense as *'el* (BDB, p. 758, s.v. '*l*, §8), though this use is found mostly in postexilic Hebrew.

23. J. D. Levenson ("A Technical Meaning for N'M in the Hebrew Bible," *VT* 35 [1985]: 61–67) hypothesizes the word here translated "beauty," *nō'am*, in Pss. 4:6–7; 16:5–6, 11; and 90:16–17 takes on a connection with "an affirmative response to an act of augury." His arguments include: a) " 'beauty' [in Ps. 27:4] . . . seems excessively abstract"; b) *hādār* means "a revelation" of some sort of deed; c) "the light of God's face" in Ps. 4:6 refers to "a theophanic fire employed as an affirmative omen"; d) an Akkadian parallel in an Old Babylonian divination text means "give a clear answer"; e) "May you establish" in the parallel in Ps. 90:17 should be rendered as "may you affirm, approve, say 'yes' to"; f) the root *n'm* in Ps. 16:5–6 occurs explicitly in association with augury; g) following a preposition, "pleasant places" in Ps. 16:11 yields no sense: "The traditional rendering [*n*e*'îmôt*] 'pleasures [in his right hand]' is 'an oddly abstract image' "; h) in 2 Sam. 23:1; Num. 24:3, 15; and Prov. 30:1, "it would seem . . . the word [*n*e*'um haggeber*] means . . . 'a person granted an affirmative omen.'" These arguments are not convincing: a) A metonymy such as "beauty" for the thing itself is common in Hebrew poetry; b) "splendor," the certain meaning of *hādār*, is semantically pertinent; c) "the light of God's face" commonly refers to God's favor, not to theophanic fire; d) the Akkadian parallel is a different word; e) *kûn* Polel normally means "establish" and makes perfectly good sense, especially after the lament that their achievements are futile; f) in Ps. 16:5, David is using figurative language, and a metonymy after a preposition is not unsensible; g) a

and the work of our hands establish for us;
and the work of our hands, establish it.[24]

Part II. Commentary

I. Introduction

Form

Psalm 90 is poetry, characterized by parallelism, terseness—poets do not footnote exceptions—and figurative language (see p. 23). Its stated specific form is "a prayer." This "chastened and sober"[25] prayer contains the five typical motifs of a lament/petition psalm:

    I.   Direct address: "O Lord," v. 1
    II. Confidence: "a dwelling place for us," v. 1
    III. Lament: for God's harsh discipline of humankind and
          of sinful Israel, vv. 3–10
    IV. Petitions for salvation: vv. 13–17
    V. Praise: vv. 14b–15

More precisely, it is, as Robert Alter says, "a collective penitential supplication."[26] So Marvin Tate plausibly postulates as its appropriate context "a worship

---

metonymy for the sum of pleasures at the exalted honor of God's right hand is not odd; h) *nᵉ'um haggeber* more probably refers simply to prophetic speech. In sum, Levenson's arguments for investing "beauty" with a technical sense are smoke and mirrors. He misunderstands or minimizes figurative language in Hebrew poetry and introduces into Old Testament theology the notion of omens by other signs than the Urim and Thummim that are housed next to the heart of the high priest.

Allowing *'al* ("upon") its normal sense, the pregnant preposition, as often occurs in Hebrew poetry, implies an elided verb of motion, such as "settle"/"rest" (see *IBHS*, §11.4d).

24. Bruce Vawter ("Postexilic Prayer and Hope," *CBQ* 37 [1975]: 460–70, esp. n. 5) wrongly says "vs 17b [is] an obvious dittography." Vv. 17a and b are saying different things (see exposition).

25. Derek Kidner, *Psalms 73–150*, TOTC (Downers Grove, IL: IVP Academic, 2009), 359.

26. Robert Alter, *The Book of Psalms: A Translation and Commentary* (New York: Norton, 2007), 318.

service of communal prayers of lament" similar to that of Joel 2:12–17 (note the use of *šwb* and *nḥm* in Joel 2:14 and Ps. 90:13).[27] But the psalm also has the characteristics of wisdom literature. The hinge on which the psalm swings from lament (11) to petitions (12) combines the prayer genre with the genre of wisdom literature. "To gain wisdom" provides the motivation "to number days" (v. 12). The lament over burdensome toil and its futility (v. 10) strikingly resembles the wisdom book of Ecclesiastes.[28] In sum, the psalm's "unmistakable stamp" of being a national song of complaint combined with the unmistakable stamp of the wisdom genre makes it, as von Rad put it, "a stranger in the Old Testament."[29]

Rhetoric and Structure

Phyllis Trible deftly defines form and rhetorical criticisms: "Whereas form criticism studies the typical and so groups literature according to its genres, rhetorical criticism studies the particular within the typical. Its guiding rubric declares that 'proper' [or appropriate] articulation of form-content yields proper [or appropriate] articulation of meaning."[30]

The psalm is framed by two of *I AM*'s titles, "Lord" and "God," and by the chronological notices of "generation to generation" and "their descendants" (vv. 1, 16). The anagram *māʿôn* ("dwelling place," v. 1) and *nōʿam* ("beauty," v. 17) may be an intentional frame. Here is an outline of the psalm's stanzas and strophes:[31]

---

27. Marvin E. Tate (*Psalms 51–100*, WBC 20 [Dallas: Word, 1990], 439) agrees with von Rad that a scribe or sage composed the psalm for the pious in postexilic communities because it is an atypical communal lament (cf. Pss. 44, 60, 74, 79, 80, 83, 106, 137): to wit, God does not hide himself; there is no complaint about national enemies nor cries of immediate distress and pleas for God to deliver. However, the prophets, of whom Moses was one, frequently pictured God as an enemy. Amos asked God to change his mind, to relent from his threatening doom (Amos 7:2). So there is good reason to think that Moses would depict God as an enemy (see Deut. 32:20–35) and ask him to relent (see Deut. 32:36–43). Like all prayers in the Bible, it is to be overheard and studied by the pious.

28.Ecclesiastes, however, unlike Psalm 90, neither attributes the trouble and toil of this life to sin nor petitions God for salvation from them.

29. Gerhard von Rad, *God's Work in Israel*, trans. John H. Marks (Nashville: Abingdon, 1980), 218.

30. Phyllis Trible, "Wrestling with Words, Limping to Light," in *Why I (Still) Believe*, ed. John Byron and Joel N. Lohr (Grand Rapids: Zondervan, 2015), 233.

31. By form and rhetorical criticism and semantics, a psalm is analyzed into stan-

Temporal catchwords unify the psalm's stanzas, strophes, and couplets: "generation to generation," "eternity to eternity," and "before" (vv. 1–2); "yesterday" and "watch in the night" (v. 4); "morning" (vv. 5, 6, 14) and "night" (v. 6); "years" (vv. 9, 10, 15) and "days" (vv. 9, 10, 12, 14, 15); and "how long" (v. 13). Konrad Schaefer notes the katabasis in the invocation and lament: from "eternity to eternity" to "a thousand years," "yesterday," "a watch in the night," and "morning" and "evening" (vv. 1–6). He also notes an anabasis in the benedictory petitions: from "morning" to "days" and "years" (vv. 14–15).[32] Terms

---

zas, strophes and units. The psalm is the house; the stanzas are its major portions, like upstairs and downstairs; strophes are its rooms; and units are parts of a room, like ceilings and floors. As is common, in Ps. 90 these divisions are quatrains, couplets (i.e., two verses or versets), apart from v. 13. The unified invocation, lament and hinge consist of seven couplets (vv. 1b–2, 3–4, 5–6, 7–8, 9–10, 10a–10b, 11–12), and the petitions for salvation consist of three strophes with two couplets (vv. 13, 14–15, 16–17).

32. Konrad Schaefer, *Psalms*, Berit Olam (Collegeville, MN: Liturgical Press, 2001), 226f.

for God's anger unify the second and third stanzas: "anger" (vv. 7a, 11), "wrath" (v. 7b), "fierce anger" (vv. 9, 11). The stanzas and strophes are also linked by the logic of Israel's covenants: sin and death (vv. 3–10), fear of *I AM* and wisdom (vv. 11–12), and repentance and restoration (vv. 13–17).

Author

Intertextual evidence supports the historical credibility of the claim that Moses composed the psalm. The psalm shares some language with Deuteronomy 32–33,[33] and as an intercessory prayer, it fits well on the lips of Moses, the great intercessor for Israel (see Exod. 32:11-13, 31-32; Num. 14:13-19; Deut. 9:25-29; Ps. 106:23; Jer. 15:1; see also Ps. 99:6). F. Delitzsch comments: "There is scarcely any written memorial of antiquity which so brilliantly justifies the testimony of tradition concerning its origin as does this Psalm."[34] But the academic consensus for over a century dates the psalm to the exilic or postexilic era.[35] Mischievously, "the consensus" subverts the evidence that supports the superscript's historical credibility by claiming that the evidence explains the origin of the alleged pseudograph (i.e., a forgery).[36] Tate argues that the term "your servants" locates the psalm in postexilic communities,[37] but he curiously overlooks the use of that term by Moses (Exod. 32:13), Solomon (1 Kgs. 8:32), and Asaph (Ps. 79:2).

But cracks are now showing in the academic consensus, though none yet dares to affirm the tradition. H.-J. Kraus characterizes the psalm as preexilic (ninth century) largely because of its resemblances to Deuteronomy 32 and the "J" story in Genesis 2–3.[38] Mitchell Dahood dates the psalm as an

33. Moses is called "the man of God" (Ps. 90:1) in the introduction to his blessing at the time of his death (Deut. 33:1). The psalm begins "you are a dwelling place," where Moses's blessing ended (Deut. 33:27 [*māʿôn* and *məʿōnâ* are a gender doublets]). *Yālad* and *ḥûl* Polel occur together in v. 2 and Deut. 32:18; *yəmôt* occurs only in v. 15 and Deut. 32:7, where also *dôr-wədôr* occurs (see v. 1).

34. F. Delitzsch, *Psalms,* trans. Francis Bolton, Keil and Delitzsch Commentary on the Old Testament 5 (London: T&T Clark, 1866–91; repr., Peabody, MA: Hendrickson, 1996), 593.

35. Gerhard von Rad, *God's Work in Israel* (Nashville: Abingdon, 1980), 212.

36. So *Zondervan TNIV Study Bible*, ed. Barker, Stek, Youngblood (Grand Rapids: Zondervan, 2006), 943.

37. Tate, *Psalms 51–100*, 437f.

38. H.-J Kraus, *Psalmen II*, BKAT 15 (Neukirchen: Erziehungsverein, 1960), 627–33.

early (ninth-century?) composition because of its archaic language.[39] Walter Brueggemann suggests it be heard as if Moses were at Pisgah (Deut. 34).[40] David Noel Freedman notes that on the occasion of the golden calf episode, Moses prayed using the same two imperatives as in verse 13: "Turn (*šûb*) from your fierce anger; relent (*wᵉhinnāḥēm*) and do not bring disaster on your people" (Exod. 32:12). He comments, "Aside from Amos, only Moses intercedes successfully with Yahweh and obtains his repentance" (see Exod. 32:14). So Freedman suggests that whoever composed Psalm 90 based it on the episode in Exodus 32 and imagined in poetic form how Moses may have spoken in those circumstances.[41] Beth L. Tanner explores the psalm's superscription in light of Exodus 32-34 and Deuteronomy 32-33 and argues the superscription was added so that the psalm would be read "intertextually with the wilderness narrative and the final prayer and blessings of Moses."[42] Gerald T. Sheppard notes its placement after Psalm 89: "Moses intercedes on behalf of Israel who has been given a divine promise that now seems to be in jeopardy."[43]

The superscript to the Targum identifies the historical setting as "when the people, the house of Israel, sinned in the wilderness." The historical context of the dying-off generation during the closing years of Moses's life aptly fits the psalm's dark tone and minor key. The exodus-wilderness generation spent their last forty years wandering around in a cemetery, a harsh wilderness, a land of scorpions and venomous snakes. For their unbelief at Kadesh Barnea they died off in natural deaths and never reached the promised land (see Psalm 95). The wilderness generation killed time in meaningless wanderings (Num. 14:33). And so do moderns with no metanarrative by which to interpret the meaning of their lives.

It may be justly urged, however, that the psalm's restriction of human life to at best eighty years (v. 10) does not comport well with Moses's and Aaron's life-spans of 120 and 123 years respectively (Deut. 34:7; Num. 33:39) or with

39. Mitchell Dahood, *Psalms II*, AB 17 (New York: Doubleday, 1968), 322.

40. Walter Brueggemann, *The Message of the Psalms*, Augsburg Old Testament Studies (Minneapolis: Augsburg, 1984), 110.

41. D. N. Freedman, "Who Asks (or Tells) God to Repent?" *BRev* 1, no. 4 (1985): 56–59.

42. Beth L. Tanner, *The Book of Psalms through the Lens of Intertextuality*, StBibLit 26 (New York: Peter Lang, 2001), 85–107, esp. 98.

43. Gerald Sheppard, "Theology and the Book of Psalms," *Int* 46 (1992): 143–55, esp. 151.

Joshua's 110 years (Josh. 24:29) and Caleb's strength at 85 years of age (Josh. 14:10). But these four are the exceptions. Deuteronomy 34:7 implies Moses was exceptional by its notation: "when he [Moses] died, his eye was not dim nor was his natural vitality diminished." If this were normal, why mention it? Caleb explained his extraordinary full strength at eighty-five years of age—forty-five years after the exodus—as due to *I AM*'s unique promise to him (Josh. 14:10). The longevity of these four great men of the exodus-wilderness generation, which merits biblical notices, actually proves the psalm's rule for the majority of Israel. Moses's epithet "man of God" calls the audience of his prayer to take their shoes off their feet; they are standing on holy ground.

The Speakers

Moses may be the author, but he prays with the dynamic of "you—we," not "you—I," confident that the eternal God has uniquely adopted Israel, "your servants" (vv. 13, 16), as his family (cf. Ps. 100:3). The speakers are chastened penitents who are firm in their faith. They belong to Joshua's generation that entered the promised land, the offspring of the wilderness generation, whom God barred from that land. By faith they invoke God as their eternal dwelling place (vv. 1–2). By faith, like Daniel (9:4–20) and Ezra (9:5–15), they confess their sin as part of corporate Israel (vv. 3–10). By faith, they petition *I AM* to enlighten them (vv. 11–12) and save them in the morning of a new age (vv. 13–17). The "we" is corporate and personal: As individuals they live seventy or eighty years (v. 10a); as a community they endure throughout generations and experience God's covenantal wrath in the hope of his covenantal promises. The relationship of the individual to the group is like leaves on a tree: Each has its own days and years, but those days and years are inseparable from the corporate whole. Today the "we" is the church being built by Jesus Christ. The church is the seed of Abraham (Gal. 3:29). The Jewish leadership said no to God's Son, and God said, "They are not my people." But at the end of history as we know it, ethnic Israel will repent and identify with Jesus Christ and his church.[44]

---

44. Bruce K. Waltke with Charles Yu, *An Old Testament Theology* (Grand Rapids: Zondervan, 2007), 321–32.

II. Exegesis

Superscript 1a

A *prayer* here means "an intercession."[45] H. P. Stähli notes that prayer has four characteristics: (a) directed toward God; (b) for Israel; (c) "usually in the face of God's wrath and punishment for sin"; and (d) the interceders "in older texts are esp. the powerful men (of God): Abraham (. . . Gen. 20:7, 17 . . .), Moses (Num. 11:2 . . . ; 21:7 ; Deut. 9:26), Samuel (1 Sam. 7:5; 12:19, 23; cf. Jer. 15:1)."[46] *By Moses* (see "Author"). *The man of God* refers to a true prophet (cf. Hab. 3:1): one who is highly respected by the faithful and is pious, devoted, godly, and charismatic.[47] Manoah's wife called the awesome angel of *I AM* who appeared to her "the man of God" (Judg. 13:6, 8). The epithet assures the faithful that God will answer this prayer, for "the prayer of a righteous person is powerful and effective" (Jas. 5:16).

Stanza I: Doxological Invocation 1b–2

Pierre Auffret notes the artistic structure of verses 1–2.[48] Reference to the *Lord/Dwelling Place* and *God*, followed and preceded respectively by an emphatic *you*, frames the invocation around chiastic references to universal time ("generation to generation" and "from eternity to eternity") and global space ("mountains" and "earth/world") which "were born/you brought forth." Verse 1 looks to God's help to past generations of Israel. Verse 2

---

45. The juridical background of *pll*, the root of *tᵉpillâ*, can be observed in the nouns *pālîl* ("judgment," "an estimation requiring a judgment"; see Exod. 21:22; Deut. 32:31; Job 31:11) and *pᵉlîlâ* ("decision").

46. H. P. Stähli, *TLOT*, 2:992, s.v. *pll* Hithpael.

47. The collocation *'îš hā'ᵉlōhîm* occurs 76 times and always refers to a prophet: Samuel (1 Sam. 9:6–10); Elijah (2 Kgs. 1:9–13); Elisha (2 Kgs. 4:7, 9, 16ff.); and, most often, Moses (Deut. 33:1; Josh. 14:6; 1 Chr. 23:14; 2 Chr. 30:16; Ezra 3:2). In the Pentateuch, Moses is called "the man of God" only at the time of his death (Deut. 33:1). In Jer. 35:4, referring to Hanan, "the Targum translates the 'man of God' by 'the prophet of the Lord' to signify a true prophet of YHWH" (Jack R. Lundbom, *Jeremiah 21–36: A New Translation with Introduction and Commentary*, AB [New York: Doubleday, 2004], 575, citing Hayward and P. Churgin).

48. Pierre Auffret, "Essai sur la structure litteraire du Psaume 90," *Bib* 61 (1980): 262–76, esp. 63. But Auffret pairs *mᶜwn*, not *'dny*, with *'l*.

takes their situation beyond that into the context of God's eternity, before the earth existed. The transcendent Sovereign over time and space humbled himself and entered both spheres to be forever Israel's home—a foretaste fulfilled in the incarnation in Jesus Christ. Craig Broyles notes: "Psalm 90 uses the praise of God as a platform from which it can express a persuasive appeal."[49] The supplicants will never be homeless, for their God—today to be known in his Son (see p. 2–3)—is eternal, and he made himself their refuge. However deep our sin and desperate our plight, *I AM* remains the home of his chosen family.

1 The unique address in the Psalter, *O Lord* (*'ᵃdōnāy*) means "Lord of all."[50] The title is appropriate because the supplicants conceptualize themselves as his servants (vv. 13 and 16). *You* is tautological and so emphatic. *Have been* holistically represents a situation that encompasses the past and the present (cf. Ps. 10:14).[51] *For us* (i.e. Israel, see p. 13). The Sovereign began to be Israel's dwelling place when he uniquely adopted the patriarchs as his sons and later formed their descendants into a nation through Moses (see Ps. 100:3). Today the "us" is the church: Jews and Gentiles (see Rom. 4:17; Gal. 3:26–29; 1 Pet. 2:9–10).[52] The Eternal's election of nomads and nobodies, schmucks and schlemiels, is the scandal of history. Elsewhere, *dwelling place* is used both of heaven (Deut. 26:15), which is reached through prayer (2 Chr. 30:27), and of God's earthly temple (1 Sam. 2:29; 2 Chr. 36:15; Ps. 26:8). Here, it is used metaphorically, as indicated by the likening of God, who is spirit, to a physical abode—a place of provision, trust, loyalty, communion, comfort, stability, and security. He himself provides what the temple provided. Israel's temple may have been gone when Book IV was compiled (see p. 15–16) but not their covenantal relationship with God. Only the faithful find *I AM* their refuge (Ps. 91:9–10) and that faith cannot be separated from his eternal law. Brueggemann comments: "The speaker is not homeless. There is a center to prevent fragmentation. There is a belonging to preclude isolation."[53] *Throughout generations* signals an endless succession of generations from Abraham to the present. The faithful conquest generation remained almost as numerous as the dead wilderness generation: like the stars in the sky (Deut. 1:10; cf. Num. 26:51, 62 with Num. 1:46). God's

49. Craig C. Broyles, *Psalms*, NIBCOT (Peabody, MA: Hendrickson, 1999), 359.
50. *IBHS*, §7.4.3e.
51. The possible gloss, "You are . . . ," would not represent the past well.
52. Waltke, *An Old Testament Theology*, 321–32.
53. Brueggemann, *Message of the Psalms*, 111

people have sufficient reason to sing: "Our help in ages past, our hope for years to come . . . and our eternal home."

2 In the ancient world's cosmology, *the mountains* are the foundations of the earth in the midst of the primeval ocean depths, so here they are mentioned first (cf. Jonah 2:6[7]; Ps. 104:6–8). As the ocean depths represent primeval chaos, the mountains represent the oldest parts of the earth, which sustained life at the beginning of historical time (cf. Micah 6:2). *Were born* may be a figurative echo of an ancient mythical idea that mother earth suffered labor pains in giving birth to the mountains. *And you brought to birth* clearly identifies Israel's God as the Agent. Thus Moses polemicizes against the pagan mother-earth myth, just as Milton polemicized against Greek myths using their own subject matter. *The earth* probably refers to the land that sustains life and, in the cosmology of the biblical world, stands in contrast to the chaotic seas around it, to the unfathomable depths below, and to the unattainable heavens above. Philip Sumpter defines the Hebrew word for *the world* (*tēbēl*) as "the earth-disc . . . which is the *ground* [italics his] for the existence of its inhabitants."[54] Christopher J. H. Wright notes: "It is used frequently in contexts both that associate it with Yahweh's creative act and that, as a result, express the stability or durability of the earth (1 Sm 2:8; Pss. 89:11[12]; 93:1; 96:10)."[55] Matching the universal population of the world (cf. Pss. 24:1; 33:8; 98:7; Isa. 18:3; Nah. 1:5) are the temporal terms *throughout generations* and *from eternity to eternity*. "Eternity" (*'ôlām*) often denotes the most remote time in the past or future. But in contexts where it refers to God, like this one, it has its full philosophical sense: "Only in expressly theological and doxological contexts to be translated 'eternally, in eternity.' "[56] Israel's God is Lord of all, transcending all in space and time. The confession *you* (see "Stanza I: Doxological Invocation 1b–2" above) *are God* (*'ēl*, see 100:3) implies that Israel's God "has an unlimited abundance of power and a presence that overcomes the barriers of time."[57]

54. Philip Sumpter, *The Substance of Psalm 24: An Attempt to Read Scripture after Brevard Childs* (London: Bloomsbury T&T Clark, 2015), 97.

55. Christopher J. H. Wright, *NIDOTTE*, 4:273, s.v. *tēbēl*. Poets represent the *tēbēl* as set upon foundations (1 Sam. 2:8) and speak of its inhabitants (Isa. 18:3; 26:9, 18; Pss. 24:1; 33:8; Lam. 4:12), its fruit (Isa. 34:1), its fullness (Ps. 50:12), and all that is in it (Ps. 89:11[12]). In draught, it withers (Isa. 24:4). The king of Babylon transformed it into an uninhabitable wilderness (Isa. 14:17), and whoever is banished from it perishes (Job 18:18).

56. E. Jenni, *TLOT*, 2:854–62, s.v. *'ôlām*.

57. Artur Weiser, *The Psalms*, OTL (Philadelphia: Westminster, 1962), 597.

Stanza II (Lament): Death and Sin 3–10

The enormous discrepancy between God's time and ours is not inherent in creation but historically conditioned.

The Creator's original intention for the unending life of the sinless human has not been rescinded but accomplished through the man Christ Jesus. In the prodigal penitents' implicit return to their eternal home, they confess that their sin cut their lives off the loom and their days are like smoke. Now, God's eternal nature stands in sharp contrast to the sinful mortal's infinitesimally brief existence (v. 4). As the enemy of sinners, God circumscribes the depraved mortal's' brief days within seventy, or at best eighty, years (vv. 3–10).

This dark stanza on mortality has two equal strophes of four verses: verses 3–6 pertain to mortals in general and 7–10 pertains to "we" (i.e., Israel). The two strophes are linked by "surely," by the theme of the brevity of the mortal's life, and by the logic of covenant theology: death (vv. 3–6) is due to God's wrath against sin (vv. 7–10). That all die is science; that God abases humanity is theology. Death is at God's "absolute disposal."[58] This harsh realism regarding life's brevity is similar to that of the Preacher in the Book of Ecclesiastes. Weiser comments: "[Death points] to the other eternal reality which transcends the evanescent life of man and which alone is able to impart to it a lasting purpose and value. There is no other way to a genuine faith than the one which continually compels a man in remorseless sincerity to abandon all hope in his own strength and cast himself whole upon God."[59] This sober view of death, however, must be held in tension with a robust affirmation of Israel's triumph: "No misfortune is seen in Jacob, no misery observed in Israel. *I AM* their God is with them; the shout of the King is among them" (Num. 23:21).

Strophe A: The Certainty of Death and Brevity of Life 3–6

The first couplet (vv. 3–4) is linked by the medial "surely" (v. 4) and the second couplet (vv. 5–6) by the repetition of the catchword "in the morning." The two couplets are thematically linked in their initial verses by the agent, *you*, who rules death (vv. 3, 5), and by their elaboration on the mortal's death, first by contrasting the brevity of life with God's eternity (v. 4) and then by comparing it to grass that blossoms in the morning and dies in the evening (v. 6).

58. A. F. Kirkpatrick, *The Book of Psalms* (1902; repr., Grand Rapids: Baker, 1982), 549.

59. Weiser, *The Psalms*, 600f.

The comparison to grass also illuminates the mortal's transience in contrast to God's immutability. All people know the brevity of this life, but almost all foolishly cling to the transient things of this world, flattering themselves that their pictures will not appear in tomorrow's obituary page. Few wisely cling to the eternal God.

1. In Contrast to the Sovereign's Eternity 3–4

3 *Return . . . to dust* is one of several idioms for death (cf. Job 34:15; Ps. 104:29; Eccl. 3:20); it can be inferred a person ought not to put their trust in mortals (cf. Ps. 146:4; Prov. 11:7). "Return" evokes the understanding that human bodies originated from the ground. Whereas "dust" (*'āpār*) in Gen. 3:19 denotes "dry, loose, ground," the term used here for *dust* (*dakkā'*) derives from the verb "to crush" (cf. Isa. 3:15) and may connote humankind's total defeat. *The mortal* (*'enōš*) denotes the male in his weakness. *You say "return"* reprises God's direct word to Adam, mankind's representative: "To the dust you will return" (Gen. 3:19). *Mankind* (*benê 'ādām*, lit. "sons of humankind") represents the nature, quality, character, or condition of a "son" (i.e., a person) as an "*'ādām*,"[60] a noun probably derived from *'adāmâ*, ("ground"). Mankind was created a mortal, but this became "a realized mortality" only when he ate the forbidden fruit.

4 A *thousand* is the largest round figure that can exist in multiples for counting and here serves as a symbol for an extremely long period of time (cf. Deut. 7:9; Pss. 50:10; 84:10). Were a specific number intended, "about" (cf. Exod. 12:37; 32:28; Josh. 4:13) could have readily been added.[61] *Years* has its conventional sense of calendar years and stands in contrast to other chronological terms (e.g., "day," "week," "month") as the largest measure of time.[62] *In your estimation* contrasts the viewpoint of time from the perspective of the eternal with that of the temporal. If a thousand years of human time is like twenty-four hours to God, then seventy or eighty years is like less than two hours. *Is like yesterday* could refer either to a full day of twenty-four hours or to the daylight hours of a previous time. "Day" has both senses in Genesis 1:5. The parallel "night" (v. 4b) favors the meaning of "daylight" (cf. Neh. 4:16; Job 3:3;

---

60. GKC, 128s; *IBHS*, §9.5.3a.

61. Leland Ryken, James C. Wilhoit, and Tremper Longman III, eds., *Dictionary of Biblical Imagery* (Downers Grove, IL: IVP Academic, 1998), 865f.

62. The smallest amount of time is called a *rega'* ("moment," cf. Exod. 33:5; Isa. 54:7-8; Jer. 4:20).

Hos 4:5). *When it is over* adds notions of life's fleeting, ephemeral and futile nature. To paraphrase the Preacher: "It's all utter vanity" (lit. "a puff of air," like a puff of cigar-smoke, Eccl. 1:2, 5). The day is spent and cannot be recovered. Even the simile of "yesterday" is too long—the thousand years are more like *a watch* in the night, the four hours a watchman stands his post to protect the people while they sleep.[63] Accordingly, the mortal's seventy or eighty years are like a little over a quarter of an hour in the scope of a day to God. As "watch" intensifies "day," so *in the night* intensifies "when it is over"—that is to say, it intensifies life's ephemeral nature. Delitzsch comments: "It is certainly not without design that the poet says *'ašmûrâ ballāylâ* ['watch in the night'] not *'ašmōret hallāylâ* ['watch of the night']. The night-time is the time for sleep."[64] Kirkpatrick comments: "Time no more exists for God than it does for the unconscious sleeper."[65] (Cf. 2 Pet. 3:8 and Sir. 18:10, which affirm the converse of this verse.)

2. In Comparison to Grass 5–6

The notion of an unconscious sleeper in the night segues into the notion of the sleep of death. The simile likening the brevity of life to grass demands that the blossoming of grass in the morning (v. 5b) be contrasted with its withering in the evening (v. 6b). To join them, the poet essentially repeats the first and last words of 5b in 6a: "in the morning . . . is renewed."

5 *You make an end of their lives* (see n. 4) keeps the focus on God's sovereignty and on humankind's brevity. The metaphor *they fall into deep sleep* connotes death (see Job 14:12; Ps. 76:5–6; Jer. 51:39, 57; Nah. 3:18). *In the morning* denotes daybreak.[66] *Like grass* (*keḥāṣîr*) refers to "wild growth that comes

---

63. Judg. 7:19 refers to a "middle watch" of the night (apparently of three); Lam. 2:19 refers to the beginning of the night watches; and Exod. 14:24 and 1 Sam. 11:11 mention "the morning watch," which NIV interprets as the "last watch of the night." Many verses of the Bible pair day and night to denote the entire twenty-four-hour period of a day, making night half of the daily cycle, or twelve hours. Accordingly a watch is 1/3 of 12 hours. "In the NT times division the Rom. division into four watches seems to have been used (cf. Mark 6:48)" (J. D. Douglas et al., eds., *New Bible Dictionary*, 2nd ed. [Leicester: IVP, 1982], 1.242).

64. Delitzsch, *Psalms*, 52.

65. Kirkpatrick, *The Book of Psalms*, 550.

66. The coming of sunrise, from the time when the stars that presage the new day are still visible (Job 38:7) and people and things are scarcely visible (Gen. 29:25;

up regularly and abundantly after the winter rains (Ps. 147:8). . . . As quickly as *ḥāṣîr* sprouts in the rain, it withers in draught (Is. 15:6) or is found along streams at best (1 Kgs. 18:5)."[67]

6 Two sets of verbs describe the states of renewal and death: "to blossom" and "be renewed" versus "to wither" and "dry up." The similes reinforce the notion of humanity's brevity and futility. That the grass *blossoms* signifies that for a brief moment humanity experiences health and vigor. The narrative *waw* with *and is renewed* may be logical ("and so it is renewed"). *In the evening* (see Ps. 30:5[6]) refers to sunset.[68] According to Ps. 37:2, grass *withers* quickly *and dries up* (cf. Isa. 15:6; Job 18:16).

Strophe B: Israel's Punishment for Sin 7–10

The second strophe adds three truths: (a) Israel's death is due to God's wrath against iniquities (vv. 7–9); (b) a person's span of years is seventy or at best eighty years (v. 10a)[69]; and (c) mankind's proud achievements are futile (v. 10b). Its first couplet (vv. 7–8) is linked by covenant logic: God's wrath (v. 7) is provoked by sin (v. 8) (cf. Jer. 4:4).[70] Its second couplet (vv. 9–10) is linked by the catchwords "days" and "years," by the medial "surely," by the escalating synonyms "in your anger and in your wrath" (v. 7) and "in your fierce anger" (v. 9), and by the lexeme *kālâ* (Qal, "perish," v. 7; Piel, "finish," v. 9). In sum, of the five words in verse 7, two are repeated by a synonym in verse 9. With these tight sutures the poet shows that due to God's wrath, a person's life is restricted to seventy or at best eighty years (v. 10a). The setting of universal death (vv. 3–6) and human experience before modern medicine suggest that Moses has in mind all the generations of Israel, not just his own. Accordingly, the strophe's verbs are gnomic; they represent the situations of God's burning wrath holistically.[71] God's righteous volition deconstructs all humankind's insolent volition.

Ruth 3:14; 1 Kgs. 3:21) to the breaking of the sun over the horizon (Judg. 9:33; 2 Sam. 23:4; 2 Kgs. 3:22).

67. M. D. Futato, *NIDOTTE*, 2:247, s.v. *ḥāṣîr*.

68. The end of daylight (Gen. 1:5), a time when people stop work (Ruth 2:17; Ps. 104:23), gates are shut (Ezek. 46:2) and lamps are lit (Exod. 30:8) but people and objects are still visible (Gen. 24:63).

69. For exceptions see "Author."

70. Auffret, "Essai sur la structure," 266f.

71. *IBHS*, §§30.5.c, d; cf. GKC, 106k, m.

1. Death for Sin 7–8

Kidner aptly comments on verses 7–8: "We are shown God's wrath as doubly irresistible, by its vigor and by its justice, leaving us with no resource (v. 7) and no excuse (v. 8)."[72]

7 In the chiastic parallels of verse 7, "anger" is intensified by "burning wrath" and "dismay" is added to *perish* (*kālâ*; i.e, "come to a complete end, vanish, be destroyed"). *In your anger* (lit., "in your nostrils") points to the physically visible state of an individual's excitement seen in their breathing heavily as a consequence of anger. God's anger differs from most examples of human anger: His anger results in deliberate judgment against sin (cf. Deut. 6:15).[73] So his anger is not capricious but rather is his righteous response "to human deeds that violate his being and commandments."[74] Jesus responded in anger to hardness of heart (Mark 3:5) and threatened God's anger against the privileged few who spurned his invitation to enter the kingdom of heaven (Matt. 22:7). God's wrath now rests on those who fail to believe in Jesus (John 3:36) and against those who suppress the truth (Rom. 1:18; 1 Thess. 2:16). Governing authorities serve as instruments of God's anger to punish criminals (Rom. 13:4).[75] *'Ap* is used most frequently, as here, in parallel with *wrath* (*ḥēmâ*), a derivative of *yḥm* "to be hot." The coordination of "anger" and "wrath" brings to a flash point the holy *I AM's* burning anger against those who dishonor his Person and disobey his commandments. *We are terrified* may mean the whole skeleton is racked and shaken in fright (Ezek. 7:27; Ps. 6:2[3]) and denotes a psychological state of extreme fright at imminent threat (Gen. 45:3; Judg. 20:41; 1 Sam. 28:21), including death (Ps. 104:29). Moses's unbelieving generation, whom *I AM* had duly warned and threatened, trembled from the prospect of divinely inflicted, premature death, not from a normal malady that creeps silently through the windows in old age (Eccl. 12:1–8).[76]

72. Kidner, *Psalms 73–150*, 361.

73. God's anger was aroused against Moses's generation when they complained about their hardships (Num. 11:1), complained about their restricted diet of manna (Num. 11:10), and worshiped the Baal of Peor (Num. 25:3–4).

74. G. Sauer, *TLOT*, 1:169, s.v. *'ap*.

75. Ryken, Wilhoit, and Longman, *Dictionary of Biblical Imagery*, 26.

76. Tate (*Psalms*, 434) thinks *bhl* Niphal may have its other sense, "to be in haste/hasty," and if so means "being hurried (away to an untimely end)."

8 The penitent prodigals, unlike the wilderness generation, do not murmur against God for their plight. Verse 8 is the metonymy of the righteous and just cause for the physical afflictions in verse 7. The idiomatic anthropomorphism *you set . . . before you* means "you make conspicuous to you."[77] Like a good detective seeking justice, God deliberately searches out *our iniquities.* '*Awôn* is the most holistic term in the semantic domain of sin; it encompasses both religious and ethical crimes and the resulting guilt. *Our hidden sins* is literally "our concealments," a qualifying parallel to "our iniquities." The anthropomorphism *in the light of your face* communicates regarding sins, which people hide from themselves by self-deception and conceal from others by hypocrisy, that the just God does not sweep them under the rug but exposes them. It is implicit that God exposes sins in order to right the wrong (cf. Prov. 20:27; 1 Cor. 2:11). *Light* is literally "place of light, luminary, lamp," possibly a metonymy for "light" more generally. The apostle Paul warns: "He [the Lord] will bring to light what is hidden in darkness and will expose the motives of the heart" (1 Cor. 4:5). C. S. Lewis noted: "In the end that Face which is the delight or the terror of the universe must be turned upon each of us . . . either conferring glory inexpressible or inflicting shame that can never be cured or disguised."[78] If one wants to understand the strength of God's wrath against the sin of unbelief, do not look to the black and fanciful lines of Baxter, Bunyan or Milton, but look at ethnic Israel's tragic history.

2. Punishment Lasts Seventy or Eighty Years 9–10

9 *All our days* (see v. 4) encompasses the entirety of our lives in their sequential, segmented daily components. That notion will pave the way into the psalm's new insight to wisdom, namely to count our days (v. 12). *Pass away* translates *pānâ* ("to turn"). With "days" as its subject, this forms the idiom "the day turned away" (i.e., "drew to a close, disappeared"; cf. Jer. 6:4). The full scope of our days fades away and affords no hope of change, without the intervention of God's grace through wisdom. *In your fury*[79] is a metonymy of cause for the daily toil that amounts to nothing (see v. 10). *We finish our years* (see v. 3; "perish," v. 4). *A sigh* signifies a long deep breath emitting a soft, dull

---

77. BDB, p. 617, s.v. *neged.*

78. C. S. Lewis, "The Weight of Glory," in *The Weight of Glory and Other Addresses* (New York: Macmillan, 1949), 10.

79. J. A. Emerton, "Notes on Jer. 12:9," *ZAW* 81 (1989): 189.

sound that "vanishes into thin air (Rashi)."[80] This sound of sadness is the appropriate response to death, to the reality of God's fierce anger against sin. Stoicism is not appropriate, for it fakes reality and refuses to be emotionally real in the presence of anger and death. Being truly sad makes a person long for something better (see 2 Cor. 5:2).

10 Moses now numbers the mortals' days as at best a brief eighty years, and all of them are toilsome and futile. They pass quickly, and once gone, they are gone forever.[81] The idiom *as for the days of our years* refers to our entire lives (cf. Gen. 47:8). Mankind's "days" *are* surrounded by the concomitant condition of *seventy years. Or if* the days are accompanied *with strength* (see n. 7)[82] *eighty years.* The conjunction *and* joins the burdensome and deceptive quality of the days to their brief quantity. *And their proud achievements* (see n. 8) understands with BDB and others that *rōhab* is a metonymy for "objects of pride."[83] More precisely *rōhab* means "insolent pride." In their hubris, mortals strive to achieve what they call "success" independently from God and credit their achievements to the power and strength of their own hands, not to God

---

80. Feuer, *Tehillim,* 4, 1.126. In its two other occurrences, it is used of the growling, rumbling sound of thunder (Job 37:2) and of "mourning" in the sequence of [words of] "lamentations and mourning/moaning and woe" (Ezek. 2:10).

81. In the Bible, the span of human life begins with the astronomical longevity of the antediluvians (Gen. 5; Bruce K. Waltke with Cathi J. Fredericks, *Genesis: A Commentary* [Grand Rapids: Zondervan, 2001], 111) but goes through a logarithmic reduction of years after the flood, from 500 to 119 years (Gen. 11:10–25). The patriarchs, however, lived long: Abraham to 175, Isaac to 180, and Jacob to 147. Joseph lived to be 110, the ideal age of the Egyptians (J. Vergote, *Joseph en Égypte* [Louvain: Publications Universitaires, 1959], 200ff.; see *ANET,* 414n33). Today few live to be 100, and were it not for modern medicine, the mortal could expect to live only 70 or 80 years. Sir. 18:9–10 resembles Ps. 90: "His [A human being's] is at the most a hundred years; compared with unending time, his few years are like one drop from the ocean or a single grain of sand." But the Talmud says that the average lifespan is sixty years: "Thus the man who reaches seventy has achieved . . . 'ripe old age' (Feuer, *Tehillim,* 1.126).

82. Heb. *bigᵉbûrōt.* J. Kuelewein says the root *gbr* signifies "to be superior," and "the basic meaning of *gᵉbûrâ,* closely related to the verb, is "superiority, strength, might." *HALOT* glosses it "in strength," but adds "the strongest vitality" and cites Luther for the notion of "at the most." Delitzsch (*Psalms,* 598) cites with approval the same notion in Symmachus and the Talmud.

83. Delitzsch (*Psalms,* 598) identifies them as "riches, outward appearance, luxury, beauty, etc."; cf. 1 John 2:16, *hē alazoneia tou biou* ("the boasting of life").

who gave them ability (cf. Deut. 8:17–18; James 4:13–17). Their self-glorifying achievements are *toilsome*, or "burdened with grief" (*ʿāmāl*).[84] Schwertner, citing Ps. 90:10, notes the basic meaning of *ʿāmal* "indicates primarily the process of work . . . and the trouble that it causes."[85] *And futile* (cf. James 4:14). Shakespeare's Mark Antony lamented over the corpse of Julius Caesar: "O mighty Caesar, dost thou lie so low?/ Are all thy conquests, glories, triumphs, spoils/ Shrunk to this little measure?"[86] Humans deceive themselves when they think their achievements will gain them social immortality and praise. They name streets after themselves and write posthumous memoirs. They might just as well write their names on water. They build monumental architecture, but most of it winds up only as foundation stones that are uncovered by the archeologist's spade, and the few that remain above ground are skeletons. Their mansions are sand-castles that the tide inexorably washes away. *For* introduces a causal clause that explains why the mortal's proud achievements are futile: *they pass away quickly* (see n. 11). The metaphor *and we fly away* (cf. Prov. 23:5) connotes speed and that once we are gone, we are gone forever. Weiser comments: "No wonder that a man who seeks in life *his* will and *his* pleasure is bound to end in this disappointment; for all pleasure seeks perpetuity."[87] But the psalm's final word is "establish the works of our hands" (v. 17).

Stanza III (Hinge): Lament and Petition to Gain Wisdom 11–12

Logic and catchwords screw the hinge stanza into the lament stanza (vv. 3–10): "your anger" (vv. 7, 11a) and "your fierce anger" (vv. 9, 11b); "our days" and "the days of our years" (vv. 10, 12). Having numbered the mortal's days to seventy or eighty years (v. 10a), the penitents are now able to number their own days (vv. 12a). Similarly, logic and form screw the hinge into the petition stanza (vv. 13–17): petition and wise hearts (v. 12b) are what God blesses (vv. 13–17). The hinge stanza itself is unified by the lexeme *yādaʿ* (Qal, "to know," v. 11; Hiphil "cause to know," v. 12). Indeed, the objects of "cause us to know" (v. 12a) are the double objects of what none or few know (v. 11). Also, the wise hearts of verse 12b are inseparable from knowing "the fear due you" (v. 11b; cf. Prov. 1:7; Job 28:20–28; Eccl. 12:13–14). The hinge swings the psalm from the sober de-

---

84. *HALOT*, 2:845, s.v. *ʿāmāl*.
85. S. Schwertner, *TLOT*, 2:925, s.v. *ʿāmāl*.
86. William Shakespeare, *Julius Caesar*, 3.1.282–83.
87. Weiser, *The Psalms*, 600.

spair of the lament to the bright hope of the petitions. Christine Forster notes numerous key words that point to the reversal:

> The root *šûb* in 13 points back to v. 3, but now refers not to the mortal's "return" to dust, but instead to YHWH's "return" to the petitioners or the "turning away" from his wrath. Verse 14 takes up *bbqr* ["in the morning"] from vv. 5–6. What in the earlier verses was part of an image for mortality now describes the morning as a time in which YHWH will again prove himself gracious. Verses 14 and 15 with (*kl-ymynw* "all our days") and (*šnwt kymwt* "according to the days/years") refer back to v. 9. . . . In contrast to the lament there over the vanished years and days, what follows here is a petition for joy lasting just as many days and years. A major inclusion is created by the key work linkage *bny-ʾdm/ bnyhm* between vv. 3 and 16, undoubtedly also with an antithetical tendency: despite the mortality of the *children* of humanity there is hope that YHWH's servant and their *children* will see revealed the glory of YHWH.[88]

By a rhetorical question—"who knows?"—the penitents confess that mankind is so sinful that none or few know the vehemence of God's wrath against sin, or that it is as great as the fear due to him (v. 11; cf. Ps. 103:11). In response, the penitent prodigals ask God to make them know by their numbering their fleeting, precious days and, presumably, devote them to the fear of *I AM*. Accordingly, they will gain wise hearts. Zenger comments: "It is striking that at the beginning [of the petition section], in verses 11–12, what we have is a petition not for an end to the crisis, but for knowledge or insight into the crisis."[89] Their confession of their sin and of their spiritual blindness entails the supplicants' repentance.

Strophe A (Lament): Few Know God's Wrath against Sin and the Fear Due Him 11

Semantic pertinence demands that the question *who* demands the answer "very few at best" (Deut. 9:2; Prov. 31:10).[90] *Knows* denotes both the mental

---

88. Forster, *Begrenztes leben,* 150, quoted in Frank-Lothar Hossfeld and Erich Zenger, *Commentary on Psalm 51-100,* trans. Linda M. Maloney, Hermeneia (Minneapolis: Fortress, 2005), 420f.

89. Hossfeld and Zenger, *A Commentary on Psalms 51-100,* 418.

90. James Crenshaw ("The Expression *Mî Yôdēaʿ* in the Hebrew Bible," *VT* 36, no.

knowledge of a fact and the visceral experiencing of that reality. The linkage between the indicative *yôdēaʿ* ("knows," v. 11) and the imperative *hôdaʿ* ("make us know," v. 12) shows that God's grace can overcome the human deprivation of knowledge. *The strength* indicates "the overpowering nature . . . and vehemence."[91] *Of your anger* (see v. 7; cf. the hendiadys *ʿuzzô wəʾappô* in Ezra 8:22) is a metonymy for God's punishment against his foes who discredit his person or disobey his commands. *And* adds a second question. *According to* expresses conformity to a standard or rule. *The fear due to you* (see n. 12) signifies pious submission to God's word out of fear and trust in him and entails a metonymy for hating evil (Prov. 8:13), departing from it (Prov. 3:7; 16:6), and doing what is right (Deut. 5:29).[92] *Your wrath* (see v. 9). Geoffrey W. Grogan explains the comparison: "As the reverential fear of God should be absolute, so is God's wrath."[93]

Strophe B (Petition): To Know by Numbering Days 12

The deficiency of the desired moral knowledge is met by acquiring that knowledge through numbering days. *To number* with the accusative means "to count" in order to obtain the sum total (cf. Gen. 13:16; Ps. 147:4; 2 Kgs. 12:10[11]; 2 Sam. 24:1) of *our days* (see vv. 4, 9, 10). The sum will diminish by one each day. The petition implies repentance for their iniquities and their spiritual blindness. Goldingay comments: "It is the counting of days in their toilsome and troubled nature that could push the community to this acknowledgment [of the strength of Yhwh's wrathful anger] and of submission [in reverence to God]. Without it, people can live in denial and simply continue enjoying their lives without a care or a thought for God."[94] *So* (see n. 13) is medial with reference to what has preceded,[95] to wit, "to number our days," not to verse 11. *Cause . . .*

---

3 [1986]: 274–88) divides the ten occurrences of *mî-yôdēaʿ* into two groups. "Five of them leave a door open to possible response that will change the situation for human good, and the other five (four in Eccl. plus Prov. 24:22) seem to assume a closed door." He hesitantly includes Psalm 90:11 in the former; he cites no instance of a wish. His distinction, however, between "open" and "closed" seems arbitrary.

91. A. S. van der Woude, *TLOT,* 2:870, s.v. ʿzz.

92. See Bruce Waltke, "The Fear of the LORD," in *Alive to God: Studies in Spirituality,* ed. J. I. Packer and Loren Wilkinson (Downers Grove, IL: InterVarsity, 1992), 17–33.

93. Geoffrey W. Grogan, *Psalms* (Grand Rapids: Eerdmans, 2008), 159.

94. John Goldingay, *Psalms,* vol. 3, BCOTWP (Grand Rapids: Baker Academic, 2008), 31.

95. *IBHS,* §39.3.4e.

to know asks for a double accusative of person and thing, both elided.[96] The object of person, *us*, is readily supplied from "our days." The only expressed object of thing is the objects of "know" in verse 11—to wit, God's vehement anger against sin and that his anger is equal to the fear due him. The design of Moses is that by numbering their evanescent days people will become keenly aware of "the immense value of every single day,"[97] and they elevate their minds to God in heaven by detaching them from the insolent pride associated with earthly objects (Eph. 5:16; Col. 4:5). By facing the complete negation of life due to sin, the penitents pay daily attention to the other reality: life in the fear of the Eternal who is their ever-present dwelling place (see v. 1 and David's prayer in Ps. 39:4–7[5–8]). Verse 12, says M. Wilcox, is "a lesson not in elementary arithmetic but in life-changing theology."[98] *That* (see n. 14) *we may gain* (lit. "that we may cause to come in"). *Wise* signifies masterful skill in living.[99] In wisdom literature, wisdom is a matter of the heart's disposition and is inseparable from doing what is right (cf. Prov. 1:3) and from its reward of life. Delitzsch comments: "The wise heart is the fruit which one reaps or garners in from such numbering of the days, the gain which one carries off from so constantly reminding one's self of the end."[100]

96. Most English versions read "teach us," but that translation obfuscates the connection with "know" in v. 11.

97. Hossfeld and Zenger, *A Commentary on Psalms 51–100*, 423.

98. M. Wilcox, *The Message of Psalm 73–150: Songs for the People of God*, The Bible Speaks Today (Leicester: InterVarsity Press, 2001), 77.

99. Bruce K. Waltke, *Proverbs 1–15*, NICOT (Grand Rapids: Eerdmans, 2004), 76–78; *Finding the Will of God: A Pagan Notion* (Grand Rapids: Eerdmans, 2016), 75f.

100. Delitzsch, *Psalms*, 599. Jeffrey D. Arthurs (*Preaching as Reminding: Stirring Memory in an Age of Forgetfulness* [Downers Grove, IL: InterVarsity Press, 2017], 23) tells of the burial practices of the Trappist monks: "When one of the brothers of the monastery dies, they place his body in a newly dug grave, and immediately after the interment they trace the dimensions of a new grave, the resting place of the next brother who will die." Arthurs teaches: "In this way they remind themselves of their own mortality and thus gain wisdom for living." On the day I (Bruce) prepared a sermon on this psalm in 1967, the total number of days to my seventieth birthday were 12,345—I could scarcely believe the sequence. Of course, the sum changes daily. When I told my wife I would daily subtract one from the remaining sum for the rest of my life, she replied "That's morbid." I did it for years to my spiritual benefit, and since passing that mark I still keep track.

Stanza IV (Petitions): Relent from Anger and Bless Israel 13–17

"Your servants" frames the petitions (vv. 13, 16) and links the closing petitions to the opening doxology (v. 1). The penitents follow their prayer for salutary knowledge with petitions that God take pity on them (v. 13) and bless them (vv. 14–17). Weiser comments: "The hand which afflicted the wounds is alone able to heal them (cf. Hos.6.1)."[101] According to covenant theology, *I AM* relents from his anger when his people repent, as indicated of the generation that prays this prayer in the two preceding stanzas (cf. Prov. 28:13; Jer. 18:1–8; Jonah 4:2). Tate helpfully expresses the opinion of most commentators: "The meditation, or reflection, in verses 1–12 is the context and foundation for the petitions in verses 13–17."[102] Kirkpatrick comments that their consolation of sorrow and their consecration of effort lies in the hope of the renewed life of the nation (Lam. 5:21), not yet in personal immortality, unlike 1 Cor. 15:58.[103] Nevertheless, as Isaac Taylor comments, "the thought of a life eternal is here in embryo."[104] Although they speak of their future years as "according to the years you afflicted us" and their hope is in their descendants, they nevertheless ask to be delivered from the sleep of death and mention the morning of the new age without mentioning the night. Their embryonic desire will come to birth in Jesus Christ in a way immeasurably greater than they could ask or imagine (Eph. 3:20; cf. 2 Cor. 4:17).

Strophe A: Relent from Punishment 13

Šûb ("to [re]turn" to a place [v. 3]) is used figuratively for *turn back* [from your anger and judgment] (vv. 3–11; see n. 15; cf. Exod. 32:12; Joel 2:14). *I AM* (*yhwh*, see pp. 1–3), God's covenant name with Israel, is used for the first time and is apt in a plea for covenant fidelity. *How long* elides "will your vehement anger against sin be turned against your servants?" (vv. 3–11).[105] The rhetorical question expresses exasperation in the acute situation of death and futility long endured and invests the petition *and take pity on* (see n. 16) with urgency.

---

101. Weiser, *The Psalms*, 602.

102. Tate, *Psalms 51–100*, 437.

103. Kirkpatrick, *The Book of Psalms*, 55.

104. Isaac Taylor quoted in J. J. Stewart Perowne, *The Book of Psalms*, vol. 2 (Andover: Warren F. Draper, 1898), 157.

105. Owing to the excitement and complaining exclamation, the poet suppresses the indispensable subject and predicate (GKC, 147c).

Your servants (see "O Lord," v. 1) implies Israel's conversion, for to be a servant entails Israel's whole life being in subjection or in a subordinate position to their Master (cf. v. 1). As such, they live in (a) responsible obedience to his direction, (b) faithful dependence on his care, (c) personal intimacy of trust with him, and (d) humility before him.

Strophe B: Confer Benedictory Blessings 14–17

The benedictory petitions to *I AM* consist of two couplets: (a) to satisfy them with his unfailing love and so to make them rejoice (vv. 14–15) and (b) to show his mighty work among them and so to establish their work (vv. 16–17). The two couplets are joined by the catchword "to see" (vv. 15b, 16a), supplemented by the assonance of the last two words of verse 15 (*rā'înû rā'â* "we saw disaster") with the first word of verse 16 (*yērā'eh* "let appear"). The penitents will rejoice (vv. 14–15) when the majestic saving acts of God once again appear among them.

1. To Rejoice in God's Unfailing Love in His Saving Deeds 14–15

Verses 14 and 15 are connected by the catchwords "rejoice" and "days" (vv. 14b, 15a). The petition to be sated with *I AM's* unfailing love (v. 14a) is supported by the motivation that "we may rejoice in all our days" (v. 14b). The motive is then reprised as an imperative in verse 15a for emphasis, and "all our days" is clarified by "according to the days you afflicted us" (v. 15b).

14 *Satisfy us* is a request to provide the wise servants with the full and consummate measure of their expectations, needs, and desires. No distinction is intended between their physical and spiritual appetites, for they end their fleeting and futile span of days in a sigh. Their whole being hungers for *I AM's* unfailing love. *In the morning* (see v. 5b) is conventionally the time God answers prayer. It scenically depicts the bright joy of flourishing life in the new dispensation after the night of distress in the old (cf. Job 11:17; Pss. 30:5[6]; 46:5[6]; 49:14[15]; 59:16[17]; 143:8). Unlike verses 4–5, no mention is made of death at sunset. The petition contains in embryo the hope for the dawn of what will become known as "the messianic era." *With your unfailing love* (*ḥasdekâ*; see Ps. 100:5). *That we may shout [for joy] and rejoice* (*ûnᵉrannᵊnâ wᵉniśmᵉḥâ*) probably assumes a liturgical setting, and if so, their joy gives praise to God, an enrichment of the supporting motivation. *Rānan* Piel, in contrast to Qal ("to rejoice"), means "to let out an entire series of cries of jubilation, to rejoice."[106] It commonly occurs with *śāmaḥ* ("rejoice"; see Ps. 100:2). *In all our days* (see vv. 4, 9) envisions their daily experience, within the time allotted to them, of God's unfailing love with fitting praise. Feuer comments: "*Radak* perceives this verse as a reference to the dawn of the messianic era, which will shine brilliantly as the morning sun. At that time, we will be sated by God's kindness and we will never again experience any misery. Then *we shall sing out and rejoice all our days.*"[107]

15 Since "to rejoice" is a spontaneous response to a situation and so cannot be imposed, *make us rejoice* is a metonymy for the good things that prompt this emotional response. *According to* [i.e., as long as] *the days* (see v. 14b) *you afflicted us.*[108] *According to the years* matches the parallelism of verse 9 and presumably refers to the span of seventy and eighty years (v. 10). The gnomic psalm does not mention the forty years of wilderness affliction (see p. 35). The parallel *we saw*[109] *disaster*[110] changes the perspective from God's afflicting them to their experiencing the affliction. Moses is groping and yearning for days and years of God's favor and expresses that hope in terms of equilibrium.[111] Kirkpatrick

106. *HALOT*, 1:248, s.v. *rānan*.

107. Rabbi Avrohom Chaim Feuer, *Tehillim: A New Translaton with a Commentary Anthologized from Talmudic, Midrashic, and Rabbinic Sources* (Brooklyn: Mesorah Publications, 1985), 1129.

108. III *'ānâ* Piel occurs fifty-four times and at the least means the use of force to alter the status of someone for the worse. Birkeland (*TDOT*, 11:237, s.v. *'ānâ* II) says of its uses: "A person who 'oppresses, violates, abuses, humiliates' is using power contrary to the demands of justice." But this is certainly not true of its use with God as the agent. The psalmist says: "I know, *I AM*, that your laws are righteous, and that in faithfulness you have afflicted me [*'innîtānî*]" (Ps. 119:75). Similarly, "he [God] is not predisposed to afflict [*lō' 'innâ millibbô*] or grieve people" (Lam. 3:33, NET). God afflicted Israel in the wilderness with hunger not as punishment but as a test of faith, since hunger was not part of his covenant design (Deut. 8:2–3). Otherwise "he afflicts" is used commonly of his punishment for sin (Isa. 64:12[11]; Nah 1:12), though it is used of waves overwhelming the psalmist without a stated reason in Ps. 88:7[8].

109. "See" commonly signifies "to experience something" (Pss. 16:10; 89:48[49]; Eccl. 5:18[17]; passim).

110. The feminine abstract noun *rā'â* ("disaster") denotes the evaluation that something is bad, whether it be a concrete physical state (e.g. "ugly" cows, Gen. 41:3; "poor/ bad" figs, Jer. 24), an abstraction of moral behavior that injures others, or a physical "disaster, calamity, trouble." The parallel "afflicts" shows it refers to "calamity/disaster."

111. Feuer (*Tehillim*, 1130) comments: "A great many opinions are offered by the

paraphrases: "Let the joy of restoration to Thy favour be proportioned to the depth of our humiliation."[112] Ḥakham similarly comments: "The psalmist is alluding to the feeling of gladness that compensates for all the suffering in life."[113]

2. To See God's Saving Deeds and to Establish the Israelites' Work 16–17

The couplet is tightly sutured by the conjunction "and," the jussive mood, the synonyms "your work" (*po'olekā*, v. 16a) and "our work" (*ma'ᵃśēh yādênû*, v. 17),[114] and a pun on *'al* ("to" and "upon").

16 The prayer in verse 16a asks for the present generation ("your servants") to see God's mighty deeds, and verse 16b escalates the description of those deeds, calling them "splendor," and extends the request to benefit unrestricted future generations. *Let appear* (see n. 20) refers to seeing and experiencing *I AM*'s mighty saving *deeds* as Moses's generation (see "Author" above) had (e.g., the exodus, manna, quails, and the rock and at Sinai; cf. Hab. 3:2). *Your servants* refers to the penitent generation (see vv. 1, 6, 13), extended to their descendants in the second part of the verse. *Your splendor* (see n. 21) is a metonymy for its parallel, "deeds." *To* (see n. 22) *their* ["your servants"] *sons* could have a synchronic sense, but in this psalm, featuring generations and time, it is diachronic.

17 God's majesty is expanded into the "beauty of God," conferred as an enduring presence upon them and presumably their descendants. Samuel A. Meier defines *beauty* (*nō'am*) as a physical reality: "The intrinsic agreeableness of an object is identified by reference to the many of the five physical senses."[115] This metonymy for *I AM*'s experienced deeds is visualized as theophany com-

---

Talmud (*Sanhedrin* 99a) to determine the duration of the Messianic era. Some say that it will last forty years corresponding to the number of years the Jews suffered in the wilderness, . . . or 400 years corresponding to the years of Egyptian bondage, . . . or 7000 years like the days of the week, and each day of God is 1000 years (see v. 4)." Many Christians, like the rabbis, interpret eschatological texts woodenly. According to them, the messianic era will last 1,000 years (see Rev 20:6).

112. Kirkpatrick, *The Book of Psalms*, 552.

113. Amos Ḥakham, *Psalms with the Jerusalem Commentary*, trans. Israel V. Berman, vol. 2 (Jerusalem: Mosad Harav Kook, 2003), 357.

114. BDB, p. 821, s.v. *pō'al*, §1a.

115. Samuel A. Meier, *NIDOTTE*, 3:122, s.v. *n'm*.

ing down to settle and *rest upon us* (see n. 23).[116] This beauty is an inalienable possession of *the Lord our God*.[117] Matching verses 13–15, the psalmist reverts to the imperative "establish" in direct address. With their hands emptied of pride (see v. 10), Moses adds the final petition: *and the work of our hands establish* (*kôneͤnâ*). "The work of our hands" is a metonymy for their creations in arts and crafts and a potential metaphor for their social achievements. *Kûn* Polel means "to make established an entity already present"[118]; it connotes permanence, firmness, stability. The permanence of the renewed people's works matches the enduring life of the renewed people (see v. 15) and stands in stark contrast to the fleeting, futile, and frustrating character of the mortal's work under God's wrath. Hakham comments: "The psalmist's purpose is to request that we ourselves will be privileged to eat the fruits of our toil, and that we will not be like those described in Psalm 39:7. . . , in Psalm 49:11, or in Ecclesiastes 2:1."[119] By an exceptional repetition, yet with a change of syntax "the work of hands, establish it" expresses the strong desire that their works withstand the test of time and implicitly be enjoyed by others independently from them. Weiser comments: "Seen in the light of God what is evanescent becomes durable, what is miserable becomes glorious, and what is meaningless becomes meaningful, because everything is bathed in the light of eternity."[120]

PART III. VOICE OF THE CHURCH IN RESPONSE

Throughout the ages, commentators have differed on whether the fourth book of Psalms begins with this psalm ascribed to Moses or whether Book III ends with this psalm. The church fathers considered the end of Book III to be Ps. 90[= LXX 89], while the Reformers placed the Song of Moses at the beginning of Book IV. Goldingay, along with McCann, suggests that Psalms 90–106 might be called a "Moses-book," as Moses is mentioned several times in these psalms, but only once in Books I–III.[121]

---

116. Feuer (*Tehillim*, 1131) comments: "The children of Israel responded to Moses' blessing (Exod. 39:43) by affirming Moses' blessing, saying, *May the pleasantness of my* [sic] *Lord, our God, be upon us* (*Sifri, Pinchos* 28:8).

117. *IBHS*, §9.5.1h.

118. Koch, *TDOT*, 7:97, s.v. *kûn*.

119. Hakham, *Psalms 58–100*, 356.

120. Weiser, *The Psalms*, 603.

121. Goldingay, *Psalms*, 23; J. Clinton McCann, Jr., *Psalms*, NIB 4 (Nashville: Abingdon, 1996), 1040.

Psalm 90 was sung in early Christian liturgy as a morning psalm, while in Jewish liturgy it had been a Sabbath psalm.[122] As a psalm reflecting upon human mortality, it has traditionally been quoted at funeral services. Isaac Watts (1674–1748) paraphrased the psalm in the well-known hymn, "O God, Our Help in Ages Past." Later composers such as Vaughan Williams and Charles Ives have also focused on Ps. 90, "God's dwelling place," as a source of musical awe and contemplative peace.

The multipurpose use of the Psalms is best studied first of all in the writings of the church fathers, who were concerned not with canonical nor historical contexts but with a healing and salvific address. Athanasius and Augustine pioneered this interpretive concern.

I. Athanasius of Alexandria (c. 295–373)

Athanasius wrote a pastoral letter to Marcellinus, who was probably a deacon or at least an urban Christian who needed to adopt an ascetic life.[123] It probably dates from c. 367. According to the letter, Marcellinus had fallen sick but had been occupying his time in convalescence studying the Scriptures. Athanasius writes to him that singing the Psalms is indeed therapeutic. Following Plato, Athanasius believed that human beings have three faculties: reason (*logistikon*), affections (*thymetikon*), and passions or desires (*epithymetikon*). Singing the words of the Psalms richly broadens those words, and the melodies enable worshipers to "love God with their whole strength and power."[124] Harmonious singing of the Psalms makes for harmonious people. As Carol Harrison observes, "Athanasius' description of the natural resonance which exists between the souls and the Psalms is clearly based on his conviction that both are the work of God and that both resonate in microcosm, with the measured music of his entire creation."[125]

---

122. Susan Gillingham, *Psalms through the Centuries,* vol. 1 (Oxford: Blackwell, 2008), 40, 44.

123. David M. Gwynn, *Athansius of Alexandria: Bishop, Theologian, Ascetic, Father* (Oxford: Oxford University Press, 2012), 149.

124. Athanasius, *Ep. Marcell.* 27, in *Athanasius: The Life of Antony and the Letter to Marcellinus,* trans. Robert C. Gregg (Mahwah, NJ; Paulist, 1980), 124.

125. Carol Harrison, "Enchanting the Soul: The Music of the Psalms," in *Meditations of the Heart: The Psalms in Early Christian Thought and Practice,* ed. A. G. Andreopoulos, Augustine Cassidy, and Carol Harrison (Louvain: Brepols, 2011), 211.

Thus Athanasius speaks of the soul-healing of the Psalms. They stir our inner life deeply, as a mirror of the soul—indeed, as a mini-Bible, a synopsis of all the Old Testament Scriptures. Like a doctor making his right prescription for each medical patient, so does Athanasius use the Psalms: "If you intend to make yourself bold and the others confident in right worship, since hope placed in God brings no shame, but instead makes the soul fearless, then praise God with the expressions of Psalm 90."[126]

II. Augustine of Hippo (354–430)

Augustine also acknowledges the profound influence of music. But in his homily on Ps. 90, he reflects upon Moses as the pivotal biblical figure: servant of the Old Covenant and prophet of the New Covenant. He quotes the words of Jesus: "If you believed Moses, you would believe me, for he wrote about me" (John 5:46).[127]

Augustine interprets v. 1, "throughout generations" (lit. "in generation and generation") as referring to "the two generations" of the two covenants.[128] God is the Creator of "the earth," where humans live, and of "the mountains" where the angels dwell. Time, too, is one of God's creations; God himself exists

> not from any age, but before the ages. . . . There is no "was" or "will be," in God, but only "is." This is why God said, *I AM WHO I AM. Thus shall you say to the children of Israel, HE WHO IS has sent me to you, and why it is said to him in a psalm, You will discard them, and so they will be changed, but you are the selfsame, and your years shall not fail* (Exod. 3:14; Pss.101:27–28(102:26–27)).[129]

Then in verses 3–6, Augustine contrasts the transience of this life with the world to come. In what sense is Augustine using this psalm therapeutically? It's all about Christians' soul health as spiritual beings. Humanly, we may reach "seventy" years, but we may be blessed to reach "eighty" by being "strong" spiritually—by already living in the eternal state.[130] Because of this spiritual

---

126. Athanasius, *Ep. Marcell.* 22 (Gregg, 120).

127. Augustine, *Exposition of Psalm 89* 2 in *Expositions on the Psalms,* trans. Maria Boulding, vol. 4 (Hyde Park, NY: New City, 2002), 303.

128. Augustine, *Exposition of Psalm 89* 2 (Boulding, 303).

129. Augustine, *Exposition of Psalm 89* 3 (Boulding, 304f.).

130. Augustine, *Exposition of Psalm 89* 10 (Boulding, 308).

strength, the fierce suffering of the martyrs simply intensified the experience of the "splendor of the Lord" shining upon his faithful witnesses—something Augustine may have witnessed himself. "Faith working through love" is the unique work of *I AM*, which the apostle tells us is "the work God wants" (John 6:29). "Thus the sole work, in which all others are comprised, is faith working itself out through love."[131]

III. Gregory of Nyssa (c. 332–395)

Gregory, writing between 376 and 378, like his elder brother, Basil of Caesarea, discerns musical harmony between the cosmos and the human person. As Hans Boersma puts it: "Harmony and virtue, beauty and goodness, go together with the Cappadocian Fathers."[132] Gregory interprets the five books of the Psalms as having the "blessedness," or aim (*telos*), of climbing Mount Sinai in five stages, as the growth of the virtuous life. It begins in Ps. 1 with "Blessed is the man," with all that follows being "praise unto our God." In the next stage, in Ps. 42[41], like the doe, the soul is longing and thirsting after God. Ps. 73[72] describes the kind of contemplation that is possible in the third stage of ascent. Ps. 90[89] begins the fourth stage with Moses guiding the soul to the height that Moses himself had climbed, having "removed himself from things that are inferior and earthly." In Ps. 107[106], the climax or mountain peak is reached, seeing a complete summation of human salvation and reaching to the final eschatological song of praise in Ps. 150.[133] As Boersma concludes: "Music making, Bible reading, and moral living were all of a piece to the church fathers."[134] The Psalms superbly demonstrate this unity.

IV. Martin Luther (1483–1546)

When we come to the Reformation, however, Ps. 90 is treated much more polemically. Luther's passionate pronouncement was that Moses had to be Moses in this psalm.

131. Augustine, *Exposition of Psalm 89* 17 (Boulding, 313–14).
132. Hans Boersma, *Scripture as Real Presence: Sacramental Exegesis in the Early Church* (Grand Rapids: Baker Academic, 2017), 143.
133. Boersma, *Scripture as Real Presence*, 154–56.
134. Boersma, *Scripture as Real Presence*, 158.

Luther, in one of his last lectures on the Psalms before beginning his massive commentary on the book of Genesis, interprets Ps. 90 as a lament psalm. He had begun his teaching on "the seven penitential psalms" in 1517, but now, toward the end of his life in 1535, his theme is "the lament psalms." He had been attached to the Psalms all his life, beginning in 1505 when he became an Augustinian friar.

Luther argues that Moses only composed one psalm, recognizing his authorship was supported not only by "the title, but also the language itself, the subject matter, and the whole theology of the Psalm."[135] In his last lecture series on the Psalms, in 1535, Luther argued, as Dennis Ngien summarizes, "Moses taught us the proper way of reading the Scriptures (2 Tim. 2:15), in which one must deal with arrogant and smug sinners in one way (i.e. by the law) but in an entirely different way with those have been already terrified (i.e. by the Gospel)."[136] The prime office of Moses, the archetype, was to be the inseparable companion of Holy Scripture, fulfilling his special office as "a minister of death, sin, and damnation."[137] No doubt Luther also saw this as his own office in the context of the Reformation, so he has a strong partiality for Moses, dwelling on this theme for most of his lecture! God's dwelling place and grace are the same thing for Luther, and "both creation and condemnation, contradictory activities, are done by the one and same God. . . . Just as life comes as a result of God's design, so death occurs as the result of God's wrath."[138]

In Luther's pessimism, he sees even the life of Methuselah, who lived a thousand years, to be as nothing with God (cf. Ps. 90:4). With sin in our lives, we live like lepers, yet the worst calamity is when we are unaware of our mortality! As with our secular society today, Luther saw that the vast majority of human beings in his time were practical atheists, going about their daily tasks as though there were "no death, and for that matter, no God."[139] But Moses, according to Luther, found consolation in God, who "before the mountains were born, and you brought to birth the earth and the world," is God who creates *ex nihilo*.

Thus for Luther, effective pastoral care is nothing other than the ministry of both law and gospel to cause us to repent in lament for sins. In this

---

135. Dennis Ngien, *Fruit for the Soul: Luther on the Lament Psalms* (Minneapolis: Fortress, 2015), 157.

136. Ngien, *Fruit for the Soul*, 158.

137. Ngien, *Fruit for the Soul*, 159.

138. Ngien, *Fruit for the Soul*, 169.

139. Martin Luther, "Psalm 90," trans. Paul M. Bretscher, *Luther's Works* (Minneapolis: Fortress, 1956) 13:128–29, quoted in Ngien, *Fruit for the Soul*, 171.

sense, God is "the God of lamentations." He causes lament, yet he cures the lamenting soul. It is Satan who causes us to lament without repentance, with no hope in our utter despair. Early in his life, Luther began to formulate his "theology of the cross," as "negative theology." But unlike Dionysius, who uses negatives to make affirmations and to achieve union with God, Luther finds God in weakness and suffering, not in majesty and glory. Thus the petition of Moses in v. 16, "Let your deeds appear to your servants and your splendor to their children," points to the advent of Christ in the flesh.[140] Negation, then, is not found through our logical conclusions based on natural knowledge but through the cross; not through a mystical ascent to God but through the sacred text itself. The experience of God is not found in the Dionysian darkness but in the life of the believer who has the text in the heart. As Gerhard Forde observes, the question of what God might do or not do is already answered in what he actually does and has done.[141]

After it has been thoroughly terrified, Luther advises the soul to sigh to God for mercy. It is an exercise like *compunctio*, which we have discussed in our previous commentaries.[142] Sighing is likewise a deep-felt emotion ("sighs too deep for words," Rom. 8:26, NRSV) that has a childlike authenticity, naivety, honesty, and dependence, all of which delight the heart of God. It is where God has his dwelling place within our hearts.[143]

The conclusion is the opposite to where the petitioner started. God is no longer "the problem." Wrath has been transformed into mercy, darkness and illness into light and health. Quoting v. 14, "Satisfy us in the morning with your unfailing love that we may shout for joy and rejoice in all our days," Luther concludes that we may now enter into God's "oceanic mercy." In the vastness of this experience, we voice the final petition: "Let the beauty of *I AM* our God rest upon us, and the work of our hands establish for us; and the work of our hands, establish it" (Ps. 90:17).[144]

Many other commentators have followed Luther in his commentary on this psalm, but we conclude with him, because his meditation is climactic!

140. Ngien, *Fruit for the Soul*, 183.

141. Gerhard O. Forde, *Where God Meets Man: Luther's Down-to-Earth Approach to the Gospel* (Minneapolis: Augsburg, 1972), 26.

142. Bruce K. Waltke and James M. Houston with Erika Moore, *The Psalms as Christian Worship: A Historical Commentary* (Grand Rapids: Eerdmans, 2010), 450.

143. Ngien, *Fruit for the Soul*, 190–95.

144. Ngien, *Fruit for the Soul*, 195–96.

PART IV. CONCLUSION

I. Canonical Context

According to Gerald Wilson, there is a historical movement reflected in the arrangement of the Psalter: Books IV and V are a response to Psalm 89, a psalm in which the issues of the failed Davidic monarchy and the crisis of the Babylonian exile are addressed (see pp. 15–16).[145] Accordingly, Book IV (Psalms 90–106) answers the crisis of the Babylonian exile by redirecting reliance on an earthly monarchy to an appreciation of God's eternal kingship,[146] from reliance on the earthly temple to reliance upon God himself. J. Clinton McCann argues: "Book IV can be characterized as a Moses-book, and in response to the crisis of exile and its aftermath, it offers the 'answer' that pervades the Psalter and forms its theological heart: God reigns!"[147]

There is an alternate eternal reality—the kingdom of God—that intersects with the sordid political reality. The two have not yet become one kingdom, but someday, in Jesus Christ, they will become one. That intersection began afresh with the advent of Jesus Christ. In his first advent, he bore God's wrath for the sins of his people (vv. 3–10) and learned obedience through his sufferings (vv. 11–12); in his second advent, he will fill them with eternal joy (vv. 13–17). Jerusalem and its carnal temple failed, but Christ's church will prevail. Ultimately the kingdom of God, the church, under the reign of Jesus Christ, the anointed King, will fill the new heaven and earth.

II. Message

The confidence that Israel's God is always his people's dwelling place gives the prodigal penitents space to lament that they wither as quickly as grass due to God's wrath against their sin and to find by their faith in him what the Jerusalem temple previously provided: peace and protection. Pity the homeless prodigal. Though few people know the verity that God's wrath is commensurate

---

145. Gerald H. Wilson, *The Editing of the Hebrew Psalter*, SBLDS 76 (Chico, CA: Scholars, 1985), 209–28.

146. Harry Nasuti, *Defining the Sacred Songs: Genre, Tradition, and the Post-Critical Intepretation of the Psalms*, JSOTSup 218 (Sheffield: Sheffield Academic, 1999), 177.

147. McCann, *Psalms*, 1040.

with the fear due him, the penitent prodigals, humbled and yet hopeful, ask God to cause them to know this by numbering their days and so giving them wise hearts. Thus enlightened, they petition *I AM* to confer upon them a new dispensation both of the joy of salvation in days and years commensurate with their affliction and of enduring work as his majestic deeds of salvation—in which they participate—once again appear among them. The most merciful God hears the prayer of the humble and does not despise their plea; rather, in the resurrected and eternal Jesus Christ, he answers them abundantly more than they dared to think or imagine. Yes, when he hides his face, we are dismayed and return to dust, but when he sends forth his life-giving Spirit, we renew the face of the ground both now and forevermore.

CHAPTER 3

Psalm 91: The Messiah's Invulnerability and Invincibility

PART I. VOICE OF THE PSALMIST: TRANSLATION

1   A song; a psalm by David.[1]
    As one[2] who dwells[3] in the secret place of the Most High,
       who in the shadow of the Almighty[4] resides,[5]

1. So LXX. MT lacks a superscript (see "Author," below).

2. Traditionally, *yōšēb* ("the one who dwells") is understood as subject and *yitlônān* ("resides") as its predicate: "the one who dwells in . . . resides in. . . ." This interpretation, however, is somewhat tautological, and the speaker of v. 1 cannot be clearly identified. A. F. Kirkpatrick (*The Book of Psalms* [1902; repr., Grand Rapids: Baker Books, 1986], 554) thinks the voice of v. 2 is the poet's voice of v. 1, but Robert Alter (*The Book of Psalms: A Translation and Commentary* [New York: Norton, 2007], 321] thinks "the poet" speaks in vv. 1, 3–13, but not in 2. *Yitlônān* is better interpreted with the Syriac version and with normal Hebrew syntax as continuing the participial construction "by a finite verb, with or without וֹ *waw*" (GKC, 116x; cf. Isa. 65:4: *hayyōšᵉbîm baqqᵊbārîm ûbannᵊṣûrîm yālînû*, "who sit among the graves and spend their nights keeping secret vigil"). Accordingly, *yōšēb* is an accusative of state, modifying the subject of "I say" in v. 2 (see *IBHS*, §10.2.2d). Kirkpatrick (*The Book of Psalms*) thinks this construction "harsh and cumbrous," but Frank-Lothar Hossfeld and Erich Zenger (*Commentary on Psalm 51-100*, trans. Linda M. Maloney, Hermeneia [Minneapolis: Fortress, 2005], 429) adopt it (cf. NRS, NET, JPS, NAB).

3. Or "one who sits enthroned," understanding the speaker is a king. So Mitchell Dahood (*Psalms II*, AB 17 [New York: Doubleday, 1968], 329) and Frank Moore Cross Jr. and David Noel Freedman ("The Song of Miriam," *Journal of Near Eastern Studies*, 14 [1955]: 237–50, esp. 248f.). Nevertheless, the parallel *lyn* ("to remain") and the parallelism of the concrete images for protection ("secret place" and "shadow") suggest *yšb* has its usual sense, "to dwell."

4. *Šadday* is conventionally glossed on the basis of the Vulg. by "Almighty," but its etymology and meaning are debated (cf. M. Weippert, *TLOT*, 3:1304–10, s.v. *šadday* [divine name]).

5. *Lûn* Hithpolel signifies being in the state of spending the night or of remaining,

2   I say[6] of[7] *I AM*, "[He is] my shelter and my stronghold,
       my God in whom I trust."

3   Surely, he will deliver you from the fowler's trap,[8]
       from[9] the destructive plague.[10]

---

a form that occurs elsewhere only in Job 39:28, where it used in parallel with *šākan* ("to dwell"), a synonym of *yšb*. This parallel suggests the gloss "stay," "reside." If so, this meaning debunks the incubation theory: that the king stays overnight at the cultic center with the hope of receiving from his privileged position a revelation (vv. 3-16; cf. Gen. 28:11; Num. 22:8; 1 Kgs. 19:9; see Leo Oppenheim, *The Interpretation of Dreams in the Ancient Near East*, TAPS 46 [1956], 186–88).

6. LXX, Vulg., Syr. gloss "he will say" (= *yō'mar* or *'ōmēr*). NAB and NJB add "you [who dwell/live]" in v. 1, but NAB repoints *'mr* as an imperative ("say") and NJB reads it as participle ("saying/who says"). The Qumran text, 11QPsAp[a] reads *h'wmr* ("the one who says"), thereby keeping the trusting person as the consistent speaker of vv. 1–2 (J. van der Ploeg, "Le Psaume XCI dans une recension de Qumran," *RB* 72 [1965]: 210–17, esp. 211; and Otto Eissfeldt, "Eine Qumran-Textform des 91 Psalms," in *Bibel und Qumran*, ed. H. Bardtke [Berlin: Evangelische Haupt-Bibelgesellschaft, 1968], 83). These are all facilitating readings (see *IBHS*, §§1.6.3g–m). The imperfect form signifies a habitual, repeated situation (i.e., "it is my custom to say," *IBHS*, §31.3e); a perfective form would signify an utterance at the moment of speaking (*IBHS*, §30.5.1d).

7. *Lamed* can signify the dative ("I say to *I AM*, '[You are] my shelter' "; so LXX, NRS, CSB, NAB, NJB), but more plausibly it signifies "with regard to" (so NIV, NET, ASV, ERV, JPS, KJV, NKJV, NLT; see *IBHS*, §11.2.10d). The *revia* sharply separates *lyhwh* from *'mr*, presumably to negate the expected dative after a verb of speaking. Dahood (*Psalms II*, AB 17 [New York: Doubleday, 1968], 330), followed by Pirmin Hugger (*Jahwe meine Zuflucht: Gestalt und Theologies des 91. Psalms*, Münsterschwarzacher Studien 13 [Münsterschwarzacher: Vier-Turma-Verlag, 1971], 31) and Marvin Tate (*Psalms 51–100*, WBC 20 [Dallas: Word, 1990], 447) interpret the preposition as a vocative *lamed* (= "O *I AM*"), but English versions do not accept this unnecessary and exceptional interpretation.

8. *The Concise Dictionary of Classical Hebrew* (ed. David Clines [Sheffield: Phoenix, 2009]) glosses *yāqûš* with "hunter," but in Prov. 6:5 (cf. Jer. 5:26–27) it clearly means "fowler." The fowling metaphor matches the ornithological metaphor in v. 4.

9. Several Heb. MSS, LXX, and Syr. read or reflect *ûmiddeber* "and from the destructive plague," but 11QPsAp[a] omits the conjunctive "and" with most medieval MSS.

10. LXX, Vulg., and possibly Tg. read *midde bar* ("from the matter of/word of/ obstacle of"). MT is the somewhat more difficult reading and so preferred (see *IBHS*, §§1.6.3g–m). Josua Blau ("Über Homonyme und Angeblich Homonyme Wurzeln II," *VT* 7 [1957]: 98) rebuts the notion of Immanuel Löw that *deber* in Psalm 91:3 and Hos 13:14 denotes "thorn" or "sting."

4   With his pinions[11] he will overshadow you;
    and under his wings you may seek shelter.[12]
    His faithfulness is a shield and a rampart.[13]

5   Do not be afraid of the terror at night,
    from the arrow that flies by day,

6   from the plague[14] that walks in darkness,
    from the pestilence that rushes[15] at noon.[16]

7   A thousand will fall at your side,

11. Construing poetic *'ebrâ*, always in parallel with prosaic *kānap*, as a collective singular (cf. Deut. 32:11).

12. 11QPsAp reads *tškwn* ("you will dwell"), which is probably not the original text (so also van der Ploeg, "Le Psaume XCI," 212). Eissfeldt ("Eine Qumran-Textform des 91 Psalms," 83) conjectures it replaces the older word of MT.

13. *sōḥērâ* is a hapax legomenon whose form and denotation are uncertain. A. A. Macintosh ("Psalm XCI 4 and the Root סָחַר," *VT* 23 [1973]: 56–62), after critically appraising its various interpretations, glosses it "[supernatural] protection" (cf. CSB, NAB). The notion of " 'supernatural' protection against demons," he argues, "has already been detected in Isa. 47:15, and . . . the evidence of comparative Semitic philology [Akkadian, Old South Arabic, and Arabic] suggests this meaning is widely attested in Semitic speech." (Macintosh surprisingly does not appeal to Jerome [*Psalmi Iuxta Hebr.* "protection"].) However, the meaning of "enchanters/ sorcerers" is not convincing in Isa. 47:15. Macintosh has not been followed, apart from "wizard" in NAB and NJB. *HALOT* (2:750, s.v. *sōḥērâ*) on basis of Syr., Mandaean, and Akkadian cognates, understands it to mean "wall" (i.e., a defensive wall or rampart). Macintosh's objection to this ("There is no evidence from the ancient versions to indicate that the word had this meaning in Ps. 91:4") can also be raised against his own conjecture.

14. LXX (cf. Aquila, Syr.) reflects *dābār* (see n. 10).

15. LXX reads *kai daimoniou* (= *wᵉšēd*, "and the demon"). Dahood (*Psalms 50-100*, 332) derives the word *'šd* with elided *aleph* ("leg") and repoints it as *yᵉšōd* ("stalks"). He has not been followed. GKC (67q) hesitantly suggests *yāšûd* is a metaplastic form of the Qal imperfect of *šdd* ("deal violently with, despoil"). Almost all English versions follow this interpretation. Robert Gordis ("The Biblical Root ŠD, ŠDY," *JTS* 41 [1940]: 34–41, esp. 39f.), however, followed by Tate, more plausibly derives *šwd*, the expected root. Syr. *šwd* means "to rush in force." Gordis argues that the concrete image "walk" in the first verset requires this more concrete sense than the traditional interpretation. The escalation from "walk" to "rush" aptly represents the plague as spreading from a unit of soldiers to a myriad of soldiers (see v. 7).

16. In the Qumran scroll, 6a and 6b are reversed.

> a myriad at your right hand;
>   [but] it will not come near you.
>
> 8   Only with your eyes will you look,
>   and you will see the retribution[17] of the wicked.
>
> 9   Because you [proclaim],[18] "*I AM* is my refuge,"
>   [and][19] you make the Most High your dwelling place,
>
> 10 calamity will not meet you;
>   and a plague will not draw near your tent.
>
> 11 Surely, he will command his angels for you,
>   to protect you in all your ways.
>
> 12 Upon the palms of their hands they will lift you up,
>   lest your foot strike a stone.

17. The feminine *šillūmâ* occurs only here in contrast to the three occurrences of masculine *šillûm*; HALOT (4:1540, s.v. *šillūmâ*) suggests "perhaps as an abstract, unitary noun, as distinct from meaning one individual manifestation (one particular consequence) of retaliation" (cf. *IBHS*, §6.4.2d).

18. English versions differ significantly in their translations of v. 9. As for *kî*, NIV and NLT gloss "if," but this calls into question the sincerity of the trusting person's confession in v. 2. In truth, as in vv. 1–2 and 3–8, the trusting person's confession of faith in 9 functions as the cause for the promises in 10–13. As for emphatic *'attâ* ("you"), LXX, Vulg., Tg., ASV, ERV think its antecedent is *I AM*. If so, the trusting man is the speaker and *yhwh* is a vocative (= "Because you, *I AM*, are my refuge"). But this understanding cannot be harmonized easily with 9b, for the speaker would change from the trusting person in 9a to the prophet within the verse itself. The LXX opts to smooth the difficulty by adding: "Thou, my soul, hast made. . . ." Most translations interpret the emphatic "you" in 9a as referring to the trusting person, in which case the prophet quotes what he said in 2. With this understanding, NRS, CSB, JPS, KJV, NAS suppose "have made" in 9b has been gapped and emend *mḥsy* ("my refuge") to *mḥsk* ("your refuge"). But this emendation has no textual support, and the MT is difficult to explain away. (Dahood explains *mḥsy* as retaining an archaic *yod* and that the "your" of the suffix of *meʿônekā* ["your dwelling place"] has been gapped, but this seems far-fetched.) NIV, GNV (cf. NJB) add "say" from the confession in v. 2 ("If you say, '*I AM* is my refuge' "). This interpretation has some support in the Tg.: *Solomon answered and said*: "For you are my confidence, O LORD"). It also finds support in the Qumran text. Van der Ploeg ("Le Psaume XCI," 211f.) restores *qrʾt* ("you call out"). Eissfeldt ("Eine Qumran-Textform des 91. Psalm," 84) agrees and translates: "Jahweh hast du gennant: Meine Zuflucht" ("you have named Yahweh: 'My Refuge'").

19. "And" is added for stylistic reasons.

13   Upon the lion[20] and the cobra[21] you will tread;
        you will trample the young lion and the serpent.[22]

14   Because he clings to me, I will rescue him,
        I will set him on high because he knows my name.

15   He will cry out to me, and I will answer him,
        I [will be] with him in distress;
        I will deliver him; I will glorify him.

16   I will satisfy him with endless days,
        and I will show him my salvation.

Part II. Commentary

I. Introduction

Author

The Masoretic Text (MT) lacks a superscript, but the Septuagint (LXX) attributes the psalm to David. There is no reason to discredit the LXX (see pp.

---

20. LXX, Vulg. and Syr. either interpreted *šaḥal* to mean "asp" or read *zḥl* ("reptile," see *BHS*). S. Mowinckel ("שחל," in *Hebrew and Semitic Studies: Presented to G. R. Driver*, ed. D. W. Thomas and W. D. McHardy [Oxford: Clarendon, 1963], 97) argued that *šaḥal* originally denoted a serpent dragon, the mythical wyvern, or "Lindwurm," that later came to be used as a poetical term for a lion. Scott C. Jones ("Lions, Serpents, and Lion-Serpents in Job 28:8 and Beyond," *JBL* 130 [2011]: 663–86) argues *šaḥal* in Job 28:8 evokes both a lion and a serpent and that there is a fuzzy line between the mythical and the real. This may also be true of *tannîn* (see n. 22). *HALOT* (2:1461–62, s.v. *šaḥal*) glosses *šaḥal* with "lion" in Ps. 91:13. *Šaḥal* occurs seven times in the Heb. Scriptures, all in poetry. Its use in Job 4:10; 10:16; Prov. 26:13; Hos 5:14; 13:7 fully supports the meaning "lion." Its use in Job 28:8, however, may connote the mythical dragon as well. In sum, *šaḥal* denotes the rapacity of the king of the beasts and may connote a supernatural reality.

21. *Peten* denotes a poisonous snake (Deut. 32:33; Job 20:14, 16), perhaps the cobra. Its Ugaritic cognate denotes "serpent, dragon" (Scott C. Jones, *Rumors of Wisdom: Job 28 as Poetry* [Berlin: de Gruyter, 2009], 157, esp. n. 305). Here, too, there may be overtones of the supernatural.

22. Or possibly "monster/dragon." *Tannîn* means "serpent" in Exod. 7:9 and Deut. 32:33, but it may have mythical overtones of a "sea-monster/dragon" in Isa. 27:1 and Jer. 51:34.

13–15 above and "royal" below). As for internal evidence, Charles and Emilie Briggs document that the psalm shares a large number of terms with psalms attributed to David in the MT.[23] Psalm 91 is a royal psalm, and more specifically a messianic prophecy (Luke 4:9–11; see "Messianic" below); the New Testament reckons David a prophet (Acts 2:30).

Form

Poetry, Liturgy, and Confidence

Psalm 91 is a poetic, liturgical psalm of confidence pertaining to the Messiah's invincibility. It has the benchmarks of Hebrew *poetry*: parallelism, terseness and figurative language (see p. 23–25). The psalm's change of voices and direction suggest it was an antiphony performed in a *liturgical* setting,[24] though one could argue that a poet adopts different voices in a literary fiction. Nevertheless, "secret place," "shadow" (v. 1) and "wings [perhaps of cherubim]" (v. 4) may signal a temple setting. Tremper Longman III identifies Psalm 91 as a psalm of *confidence*: "Metaphors of protection pervade the opening stanza."[25]

Royal

Before arguing for identifying Psalm 91 as a messianic psalm, let its *royal* character first be noted. As in other royal psalms (e.g., 2, 45, 84, 110), the poet presents his audience with different voices in different directions, as indicated by pronouns. In Psalm 91, three voices are heard with changing direction: (a) the voice of "I" who in direct address to God confesses his faith in *I AM* (vv. 1–2); (b) the voice of an authority who assures "you" (masc. sing.) of God's deliverance and "unflagging"[26] protection (vv. 3–13); and (c) the voice of "I" who assures "him" of security, exaltation, and fullness of life (vv. 14–16). The

---

23. Charles Augustus Briggs and Emilie Grace Briggs, *A Critical and Exegetical Commentary on the Book of Psalms*, vol. 2, ICC (1907; repr. Edinburgh: T&T Clark, 1976), 279.

24. S. Mowinckel, *Offersang og sanmgoffer* (Oslo: Aschehoug, 1951), 305; cited by A. Caquot, "Le Psaume XCI," *Sem* 8 (1958): 21.

25. Tremper Longman III, *Psalms: An Introduction and Commentary*, TOTC (Downers Grove, IL: IVP Academic, 2014), 329–30.

26. Robert Alter, *The Book of Psalms* (New York: Norton, 2007), 321.

crux interpretum is: Who is the "I" of v. 2, who is also the antecedent both of "you" in 3–13 and of "him" in 14–16? F. Kirkpatrick thinks the antecedent is the nation of Israel or any godly Israelite.[27] However, the national interpretation is unlikely because the pronouns are singular, not the plural. Most commentators think of a godly Israelite.[28] Tate comments: "The psalm is intended for instruction and exhortation and is designed to challenge and strengthen the faith of those who trust in Yahweh."[29] H. Schmidt classifies it with Psalm 121 (cf. 15 and 24) as a dialogue between the priest and the worshiper before entering the temple.[30] Otto Eissfeldt thinks the speaker is a convert on whom the priest bestows exuberant blessings.[31] Walter Brueggemann represents him as a "traveler" facing many threats on his journey,[32] and Amos Ḥakham refines that to "those going on pilgrimage festivals."[33] But none of these interpretations does justice to the martial language that characterizes Psalm 91. John Goldingay rightly comments: "It [the psalm] makes sense as addressed to the king, like Ps. 20. It is the king who especially needs Yhwh's rescue and protection in battle."[34] Other arguments also support a royal interpretation. First, John Eaton argued convincingly for an extensive royal interpretation of the Psalter.[35] Second,

27. F. Kirkpatrick, *The Book of Psalms* (Cambridge: Cambridge University Press, 1902), 555.

28. Rabbi Avrohom Chaim Feuer (*Tehillim: A New Translation with a Commentary Anthologized from Talmudic, Midrashic and Rabbinic Sources,* trans. Avrohom Chaim Feuer in collaboration with Nosson Scherman [Brooklyn: Mesorah, 1982], 1138) writes: "The Talmud relates that Rabbi Yehoshua ben Levi recited this psalm before he went to sleep to insure his safety from the dangers of the night. Consequently, the Halachah stipulates that this psalm be said every night before retiring (*Orach Chaim* 239:1)." Amos Ḥakham (*Psalms with the Jerusalem Commentary,* trans. Israel V. Berman, vol. 2 [Jerusalem: Mosad Harav Kook, 2003], 91f.) notes: "In *Shevuot* 15b, a *Baraita* is quoted which states that the first half of Psalm 91 is ... 'The Song of Perils,' or ... 'The Song of Plagues'.... The Talmud mentions that Rabbi Yehoshua ben Levi would recite 'The Song of Perils' in the prayers ... said when retiring to bed at night.... This psalm is customarily recited at funerals."

29. Marvin E. Tate, *Psalms 51–100,* WBC 20 (Dallas: Word, 1990), 450.

30. H. Schmidt, *Die Psalmen,* HAT 15 (Tübingen: Mohr [Siebeck], 1934), 172.

31. Eissfeldt, "Eine Qumran-Textform des 91 Psalms," 83.

32. Walter Brueggemann, *The Message of the Psalms* (Minneapolis: Augsburg, 1984), 156–57.

33. Ḥakham, *Psalms with the Jerusalem Commentary,* 91.

34. John Goldingay, *Psalms,* vol. 3, BCOTWP (Grand Rapids: Baker Academic, 2008), 39.

35. John Eaton, *Kingship and the Psalms,* SBT Second Series 32 (Naperville, IL:

the royal interpretation is the oldest. The Targum paraphrase of Psalm 91 reckoned David as speaking to Solomon. The New Testament (see below) interprets the trusting person as the Son of God, who according to the flesh was the son of David (Rom. 1:3). Third, the martial motifs of Psalm 91 are eminently suitable for a king, not an ordinary person. Eaton notes: "For a king, the air is ever thick with deadly darts, whether of plague (often a danger on campaigns), hostile curse or weapons. But God confers safety on him day and night, though armies fall in ten-thousands at his side (cf. II Sam. 18.3)."[36] The prophecy in 3–13 climaxes with the promise that he will trample satanic nations (v. 13).[37] Finally, there is this note that comes with the help of A. Caquot and Dahood[38]: Of course, the psalm assumes the faithful king does not fight alone but with an army that offers itself willingly with him in their battle for the kingdom of God (Ps. 110)[39] and whose life's breath is the king (Lam. 4:20).

Messianic

Even more specifically, Psalm 91 is a *messianic* psalm. For those who think an ordinary person or faithful king is in view,[40] there is the proverbial elephant in the room: This king is indestructible and unconquerable. From the perspective of any faithful king, its promises are overly optimistic to a flaw.[41] Psalm 44

Alec R. Allenson Inc., 1976), 20–26; Bruce K. Waltke and James M. Houston with Erika Moore, *Psalms as Christian Worship* (Grand Rapids: Eerdmans, 2010), 91.

36. Eaton, *Kingship and the Psalms*, 58.

37. Alter's (*The Book of Psalms,* 322) notion of "life imagined as a battlefield fraught with dangers" is misguided. It is unlikely that a poet would sustain the metaphor of the battlefield from vv. 3–16 without giving a clue to the figured reality.

38. Caquot, "Le Psaume XCI," 21–27; Dahood, *Psalms II*, 329–34.

39. Waltke and Houston, *Psalms as Christian Worship*, 484–514.

40. Most recently, Longman (*Psalms*, 329–31) identifies the army/congregation as the psalm's subject.

41. Derek Kidner (*Psalms 73–150*, TOTC [Downers Grove, IL: IVP Academic, 2009], 365), who interprets the psalm as giving assurances to every servant of God, tries to resolve the contradiction between the psalm's promises and the experienced reality with two bromides. First, "Rom. 8:28 ('. . .everything . . . for good with those who love him') does not exclude 'nakedness, or peril, or sword' (8:35)." But the promise of working all things for the saint's good is not the same as this psalm's promises of invulnerability and invincibility. Second, "what it does assure us is that nothing can touch God's servant but by God's leave." But nothing in the psalm suggests

rehearses the protest of Israel's king and his army that God had forgotten them on the battlefield (see Rom. 8:36). If the psalm's promises of invulnerability, invincibility (vv. 11–13), and long life are applied universally to martyrs, it mocks them. The faithful have been slaughtered from "the blood of righteous Abel to the blood of Zechariah son of Berekiah" (Matt. 23:35), to the beheading of John the Baptist (Matt. 14:1–12), to the recent deaths of Christians at the hands of Islamic (and other religious and nonreligious) extremists. Broyles resolves the clash between the poet's heavenly promises and earth's reality by arguing on the strength of 8b: "These are not general disasters but divine judgments aimed at the wicked. . . . This psalm promises not that believers are exempt from any calamity—simply that they are free from divine retribution" at the final judgment (cf. Gen. 6:9–8:18; Gen. 19:29; Exod. 8:22; 9:4, 26; 10:23; 2 Kgs. 19; Matt. 13:30, 31–46; Matt. 25:46).[42] However, the restriction to battles of retribution is unnatural, as evident from its lack of recognition in other commentaries. The point of verse 8b seems to be that the king's war is just.

The Lord Jesus Christ materializes the invincibility of the king in Psalm 91 in all situations prior to his death. Of his own accord, he gave his life over to death to make atonement for the sins of many (cf. Isa. 52:13–53:12). Of his own life he said: "No one takes it from me, but I lay it down of my own accord" (John 10:18). Before his willing and sacrificial death, however, Jesus Christ remained unscathed from attacks on his life (Matt. 2:13–18; Mark 4:37–39; Luke 4:29-30; John 10:31–39).[43] Satan assumed (and presumably the Lord Jesus

---

that caveat. A. Maclaren (*The Psalms*, vol. 3, Expositor's Bible [New York: George H. Doran, n.d.], 23) offers another bromide: "They [evil and sorrows] will not touch the central core of the true life, and from them God will deliver, not only by causing them to cease, but fitting us to bear." But the psalm does not distinguish between a person's outer being and inner core, and deliverance from trouble is not the same as being fitted to bear them. And Calvin offers the bromide for verse 10: "Troubles, it is true, of various kinds assail the believer as well as others, but the Psalmist means that God stands between him and the violence of every assault, so as to preserve him from being overwhelmed" (*Commentary on the Book of Psalms*, trans. Rev. James Anderson, vol. 2 [Grand Rapids: Baker Books, 2003], 484). None of these platitudes does justice to the text.

42. Craig C. Broyles, *Psalms*, NIBCOT (Peabody, MA: Hendrickson, 1999) 362.

43. Achilles' mother tried to make him immortal by treating him with ambrosia and burning away his mortality. Because the heel by which she held him remained untouched by the magic, she failed to make him immortal. *I AM*, however, successfully made his Messiah invulnerable and invincible in conjunction with the Messiah's ethical faith in the promises of God.

Christ agreed) the divine inspiration of Psalm 91 and its messianic interpretation (Luke 4:9–11; cf. 10:19). In short, the messianic interpretation of Psalm 91 is its plain sense[44] and is confirmed by the New Testament.

The assurances of Psalm 91 to this ideal king aimed to generate faith in Israel's kings, perhaps upon their enthronement or before they went to battle. As types of the messianic Antitype, they prevailed by faith.[45] Today these promises of Christ's invulnerability and invincibility embolden the church to live by his faith, knowing their hope will not be put to shame. Being "in Christ," as Paul expresses it, they face persecution and danger as their Lord did, knowing that in him, the Eternal One, they are in a true sense indestructible.

Rhetoric

When "you" in vv. 3–13 and "him" in 14–16 are understood as the king, the psalm's dramatic rhetoric becomes apparent. The king testifies to his faith in God (vv. 1–2, 9a); a prophet—be it the priest, a prophet attached to the temple, or a court poet—assures him of his safety, security, and salvation (vv. 3–13; cf. Ps. 45:1); and this oracle becomes an oracle of *I AM* himself, probably uttered by the prophet (vv. 14–16), a common occurrence in prophetic literature (e.g., Mic. 1:2–16). Since the prophet repeats the king's confession of faith in verse 9a, the psalm could be analyzed as consisting of two equal stanzas: the "king's" confession of faith (1–8) and the promises of assurance (9–16).[46] Since, however, God reprises the king's faith (14a), the psalm is better analyzed as consisting of three stanzas and the prophet's oracles as consisting of two alternating strophes (3–8, 9–13).[47] These strophes begin with "surely" followed by images of the king's deliverance and protection from calamity and from pestilence (3–4, 10), which images are

44. "It is supposed by the Jews to relate to the Messiah," says John Calvin (*Commentary on the Book of Psalms*, 477).

45. See Bruce K. Waltke, "A Canonical Process Approach to the Psalms," in *Tradition and Testament: Essays in Honor of Charles Lee Feinberg*, ed. John S. Feinberg and Paul D. Feinberg (Chicago: Moody, 1981), 3–18.

46. Kirkpatrick (*The Book of Psalms*, 554) so analyzes the psalm.

47. "Stanza" refers to the largest divisions of a psalm and "strophe" to the largest divisions of a stanza. See p. 32n31.

followed in turn by assurance of his safety in the plague (6–7), escalated in the latter case to angelic protection (11–12). The first strophe culminates with the king gazing down at corpses of the wicked (8) and the second strophe with his trampling the symbolic "cobra" and "lion" (13). The divine oracle escalates his deliverance and protection to glorification, fullness of life, and salvation.

Here is a roughly hewn outline of the psalm:

II. Exegesis

Stanza I (King Speaks): Confession of Faith in God 1–2

Verses 1–2 are connected by (a) grammar (see n. 2); (b) the voice of the king in contrast to the authoritative voice in verse 3; (c) fourfold references to God matched by four metaphors for security, with each verse having two; (d) the theme of the king's faith in God as protector; and (e) the parallel metaphors "shade" and "shelter."

Strophe A: Introduction to Confession 1

Verse 1 sounds the psalm's theme: *I AM*'s protection.[48] To connote God as Israel's dwelling place from ages past (cf. Psalm 90:1–2), the king refers to *I AM* by his patriarchal names: [El] Elyon, "[God] Most High" (cf. Gen. 14:18); and [El] Shaddai, "[God] Almighty" (see n. 4; cf. Gen. 17:1; Num. 24:16). The verse's core images of "secret place" and "shadow" connote the intimate connection between the monarch and God. The framing verbs "dwell" and "reside" point to this relationship being continual. *As one who dwells* connotes hospitable acceptance into a household, security (cf. Gen. 19:3–8; Judg. 19:16–24), and duration of residence. *In the secret place* (*bᵉsēter*; cf. royal Ps. 61:4[5]) denotes a place of intimacy that is inaccessible to those not chosen, even as a secret (*sēter*) message is accessible only to the addressee (see Judg. 3:19). Grammatically, the secret place of Ps. 91:1 is not the Most High himself[49]—though theologically that is true (Ps. 31:19–20[20–21])—but a metonymy for the house of God on Mount Zion. If the psalm is by David, it refers either to the tent that David pitched for the ark or to the temple that he envisioned (see p. 15). The epithet *the Most High* (cf. royal psalms 18:13; 21:7[8]; 92:1[2]) "is an integral part of Zion theology (cf. esp. 46:4[5]; 47:2[3])."[50] It is an epithet of kingship (Pss. 18:13[14]; 47:2[3]); Isa. 14:14; Lam. 3:38).[51] That title "cuts every threat down to

---

48. Brennan Breed ("Reception of the Psalms: The Example of Psalm 91," in *The Oxford Handbook of the Psalms*, ed. William P. Brown [Oxford: Oxford University Press, 2014], 297–310, esp. 298), with erudition, documents that "most readers throughout history have understood Psalm 91 to be a statement or enactment of divine protection from demons." He fails, however, to distinguish in the *history of the psalm's reception* between the psalmist's perils interpreted as demonic and the anti-demonic apotropaic use of the psalm. The identification of the perils as demonic is bad exegesis, and its anti-demonic apotropaic use is bad theology. The use of the psalm as magic contradicts the very nature of *I AM*'s covenantal relationship with Israel. He rules her history according to Torah ethics and detests magic (pace H. Gunkel and J. Begrich, *Introduction to the Psalms: The Genres of the Religious Lyric of Israel*, trans. James D. Nogalski [Macon, GA: Mercer University Press, 1998], 147).

49. In that case, one expects an apposition (i.e., "in the Most High"), not a genitive probably of possession (i.e., "the secret place that belongs to the Most High").

50. Hossfeld and Zenger, *Commentary on Psalms 51–100*, 430.

51. Hans-Joachim Kraus, *Theology of the Psalms*, trans. Keith Crim (Minneapolis: Augsburg, 1979), 28; T. D. Mettinger, *In Search of God: The Meaning and Message of the Everlasting Names,* trans. F. H. Cryer (Philadelphia: Fortress, 1988), 122.

size," says Kidner.[52] *In the shadow* connotes protection (cf. Gen. 19:8; Jonah 4:5; Isa. 4:6; 34:15; Ps. 17:8).

Strophe B: Confession of Trust 2

Like the psalmists in Pss. 31:14[15] and 102:24[25] (cf. Job 10:2) the king formally introduces his address to God by *I say* (cf. "he says" that opens the royal Ps. 18 [2 Sam. 22]). He customarily declares his faith publicly (cf. Rom. 10:9) *of*/about I AM (cf. Ps. 100:1). As in Isaiah 4:6, "shade" (v. 1) and *shelter* are probably semantic catchwords. Whereas in verse 1 the sanctuary where God sat enthroned provided protection, in verse 2, *I AM* himself is the defender: he is always with him (v. 14). Its threefold repetitions of "my" emphasize the king's personal relationship with God. In *and my stronghold*, "stronghold" (*mᵉṣûdâ*) is a military term appropriate for a king (2 Sam. 5:9). Strongholds are usually built on cliff-like heights. The Qumran scrolls use the term for the now famous Masada, whose steep cliffs on the east side are 1,300 feet high and on the west 300 feet high. *My God* (see Ps. 100:3) is emphatic. *In whom I trust.* "Trust" signifies "to feel secure, be unconcerned, or, with an affirmation of the reason for the security, to rely on something (e.g., wealth, Prov. 11:28) or someone (e.g, Pharaoh, Jer. 46:25)."[53] The definition implies "trust" is exercised in the face of danger. The tense again indicates an ongoing situation. Outside of Judges 20:36 and Proverbs 31:11, Scripture condemns trust in anyone or in anything apart from God (cf. 2 Kgs. 18:21; Ps. 118:8–9; Isa. 36:5; Jer. 5:17; 12:5; 18:10; 48:7; Ezek. 33:13; Mic. 7:5). E. Gerstenberger observed: "One can successfully place confidence only in Yahweh, . . . no other entity can be an ultimate object of trust."[54] Trust in God, however, cuts no ice in one's thinking unless God has spoken words guaranteeing that trust. So the psalm segues into words of promise and assurance (vv. 3–16).

Stanza II (Prophet Speaks): Assurances to the King 3–13

Inferentially, the speaker in verses 3–13 is a prophet, for he gives assurances only God can fulfill. His addressee, "you," has no other plausible antecedent than the "I" (i.e., the king) in verse 2.

---

52. Kidner, *Psalms 73–150*, 364.
53. A. Jepsen, *TDOT*, 2. 89, s.v. *bṭḥ*.
54. E. Gerstenberger, *TLOT*, 1:229, s.v. *bṭḥ*.

Strophe A: First Cycle 3–8

The catchword "shelter" verbally connects the king's confession of faith to God—"he is my shelter" (v. 2)—with the prophet's assurance that under God's wings "you may seek shelter" (v. 4). The first cycle consists of a couplet assuring the king that God will deliver and protect him (vv. 3–4) and a quatrain (two couplets) pertaining to battlefield perils (5–8): to wit, to human weapons and nature's plague (5–6) and to the king's triumph through the plague (7–8). Tate calls Johnson's literal interpretation of verse 5–8 "an exercise in poetical imagination."[55] To be sure, the poet uses many figures of speech, but these figures occur within a sustained, holistic description of battlefield perils. We will proceed with Goldingay "on the assumption that the military language reflects the king's literal position as commander in chief; reference to epidemic and to his tent may link with that."[56] Some speculate the real perils are demons (see notes 13, 15, 48).[57] but as Goldingay rightly comments: "There is no explicit indication of this reference [demons], and it would be unique in the OT, which makes hardly any reference to demons."[58] On the other hand, the New Testament gives a spiritual depth to the physical images of the Old Testament. Our gifted poet reports the telling details of the battle to represent the whole: terror at night, arrows that fly by day, and an unscathed king gazing at the tens of thousands of soldiers round about him, felled by a plague that accompanies battle. Weiser comments: "The greatness of the divine power to help can be judged only by the magnitude of the affliction."[59]

1. Delivered and Protected from Peril 3–4

God promises both to deliver the king from his enemies (v. 3) and to protect him from harm (v. 4). The two images of evil—the human "trap" and nature's "plague," from which the king is saved—mutually support one another, for, as Kidner observes, both dangers "strike unseen," and against them "the strong are as helpless as the weak."[60]

---

55. Tate, *Psalms 51–100*, 455.
56. Goldingay, *Psalms*, 39.
57. Cf. Artur Weiser, *The Psalms*, OTL (Philadelphia: Westminster, 1962), 608f.
58. Goldingay, *Psalms*, 45.
59. Weiser, *The Psalms*, 607.
60. Kidner, *Psalms 73–150*, 364.

3 The antecedent of emphatic *he* has no plausible candidate other than *I AM* ("my God," v. 2). *Will deliver* means "to snatch away, to remove, to liberate out of any kind of being held fast."[61] The antecedent of *you* is "I" of verse 2 (see "Form" above). *The fowler* (see Pss. 124:7; 141:9; 2 Tim. 2:26) may be death itself[62] and/or the wicked (v. 8) and the cobra and snake (v. 13). A *trap* or snare conceals its deadly danger in order to take its victim suddenly and by surprise to hold him fast until its owner can do as he will to the powerless victim (cf. Eccl. 9:12). Another danger of the battlefield is *the plague*. Probably bubonic plague is in view—a plague associated with war. The angel of *I AM* killed 185,000 in the Assyrian army in 701 BCE, probably through bubonic plague (2 Kgs. 19:35).[63] Bubonic plague was a serious threat that God leveled against Israel (Lev. 26:25; Num. 14:12). Here it is described as *destructive* forces that bring ruin.[64]

4 Kidner notes: "As for God's care, it [verse 4] combines the warm protectiveness of a parent bird (4a) with the hard, unyielding strength of armour (4b)."[65] *With his pinions* evokes the image of a mother bird who protects her brood by spreading her wings over them (cf. Ruth 2:12; Pss. 17:8; 36:7[8]; 57:1[2]; 61:4[5]; 63:7[8]). Possibly, the figure refers to God, who is present above the wings of

---

61. U. Bergmann, *TLOT*, 2:760, s.v. *nṣl*.

62. So F. Delitzsch, *Psalms,* trans. Francis Bolton, Keil and Delitzsch Commentary on the Old Testament 5 (London: T&T Clark, 1866–91; repr., Peabody, MA: Hendrickson, 1996), 603.

63. The Greek historian Herodotus, writing his history in the fourth century BCE, heard an Egyptian story about Sennacherib's campaign that also ascribed the Assyrian withdrawal from Jerusalem to a miracle: "After this, Sennacherib, King of the Arabians and Assyrians, marched a large army against Egypt. . . . A number of field-mice, pouring in upon their enemies, devoured their quivers and their bows, and moreover, the handles of their shields; so that on the next day, when they fled bereft of their arms, many of them fell" (Herodotus, *Hist.*, 2.141.2, 5 [trans. Henry Cary]). The presence of mice in his account suggests that a bubonic plague destroyed the Assyrian army because rat fleas are the usual carriers of the disease. So also *I AM*'s ark of the covenant probably inflicted a bubonic plague on the Philistines, for their apotropaic devices of tumors and rats are connected with bubonic plague (1 Sam. 6:5). Mice are a Greek symbol of pestilence; it is Apollo Smintheus (the mouse god) who sends and then ends the plague in Homer (*Il.* 1.39).

64. *HALOT*, 1:242 s.v. *hawwâ* II; its form is often plural.

65. Kidner, *Psalms 73–150*, 364.

the cherubim upon the ark (Exod. 25:20; 1 Kgs. 8:6-7; see pp. 24, 237).[66] The figurative references to the temple in verse 1 support this interpretation. There are two sides to the image: God's side (*he will overshadow you*) and the king's side (*and under his wings you may seek shelter*). Verset 4b clarifies the image. The protective wings of *I AM* refer to *his faithfulness*. The abstract attribute of God's reliability, dependability, trustworthiness, faithfulness, and constancy finds concrete reality in God's words, such as those of the Davidic covenant and of this psalm. Maclaren comments: "We have not to fly to a dumb God for shelter, or to risk anything upon a Peradventure. He has spoken, and His word is inviolable. Therefore, trust is possible."[67] *A shield* (*ṣinnâ*) denotes a shield used to protect the entire body.[68] The defensive shield of the warrior is combined with and escalated to a defense wall, *a rampart* (see n. 13).

2. Do Not Fear Round-the-Clock Perils   5-6

This couplet is united grammatically by four prepositional phrases that modify "do not be afraid" in connection with the perils of battle: to wit, from terror and arrows (v. 5), and from the ensuing bubonic plague and destruction (v. 6). The perils alternate as several merisms: by humans (v. 5) and by

66. See also Psalm 99:1 (p. 236). "This image [of covering wings]," says Caquot ("Le Psaume XCI," 28), "seems to be specifically Israelite; it has no equivalent in Akkadian lyrics." He draws the conclusion: "Probably, its origins are to be found in the realities of the temple: the 'pinions of Yahweh' are those of the cherubim connected with the ark." The cherubim are winged angelic creatures who protect what is sacred. They appear with wings in Ezekiel's vision (Ezek. 1:5-11; 10:19-20). David says of God: "He mounted the cherubim and flew; he soared on the wings of the wind" (Ps. 18:10). Two cherubim overshadowed the ark to protect it from defilement, even as the cherubim protected the way to the tree of life in the Garden of Eden to prevent sinful human beings from eating its fruit. In later Jewish and Christian thought they are regarded as angels, but not in the Bible.

67. Maclaren, *The Psalms*, 19.

68. It was used during the siege of cities, particularly when warriors were trying to undermine the wall. Often, a shield bearer would have the single responsibility of moving the shield in order to protect himself and an archer who accompanied him (T. Longman, *NIDOTTE*, 3.819-20, s.v. *ṣinnâ* II; see Y. Yadin, *The Art of Warfare in Biblical Lands* [New York: McGraw-Hill, 1963], 406, 418, 462). By contrast, the *māgēn* (Gen. 15:1) is a round, light shield that is made of wood or wicker and covered with thick leather rubbed with oil (cf. Isa. 21:5) to preserve it and to make it glisten. It is carried by the light infantry to ward off the enemy's sword, spear, or arrows.

God through nature (v. 6); in verse 5, night and day, hidden and open; in verse 6, darkness and noon, hidden and open. The king is protected from all perils 24-7.

a) Peril of Human Weapons 5

Do not be afraid is an *oratio variata*—a poetic way of reinforcing the underlying strong promises of verse 5, not a real command—for the king has expressed his confidence in *I AM* to be his shelter and stronghold. Instead of describing the perils of 5–6 in the pedestrian language of bare facts, a poet prefers to represent them in the form of a command. *Terror* (*paḥad*) has the core idea "to shake, tremble," either for joy (Isa. 60:5; Jer. 33:9) or, predominantly, before something "scary" (Deut. 28:66; Isa. 33:14).[69] *At night* qualifies the metonymy. But to what is "terror at night" an adjunct? According to the paraphrase of the Targum, it is demons ("Be not afraid of the terror of *demons that walk at* night"), and it is so heard by the rabbinic aggadists and by some moderns (Wensinck, Oesterley, and Gemser). This is so because, among other things, they understand the night as the domain of demons. Job 24:16–17 associates the night with evil, but with thieves and adulterers, not with demons. Caquot notes that the night does not end demonic activity.[70] Moreover, the parallel ("the arrow that flies by day") seems to point to a military peril (cf. Ps. 121:6). More probably, the metonymy refers to a sudden and unexpected attack of the enemy army at night.[71] *The arrow*

> in contrast to most other weapons, . . . strikes from afar (Gen. 21:16). While one may defend against many other weapons, the arrow strikes suddenly (Ps. 64:7), so swiftly that time stands still (Hab 3:11). The bowman may let his arrow fly from ambush (Jer. 9:8). The arrow may wound randomly (1 Kings 22:34). These qualities—long range, lightning quick, unseen, perhaps even random—made the bow and arrow . . . a weapon to be feared.[72]

69. Goldingay, *Psalms*, 44.

70. Caquot, "Le Psaume XCI," 29.

71. Song 3:7 supports this interpretation. Solomon's warriors were "all of them wearing the sword, all experienced in battle, each with his sword at his side, prepared for the terrors of the night." Ps. 11:2 refers to shooting arrows in the darkness.

72. Leland Ryken, James C. Wilhoit, and Tremper Longman III, eds., *Dictionary of Biblical Imagery* (Downers Grove, IL: IVP Academic, 1998), 48.

That flies is a metonymy of cause, implying the effect of the often poisoned arrow's deadly strike. *By day* constitutes a merism with "at night." Weapons and plagues both pose a round-the-clock threat.

b) Peril of the Bubonic Plague 6

Verse 6 is parallel to verse 5: the causal *from* again introduces the next two perils. Grammatically, the perils are directly connected with a relative clause (*that*). The versets pertain to "night" and "day" (cf. v. 5) but have been escalated to "darkness" and "noon." The poet personifies "pestilence"/ *plague* (see v. 3) as a person who *walks* through the camp by foot, a fitting metaphor for the spread of the plague from one soldier to another. *Darkness* denotes the darkness of night but connotes sinister "gloom."[73] *Pestilence* (*qeṭeb*) in three of its four occurrences is paired with "plague" (*deber* [v. 6; Hos 13:14] and *rešep* [Deut. 32:24]), suggesting it is used here as a metonymy for a plague—perhaps "epidemic." It escalates from "walks" to *rushes [in force]*, implying the plague has reached epidemic proportions. *At noon*, the brightest time of the day (Ps. 37:6) stands in contrast to evening and morning in Psalm 55:17.

3. Gaze on the Destruction of the Wicked 7–8

The king's protection (vv. 5–6) from his enemies is complemented with their destruction (7–8). He gazes (8) upon the fallen wicked all around him (7).

a) Myriads of the Wicked Fall 7

The poet elaborates on the plague rather than weapons because it is an act of God, not the king's military skill, to destroy the wicked. Verset 7a consists of synonymous parallels ("a thousand," 7aα ; "a myriad," 7aβ) about the felled enemy, antithetical to the parallel about the king's escape (7b). "At your side" (7a) is set over against "not near you" (7b). The fallen from the plague are right beside him, but the plague itself is not within talking distance of him. As for verset 7a, the escalation from "a thousand" to "ten thousand" is formulaic in

---

73. *'ōphel* is used of the darkness in which the wicked wait in ambush (Ps. 11:2); of the darkness of the netherworld, a land of deep darkness (Job 10:22); and as a metonymy for calamity (Job 23:17; 30:26).

synonymous parallelism (cf. 1 Sam. 18:6–7), but in this case it reflects, like the parallels "walk" and "rush" in verse 6, that the plague has reached raging, epidemic proportions.

The synonymous parallels of verset 7a are structured as a chiasm: "at your side a thousand//ten thousand at your right hand." A *thousand* (*'elep*) is the largest round figure that can exist in multiples for counting. Usually, it occurs with a noun (cf. Ps. 90:4), but here it is used absolutely, probably as a reference to a military unit of a thousand soldiers. Jesse sent David with cheese to the commander of an *'elep* (1 Sam. 17:18; cf. Deut. 32:30). "Thousands" and "myriads" are also used in the military contexts of Deut. 33:17, 1 Sam. 18:7, and Ps. 3:6[7]. The numbers may be actual. Sennacherib's slain troops numbered 185,000. *Will fall* is used "especially of violent death" (c. 96 times).[74] The idiom *at your side* (cf. Ruth 2:14; 1 Sam. 20:25) connotes close proximity. An insuperable *myriad* designates an indeterminate, immense number (cf. 1 Sam. 18:6–9; Ps. 3:6[7]; Mic. 6:7). "At your side" is escalated to the *right hand*, the favored and stronger hand (cf. Gen. 48:13, 18; 1 Kgs. 2:19).[75] In sum, the king will appear to have slain a whole army, though in truth they were killed in the raging bubonic epidemic.

As for the assurance, "it will not come near you," the only grammatical antecedent of *it* (masc. sing.) is the devastating plague "that frequently broke out during military campaigns."[76] The assurance in the midst of scenic descriptions of the enemy falling all around the king (v. 7) and of his only gazing at them (8) is eminently suitable for a plague. *You* is emphatic. *Draw near* (*nāgaš*) denotes "to come close" for contact: for sex (Exod. 19:15) or for conversation (Gen. 43:18; 44:18). He can see the fallen enemy beside him, but the plague does not come close enough to be heard.

b) The Wicked Paid Back 8

The destruction of the wicked is just, not arbitrary. *Only* means "except" (cf. 1 Kgs. 8:9). Though the plague will not draw near the king, he will gaze at its devastating effect. The concrete image of his body part, *with your eyes*, matches the comparable image of "at your side," but more importantly has the sense "with your own eyes." *Will you look* (*tabbîṭ*) means to set eyes upon something

74. Of Sisera, Deborah sings: "Where he sank, there he fell—dead" (Judg. 5:27).
75. "Since time immemorial, the 'right hand' has been used figuratively in the sense of 'power' or 'might' (cf. Isa. 63:12)" (Soggin, *TDOT*, 6:101, s.v. *ymyn*).
76. Dahood, *Psalms II*, 332.

or in a certain direction in order to see it (cf. Hab. 1:13). *And you will see* ("like Israel on the night of the Passover"[77]) *the retribution* (see n. 17)—namely, the compensation or reward that the wicked must pay to God and his king for the harm they intended by setting a trap for the righteous. "Retribution" is a metonymy for the "rotting bodies of the king's adversaries decimated by the plague"[78] and so explains the reason for the epidemic. Pirmin Hugger comments: "The poet sees the victims of the plague, their death and their putrefaction, and explains both theologically as a 'consequence' (. . . *šillūmâ*) of godlessness."[79] *Of the wicked* denotes a community that is guilty of sins of thoughts, words, and deeds that betray their inner hostility to God and his people.[80] Contextually, "the wicked" is a metonymy for the fallen enemy the king gazes upon, not for the wicked generally, though theologically that too is true.[81]

Strophe B: Second Cycle 9–13

Verse 9 reprises the chiastic repetition of "the Most High" (1, 9b), and "my shelter" (2a, 9a) to introduce the second strophe. As will be seen in comments on verse 10, that the perils and plague will *not* happen to the king reprises 3–8. The two strophes of the second stanza have an alternating structure: an emphatic "surely" (vv. 3, 11); assurances of the king's divine protection by God's wings (4) and his angels (11–12); and climactically, that the wicked will be punished (8) and the king will trample them (13).

1. Faith and Protection 9–10

In addition to the unified function of verses 9–10 as an echo of 1–8, the protasis (v. 9) and apodosis (v. 10) construction links them.

---

77. Delitzsch, *Psalms*, 603.

78. Cf. Dahood, *Psalms II*, 332f.

79. Pirmin Hugger, *Jahwe meine Zuflucht*, 45.

80. K. Richards, "A Form and Traditio-Historical Study of *rš‘*" (PhD diss., Claremont, CA, 1970; cf. *ZAW* 83 [1971]: 402). C. van Leeuwen (*TLOT*, 3:1262, s.v. *rš‘*) says: "In contrast to the positive root *ṣdq*, *rš‘* expresses negative behavior—evil thoughts, words and deeds—antisocial behavior that simultaneously betrays a person's inner disharmony and unrest (Isa. 57:20)."

81. *Pace* Weiser, *The Psalms*, 610.

a) Cause: Reprise of King's Confession 9

The polysemous *you make* signifies specifically "you have set, appointed."[82] For *the Most High*, see "Strophe A: Introduction"; and on *your dwelling place*, see comment on 90:1 (p. 38).

b) Consequence: No Calamity 10

Calamity (*rāʿâ*) conveys the judgment that something is bad, not good, whether a concrete physical state (Gen. 41:3; Jer. 24:2) or moral behavior that injures another (ethical "evil") or, as here, an abstraction for what is physically bad ("harm/injury/calamity/disaster"). *Will ... meet* (III *ʾānâ* Pual = "be made to happen" to) *you* (cf. Prov. 12:21). *Plague* (*negaʿ*) echoes "plague" (*deber*, vv. 3b, 6a). Does "calamity" echo "terror" and "arrows" (v. 5)? That 10 is a reprise of 3–8 finds further support in the respective predicates of the two synonymous nouns translated "plague": *Draw near* (*yiqrab*) reprises "to be close to" (*nāgaš*, 7b). The two verbs occur as parallels in Isaiah 65:5. *Your tent* is the appropriate locus for a king in battle (cf. 1 Sam. 4:10; 17:54; 2 Kgs. 7:7); its frequent interpretation as an allusion to a nomadic life does not fit the holistic battlefield scene.

2. Angelic Enablement 11–12

Verses 11–13 are unified grammatically and semantically. Angels are the subject of 11–12 and the motif of advancing movement unifies them: "way" (v. 11), "foot" (12), "tread [under feet]" (13). Climactically, the prophet assures the king: angels will protect/watch over you (11), keep your feet from stumbling on a stone that would end your mission (12), in order that you may tread upon the cobra and the lion (13). Only now the poet discloses why the king engages the battle: to vanquish the enemy.

a) The King Guarded in All His Ways 11

Surely, he will command signifies that I AM the Most High speaks as a superior with authority and force. *His angels* (*malʾākāyw*) are supernatural and nonphysical spirits that may assume a bodily appearance and function as his messengers (see Ps. 103:20).[83] Their plural number in verse 11 evokes the image

---

82. BDB, p. 963, s.v. *śîm, śûm* I, §3d.
83. *Malʾāk* means "messenger," glossed in English versions "messenger" for a hu-

of a camp of angels (cf. Gen. 32:2). As God assured Moses, "I am sending an angel before you to guard you along the way" (Exod. 23:20), so now he assures his king: *to protect you in all your ways* and so bring salvation history to its climactic conclusion.[84]

b) Angels Prevent King from Stumbling 12

The image of a stumbling stone originated in the rocky landscape of the Judean hills, in which there were no paved roads until the Romans introduced them.[85] The overshadowing wings of God (cherubim?) now give way to the palms of angels' hands (vv. 4, 12a) and a stumbling block replaces a trap (3, 12b). *They will lift you up* connotes "to support, sustain"[86] with the phrase *upon the palms [of their hands]* (*'al-kappayim*).[87] Hakham plausibly, albeit without documentation, suggests: "This is an image based on the practice that when high-ranking nobility walk in a place where walking is difficult, their servants carry them."[88] Angels appear as human beings with hands, not with wings.[89]

---

man being and "angel" for a divine being. In heaven, the innumerable angels who remained loyal to God function to praise God (Rev. 5:12) and to be intermediary creatures linking heaven and earth, as in Psalm 91:11–12. In Jacob's famous dream, he saw angels ascending and descending on a stairway reaching from heaven to Bethel, showing Bethel to be the axis between heaven and earth (Genesis 28). Today that axis is Jesus Christ (John 1:51). Angels are excellent in wisdom and power. David is flatteringly compared to an angel of God by the Philistine king Achish, by the wise woman of Tekoa, and by Saul's son, Mephibosheth (1 Sam. 29:9; 2 Sam. 14:17; 19:27). The psalmist describes angels as "mighty ones who do *I AM*'s word" (Ps. 103:20). Often, they perform some particular commission on behalf of God, such as to prosper the search of Abraham's servant for Isaac's bride (Gen. 24:7). The angel of *I AM* encamps around the faithful (Ps. 34:7) and chases the king's enemies (Ps. 35:5). They continue to be "ministering spirits sent to serve those who will inherit salvation" (Heb. 1:14; cf. Matt. 18:10; Acts 5:19–20; 10:22; 12:7–11).

84. *Šāmar* can also glossed "to watch over" (see Ps. 99:7; cf. Gen. 28:20, NIV). In these contexts, "way" is used "figuratively of course of life, or action, undertakings" (BDB, p. 203, s.v. *derek*, §5). The metaphor entails appropriate action to achieve a desired purpose.

85. See Alter, *The Book of Psalms*, 323.

86. BDB, p. 671, s.v. *nāśā'*, §2c.

87. Cf. 1 Sam. 5:4: *kappôt yādāyw* ("palms of his [Dagan's] hands").

88. Hakham, *Psalms*, 366.

89. Manoah did not recognize the angel of *I AM* until the angel did not return after his ascent in flames (Judg. 13:21). Mark says that the women who entered Jesus's

Lest your foot strike a stone could involve falling off a cliff to one's death. Satan possibly so understood it (Luke 4:9–12). In other words, the king walks securely (cf. Prov. 3:23). Hannah sings in her patriotic hymn: "He will guard the feet of his faithful ones" (1 Sam. 2:9). Satan uses this promise to tempt the Son of God to throw himself from the pinnacle of the temple (Luke 4:9–12) to deflect him from his mission to crush the serpent (Gen. 3:15). Had Jesus done so, he would have put God to the test and so disobeyed God's word, thereby thwarting his mission.

3. Trample Wild Animals 13

Verse 13 is linked with verses 11–12 in several ways: rhetorically by the motif of advancing movement (see above), semantically by answering the question why angels guard the king, and grammatically by the initial "upon." *Upon . . . you will tread* connotes subjugation (cf. Deut. 33:29; Job 9:13; Mic. 1:3; Hab. 3:15). "Tread" is escalated to *trample* (*tirmōs*) also in Isa. 63:3. *Rāmas* denotes "to beat down with the feet, to stamp upon"; connotes doing so harshly, cruelly, insensitively; and entails crushing, bruising, injuring, and destroying. The heroic king triumphantly tramples the hungry *young lion* (*kappîr*, 13b), and the *lion* (*šaḥal*, 13a—a term that may connote its association with the supernatural; see n. 20). *Serpent* (*tannîn*) may escalate *cobra* (*peten*), for it too may have overtones of a sinister sea monster—albeit both terms, like *šaḥal*, may blur the boundary between the natural and supernatural (see nn. 21, 22). Moses's rod first turned into a snake (*nāḥāš*, Exod. 4:3) and then a serpent (*tannîn*, Exod. 7:9). These zoomorphic figures symbolize the thousands of wicked fallen round about the king; angels do not come to the aid of the king merely so that he can tread upon a snake and a lion. Kings trample down their political enemies, who, as we learn in the New Testament, are energized by demonic forces.[90] In sum, the cobra/serpent and lion/young lion are not real

---

tomb "saw a young man dressed in a white robe" (Mark 16:5), and Luke says "two men in clothes that gleamed like lightning stood beside them" (Luke 24:4). None of these accounts mention wings.

90. The Uraeus—the stylized, upright form of a cobra—featured prominently as the head ornament on the pharaoh's crown. It symbolized his sovereignty, royalty, deity, and divine authority and reinforced his claim over the land. Similarly, Israel's poets used the serpent/sea monster to symbolize ancient Egypt (Isa. 51:9; Ezek. 29:3). In Ezek. 32:2 the pharaoh is likened to "a lion among the nations" (*kappîr gôyīm*) and "a monster in the water" (*tannîm bayyammîm*), and in Jer. 51:34, Nebuchadnezzar

animals but symbols of Israel's political and historical enemies and of the spiritual powers that inspire and empower them.[91]

Stanza III (God Speaks): Assurances to the King 14-16

In Israel's liturgy, God may respond to the faithful with assurance that their prayers are answered (cf. Pss. 12:5[6]; 46:10[11]; 60:6[8]; 75:2[3]; 81:7[8]; 95:8). In this stanza, however, God gives assurance to the king by talking about him, not to him—"a form of hearing that has its own power."[92] The introductory verse of the third stanza, like verses 9-10 of the second stanza, reprises 1-4: "Because he clings to me" (14a; cf. v. 2) and "knows my name" (14b; cf. vv. 1-2), God promises to deliver (14a; cf. v. 3) and to protect him (14b; cf. v. 4). *I AM*'s assurances consist of two divine sevens: seven escalating versets (v. 15 has three) and seven verbs of salvation to "him" with "I" as subject, centered around "I [will be] with him."

Strophe A: Love for God and Salvation 14

Kî again introduces the new section (cf. vv. 3, 9), but the particle is now causative (*because*), not emphatic ("surely"). *He clings to me* speaks of attraction toward another (cf. Gen. 34:8; Deut. 7:7; 21:11). The king's inner, spiritual purity enables him to see what is truly beautiful: the transcendent, absolute beauty of God himself. Because the eye of the wicked is dark, they do not see true beauty but choose the repulsive.[93] *And*, in response, *I will deliver him*

---

is compared to a serpent (*tannîn*) and to a lion (*'aryēh*). At the outset of salvation history, *I AM* covenanted with humanity that the seed of the woman will crush the serpent's head (Gen. 3:15). Paul echoes these words in Rom. 16:20: "The God of peace will soon crush Satan under your feet." In the Testament of Levi 12:18, the new priest "shall give power to his [God's] children to tread upon the evil spirits." Jesus echoes these words to his disciples in Luke 10:19: "I have given you authority to trample on snakes and scorpions and to overcome all the power of the enemy; nothing will harm you." These texts about the Devil and evil spirits and their defeat by *I AM* find their echo in Rev. 12.

91. For the association of animals with rulers, see O. Keel, *Symbolism of the Biblical Word: Ancient Near Eastern Iconography and the Book of Psalms*, trans. T. J. Hallett (New York: Seabury, 1978), 84-86.

92. Goldingay, *Psalms*, 48.

93. The proverb "beauty is in the eye of the beholder" is famous because it rings

(*'ᵃpallᵊṭēhû*). *Plṭ* Piel denotes more precisely "to bring into a state of security" (Pss. 18:43[44], [48]49; 22:4[5]; 43:1; 144:2; cf. 17:13; 37:40; 71:4). *I will set him [safely] on high* metaphorically depicts *I AM* setting his king securely on high (Ps. 59:2), above the reach of his enemies (cf. Ps. 139:6). Proverbs 18:10 fills out the figure: "The name of *I AM* is a fortified tower; the righteous run to it and are set on high [inaccessible to danger]." *Because he knows my name* (see the four names used for God in vv. 1–2), that reveals his character. "Know" connotes intimate possessing, not merely intellectual knowledge (see 90:11), and entails entrusting oneself to the other (see Ps. 9:10[11]) and submitting to them (cf. 1 Kings 8:43).[94]

Strophe B: More Than Answered Prayer 15

"Because he knows my name" segues naturally into "he will cry out to me, and I will answer him" (cf. Ps. 50:15; Rom. 10:9). *He will cry out* (cf. 1 Kgs. 8:52) denotes "to draw someone's attention with the sound of the voice in order to establish contact," while *and I will answer him* describes *I AM*'s reaction or response.[95] But cry he must, for failure to turn to his only source of hope would be tantamount to an abdication of his throne, making him an accomplice with the evildoers (cf. Deut. 22:24). This promise is underscored by the parallel. *I* (*'ānōkî*) is emphatic, for elsewhere in the stanza "I" is prefixed to the verb. Since the prefixed conjugation in this psalm has been mostly interpreted as a specific future, for stylistic reasons we supplied *will be* in this nominal clause. *With him* signifies "fellowship and companionship," and more specifically "giving aid" (see 1 Chr. 12:19; cf. Gen. 21:22; Deut. 20:1, 4; Josh. 1:5, 9; Judg. 2:18; 6:12).[96] *In distress* derives from a root meaning "to be narrow, restricted, cramped,"[97] and is used of extreme physical and/or mental suffering and/or of the state of extreme necessity or misfortune (Isa. 8:22). *I will deliver him*

---

true to a universal human experience: People have different ideas of what beauty is. The saying is attributed to Plato, but first appears in print, according to the *Oxford Dictionary of Quotations*, with Margaret Wolfe Hungerford (1845-1897). Lew Wallace (1827-1905) said: "beauty is altogether in the eye of the beholder." His exaggeration, however, is not famous because it does not ring true. People intuitively prefer to think that beauty is transcendental, an attribute of being itself, like truth and goodness.

94. Caquot, "Le Psaume XCI," 36.
95. C. J. Labuschange, *TLOT*, 3:1159–60, s.v. *qr'*.
96. BDB, p. 767, s.v. *'im*, §1a.a.
97. *HALOT*, 2:1053, s.v. *ṣārâ*.

originally meant "to withdraw, pull out" (cf. Lev. 14:40). Regarding *I will glorify*/honor *him*, Hugger argues cogently from 1 Samuel 2:30 ("whoever honors me I will honor") that what is meant by "honor" is an enhancement of life ("blessing"). He also comments that whom God honors stands honored in the sight of his fellow man.[98]

Strophe C: Longevity and Salvation 16

I will satisfy him signifies to provide one with the full and consummate measure of their expectation, need, and desire for life. The ancient versions gloss *'ōrek yāmîm* literally by "length of days." The phrase is ambiguous. It may refer to a long life terminated by clinical death (Job 12:12) or to "endless days" without a terminal, clinical death (Pss. 21:4[5]; 93:5). KJV, NAS, JPS, NJB, RSV, NIV, ESV, and NLT inconsistently translate the phrase by "forever" or its equivalent in Psalm 23:6 but by "long life" in Psalm 91:16. The desire for food can be satisfied temporarily with a meal, but the desire for life can be sated only by truly *endless days*.[99] *And I will show him* denotes "to make visible to him what heretofore had been invisible." With the preposition b^e (see *bîšû'ātî*), however, it means more specifically "to cause to look intently at, to cause to gaze at with joy."[100] *My salvation* (*yəšû'ātî*) refers to the just deliverance of the king by God from external evils. The lexeme *yāša'* denotes deliverance in both the military (cf. Judg. 12:2; 1 Sam. 11:3) and the juridical spheres (2 Sam. 14:4): God delivers because it is the king's due or right.[101] Salvation from evil, including its elimination, consummates the purpose of sacred history (cf. Ps. 50:23). The Lord Jesus Christ has already conquered death and at the end of history will vanquish it (1 Cor. 15:55). Peter describes the church as those "who through faith are shielded by God's power until the coming of the salvation that is ready to be revealed in the last time" (1 Pet. 1:5).

---

98. Hugger, *Jahwe meine Zuflucht*, 275f.

99. Isaiah prophesied of Jesus Christ: "After he has suffered, he will see the light of life and be satisfied" (Isa. 53:11). By "suffered," Isaiah means "he makes his life an offering for sin" (Isa. 53:10).

100. BDB, p. 909, s.v. *rā'â* Hiphil. §2a; cf. pp. 907–8, s.v. *rā'â* Qal, §8a(5).

101. J. Sawyer, "What Was a Môšia'?," *VT* 15 (1965): 479. Sawyer notes that *other* words in the semantic domain of deliverance [cf. v. 14] stress violent action, not invariable intervention on behalf of justice.

PART III. VOICE OF THE CHURCH IN RESPONSE

With its reference to "the evil by night," Psalm 91 has been used as an evening prayer in Jewish liturgy. The Christian church has used it on Ash Wednesday, at the beginning of Lent—itself a prelude to reflection upon the testing and the temptations we all experience.

I. Psalm 91 as Apotropaic

Psalm 91 has been used as an apotropaic psalm (i.e., one with the power to avert evil influences) throughout all periods of cultural fears, from the period of the Second Temple until now.[102] It was used in response to the cultural fear of demons in the early church and again, and strongly so, during the Middle Ages. The most widely used medieval Bible commentary, the *Glossa Ordinaria,* refers to Psalm 91 as "a hymn against demons." At the height of the plague of 1533 in the city of Nuremberg, the city's Reformed leader, Andreas Osiander, delivered a sermon linking 1 John 4:18 ("perfect love casts out all fear") with Psalm 91, which likewise exhorts trust in God.[103] Hugely popular, the sermon was reprinted by other leaders in cities also affected by urban epidemics. Charles Spurgeon, in his sermon on Psalm 91, comments that the Puritan preachers were quoting verse 8 during the London plague of 1664.[104] Spurgeon further claims a German physician in the late nineteenth century prescribed this psalm as the best preservative against cholera epidemics.[105]

Phrases of the psalm were written on apotropaic amulets, charms, incantation bowls, houses and so on for many centuries by Jews and Christians alike. In popular superstition and fearful piety, no verse of a psalm has been more recited than Psalm 91:7!

---

102. See the excellent survey in Brennan Breed, "Reception of the Psalms: The Example of Psalm 91," in *The Oxford Handbook of the Psalms,* ed. William P. Brown (Oxford: Oxford University Press, 2014), 297–312. For a critical appraisal of this work see n. 48.

103. Ronald Rittgers, "Protestants and the Plague: The Case of the 1532/3 Pestilence in Nuremberg," in *Piety and Plague: From Byzantium to the Baroque,* ed. F. Mormando and T. Vorcester (Kirksville, MO: Truman State University Press, 2007), 132–55.

104. Charles Spurgeon, *Psalms,* ed. Alister McGrath, J. I. Packer, vol. 2 (Wheaton, IL.: Crossway, 1993), 28.

105. Charles Spurgeon, *The Treasury of David: Spurgeon's Classic Work on the Psalms,* ed. D. O. Fuller (Grand Rapids: Kregel, 1976), 383.

II. Psalm 91 as Confessional in Temptation

Satan, presuming Psalm 91:11–12 refers to Christ, quotes these verses during his temptation of Christ (Luke 4:9). Later, in Luke 10:19, the Psalm is echoed in Jesus's response to the disciples' amazement of their power over Satan, indicating his authority over the demonic realm. The desert fathers from the third century onward conjoined this temptation with the earlier temptations of Jesus in the wilderness. This became foundational for the later spread of monasticism.

III. Jerome (342–420)

Jerome, in his homily 20 on this psalm, associates its context with the return from the Babylonian captivity, identifying "the shelter of the Most High" with the name Ezra, meaning "help." "With his pinions he will overshadow you" is an appropriate metaphor for a hen with her chicks as a father with his child.[106] Like his fellow monks in the wilderness, Jerome applies the psalm to the satanic attacks common to their monastic way of life. He devotes particular attention to "the arrow that flies by day" (Ps.91:5), or what the desert fathers prominently referred to as "the noonday devil"—*acedia*.

Jerome does not elaborate on *acedia* as "the noonday devil," but he, along with John Cassian (born c. 360),[107] interprets Psalm 91 as teaching the goal of the desert fathers and mothers and uses the psalm as a didactic treatise for teaching each one's calling. Jerome sees the whole psalm in the context of temptation, notably the three temptations of Jesus in the wilderness.[108] Jerome sees further that the entire psalm refers to Jesus in the wilderness, who now lives and reigns as King.

IV. Augustine of Hippo (354–430)

Augustine preached one of the lengthier of his homilies on Psalm 91 over two consecutive days.[109] Like his contemporaries, Jerome and Cassian, he preached

---

106. Jerome, *The Homilies of Saint Jerome*, vol. 2, trans. Sister Marie Liguori Ewald, I.H.M., FC 48 (Washington, DC: Catholic University of America Press, 1964), 156–57.

107. See John Cassian, *The Institutes,* trans. Boniface Ramsey, ACW 58 (Mahwah, NJ: Newman, 2009), 217—38.

108. Jerome, *The Homilies of Saint Jerome,* 161–63.

109. Augustine, *Exposition 1 of Psalm 90,* in *Expositions on the Psalms,* trans. Maria Boulding, vol. 4 (Hyde Park, NY: New City, 2002), 315–44.

on this psalm in the context of Jesus being tempted in the wilderness. His opening words are, "This psalm is the one which the devil quoted when he dared to tempt our Lord Jesus Christ. Let us listen to it and be armed against the tempter."[110] The Christian is being invited to "learn from me, for I am gentle and humble of heart" (Matt. 11:29). His emphasis, then, is that we avoid temptation when we imitate Christ's example.[111] Humbly, we do so within the help of the Most High (vv. 1–3). Augustine repeats his thoughts to emphasize no Christian can ever afford to be complacent (v. 7), self-sufficient, or individualistic. For in step with his central theme of "the whole body of Christ," the key to all Christians being united universally, all Christians must be wholly united in these basic precepts of the Psalms.[112]

Augustine gives several interpretations of "the arrow by day," not only as the worst of vices as Cassian and Jerome interpret it but as being "mild," not insistent. Yet ambiguously, he sees as they do that it may reflect fierce persecution as well. He interprets temptations "by night" as those of the ignorant, who cannot "see" them in the darkness of their minds. He strongly concludes that the three temptations of Jesus in the wilderness express his solidarity with us, in becoming human. For the nature of being human is to be susceptible to temptation. Christ, then, was tempted to empower us when we are tempted in our humanity.[113]

The threefold temptation of our Lord—the lust of the flesh, the lust of the eyes, and the pride of life—are what we have to overcome through the indwelling Christ. This became the moral basis of the threefold vows of the monk. The final message is that Satan will be finally overthrown (v. 13), and with the deliverance of Christ's saints, "the length of days" (v. 16) becomes the prospect of eternal life.[114]

In conclusion, very practically, Augustine reminds us all that our security lies not in food cupboards nor in warehouses, not in money bags nor vaults, but "under the wings of God."[115]

---

110. Augustine, *Exposition 1 of Psalm 90* 1 (Boulding, 315).
111. Augustine, *Exposition 1 of Psalm 90* 3–4 (Boulding, 317–19).
112. Augustine, *Exposition 1 of Psalm 90* 9–10 (Boulding, 321f.)
113. Augustine, *Exposition 1 of Psalm 90* 7 (Boulding, 321).
114. Augustine, *Exposition 1 of Psalm 90* 20 (Boulding, 343).
115. Augustine, *Exposition 1 of Psalm 90* 5 (Boulding, 319).

V. Bernard of Clairvaux (c. 1090–1145)

We have recorded in our first volume how the monastic movement spread into the Celtic, the Northumbrian, and later into the Germanic lands of the Carolingian empire.[116] Susan Gillingham's excellent history of reception exegesis[117] further traces the rise of the scholastic movement associated with Anselm in Normandy, the Victorines in Paris, and Herbert of Bosham in England. But curiously, she completely ignores the Cistercians, of whom Bernard of Clairvaux is their great spokesman.

No one more effectively reformed Benedictine monastic life in the new revival of the Cistercian movement than did Bernard of Clairvaux. Because he gives us the most extensive series of meditations on Psalm 91 that we have received until modern times the rest of this reception study is devoted to his writings. He reflects more on this psalm than even most modern scholars!

The Reform of Monasticism under the Cistercians

It had become the custom under feudalism that aristocratic children—boys and girls—unmatched in marriages should be adopted by the Benedictines and remain with them as monks and nuns for the rest of their lives. Their inheritance was donated to the Benedictine monasteries and convents, giving the Benedictines great wealth. Bernard and his companions reversed this inhuman practice. Instead, Bernard, his brothers, an uncle, and some friends set a new example by entering monastic life as sacrificial adults, leaving their wealth behind them to enter into poverty and to practice a new way of life. It was a reform that completely renounced the feudal culture.[118]

The central theme of Cistercian psalmody was exalting the name of the Child Jesus, who grew mysteriously through puberty into the Man Jesus. Aelred of Rievaulx, Bernard's disciple, meditates upon Him in his work, *Jesus at the Age of Twelve*.[119]

116. Waltke and Houston, *Psalms as Christian Worship*, 52–53.

117. Susan Gillingham, *Psalms Through the Centuries*, Blackwell Bible Commentaries (Malden, MA: Wiley-Blackwell, 2008).

118. James M. Houston, "Bernard of Clairvaux: Lover of God as the Lover of Jesus," in *Sources of the Christian Self*, ed. James M. Houston and Jens Zimmermann (Grand Rapids: Eerdmans, 2018), 294–311.

119. Aelred of Rievaulx, *Jesus at the Age of Twelve*, in *Treatises: The Pastoral Prayer*, trans. Theodore Berkeley (Kalamazoo, MI: Cistercian Publications, 1971).

But Cistercian reform also challenged the rise of individualism in the twelfth century, and with it the rise of corrupt and prideful scholasticism—an aberration rooted in individualism. Peter Abelard became the great exemplar of both of these movements, which were similar to the tech revolution being extolled in our current culture and its consequent narcissism. Of course, humility and pride have huge as well as subtle expressions, as they always have had and will have. But blatant *hubris* is always self-destructive: It destroyed Abelard in Bernard's day. Not that Bernard himself was always as humble as he writes and preaches about![120] We all tend to struggle against personal, ironic inconsistencies!

Bernard's Homilies on Psalm 91

Just as many of the psalms unite the mythopoeic with the historical, so Bernard combines the metaphorical with the literal in his meditations on the psalms. Bernard is all about allegory, as today we are realizing more than ever that the language of God can only be metaphorical. In a remarkable collection of homilies to introduce the Lenten season, Bernard shares with his monks seventeen meditations on the meaning of "*conversio*," from the Christian's evangelical conversion to the radical calling to become a twelfth-century monk. It is what Charles Taylor has called *metanoia*, of having a paradigm shift, to reinterpret our sense and meaning of reality.[121]

Bernard had returned from a visit to the University of Paris, where he saw and heard the voice of Abelard and his student cohorts. In response, Bernard uses Psalm 91 to rally the same audiences to a new reality and to bring comfort, assurance, and courage to his fellow monks, already in the new state of "the *conversio*." It is all about experiencing death to an old way of living, as the apostle does in Romans 7, to seek a new way of being, as in Romans 8.[122]

The best way to start, Bernard argues, is to recognize those *who do not* dwell under the shadow of the Almighty (Ps. 91:1) by seeing their rebellion—their trust in wealth and scholarship—and then asking, for one's own well-

120. Jane Foulcher, *Reclaiming Humility: Four Studies in the Monastic Tradition* (Collegeville, MN: Liturgical Press, Cistercian Publications, 2015), 239–40.

121. Charles Taylor, *The Skilled Pastor: Counseling as the Practice of Theology* (Minneapolis: Fortress, 1991), 137ff.

122. Bernard of Clairvaux, *Sermon on the Psalm "He Who Dwells,"* in *Sermons on Conversion*, trans. Marie-Bernard Saïd (Collegeville, MN: Cistercian, 1981).

being, What does it all add up to? Why should one go on living like that: dwelling on one's own merits, on one's own woes, or on one's own vices? At the same time, this does not make us "angelic beings" as the desert fathers sought to be. We remain human, "sheltering" under the Almighty, not yet "dwelling" there permanently.[123] This "sheltering" lies in thanksgiving and praise, so that when we stumble, we can begin singing again—indeed, as the Broadway musical puts it: "Singin' in the rain! Just singin' in the rain!"

Bernard could exhaust us, as he expounds on Psalm 91 in seventeen homilies. Our summary cannot do justice to his skill as a doctor of the soul. A soul doctor does not just "help us"; he has to "examine us" to give us hope as we cry out: "My hope is in God" (Ps. 91:2). We need deliverance then from the voice of the "worldlings"—the "fowlers"—and from their snares of enticement, riches, flattery, and so on (Ps. 91:3). We are then "overshadowed" on Christ's broad shoulders by his promises both for this world and for the world to come. That is where our hope rests. Thus we watch and pray that we do not fall into temptation (Matt. 26:41; Ps. 91:5). Adversity will come to us all (Ps. 91:6) in the grief of "darkness," in our garden of Gethsemane, and in "the arrow that flies by day" of subtle vanities. Like other commentators before him, Bernard sees that the fiercest battles—against "a myriad"—occur where we believe we have more self-confidence. On the other hand, where we are more self-conscious (i.e., exercising more humility), the battle is lighter. But he multiplies his metaphors and allegories in a key verse he associates with human temptation. All these things we can observe, not detachedly, but to exercise "consideration,"[124] which he elaborates on to his disciple the Bishop of Rome, the Cistercian Pope Eugenius III, in *On Consideration* in 1145.[125]

The second portion of the psalm (vv. 9-13) now enters into a tempo of tranquility, to which Bernard responds differently. Now he reflects gently on "the end of our pilgrimage, the reward of our labors, the fruit of captivity.... As the apostle says, 'As we have abundant trials for Christ, so through him we have abundant comforts too' " (2 Cor. 1:5).[126] We must not speak of our hope being in God as a cliché but as a lived reality in destitution, savored by a deep abiding faith with hope not only being *from Him* but also *dwelling in Him*.[127]

123. Bernard, *Sermon on the Psalm "He Who Dwells,"* 123.

124. Bernard, *Sermon on the Psalm "He Who Dwells."*

125. Bernard of Clairvaux, *On Consideration*, in *Bernard of Clairvaux: Selected Works*, trans. G. R. Evans, The Classics of Western Spirituality (Mahwah, NJ: Paulist, 1987), 145–172.

126. Bernard, *Sermon on the Psalm "He Who Dwells,"* 182–83.

127. Bernard, *Sermon on the Psalm "He Who Dwells,"* 187–91.

Bernard emphasizes that verse 10 ("Calamity will not meet you; and a plague will not draw near your tent") can only be fulfilled—whether it refers to our well-being of body ("the tent") or to our spirit—when we live out of the reality that "the true life of the soul is God."[128]

Verse 11, quoted by Satan in his second temptation of Jesus, gives us all much cause for sobriety, for we can use it in demonic, self-confident ways. Bernard recognizes four ways this can happen: (a) by "shutting one's eyes" to one's own sinfulness by all sorts of excuses; (b) by ignorance of one's own wounded condition; (c) by the presumption of defending one's self; and (d) by contempt and impenitence.[129] Angels minister "not with turning you from your ways, but by directing you from your ways into His ways."[130] Here Bernard is speaking to us as Christians who already think we are exercising virtuous living with social benefits to others but whose motives are wrongly founded on our own "good nature," not on God's character. "For we are not sufficient of ourselves to think anything by ourselves, or of ourselves" (2 Cor. 3:5).

In his twelfth homily, Bernard turns to verse 12. "Angelic ministry" consists of ascending in contemplation to seek truth and then descending in mercy "to guard us in all our ways." It is simply imitating Christ in all his ways. Their only motive is love, as divine love alone should embrace, direct and sustain all our way of living and being. But unlike the angels, who ascend to and descend from the heavenly realm, we need to live solidly on earth, being more "human" than ever before.[131] But in our understanding of our humanity, we may "strike our foot against a rock," which Bernard interprets as the humanity of Christ (Matt. 21:44), that offended Peter (Matt. 16:22), as it can all would-be disciples. We could say it is an "offense" to Unitarians, Jehovah's Witnesses, and the whole Muslim world that Christ is both human and divine.

Bernard then examines "the enemies of our soul": "the asp," biting its poison in deceit; "the basilisk" with poison in its envious eye; "the lion" with its mighty hatred; and "the dragon" in its fierce anger. Such bold metaphors are required to keep us vigilant and prevent us from "slumbering" in what we may be deceived to think is a normal human life. Bernard associates these four deadly beasts with "four" temptations in the wilderness: the first being simply that humans are temptable, from which the

128. Bernard, *Sermon on the Psalm "He Who Dwells,"* 196.
129. Bernard, *Sermon on the Psalm "He Who Dwells,"* 205–6.
130. Bernard, *Sermon on the Psalm "He Who Dwells,"* 211.
131. Bernard, *Sermon on the Psalm "He Who Dwells,"* 212.

other three follow. As soon as we are on our guard against one vice, then another lies in wait.[132]

With relief, we come to the last two stanzas of this psalm of deliverance. "Let us give thanks," exhorts Bernard, "to our Maker, our Rewarder, our Benefactor, our Redeemer." For he preserves us: "We are His, whom He made, and not we ourselves." We bear the *imago Dei*, giving us all that is necessary to express "His image and likeness."[133] Juxtaposed with the fourfold human temptations, Bernard recognizes God in his fourfold character (Creator, Rewarder, Benefactor, and Redeemer) in the last three verses of the Psalm. Bernard identifies these as "I Am" promises with the ultimate invitation: "Come unto me . . . and I will give you rest" (Matt. 11:28). Inviting us, then, to bear Christ's "burden"—"whose yoke is easy"—Bernard asks, "What then is Christ's burden?" He answers, "It is the burden of his benefits."[134] In a triple guardianship—rescuing us, protecting us, and accompanying us in trouble—God provides this "rest to our souls." Each lives in harmony with the other. This "protection" is found only in "His Name."[135]

"The magnitude of our need forces out a mighty cry."[136] Bernard sees this cry (v. 15) as no less than a covenant of peace, a treaty of godliness, a pact of compassion and of mercy. Indeed, six promises are given us in this divine covenant: rescue, protection, response, longevity, satisfaction, and demonstration of God's salvation. The apostle embraces all these in his statement that "godliness contains the promise of the life which now is, as well as of the life to come" (1 Tim. 4:8). This truly is magnificent glory, the eternal praise of our God.

Not many Christian psychiatrists today have such depth of discernment as Bernard exercised in his exploration of the soul in the twelfth century! For as we noted, Bernard was a very complex man himself: a man of peace, yet persuaded by Pope Eugenius III to support the Second Crusade and able to be quite vicious with his enemies, as he displayed with Peter Abelard. Yet in his hymnody, he could express himself like a child, and he was highly sophisticated in teaching his homilies.

A skilled biblical exegete, Bernard clearly held the Scriptures with two hands. In one he was reading and contemplating Psalm 91, but in the other hand he was constantly referring to Paul's epistles. He seems to have been

---

132. Bernard, *Sermon on the Psalm "He Who Dwells."*
133. Bernard, *Sermon on the Psalm "He Who Dwells."*
134. Bernard, *Sermon on the Psalm "He Who Dwells,"* 239.
135. Bernard, *Sermon on the Psalm "He Who Dwells,"* 245.
136. Bernard, *Sermon on the Psalm "He Who Dwells,"* 246–47.

aware that the apostle himself was benefiting from his own personal absorption with Psalm 91. Bernard is indeed "the last of the fathers," as he was later eulogized by the Reformers of the sixteenth century.

PART IV. CONCLUSION

As noted in the introduction (see pp. 15–16), Book IV of the Psalter (Pss. 90–106) responds to the crisis of the failed House of David (Ps. 89) by redirecting reliance and praise to God's eternal kingship. But *I AM* does not reign apart from the House of David. He promised on oath that David's house would rule his kingdom forever. Prophecies may fail due to changed circumstances, but God's oaths never fail.[137] In Psalm 91, God's ideal son expresses his faith in the God of Abraham, Isaac, and Jacob—to whom also God made an irrevocable oath—and God promises to protect him through peril and plague and to empower him to extinguish the lion and the serpent, symbols of the supernaturally empowered wicked. Collected into Book IV at the end of the Babylonian exile, it became part of many prophecies about the Messiah (see "Messianic" above), the Lord Jesus Christ, Son of David, Son of God.

137. Prophecies are changeable (see Jeremiah 18) but oaths are not (see Ps. 110:4; Heb. 6:17–18). See R. L. Pratt Jr., "Historical Contingencies and Biblical Predictions," in *The Way of Wisdom, Essays in Honour of Bruce K. Waltke*, ed. J. I. Packer and Sven K. Soderlund (Grand Rapids: Zondervan, 2000); Robert B. Chisholm, "When Prophecy Appears to Fail, Check Your Hermeneutic," *JETS* 53 (2010): 561–77; Matthew H. Patton, *Hope for a Tender Sprig: Jehoiachin in Biblical Theology*, BBRSup 16 (Winona Lake, IN: Eisenbrauns), 202–5.

CHAPTER 4

Psalm 92: You Are on High Forever, I AM!

PART I. VOICE OF THE PSALMIST: TRANSLATION

A psalm. A song. For the Sabbath Day.

1   It is good to give grateful praise to *I AM*,
       and to make music to your[1] name, Most High;

2   to proclaim in the morning your unfailing love,
       and your reliability during the night[2];

3   upon the ten-stringed lute,[3]
       upon the soft sounds[4] with the lyre.

4   Surely you, *I AM*, cause me to rejoice in your deeds[5];
       I shout cries of joy for the works of your hands.

5   How great are your works, *I AM*;
       your thoughts are exceedingly profound.

6   A brutish person does not[6] know,
       and a fool does not understand this:[7]

---

1. The psalmist's change of addressees from the congregation to *I AM* and vice versa is common in the Psalter's liturgical poems. This is so because he and the congregation are in worship before the living God.

2. Construing the plural as a plural of composition.

3. Construing "upon ten and upon harp" as a hendiadys.

4. *Higgāyôn* derives from the lexeme *hāggâ*, which is used for "coo/moan" of a pigeon (Isa. 38:14); "growl" of a lion (Isa. 31:4); and for humans: "read in an undertone" (Ps. 1:2), "utter a sound" (115:7), and "moan" (Isa. 16:7). The noun is also glossed "whispering" (Lam. 3:62), "meditation" (Ps. 19:14), "a musical direction" with *selâ* (Ps. 9:16).

5. Construing *pōʿal* as a collective singular.

6. 4QPs[b] reads *ʾyš bʿr wlʾ ydʿ* ("a brutish person and does not know," cf. Ps. 73:22a), leaving 92:6a a fragmented clause.

7. Construing *ʾet zōʾt* ("this") as prospective, looking ahead to v. 7, not retrospective, looking back to v. 6.

7   When the wicked flourished like[8] plants,[9]
     and all evildoers blossomed,[10]
     it led[11] to their being exterminated forever.

8   For[12] you are on high[13] forever, *I AM!*

9   For look! Your enemies, *I AM*—
     For look! Your enemies perish;
     all evildoers are scattered.

10   You[14] exalted my horn like a wild ox,
     which I rubbed[15] with rich[16] olive oil.

8. Marvin E. Tate (*Psalms 51–100*, WBC 20 [Dallas: Word, 1990], 460) understands *kǝmô ʿēśeb* to be an apodosis (= "[they are] like grass"). He cites Job 27:14 for a similar construction and notes the *paseq* after *bipǝrōaḥ rǝšāʿîm*. However, the *athnaḥ* with *ʾāwen* in 92:7[8]aβ suggests the Masoretes read 7[8]b as the apodosis to both 7[8]aα and 7[8]aβ; it is so interpreted in the ancient and modern versions.

9. *ʿēśeb* refers to plants in general, for both feed and food.

10. The narrative *waw* after a preposition with an infinitive points to a past historical situation (GKC, 114r; cf. Lev. 16:1; 1 Kgs. 18:18; Ps. 105:12; Job 38:7, 9ff).

11. The verb of motion is inferred from the preposition *lǝ* (*IBHS*, §11.4.3d).

12. Almost all English versions follow LXX and Vulg. and render the ambiguous *waw* by "but." However, *I AM*'s transcendence (v. 8[9]) does not oppose the annihilation of the wicked (v. 7[8]). Hebrew grammar, unlike English grammar, commonly uses parataxis to indicate hierarchical relations (= "for," *IBHS*, §39.2.1c).

13. Construed as adverbial accusative, albeit in a nominal clause (*IBHS*, §10.2.2b).

14. Lit. "and you." Some English versions gloss it by "but" (KJV, ASV, ERV, NAS, NRS, ESV, NLT), and others omit it (NIV, NET, CSB, NAB, NJB). The adversative translation runs rough-shod over narrative *waw*. Occasionally, as here, narrative *waw* lacks an antecedent action and is better omitted.

15. As for grammar of *ballōtî*, Tate (*Psalms 51–100*, 462f.) follows D. G. Pardee and understands "horn [like a wild ox]" as the object of *ballōtî* ("which I have rubbed with olive oil"). This finds support in an Ugaritic parallel: "Your powerful horn, girl Anat,/ Your powerful horns will Baal anoint [*ymšḥ*]/ Baal will anoint them in flight/ We'll thrust my [Baal's] foes into the earth" (cf. *ANET*, 142). As for the lexicography of *ballōtî*, Tate follows E. Kutch (*Salbung als Rechtsakt*, BZAW 87 [1963]) who argues *māšaḥ* basically means "to make fat/make greasy/rub oil into." It is further argued that "the parallel usage of *bālal* with *māšaḥ* in such texts as Exod. 29:2; Lev. 2:4; 7:12; and Num. 6:15 indicates that it too can have the meaning of "make fat (with oil)" and then to "smear/rub on/anoint." Moreover, "make fat/greasy" may be a metonymy for "to rub/smear." The imagery of rubbing a horn with olive oil probably aimed to elevate the vitality, joy, and pride that the horn signified by making it glisten, and so is part of the victory imagery of v. 10[11]a.

16. D. Winton Thomas ("Some Observations on the Hebrew Word רַעֲנָן," in *He-*

11   And my eyes[17] gazed in triumph[18] at those who tried to ambush me[19];
          my ears will hear of the destruction[20] of the wicked who attack me.

12   The righteous flourishes like a palm tree;
          he[21] grows like a cedar of Lebanon;

13   planted[22] in the house of *I AM*;
          in the courts of our God they flourish.

14   They will still thrive in old age[23];
          they will be full of sap[24] and thick with leaves,

15   proclaiming[25]: "*I AM* is upright;
          my Rock, in whom there is no injustice."[26]

---

bräische Wortforschung. Festschrift zum 80. Geburtstag von Walter Baumgartner, VTSup 16 [Leiden: Brill, 1967], 387–97) argues with erudition that when *ra'ănān* is used with trees, or with leaves or branches, it should be translated by "thick with leaves, luxurious, dense, spreading," and not by "green."

17. Lit. "my eye."

18. *Rā'â* with the preposition *bə* can mean "to look at with joy" (BDB, p. 908, s.v. *rā'â*, §8a), a meaning that can be extended here to its synonym *nābaṭ* (Pss. 91:8; 92:11a).

19. Construing the root of *bešûray* as *šûr* II, "to behold, regard," meaning, with "the wicked" as the subject, "to watch (insidiously)" (*The Concise Dictionary of Classical Hebrew* [Sheffield: Phoenix, 2009], 454, s.v. *šûr*, #3). Compare "lurk" (Hos 13:7, NIV), "lie in wait" (Jer. 5:26, NIV). In Ps. 92:11[12], NET renders it "tried to ambush" and JPS "lie in wait for."

20. The object of "hear" is uncertain. The literal renderings of the NAS "my ears hear of the evildoers who rise up against me" and of LXX "my ears will hear the wicked that rise up against me" are respectively not cogent and ambiguous. BDB (p. 1033, s.v. *šm'*, §1d) says *šāma'* with *b* governing a personal noun means "*hear exultantly* of their fate . . . (prob. imitated from the parallel *hibbîṭ be*)." If so, any object that captures that notion may be supplied: "the sound of the destruction" (Tg.), "the defeated cries of" (NET), "rout" (most English versions), etc. A Qumran text has *šm'* (= *šām'â* "heard"), a facilitating reading with *wattabēṭ*.

21. The so-called Heb. masc. is an unmarked form and may refer to a female animate (*IBHS*, §6.5.3a).

22. Plural in Hebrew, modifying both the psalm tree and the cedar of Lebanon.

23. Lit. "gray hair," a symbol of old age.

24. So BDB, p. 206, s.v. *dāšēn*.

25. Construing inf. *lehaggîd* as circumstantial, a gerundive (e.g., faciendo "doing," GKC, 114o), identifying *I AM* as the Agent of their blessed state. And also construing *kî* after a verb of speaking as introducing the quotation.

26. *Kethiv* reads *'ōlātâ*, *Qere* reads *'awlâ*, with no difference in meaning.

PART II. COMMENTARY

I. Introduction

Form

Apart from the prose superscriptions, which ground the Psalms in historical data, all psalms are poetry (see pp. 23–25).

Grateful Praise Song

The superscript [Heb. v. 1[27]] summons musicians to sing this song with the accompaniment of musical accompaniments (see pp. 25–26). Verse 1 specifies the song as "a song of grateful praise" (i.e., a testimony, see p. 5)—of course to Israel's God, *I AM* (see pp. 1–3). The first stanza (vv. 1–4; see p. 32n31) has two introductions: a corporate hymn (1–3) and an individual's testimony (4). A testimony commonly begins with a resolution to testify.[28] The individual's grateful praise for a particular act of salvation (cf. vv. 10–11) expands into universal truth (cf. vv. 12–15). Like the authors of Psalms 37, 49, and 73—so-called wisdom psalms—our psalmist gives serious thought to the prosperity of the wicked. He is an ear and eyewitness to the fact that ultimately the righteous triumph.

Royal and Messianic

More specifically, it is royal psalm: the testimony of the king himself, as implied by lines such as: "You exalted my horn like a wild ox" (v. 10) and "my eyes gazed in triumph" and "my ears will hear of the destruction of the wicked who attack me" (11). The Jews traditionally and rightly interpreted the psalm as messianic. The king's past victory that is celebrated in this psalm is an earnest guaranteeing the triumph of the righteous in the coming kingdom of God.

---

27. Hebrew versification in Ps. 92 is always one number higher than in English, with the superscript as verse 1. For simplicity's sake, only the English verse numbers will be rendered in this chapter in most cases.

28. H. Gunkel and J. Begrich, *Introduction to the Psalms: The Genres of the Religious Lyric of Israel*, trans. James D. Nogalski (Macon, GA: Mercer University Press, 1998), 201. Gunkel thinks the rejoicing and triumph of Ps. 92 is strongly personal and genuine and by a great poet (p. 213).

The Targum expands verse 8: "But you are high *and supreme* in *this* age, O LORD, *and you are high and supreme in the age to come.*"[29] Mishna Tamid 7:4 comments on "For the Sabbath": "A psalm for the future, for the day that is completely Shabbat [tranquil] for all eternity." Delitzsch notes that the Talmud disputes whether the Sabbath refers to the creation Sabbath (R. Nehemiah) or to the final Sabbath of world history (R. Akiba). "The latter," says Delitzsch, "is relatively more correct."[30] Konrad Schaefer also links the two: "The Sabbath anticipates the final rest, the eternal Sabbath, when creation is complete and God's enemies are defeated, a victory which Psalm 92 anticipates and celebrates."[31] The psalm is messianic in the sense that within the canon of Scripture, the historic king and his report of victory typify Jesus Christ and his victory over Satan, sin, and death. The universal covenant community identifies itself with this King.

Setting

Songs of grateful praise originally functioned as librettos for the grateful praise sacrifice (see p. 5). God and his people feasted together to celebrate the psalmist's victory. N. H. Snaith says: "It may safely be assumed . . . that verses 2–3 [Eng. 1–2] are an invitation to worship in connection with sacrifice."[32] N. M. Sarna agrees[33] and provides evidence that the "coordination of the vocal-musical recitation with the regular offering was rooted in first Temple usage."[34] The psalm's content, as well as its form, point to its temple setting. The singer directs his praise both to the congregation and I AM himself, as indicated by

29. Another Tg. reads: "And you, *your hand is* supreme *to punish the wicked* in the age *to come, in the great day of judgment,* O LORD; *and you, your hand is supreme to give a good reward to the righteous in the age to come,* O LORD.

30. F. Delitzsch, *Psalms,* trans. Francis Bolton, Keil and Delitzsch Commentary on the Old Testament 5 (London: T&T Clark, 1866–91; repr., Peabody, MA: Hendrickson, 1996), 606.

31. Quoted in Konrad Schaefer, *Psalms,* Berit Olam (Collegeville, MN: Liturgical Press, 2001), 230.

32. N. H. Snaith, *Studies in the Psalter* (London: Epworth, 1934), 73.

33. N. M. Sarna, "The Psalm for the Sabbath Day," *JBL* 81 (1962): 155–68, esp. 158.

34. N. M. Sarna, "The Psalm Superscriptions and the Guilds," in *Studies in Jewish Religious and Intellectual History: Presented to Alexander Altmann on the Occasion of His Seventieth Birthday,* ed. Siegried Stein and Raphael Loewe (Tuscaloosa, AL: University of Alabama Press, 1979), 281–300.

the change of pronouns (see v. 1). Both ways have unique powers. The references to music put a temple setting beyond doubt (e.g., v. 3).

As for the Sabbath setting, see "The Origin of Psalm 92 for the Sabbath" (p. 120).

Rhetoric

A terse center line of a mere four words (v. 8), in striking contrast to the two paired tricola surrounding it, divides the psalm into two equal parts of seven verses each.[35] The name of *I AM* occurs seven times—the number of divine perfection: three times in each half and once in the center line (vv. 1, 4, 5, 8, 9, 13, 15). The two halves are structured as a chiasm of four- and three-verse stanzas (vv. 1–4, 5–7; 9–11, 12–15).[36] The second and third consist of chiastic units of one- and two-verse strophes. Thus:[37]

A. King praises *I AM*	1–4
B. Praise for God's great work and profound thoughts	5–7
C. All evildoers eliminated (tricolon)	7
X. *I AM* is on high forever	8
C'. All evildoers perish (tricolon)	9
B'. King rejoices in victory	10–11
A'. Righteous and king praise *I AM*	12–15

Four verses of praise frame the psalm (vv. 1–4, 12–15) using "to proclaim" (2, 15) + *I AM* (1, 15). God's great work and profound thought that allowed the wicked to flourish for the moment and then be eliminated (5–7) is matched by the king's triumph over them (9–11). Sarna comments: "The events of the past referred to in v 8 [Eng. 7] are those described in v 10 [Eng. 9]."[38] Here is an outline of the psalm's structure:

---

35. For the view that v. 8 is the center line, see Jonathan Magonet, "Some Concentric Structures in the Psalms," *Heythrop Journal* 23 (1982): 365–76, esp. 369–72.

36. J. J. Stewart Perowne (*The Book of Psalms*, vol. 2 [Andover: Warren F. Draper, 1898], 174), independently, also so analyzed the psalm.

37. Tate (*Psalms 51–100*, 464), following the suggestion of R. M. Davison ("The Sabbatical Chiastic Structure of Psalm 92," paper presented at the annual meeting of the SBL, Chicago, IL, 18 Nov. 1988), notes the same structure.

38. Sarna, "A Psalm for the Sabbath Day," 162.

The catchwords "works" and vocative *I AM* (vv. 4, 5) link the first two stanzas; "all evildoers" links the second and third stanzas (7, 9); "on high" and "you raise up"—both derived from the Hebrew root *rûm* ("to be high")—link the third stanza to the center line; and "flourish" links the second and fourth stanzas (7, 12–13).

II. Exegesis

Superscript [Heb. 1]

A psalm refers to a song with musical accompaniment; and *a song* refers to the human voice (see pp. 25–26, 170–71). *For the Sabbath day* (see p. 102). Amos Ḥakham comments: "All communities of Israel have long established the custom of including this psalm among those received on Sabbath and festival mornings, on Friday evenings, and as the special psalm of the Sabbath day. Some also recite it in the Sabbath Afternoon Service."[39] The church reflects on God's ceasing from his six days of work (Exod. 20:9–11), on Israel's rest from the slavery in Egypt, and on her own rest in Christ (Heb. 4:8–11; see "The Origin of Psalm 92 for the Sabbath").

First Half 1–7

The first half of Psalm 92 consists of two stanzas: introductions to the king's song (vv. 1–4) and admiration for God's hidden design for the elimination of all evildoers (5–7).

Stanza I (Introductions): Tireless Praise for God's Work 1–4

The first introduction (vv. 1–3), corporate praise (cf. 106:1; 107:1; 118:1; 136:1; 147:1),[40] atypically evaluates praise: it is good (cf. 95:1; 96:1; 97:1; 98:1; 100:1). The second introduction (v. 4), a testimony, is more emotionally charged. The first introduction celebrates God's sublime attributes; the second, his saving deeds. Spurgeon quotes Aquinas: "We thank God for His benefits and praise Him for His perfections."[41]

---

39. Amos Ḥakham, *Psalms with the Jerusalem Commentary*, trans. Israel V. Berman, vol. 2 (Jerusalem: Mosad Harav Kook, 2003), 378.

40. For inclusion of hymnic element in songs of grateful praise, see Gunkel and Begrich, *Introduction to the Psalms*, 212.

41. Quoted in Charles Spurgeon, *The Treasury of David*, ed. Roy H. Clarke (Nashville: Thomas Nelson, 1997), 820.

Strophe A (First Introduction): Corporate Praise for I AM's *Sublimities 1–3*

The strophe is developed analytically: "to give grateful praise" (v. 1a) is elaborated by proclaiming his love day and night (2); and "to make music" (1b) by naming instruments (3).

1. Summary Statement: Good to Praise with Music 1

The first word, good (see Ps. 100:5), is the predicate of the entire first sentence (vv. 1–3) and so highly emphatic. Praise of God is "good," for it promotes life and is pleasing to God and his people. "Nothing affords a surer test of the reality of worship than the worshiper's joy in it," says A. Maclaren.[42] *To give grateful praise* (see p. 5). The first service at the temple began: "Give praise to *I AM*, proclaim his name; make known among the nations what he has done" (1 Chr. 16:8). The king publicly confesses *to* I AM that he has saved him and in this way he testifies to others that God is upright. Talking about God is its own form of praise (see Ps. 91:14). *And to make music* (*ûlᵉzammēr*, see *mizmôr*, "psalm," in superscript). *Your name* refers to the divine name, YHWH (see pp. 1–3). A name functions as a surrogate for the person, making that person accessible.[43] The title *Most High* (see Ps. 91:1) perhaps anticipates the center line: "You are on high forever, *I AM*" (v. 8).

2. Elaboration of Words of Praise 2

The parallel lines are linked by gapping "to proclaim" in verse 2b, by the merism "day and night" (= "all day long"), and by splitting the collocation of "unfailing love" and "reliability." *To proclaim* signifies to communicate a *vitally important* message.[44] *In the morning* signifies "at daybreak" (cf. Ps. 90:5). *Your unfailing love* refers to helping the helpless out of a responsible keeping of faith (see Psalm 100:5). *Your reliability* is added because human fidelity cannot always be counted on. *During the night* (see n. 2) reflects the 24-7 priestly temple service (cf. 1 Thess. 5:17).

---

42. A. Maclaren, *The Psalms*, vol. 3, Expositor's Bible (New York: George H. Doran, n.d.), 27f.

43. J. Gordon McConville, "God's Name and God's Glory," *TynBul* 30 (1979): 149–63.

44. C. Westermann, *TLOT*, 2.715, s.v. *ngd* Hiphil.

3. Elaboration of Music of Praise 3

Both the *lute* (*nēbel*) and *lyre* (*kinnôr*) are chordophone instruments, which produce a sound from the plucking or bowing of strings stretched over or into a sounding box. The identification of the *kinnôr* with the lyre is very probable. From archaeological evidence, we know that the lyre had two arms raised from ends of the sound box, supporting a yoke from which the strings (three to eleven in number) descend into or over the sound box. The identification of the *nēbel* is less certain. It often occurs in conjunction with the *kinnôr* (2 Sam. 6:5; 1 Sam. 10:5; Ps. 33:2; passim), but only the *nēbel* is linked with *ʿāśôr* ("ten" [strings?]). Presumably, it would be relatively large, albeit still portable. The instrument was one of four played before a procession of cultic prophets descending from a high place, so it could probably be carried by one person (1 Sam. 10:5). Attempts to derive a meaning etymologically can be misleading, but possibly its name derives from the similarity of its shape or construction to a *nēbel*, a storing vessel with a bulging bottom. If so, "the lute is the most appropriate stringed instrument known from archaeological work to correspond to such a picture."[45] But verse 4 reminds us that, as Spurgeon put it, "fine music without devotion is a splendid garment on a corpse."[46]

Strophe B (Second Introduction): Personal Praise of I AM*'s Work 4*

You . . . cause me to rejoice signifies that *I AM*'s heroic deeds put the psalmist in the state of spontaneously responding in joy, like shouting for a sport's hero in a stadium. *Works* refers to what is produced by the deed (Gen. 40:17). The agency *of your hand* denotes the appendage from the elbow to the finger tips (cf. "bracelets upon her hands," Gen. 24:22) and connotes power, rule, and control, as in "hand of the dog" (Ps. 22:20[21]) and "I will deliver from the hand of Sheol" (Hos. 13:14). *I shout cries* (cf. Hos. 13:14) can refer to cries of distress (Lam. 2:19) or of exhortation (Prov. 1:20), but most often refers to cries *of joy* (Isa. 12:6; Jer. 31:7), confirmed here by the parallel with "rejoice" (cf. Pss. 35:27; 92:4[5]; Prov. 29:6; Zech 2:10).

45. Ivor H. Jones, "Music and Musical Instruments," *ABD* 4:937.
46. Spurgeon, *Treasury of David*, 821.

Stanza II: Greatness of God's Works and Thoughts 5–7

The second stanza is also developed analytically: It begins with a summary of its content in verse 5 and then unpacks it in 6–7.

Strophe A: Summary Statement 5

The king's shout begins with the exclamation: *How great are your works* (see v. 4), I AM. As the first stanza began with the predicate adjective "good," the second stanza begins with a stative verb, a grammatical equivalent to an adjective. "Great" signifies that the magnitude of somebody or something is considerably above the normal in extent, importance, and eminence. Theologians refer to God's works as *Heilsgeschichte* ("historical facts interpreted as saving deeds"). His saving acts began with his triumph over the chaotic waters at the time of creation (see Ps. 93; cf. Pss. 19:1–2[2–3]; 102:25[26]) and will climax in Christ's victory over all evildoers at his parousia. Verset 5b delves beneath God's work to *your thoughts*, the creative calculations and plans to attain a goal. Goldingay comments: "They [his deeds] were no spur-of-the-moment, instinctive response to a sudden tricky situation. Yhwh coolly formulated some intentions and implemented them"[47] (cf. Isa. 55:8–9). *Exceedingly* signifies what is considerably above normal and so parallels "how great." *Deep* signifies inaccessibility (cf. Isa. 7:11; Jer. 49:8). Like the wicked (Isa. 29:15), God goes to great depths to hide his plans from fools.[48] "Man," says Delitzsch, "can neither measure the greatness of the divine works nor fathom the depth of the divine thoughts; he who is enlightened, however, perceives the immeasurableness of the one and

47. Goldingay, *Psalms*, vol. 3, BCOTWP (Grand Rapids: Baker Academic, 2008), 55.

48. Avrohom Chaim Feuer (*Tehillim: A New Translation with a Commentary Anthologized from Talmudic, Midrashic and Rabbinic Sources,* trans. Avrohom Chaim Feuer in collaboration with Nosson Scherman [Brooklyn: Mesorah, 1982], 1150n1) notes the apparent success of the wicked such as Haman in the midrash *Esther Rabah* 6:2: "Behold! The enemies of God are raised up to meet their downfall! This may be likened to the vile galley slave who viciously cursed the king's beloved son. The king reasoned, 'If I kill him, people will not take notice of it and they will learn nothing from it—for of what consequence is the life of a lowly galley slave?' Therefore, the king first promoted the slave to the rank of captain, then he elevated him to the post of governor-general. Only then, after giving him prominence and renown, did the king execute the rogue for his crime." The midrash finds an analogy in the way God treated Pharaoh (Exod. 7:3–6; 9:16; Rom. 9:15).

unfathomableness of the other."[49] "Oh, the depth of the riches of the wisdom and knowledge of God! How unsearchable his judgments, and his paths beyond tracing out!" (Rom. 11:33).[50] The notion of God's hidden plans "lays the foundation for the rest of the psalm," says Robert Alter.[51] Without swift justice, crime appears to pay. Fools think it does.

Strophe B: Fools Don't Understand the Prosperous Wicked Will Be Eliminated 6-7

1. Fools Don't Understand 6

A brutish person (*'iš-ba'ar*—a congener of *be'îr*, "beast, cattle, animal"[52]) lacks "the rationality that differentiates men from animals."[53] Agur reckoned himself a brute, less than human, before he acquired wisdom and knowledge of the Holy One (Prov. 30:2–3; cf. Ps. 73:21–22). There is no in-between: "One must be a saint or senseless," says Spurgeon, "there is no other choice. One must be either the adoring seraph or the ungrateful swine."[54] *Does not know* signifies, as defined in Psalm 90:11, that they lack "the mental knowledge of a fact and the visceral experiencing of that reality." In Proverbs, *fool* refers to "blockheads . . . deaf to wisdom, from their distorted moral vision, of which they are cocksure" who "delight in twisting values that benefit the community."[55] *Understand* signifies the act of giving heed and considering something in such a way that insight about the object takes place. One can see or hear something and yet not "perceive" or "understand" it (Isa. 6:9). Sometimes the accent falls on "giving heed to" or "considering" something (Prov. 7:7; 14:15; 18:5) and other times on the derived "understanding" (Prov. 1:2, 6). Perception is a matter of the disposition of the heart. A good heart that understands morality is a gift

49. Delitzsch, *Psalms,* 607.
50. "My brethren," says Augustine as quoted by Spurgeon (*Treasury of David,* 822), "there is no sea so deep as these thoughts of God, who makes the wicked flourish, and the good suffer; nothing so profound, nothing so deep. Every unbelieving soul is wrecked in that depth, in that profundity. Do you wish to cross this depth? Do not remove the wood of Christ's Cross and you will not sink. Hold fast to Christ."
51. Robert Alter, *The Book of Psalms: A Translation with Commentary* (New York: Norton, 2007), 326.
52. *HALOT,* 1:146, s.v. *ba'ar.*
53. Chou-Wee Pan, *NIDOTTE,* 1:691, s.v. *ba'ar.*
54. Spurgeon, *Treasury of David,* 823.
55. Bruce K. Waltke, *Proverbs 1–15,* NICOT (Grand Rapids: Eerdmans, 2004), 112.

from God. Weiser comments: "Only through the relationship with God is man enabled to recognize ultimate truth and reality; without that relationship he lapses into a deceptive illusion" (cf. Ps. 28:5).[56] *This* refers to the content of verse 7. Kirkpatrick comments: "Only unspiritual men fail to perceive that the prosperity of the wicked is but the prelude to their ruin, while Jehovah sits enthroned on high forever."[57] The stupid think that flourishing through unrighteousness will have the last word.

2. Prosperous Wicked Eliminated 7

The moral Governor of the universe designs that prosperity through wickedness is drinking poison. The synonymous parallels emphasize the point. *Wicked* escalates to *all* (i.e., without exception) *evildoers*, or all who "do" (put into action the necessary means to secure the success of their enterprise) "evil" (misuse their power through deception and lies "in relation to a community or an individual with a negative effect or intention"[58]). In other words, they flourished at the expense of others; their elimination is for the good of humankind. The favorable metaphor *flourished*, abetted by the simile *like plants* (see n. 9) is matched with *blossom* (see Ps. 90:6). "The wicked are like the green things that shoot up so bravely in the steppe after the late rains of spring, covering everything, but then break down just as fast beneath the hot desert wind or sun, dry out, and vanish (cf. 37:2; 90:5–6; 103:15–16)."[59] Their short-lived, grass-like prosperity *led to their being exterminated* (*lᵉhiššāmᵉdām*). Šmd Hiphil is used in liturgical laws to ban someone from the cultic community and in holy war to ban someone from the land through physical destruction. Although *I AM* may be the Agent, says Vetter, "the original sense of the ban commandment is preserved when people execute the commandment (Num. 33:52; Deut. 2:12, 23; 7:24; 33:27; Josh. 9:24; 11:14, 20; 2 Sam. 22:38; Ps. 106:34)."[60] In Psalm 92, the ultimate Agent is *I AM* and the immediate agent is his king (see vv. 9–11). Their destruction is *forever* (*ʿᵃdê ʿad*, i.e., to the unforeseeable future). Although with reference to history the unforeseeable future may not

56. Artur Weiser, *The Psalms*, OTL (Philadelphia: Westminster, 1962), 615.

57. A. F. Kirkpatrick, *The Book of Psalms* (1902; repr., Grand Rapids: Baker Books, 1986), 559.

58. K. H. Bernhart, *TDOT*, 1:143, s.v. ʾāwen.

59. Frank-Lothar Hossfeld and Erich Zenger, *Commentary on Psalms 51-100*, trans. Linda M. Maloney, Hermeneia (Minneapolis: Fortress, 2005), 439.

60. D. Vetter, *TLOT*, 3:1367–68, s.v. šmd Hiphil.

be eternal in a philosophical sense, yet *leʿōlām*, the equivalent of *ʿad*, with reference to God is eternal in a philosophical sense (v. 8). Goldingay says: "Thus the recognition that parallels that in Psalm 73, but it came not because the worshiper saw something by faith, as was the case there, but through seeing something actually happen."[61] This insight into *I AM*'s thoughts and works, based on the psalmist's own experience, enables him to confess that God is upright in a morally topsy-turvy world. Most stories of the Bible, including the story of the exodus, represent the final triumph of the righteous over the temporary prosperity of the wicked. These stories climax with the death and resurrection—an earnest of his final victory—of Jesus Christ.

Center Line: I AM *Is on High Forever* 8

In the terse, four-word center line, references to God frame two core words predicating his transcendence over space (*on high*, a metonymy for heaven; see Job 16:19; 31:2; Isa 33:5) and time (*forever*, *leʿōlām*; see Ps. 90:2; 100:5). *For you* points to God as the ultimate Agent upholding justice. The metonymy "on high" is used to signify God's transcendence over the earth and human activity and his impregnability against hostile forces. "It is the realm where God lives and works and from whence he sends forth his power and help for those who are in need, or against those whom he punishes (e.g., Pss. 18:17; 93:4; 102:20 . . .)."[62] The vocative *I AM* closes the center line with an exclamation point.

Second Half *9–15*

The second half begins where the first half ended: all evildoers will be exterminated (vv. 9–11). Their destruction is a precursor of the eschatological age. The second half closes with the righteous *flourishing in old age* (12–15).

Stanza III: *All Evildoers Eliminated* 9–11

The third stanza elaborates on the extermination of the wicked: God's enemies perished (v. 9) through the king's victory over them (10–11).

61. Goldingay, *Psalms*, 56.
62. Tate, *Psalms 51–100*, 467.

Strophe A: God's Enemies Perish 9

The synonymous parallels in 7aα and β are matched by the synonymous, climactic[63] parallels in 9aα and β. These framing tricola around the center line are also linked by the catchphrase "all evildoers" are destroyed forever.[64] Causal *for* is related to verse 7; it continues the thought that evildoers will be destroyed forever. The emotional exclamation *look*/behold asks *I AM* on high to join the psalmist to take note of a situation on earth.[65] *Your enemies* are identified in verse 9b as "evildoers" and in 7 as "the wicked." Vocative *I AM* links vv. 8 and 9. Of the many Hebrew synonyms in the semantic domain of "to destroy," *perish* (*yōʾbēdû*) may have been chosen for its assonance with *ʾōyēb* ("enemy"). The lexeme *ʾābad* means "to disappear, vanish, and cease to exist" (cf. Num. 16:33). *Will be scattered* means "to be divided/separated from each other"[66] and occurs as a parallel with *ʾābad* in Job 4:11: "The lion perishes (*ʾōbēd*) for lack of prey, and the cubs of the lioness are scattered (*yitpārādû*)." When a community of cubs is broken up, it cannot reproduce itself. So also when the community of evildoers is scattered, it cannot reproduce its thoughts, words, and deeds to the next generation. So they vanish forever (v. 7).

Strophe B: The King Victorious over Wicked 10–11

1. The King's Great Strength 10

The parallel lines point both to *I AM* as the ultimate Agent of the king's victory ("you exalted my horn," v. 10a) and to the king's enthusiastic participation in his own elevation ("I rubbed [my horn] with rich olive oil," v. 10b). *You exalted* studiously avoids identifying God as the immediate Agent. "Their being exterminated" in verse 7 does not name the agent who exterminates them,

---

63. Climactic parallelism designates a highly repetitive, slowly advancing set of lines reaching toward a climax (see Ps. 29:1–2 for a textbook example).

64. H. L. Ginsberg, "Ugaritic Studies and the Bible" (*BA* 8 [1945]: 54f.) noted that verse 9 owes its style and language to a combat myth reflected in the Ugaritic texts (c. 1300 BCE). In that myth, Baal, god of fertility, and Yam, god of watery chaos, struggle for dominion. The craftsman god, Lothar wa-Khasis, encourages Baal: "Now thine enemy, O Baal,/ Now thine enemy wilt thou strike;/ Now wilt thou cut off thine adversary" (*ANET*, p. 151, text III ABA, lines 7–9).

65. *IBHS*, §40.2.1.

66. *Yitpārᵉdû* is used of scales of crocodile (? Job 41:17[9]) and of bones [out of joint] (Ps. 22:14[15]). A *niprād* is an anti-social person (Prov. 18:1).

but the verb *šāmad* assumes a human agent. So now in the matching chiastic first strophe of the third stanza, the immediate agent is the king, not *I AM*. *My horn* is a metaphor for dignity, honor, and deadly strength (cf. Pss. 112:9; 148:14).[67] *Like the wild ox*[68] symbolizes being fierce, strong, and deadly (Num. 23:22; 24:8; Job 39:9, 10). "The image is taken from the wild ox (Ps. 92:11) who stands with uplifted horn feeling his full strength, challenging the opponent, an image also known to the Babylonians" (cf. Deut. 33:17).[69] *Which I rubbed* (see n. 15) *with . . . olive oil*, making their goring more effective and making them "gleam with virility and health."[70] *Rich* (see n. 16) intensifies the imagery of goring and gleaming horns.

2. The King Sees and Hears the Rout of His Enemies 11

Narrative *waw* (*and*) continues the king's testimony. The parallel lines in their outer frame match *my eyes* with *my ears*; and in their inner core, "those who tried to ambush me" is paired with "the wicked who attack me." Both sight and sound, each in its own way, confirm the king's victory over evildoers. He revels over them *in triumph* (see n. 18) as they lie on the ground beneath him. *Those who tried to ambush me* essentially means they "watch closely" and so makes a pun with "gaze at." The future tense *will hear* connotes that *the destruction* of the wicked will continue to be heard into the eternal future (see vv. 7–8). *The wicked* (*mᵉrēʿîm*) in the book of Psalms is a fixed expression for those who cause injury and harm and who stand in contrast to those who wait on God (cf. Ps. 22:16[17]). *Who attack me* does not so much speak of insurgents—though it can mean "revolt" (Judg. 9:18)—as it speaks of "attackers" (cf. Deut. 19:11; 22:26; Pss. 3:1[2]; passim). Zenger comments: "This is not a 'blessing' of the dictum that 'revenge is sweet,' but must be read as poetic dramaturgy meant to lead to the 'teaching' developed in the closing section of the psalm, in vv. 13–16 [Eng. 12–15]."[71] Christians pray for the establishment of God's kingdom and are told to rejoice at God's final judgment on the enemies of his kingdom (Rev 18:20).

---

67. It's possible the helmet of the king of Israel had horns on it, as on the victory stele of Naram Sin, king of Akkad (2254–2218 BCE), whose helmet had horns (H. Gressmann, *Altorientalische Texte und Bilder*, vol. 2 [Tübingen: J. C. B. Mohr, 1927], illust. 43).

68. The aurochs (*bos pimigenius*)—a grand, extinct wild animal—is depicted in the palaeolithic Lascaux cave paintings and described in Julius Caesar's *The Gallic War* 6.28.

69. H. P. Stähli, *TLOT*, 3:1224, s.v. *rûm*, citing Gunkel.

70. Tate, *Psalms 51–100*, 467.

71. Hossfeld and Zenger, *Commentary on Psalms 51–100*, 440.

Stanza IV: *The Righteous Flourish and Proclaim* I AM *Is Upright* 12–15

The scene shifts from the king's triumph over evildoers to the righteous flourishing in the temple precincts. This final stanza consists of two couplets: The righteous flourish (vv. 12–13), and they do so into old age, proclaiming that *I AM* is upright (14–15).

Strophe A: The Righteous Flourish in the Temple 12–13

This couplet is unified grammatically by being a single sentence; rhetorically by its chiastically structured catchword "flourish" (vv. 12a, 13b), and semantically by the arboreal imagery of trees. Verse 12 focuses on the trees' vitality, and 13 focuses on the temple as the source of their growth. The arboreal figure is glossed over the righteous person, and the addition of "our" (see 13b) segues the righteous person into the worshiping congregation of the righteous.

1. The Righteous Flourish like a Palm Tree and a Cedar 12

The righteous, the opposite of "the wicked" (v. 7), refers to a person who brings about right and harmony for all by submitting him or herself to the Word (*Logos*) of God.[72] The arboreal figure *flourishes* (*yiprāḥ*; see v. 7) represents the temporal and universal prosperity of the righteous person. The splendor and longevity of the stately palm tree and the towering cedar of Lebanon contrast with the ephemeral flourishing of lowly grass (cf. Pss. 1:3; 37:35; 57:8[10]; Jer. 17:8). *Like a palm tree* is apt. First, a palm tree is stately and regal in appearance (cf. Isa 9:14[13]f.)—tall, slender, and knot-free—and has "plume-like foliage"[73] only at the very top. Date palm trees grow as tall as 60–70 feet. In the Song of Solomon, the lover says to the most beautiful of women (see Song 6:1): "Your stature is like that of the palm tree" (Song 7:8[7]a). Second, the palm tree sustains human life: "It provided food in the form of the date, and its sap could be used

---

72. That Word instructs them to love God with all their hearts and to love their neighbors as themselves, and they do so from their hearts (Ps. 1:2). They serve *I AM* (Mal. 3:18), are kind and generous (Pss. 37:21; 112:6), honest and truthful (Prov. 13:5; Isa. 45:23), and speak wisely (Prov. 10:31); they are not involved in sin such as idolatry, sexual immorality, or social injustice (Ezek. 18:5). The Word became incarnate in the Lord Jesus Christ.

73. Tate, *Psalms 51–100*, 467.

as sweetener for making wine."[74] The lover adds to the image of the palm tree's stature: "And your breasts [are] like clusters of fruit" (Song 7:7[8]b). "When it has attained its full size, it bears from three to four, and in some instances even as many as six, hundred pounds of fruit."[75] Third, it demands abundant water (see v. 13) and enjoys longevity (14). *He* (see n. 21) *grows* (*yiśgeh*), in its only other occurrence, refers to the increase of riches (Ps. 73:12). The metaphor entails an increase in righteousness and life. The increase of the righteous person's prosperity is so great that they are *like a cedar of Lebanon*. The cedar excels in beauty, height,[76] value, fertility, and longevity. Ezekiel lauds this tree's excellence: "With beautiful branches overshadowing the forest; it towered on high, its top above the thick foliage" (Ezek. 31:3). "The cedars of Lebanon represent the finest of earthly material. Solomon studied the lightness and strength of cedars (1 Kgs. 4:33), bargained with Hiram, who ruled the area, and created a conscript labor force thirty thousand strong to log the Lebanon cedars for the temple in Jerusalem (1 Kgs. 5)."[77] Kings competed in building their palaces with cedar and were willing to sell their souls for it (Jer. 22:7, 14, 23).

2. The Righteous Planted in the Temple 13

The notion of growth can be discerned in its escalating framing words "planted" (v. 13a) and "flourish" (13b). The verse's inner core elaborates "in the house of *I AM*" by "in the courts of our God." The figurative framing verbs for trees glide fluidly into the reality of the righteous worshipers in the temple precincts. This first-person plural pronoun signals the poet's change of direction from speaking about the righteous to speaking to them; transforms the righteous person into the righteous people; and transmogrifies the figure into realia. Konrad Schaefer says, "By an optical trick, the poet superimposes the arboreal image on the upright person in the temple, and tree and person fade into each other and exchange features."[78] So what does the figure of both these evergreen trees flourishing in the temple precinct signify about the righteous?[79] First, both trees demand a copious supply of water. "The palm tree

---

74. Leland Ryken, James C. Wilhoit, and Tremper Longman III, eds., *Dictionary of Biblical Imagery* (Downers Grove, IL: IVP Academic, 1998), 623.

75. Delitzsch, *Psalms*, 608.

76. They may grow as high as 120 feet.

77. Ryken, Wilhoit, and Longman, *Dictionary of Biblical Imagery*, 499.

78. Schaefer, *Psalms*, 231.

79. "Planted" and "flourish" in v. 13 [Heb. 14] are plural, referring to both trees.

has deep, water-seeking roots." And so it thrives in an oasis. "Jericho, built on the site of a large oasis in the wilderness, was well known as the 'City of Palms' (Deut. 34:3; 2 Chr. 28:15)."[80] As for the cedars of Lebanon, Ezekiel emphasized by repetition that the towering tree owed its superiority to abundant water.

> The waters nourished it, deep springs made it grow tall; their streams flowed all around its base and sent their channels to all the trees of the field. So it towered higher than all the trees of the field; its boughs increased and its branches grew long, spreading because of abundant waters. . . . It was majestic in beauty, with its spreading boughs, for its roots went down to abundant waters. (Ezek. 31:4-5, 7)

Second, the poet alludes to God's original temple on earth, the Garden of Eden, on the mountain of God (see Ezek. 28:13-14). From the top of Mount Eden, a river flowed through and nourished the trees of the garden with such abundant water that it became the headwater for four rivers that fructified the four corners of the earth.[81] Similarly, a relief from a palace of Ashurbanipal in Nineveh (c. 650 BCE) depicts a temple on the top of a mountain surrounded by a park with many trees on the slope of the mountain (see relief on p. 117).[82] In front of the temple is a little pavilion with a statue of the king in prayer. From the back of the temple, a river flows at a 45-degree angle through the park with channels of water branching off it to water the entire garden. A sacred way with an altar goes straight up through the park to the sanctuary. The relief teaches that the trees in the paradisiacal garden surrounding the temple receive their life and fertility from the river that flows from the temple in conjunction with the king's prayer. In short, the life-giving water supply originates in the temple. It is now clear that as the luxurious evergreen trees find their physical nourishment in abundant water in the paradisiacal garden, so the righteous find their spiritual nourishment *in the house of* I AM, more specifically in *the courtyards* where the people worshiped and heard God's word (cf. Ps. 1:2-3; Mic 4:1-4; Isa. 2:2-3). The living God cannot be disassociated from his temple (1 Kgs. 8:10-11). As the righteous worship him and learn of him in his temple, they draw their spiritual strength from the living God who was and is and will be forevermore. Drawing their abundant spiritual life from communicating with him, they figuratively

---

80. Ryken, Willhoit, and Longman, *Dictionary of Biblical Imagery*, 622.

81. Jon Levenson, *Sinai and Zion: An Entry into the Jewish Bible* (New York: HarperCollins, 1985), 128-37.

82. Cited in Hossfeld and Zenger, *Commentary on Psalms 51-100*, 441, plate 4.

Relief from Room H of Ashurbanipal's North Palace at Nineveh. Drawing by Deborah Anderson.

flourish (see vv. 7, 12). It is probably an unintended oxymoron that their royal splendor of height and beauty is due to their humble dependence upon God.

A third aspect of the arboreal image is that the palm tree and cedar of Lebanon grow together in the temple courtyard. But, as Prof. Warren Gage pointed out in a personal conversation, these trees do not naturally grow together any more than the wolf lives together with the lamb (Isa. 11:6–8). Gage suggests that the image is similar to Zion's promised glory: "The glory of Lebanon [i.e., the cedar tree] will come to you, the juniper, the fir and the cypress together, to adorn my sanctuary; and I will glorify the place for my feet" (Isa. 60:13). These trees grow in different climates. The image of these geographically distributed trees growing together in the temple courtyard represents the ecumenical unity of the righteous. Today, Jew and Gentile who have been baptized into Jesus Christ worship together as one people at the true temple (Gal. 3:26–29).

The parallel to *I AM* identifies him as *our God* (see 90:1, 17; 100:3). As the king is implicitly the antecedent of the first-person pronoun in verses 10–11, so the worshiping covenant people are implicitly the antecedent of *our* and are reckoned as the righteous (see p. 13). The personal pronoun empowers them to understand themselves as the stately palm and the mighty cedar of Lebanon. They owe their abundant life to faith and obedience in him as he makes himself available to them at the temple through prayer and known through the word of God, which finds its fulfillment in Jesus Christ.

Strophe B: The Righteous Flourish in Old Age and Proclaim God Is Upright 14–15

The second couplet of the final stanza, a unified sentence, retains the righteous as its subject (see v. 12) and continues to impose the arboreal image upon the righteous in v. 14 but not in v. 15.

1. The Righteous Flourish in Old Age 14

Let us reflect first on the arboreal image with reference to longevity. A date palm tree can be as much as two hundred years old, and cedars of Lebanon may be up to three thousand years old. Zenger comments: "That the cedars of Lebanon, even at the age of three thousand years, can still produce seed-bearing cones is in fact a phenomenon of astonishing fertility."[83] So, like the longevity of evergreen trees, the righteous *will still thrive* (a synonym and a catchword with "flourish" in vv. 12–13) *in old age* (see n. 23). The image of the royal and towering trees thriving so many years (v. 14a) is expanded in the parallel (14b): *They will be full of sap* (see n. 24) signifies their internal health and well-being, and *thick with leaves* represents their external health and vitality, like that of Moses. When Moses died at 120 years old, his eyes were not weak nor was his strength gone (Deut. 34:7). The imagery of vitality and fertility into old age is like the first gleam of light at daybreak. It was God's purpose before the beginning of time to give his church eternal life, but it has now been revealed through the appearing of our Savior, Christ Jesus, who has destroyed death and has brought life and immortality to light through the gospel (2 Tim. 1:10; cf. John 11:24–26; 1 Cor. 15). In that fulfillment, clinical death is only a shadow, like being hit by a truck's shadow, not by the truck itself.

---

83. Hossfeld and Zenger, *Commentary on Psalms 51-100*, 449.

2. Proclaiming *I AM*'s Justice 15

In the inner core of the chiastic parallels. "*I AM*" is matched by "my Rock," and in the outer frame, "upright" is paired with its definition, "no injustice." Using language drawn from the Song of Moses (Deut. 32:4),[84] this song of grateful praise reaches its climax in this proclamation of praise. The righteous, drawing their life from the living God, stand in the temple courtyard in regal splendor and full of life and fertility, *proclaiming* (see n. 25; cf. v. 2) I AM (see v. 1) *is upright* (*yāšār*). Like the word "crooked," *yāšār* has both a literal and a derived, figurative, ethical meaning. Literally it signifies "to be straight without a curve or bend," or "level without a bump," as in "a level (*yāšār*) path" (Jer. 31:9), "a straight (*yᵉšārâ*) way" (Ps. 107:7), and "straight (*yᵉšārâ*) leg" (Ezek. 1:7). Much more frequently, *yāšār* is used figuratively for being faultlessly just and moral according to Torah ethics. It is the opposite of *'āwel* ("wrongdoing"; see Deut. 32:4). Righteousness and uprightness are both connected with justice: "You are righteous, *I AM*, and your judgments are right (*yāšār*)" (Ps. 119:137; cf. Ps. 94:15). *Yāšār* is also used with "innocence" (Job 4:7) and "pure" (Prov. 20:11). God's people trust *I AM* to do what is right; by faith they know he is moral and just, without blemish. The Sovereign over space and time takes life away from evildoers (vv. 7, 9) and endows the righteous with eternal, abundant life. The king joins the proclamation, exclaiming *I AM* is *my Rock* (*ṣûrî*). A *ṣûr* varies in shape and size: a rocky wall, cliff (Num. 23:9; Isa. 2:10); a block of stone, boulder [as an altar] (Judg. 6:21; 13:19); a monument stone [for inscriptions] (Job 19:24); and rocks in a ravine (Job 28:10). Although it may occur in parallel with "a stone" (*'eben*; see Isa. 8:14), it differs from a stone, which is a fragment of a rock. The rock is "a ready image of imperious solidity."[85] Figuratively, God is the Rock (Deut. 32:31). His reliability and justice are as impervious as a rock and so never fail. As such, he is the defense of his people: a refuge (*mā'uzzēk*, Isa. 17:10; *mā'ôz*, Ps. 31:2[3]), a shelter (*maḥăsseh*, Ps. 94:22). This imagery of a rock slides easily into seeing God as a savior (Pss. 62:2[3], 6[7]; 95:1) and redeemer (Ps. 78:35). *And in whom there is no injustice* (*wᵉlō'-'awlātâ*) makes explicit the inherent notion of *yāšār*—of being just/righteous, without a flaw. *'Awlātâ* occurs as a synonym parallel to "evildoers" (Ps. 37:1: cf. 92:11[12]), "violence" (Ps. 58:[2]3), "bloodshed" (Mic. 3:10), and "iniquity" (Job 11:14), and

84. The Song of Moses with relevant allusions from Ps. 92 noted in parentheses: "He [*I AM*] is the Rock (v. 15), his deeds (v. 4) are perfect, and all his ways are just. A reliable (see v. 2) God who does no wrong (v. 15); upright (v. 15) and righteous/just (v. 12) is he."
85. Ryken, Wilhoit, and Longman, *Dictionary of Biblical Imagery*, 732.

as an antithetic parallel to both "justice" (Isa. 61:8) and "righteousness" (Job 6:29). Jehoshaphat instructed his newly appointed judges: "Judge carefully, for with *I AM* our God there is no injustice" (*'awlātâ*, 2 Chr. 19:7).

PART III. VOICE OF THE CHURCH IN RESPONSE

I. The Origin of Psalm 92 for the Sabbath

The origin of the custom of using this psalm "for the Sabbath day"—the only reference to the Sabbath in the Psalter—cannot be dated with certainty. According to Mishna Tamid 7:4, the Levitical choir in the Second Temple chanted a psalm each day of the week; they were successively Psalms 24, 48, 82, 94, 81, 93, and 92. The superscription in the LXX (see p. 105) designates five of these psalms for the Sabbath (Pss. 24 [= LXX 23], 48[47], 92–94[91–93]) and reflects an earlier custom than the Talmud but a later one than that reflected in the received tradition.[86] Its use for the Sabbath day may go back to the First Temple, for the Torah designated the Sabbath day as the day of rest (Lev. 23:3). Robert Alter says: "It is reasonable to suppose that this psalm was actually sung as part of the temple rite for the Sabbath."[87]

Sarna argues that the psalm's "creation motif" connects with the creation account in Genesis 1, which climaxes in God's Sabbath rest. He also argues that the psalm's "socio-moral motif" connects it with the Book of the Covenant (Exod. 23:12) and the Decalogue (Deut. 14–15).[88] Even if the creation motif can be teased out of the psalm, these motifs are not unique to Psalm 92 and so do not explain this unique use of Psalm 92 for the Sabbath day. Perhaps it was chosen because of the prominence of the number seven in its rhetoric (see below), but this seems unlikely.

II. The Creation and the Eternal Sabbath

This has been a long debate in church history, both with Jews and within Christianity. It is a question raised early on by Augustine of Hippo then raised

---

86. The earliest parts of the Septuagint were translated in the third century BCE and the latest parts by the first part of the first century BCE.

87. Alter, *The Book of Psalms*, 325.

88. Sarna, "The Psalm for the Sabbath Day," 159–67.

again during the Reformation. For Augustine, Ps. 92[91] is a "sabbatical event," to be sung on the Sabbath day. He asks, "but what kind of Sabbath?"[89] Clearly the Jews had celebrated it as a temporal Sabbath of God resting after the six days of creation. Exegetes today still interpret it as a temporal event.

Likewise, John Calvin notes: "In the first account of Creation, the Sabbath is the day given to celebrate God's mighty work with joy and worship both in creation and redemption. The simple biblical statement that the climax of God's act is not the creation of man, but his rest on the seventh day. It is the day of God's example." Calvin calls it the "inward sign" and the "outward reality."[90]

Although the Sabbath has its central point of orientation in Israel, the God of Israel is the Lord of all. "That means that God reveals Himself as the Creator, the Ruler, and the Preserver of the world. On the other hand, the Sabbath testifies to the fact that God graciously grants freedom and rest to men. The Sabbath is a sign of the covenant grace in which God the Father condescends to us and gives himself to us in Christ and in the Spirit. It is the gift of the Triune God given to all mankind."[91]

Ever since God gave it, the observance of the Sabbath has been a temporal event, one day in seven. Yet as Kenneth Mathews has written, "The climactic seventh day is remarkably different from the six foregoing days of creation." He cites five reasons that the Sabbath as "the day of consecration" is different from the six days of creation. First, God's creative word is not required as the introductory formula: "and God said." Second, this "day" is not the creation's day of "evening and morning," for creation was intended to have a perpetual rest. Third, only the seventh day is blessed by God. Fourth, unlike the creation days, only "the seventh day" is distinctly repeated three times, and twice more by the pronoun "it." Fifth, unlike the paired days of creation, the seventh day stands apart, having no corresponding day in the creation week.[92]

Moses tied the Sabbath day to God's redemptive purposes, as Heschel points out: "It is a day on which we are called upon to share what is eternal in time, to turn from the results of creation to the mystery of creation: from

89. Augustine, *Exposition of Psalm 91* 2, in *Expositions on the Psalms,* trans. Maria Boulding, vol. 4 (Hyde Park, NY: New City, 2002), 345f.

90. John Calvin, *Institutes of the Christian Religion,* ed. John T. McNeill, vol. 1 (Louisville: Westminster, 1960), 2.8.29–30.

91. Kwok Ting Cheung, "The Sabbath in Calvin's Theology" (PhD thesis, Faculty of Theology, St. Andrews University, 1989).

92. Kenneth A. Mathews, *Genesis 1–11:26,* NAC (Nashville: B&H, 1996), 176–77.

the world of creation to the creation of the world."[93] Deuteronomy 5:15 relates the observance of the Sabbath to the historic deliverance of Israel from Egypt, saying God's provision of the Promised Land was so that Israel could "rest" there redemptively (Exod. 33:14), but the people failed to dwell there "in rest" through their disobedience (Num. 14:28-30).

For the apostle Paul, as for the Talmud and Mishna (see p. 120) Sabbath was a foreshadowing of the eternal redemptive realities of God, but Paul relates that fulfillment to the church, which now embodies all God's redemptive purposes for mankind.[94] The incarnation has given humankind a radically new perspective on God's love and his redemption of humanity.[95] The epistle to the Colossians hymns a mystery: that Christ is the image of God and the firstborn of creation (Col. 1:15-18a). As the Agent of creation, his agency is redemption. For apart from Christ, the whole of creation would have no coherent center or purpose and perhaps revert to the chaos from which it emerged (1:17).[96]

In this non-temporal sense, Augustine, speaks of "the Sabbath of the heart," where we take repose in God's grace, free from guilt and a conscience in tumult. It is the sphere of tranquility and joy, the indwelling sphere of divine love.[97] We have not the slightest idea what it means to be the Creator of the cosmos, but oh, the joy of knowing the Creator as we are taught by our Lord—to pray to him as our "Abba," "our Father who is in heaven" (Matt. 6:9; Rom. 8:15; Gal. 4:6)! For as such he is my Savior, delivering me as a sinner from myself! Yet as the Creator, He does everything redemptively!

On Mars Hill in Athens, the apostle Paul declared that the god the Athenians worshiped, "the unknown god," was Israel's God (Acts 17:23). And according to the account of creation in Genesis 2, He is *I AM* the covenant God. In short, God shows himself as the Creator who had previously planned and fulfilled the election, the salvation, and the preservation of His people, before creation ever existed. He is like a master builder. When a poor builder's first design fails, he must turn to plan B. God, who is love (1 John 4:16) and is good

93. A. Heschel, *The Earth Is the Lord's and the Sabbath* (New York: Harper Torchbooks, 1966), 10.

94. Under "The Voice of the Church in Response" for Psalm 95, we will discuss the fulfillment of the Sabbath rest motif in the Epistle to the Hebrews.

95. See D.A. Carson, ed., *From Sabbath to Lord's Day: A Biblical, Historical, and Theological Investigation* (Grand Rapids: Zondervan, 1982).

96. Paul J. Achtemeier, Joel B. Green, Marianne Meye Thompson, eds., *Introducing the New Testament: Its Literature and Theology* (Grand Rapids: Eerdmans, 2001), 409.

97. Augustine, *Exposition of Psalm 91* 2 (Boulding, 346).

and righteous, has only plan A. If redemption were plan B, then we would have a fallible god who is not God at all! But our Redeemer-Creator has perfectly created all for all humanity, his *imago Dei*, from the beginning of the human race. He will further create "a new heaven and a new earth" (Rev. 21:1) in which evil will never again separate him from his own people.

In this light, the creation is nothing but what reveals and speaks of God's love to us, for us, and in us. As the apostle writes to his Roman audience, pagan and Christian: "For since the creation of the world God's invisible qualities—his eternal power and divine nature—have been clearly seen, being understood from what has been made, so that people are without excuse" (Rom. 1:20).

From these observations we draw the following conclusion: Redemption precedes creation. First of all, the creation in the Bible is never a history, just a backward look to what is "the beginning," namely God. And as 1 John reminds us, "God is love." Yet Genesis 1:1 tells us, "In the beginning, God created the heavens and the earth." This "beginning" is *creation continua,* for as the living Creator, he goes on creating, whether we call it evolution (for life forms) or "the Big Bang" (from which the universe is still coming into further form). God is the Agent not only of the past but of our present and future, for us as humans and for all creation throughout all time.

III. The Church's Reception of a Sabbath Psalm

The early church received a wholly new interpretation of the Sabbath.[98] It was first symbolized by Jesus feeding and healing others on the Sabbath day (Mark 1:21–34; 2:23–28; 3:1–6; Luke 13:10–17; 14:1–6; John 5:1–19; 7:21–24; 9:1–41). It was no longer about cultic ritual but about receiving deeds of grace and mercy. The identification of the first day of the week with the resurrection of Christ also created a new identity for Christians in contrast to Jews—the latter observed the seventh day (the Sabbath) while the former kept the First Day.[99]

The apostolic fathers loudly proclaim the centrality of celebrating the First Day of the Week. The *Didache* (c. 100) instructed that "every Lord's [Day]" was the pivot of the whole week's activities.[100] Later, Justin Martyr (110–165)

98. Robert Paul Martin, *The Christian Sabbath* (Montville, NJ: Trinity Pulpit, 2015).

99. Richard Bauckham, "The Lord's Day," in *From Sabbath to Lord's Day: A Biblical, Historical, and Theological Investigation*, ed. D. A. Carson (Grand Rapids: Zondervan, 1982), 228.

100. *Didache* 14 (ACW 6:23–24).

detailed how the whole day was to be kept and taught.[101] At the same time, Irenaeus (c. 130–202) admonished that Christians should not repeat the legalism of the Sabbath-keeping under the New Covenant: "There will be no command to remain idle for the man who, in the temple of the Lord, which is man's body, does service to God, and in every hour works righteousness."[102] At that time, two psalms were adopted: Psalm 118 ("This is the day which *I AM* has made; we will rejoice and be glad in it," v. 24) and Psalm 92.

IV. Augustine of Hippo (354–430)

Augustine preached a sermon on Psalm 92 (= LXX 91) on a Saturday, no doubt as a rhetorical gesture against the Jewish abuse of their "Sabbath." For they were spending the day "with a lazy, lax, and dissolute sort of rest. They refrain from work only to give themselves to frivolous pursuits, and although God commanded the observance of the Sabbath, they spend it in ways God forbids. We rest from wrongdoing; they rest from good works." Rather the subject of the Psalm is "the Sabbath of the heart": "Our Sabbath is within, in our hearts. . . . Tranquil joy, born of our hope, is our Sabbath. What this psalm has to enjoin upon us, what it has to sing about, is how Christians are to conduct themselves in the Sabbath of their hearts, in that tranquility and serenity of conscience, where no disturbance touches them."[103]

So he adds, "Begin your Sabbath . . . not attributing any good to yourself," for "twisted, disturbed persons who are not keeping the Sabbath, attribute their bad actions to God, and their good ones to themselves."[104]

Augustine interpreted "the morning" as the times that go well with us and the "night" as the times we are sad and troubled (v. 2). "When things go well, praise his mercy; when things go badly, praise his truth. . . . When you proclaim his mercy in the morning, and at night, you are praising Him all the time, confessing to God all the time.[105]

Augustine explains that "the ten-string psaltery" (= "the ten-stringed lute," v. 3) represents the ten commandments, played by acting out its precepts. He

---

101. Justin Martyr, *First Apology* 67 (ANF 1:186; PG 6:429–32).
102. Irenaeus, *Against Heresies* 4.16.5 (ANF 1:482; PG 7:1018).
103. Augustine, *Exposition of Psalm 91* 2 (Boulding, 346).
104. Augustine, *Exposition of Psalm 91* 3 (Boulding, 347).
105. Augustine, *Exposition of Psalm 91* 4 (Boulding, 349).

sees the "lyre" as what is acted upon.[106] We are gladdened, then, by what God has performed in our lives (v. 4), as the apostle reminds us also: "We are his handiwork, created for good works" (Eph. 2:10), and again, "What have you done that you did not receive? And if you did receive it, why boast as though you had not?" (1 Cor. 4:7). The "senseless" person (i.e., the "brutish person," v. 6) does not know these things, and Augustine judges that person as having lost the meaning of "the Sabbath from his inmost being, and shut out the peace from his heart, and rejected his good thoughts [so] he begins to imitate the person he has observed to flourish amid evil deeds, and so turns aside to do the same bad things himself."[107]

How high and deep is the wisdom of God, who provides us with Sabbatical rest, for the Sabbath is all about contemplating the eternity of God (v. 5)! "All things are drying up and falling," like the grass of the field, "but you have something on which to stay yourself: 'the Word of the Lord abides forever.' "[108] What then are the soothsayers, astrologers, and fortune-tellers who are the enemies of God? No more than the ephemeral unreality that will perish. The imagery of the "cedars of Lebanon" is replete with longevity, fruitfulness, and beauty in old age, as well as tranquility in times of turbulence. It truly reflects who are "the righteous."[109] "Planted in the house of *I AM*" (v. 13), such believers rest within their souls, multiplying their beneficence upon many others, whose calm demeanor radiates the presence of God to all.

V. Medieval and Early Modern Poets

Dante Alighieri (1278–1302)

Dante, like all medieval Christian poets, claimed that David is God's minstrel. The medieval poets saw that praise is the mainstay of the Psalter. But Dante, who interpreted Psalm 92, wins out in exalting it as a psalm of thanksgiving. Dante indeed gave Psalm 92 a special role in *The Divine Comedy*. He saw that the psalmist paints a much bigger picture than Sabbath-keeping, for the psalmist depicts the sheer miracle of creation. What can one do in the face of it all but offer up one's utmost art of praise day and night?

---

106. Augustine, *Exposition of Psalm 91* 4 (Boulding, 350–51).
107. Augustine, *Exposition of Psalm 91* 7 (Boulding, 352).
108. Augustine, *Exposition of Psalm 91* 8 (Boulding, 353)
109. Augustine, *Exposition of Psalm 91* 13 (Boulding, 357).

Thus Dante considered Psalm 92 important enough to give it a particular role, envisaging it in the Garden of Eden upon the poet's Mountain of Purgatory. This location is the reward of those who have worked through all the seven deadly sins and been washed clean of their stains. It is where they are born again. Once Dante enters Eden, he sees a meadow thick with red and yellow flowers. Wending her way through this scene is a beautiful young woman. Dante can tell she is in love. She walks as if in a dance, and as she makes a bouquet from the profusion at her feet, she sings a song. Might it identify her beloved? The woman interprets Dante's curiosity at a glance and graciously decides to satisfy it. She rejoices in the beauty of the Garden of Eden with the words of Psalm 92:4–5, the psalm titled *"Delectasti Me"*—"You have made me glad."[110]

More than a century before Dante, Peter Abelard had also used Psalm 92 in his treatise on the work of creation, *Hexaemeron*, to describe those delights which man in his fallen condition may still enjoy, which "as with song caress his ear, [and] inspire in us love and praise of our Creator, even as the Psalmist says, addressing Him: 'Delectasti me, Domine, in facture tua et in operibus manuum tuarum exsultabo.'" Abelard tells us, as Dante does, that the Sabbath is the opportunity for us to praise and love the Creator.[111] For Dante, the peace of the earthly paradise is an anticipation of the heavenly peace—an anticipation and a token of eternal peace. As Virgil promises Dante, he is to experience this peace every day.[112]

John Milton (1608–1674)

John Milton had a lifelong interest in the Hebrew Psalms, being one of the few scholars of his day to translate them into English and Greek.[113] In *Paradise Lost*, the angelic choir sings Psalm 92 on the seventh day in accord with the gloss of the Geneva Bible on Psalm 92: "which teacheth that the use of the

---

110. Peter S. Hawkins, *Dante: A Brief History* (Malden, MA: Blackwell, 2010); cf. Dante, *Purgatorio* 28.77–96.

111. Charles S. Singleton, ed., *The Divine Comedy: Purgatorio*, vol. 2 (Princeton, NJ: Princeton University Press, 1973), 678–79; cf. Peter Abelard, *Exposito in Hexaemeron* 762D.

112. Dante, *Purgatorio* 27.115–17.

113. Carole S. Kessner, "Psalm 92 and Milton's Sabbath Hymn," *Milton Quarterly* 10, no.3 (1976): 75–77.

Sabbath standeth in praising God, and not only in ceasing from work."[114] Probably Milton knew the Jewish tradition that the psalm was composed by Adam, on the first Sabbath of creation. Translating the complete psalm, he inserted it into his epic.

Milton divides the psalm into four sections: (a) the call to worship with song and musical instruments, (b) the praise of God's works, (c) the description of the fate of the wicked, and (d) the description of the future of the righteous. Central to Milton's theodicy in *Paradise Lost* is that *I AM* is "upright," and he concludes his hymn on Psalm 92 with this celebration: "Thrice happy if they know,/ Their happiness, and persevere upright!"

Milton assigns the hymn to the angels to sing:

> . . . what thought can measure thee, or tongue
> Relate thee—greater now in thy return
> Than from the Giant Angels? Thee that day
> Thy thunders magnifi'd; but to create
> Is greater than created to destroy.

For the wicked who rebelled are Satan and the fallen angels.

For Milton, the Sabbath rest is the creation of a new world, without sin. He describes this new world:

> Of amplitude almost immense, with Stars
> Numerous, and every Star perhaps a World
> Of destin'd habitation; but tho know'st
> Thir seasons: among these the seat of men,
> Earth with her nether Ocean circumfus'd
> Thir pleasant dwelling place. Thrice happy men,
> And sons of men, whom God has thus advanc't,
> Created in his Image, there to dwell
> And worship him, and in reward to rule
> Over his works, on Earth, in Sea, or Air.[115]

Milton had identified in Revelation 15:3 a paraphrase of the lines of Psalm 92:5, "How great are your works, *I AM*."[116] "The song of Moses" now turns out

114. See John Milton, *Paradise Lost* 7.594–632.
115. Milton, *Paradise Lost* 11.620–29.
116. Kessner, "Psalm 92 and Milton's Sabbath Hymn," 75.

to the song of the Angels, giving a profoundly celestial character to the psalm, a theme that Dante had taken up before Milton. Both poets give an angelic character to the psalm and to Sabbath-keeping; rarely has any other commentator received Psalm 92 in this heavenly way. Later poets, like the Countess of Pembroke, Mary Sidney Herbert, would render the Psalms "poetically," but not with the theological depth of Milton.[117]

VI. Living a Godly Life according to the Reformers

Martin Luther (1483–1546)

In his first collection of lectures on the Psalms (1513–15), writing more as a pietist than as a church leader, Luther never refers to Psalm 92's superscription. He begins, "Although this psalm can be explained as dealing with the works of creation, it is more fittingly explained as dealing with the new creation, which is the church in Christ. Eph. 2:10: 'We are His workmanship, created for good works.' . . . 'That we should be a kind of first-fruits of His creation' [Jas. 1:18]."[118]

John Calvin (1509–1564)

Like Augustine, John Calvin begins by stating the Sabbath day "is not to be holy, in the sense of being devoted to idleness, as if this could be an acceptable worship to God, but in the sense of separating ourselves from all other occupations, to engage in meditating upon the Divine works . . . in the celebration of the Divine Name."[119] This we do, from earliest dawn until night. Much less metaphorically than Augustine, Calvin sees Christian worship as more fundamentally coming from vernacular, human voices than from musical instruments, acknowledging God as the Father and Judge watching over his

117. Lawrence Wieder, ed., *The Poets' Book of Psalms, The Complete Psalter as Rendered by Twenty-Five Poets from the Sixteenth to the Twentieth Centuries* (Oxford: Oxford University Press, 1955), 139-40

118. Martin Luther, *First Lecture on Psalm 92*, in Luther's Works 11, ed. Hilton C. Oswald (Saint Louis: Concordia, 1955), 228.

119. John Calvin, *Commentary on the Book of Psalms*, trans. James Anderson, vol. 3 (Grand Rapids: Baker Books, 1996), 493–94.

human family.[120] "God has displayed an incomprehensible depth of power and wisdom in the fabric of the universe, but what the Psalmist has especially in view is to administer a check to that disposition which leads us to murmur against God."[121] He summarizes his commentary on verses 6 and 7: "It seems to me that the Psalmist compares the stability of God's throne with the fluctuating and changeable character of this world, reminding us that we must not judge of Him by what we see in the world, where there is nothing of a fixed and enduring nature."[122]

In verse 10, Calvin interprets the "horn" as a symbol of power and strength, possibly a wild goat's horn. But unlike earlier commentators, he gives little attention to it. While "oil" reflects the enjoyment of all God's blessings, "the palm tree" and the "cedars of Lebanon" are briefly given their conventional meanings.[123] Like Luther before him, Calvin is scarcely aware of the superscript "For the Sabbath day"; rather his commentary on Psalm 92 is simply an admonition to live a godly life.

PART IV. CONCLUSION

Book IV is the response of God and his people to the exile: the praise of God, who reigns universally in time and space. Psalm 92 pivots on this praise: "You are on high forever, *I AM!*" The God who adopted Israel as his family now reigns through David's ideal son, the Messiah. Unlike David's failed descendants, this son, the Son of God, will not fail. In Psalm 91:8, the king, the type of Jesus the Messiah, was promised, "With your eyes you will look (*nābaṭ*) and see the retribution of the wicked"; in 92:11, the king testifies, "My eyes gazed (*nābaṭ*) in triumph at those who tried to ambush me." In Psalm 91, the faithful king was promised to be invulnerable and invincible. In Psalm 92, the king sings his grateful praise that his past victory gives assurance that he will exterminate the wicked and the righteous will flourish forever. Fools don't understand God's design that the prosperity of the wicked at the expense of the righteous will lead to their destruction. Worldly kingdoms, from that of Sargon of Akkad to Hitler's Third Reich, have all passed away, but God's kingdom endures—yesterday, today, and forever. It is the old gospel story:

120. Calvin, *Commentary on the Book of Psalms*, 496–7.
121. Calvin, *Commentary on the Book of Psalms*, 498.
122. Calvin, *Commentary on the Book of Psalms*, 499–500.
123. Calvin, *Commentary on the Book of Psalms*, 501–4.

Rome triumphed momentarily on Good Friday; Christ triumphed eternally on Easter Sunday. The king identifies himself with the righteous. He speaks of "my ears" and "my eyes" witnessing the rout of the wicked (v. 11) but pictures the righteous as an ecumenical community flourishing in the temple, in the courts of *our* God, as they drink from him in word and ritual.

As in Psalm 90, in which the righteous speak of the future in terms of years, showing how eternal life in its full sense was yet to be clearly revealed, so also our poet speaks of the future in terms of a cedar tree's longevity in the Eternal's temple, not in the clarity of Christ's resurrection and ascension into the heavenly reality. But the flourishing cedar tree is full of sap and rich foliage in old age, and so, in embryonic form, it points to the true reality.

In the New Testament, the earthly temple finds its reality in Christ (John 2:21). Today, earthly Mount Zion has been made obsolete by Jesus Christ (John 4:23–24). He sits in the heavenly temple at God's right hand. From there, he poured out the Holy Spirit upon his church so that she could worship in Spirit and in truth. She comes "to Mount Zion, to the city of the living God, the heavenly Jerusalem" (Heb. 12:22). Through his word and sacraments, they participate in his eternal life. The church is God's earthly temple, both corporately (1 Cor. 3:16) and individually (1 Cor. 6:19), where the world finds the living water of Christ's Spirit.

All this is true because the God of Abraham, Isaac, and Jacob is on high forever!

CHAPTER 5

Psalm 93: I AM's *Throne and the Earth Stand Firm*

PART I. VOICE OF THE PSALMIST: TRANSLATION

For the day before the Sabbath, when the earth was inhabited. The praise
   of a song by David.[1]

1   *I AM* reigns! He is clothed in majesty;
      clothed is *I AM;* with strength he girds himself.
      Indeed, the earth-disc is established; it cannot be toppled.

2   Your throne is established from of old;
      you are from everlasting.

3   The floods have lifted up, *I AM;*
      the floods have lifted up their voice;
      the floods lift up their pounding waves.

4   Than the thunder of the vast waters,
      than the thunder of the mighty breakers of the sea,[2]
      more mighty on high is *I AM.*

5   Your stipulations are totally trustworthy;
      holiness adorns[3] your house, *I AM,*
      for endless days.

---

1. So LXX. MT lacks a superscript.

2. Verse 4a of MT may be read in several ways. This translation interprets *miqqōlôt* in 4aα as gapped in 4aβ and *'addîrîm* as breaking the construct chain.

3. Scholars differ on the parsing of *na'ăwâ*. GKC (75×) interprets this as *'wh* Niphal ("incline, desire"; always otherwise Piel or Hithpael), as does *HALOT* (1:20, s.v. *'wh*). But *HALOT* (1:657, s.v. *n'h*), albeit as a question, also offers *n'h* Qal. BDB parses as *n'h* Pilel, and *The Concise Dictionary of Classical Hebrew* as *n'h* Pael. Most agree that the word means "beautiful," "delightful" (see Song 1:10). The preposition "to" (*lᵉbêtᵉkâ* "to your house") adds the nuance of being "suitable," "right for," or "proper/fitting to" (cf. Ps. 33:1; Prov. 17:7), justifying the rendering "adorns."

131

Part II. Commentary

I. Introduction

Author

The Septuagint (LXX) attributes Psalm 93 to King David, and there is no reason to deny that attribution (see p. 13–15).

Rhetoric: Structure and Message

Upon a first reading, the three stanzas of Psalm 93 seem disjointed.[4]

Stanza I (*I AM* Reigns): The World and His Throne Stand Firm	1–2
Strophe A: *I AM* the Warrior and Builder Firmly Established the Earth-disc	1
1. Proclamation: *I AM* Reigns	1aα
2. *I AM* Is Clothed in Majesty and Armed with Strength	1aβ–bα
3. The World Is Firmly Established	1bβ
Strophe B: The Eternal's Throne Has Been Established from of Old	2
Stanza II: *I AM* Is Mightier Than the Swelling Seas	3–4
Strophe A: The Floods Lift Up Their Loudly Crashing Waves	3
Strophe B: *I AM* Is Mightier Than the Raging Floods	4
Stanza III: *I AM*'s Law and Temple Endure Forever	5

Upon further reflection, however, the psalm is unified by (a) the metaphor of God as King; (b) its adaptation of a Canaanite myth that informs the whole; and (c) the inclusio of the semantically related words *kûn* Niphal "established" (vv. 1–2) and *'āman* Niphal "trustworthy" (v. 5).

The Metaphor: God Is King

The psalm's opening proclamation ("*I AM* reigns," v. 1) and declaration ("Your throne is established from of old," v. 2) pick up on the pivot of the previous

---

4. Analysis adapted from Dirk J. Human, "Yahweh Robed in Majesty and Mightier than the Great Waters," in *Psalms and Mythology*, ed. Dirk J. Human, LHBOTS 462 (London: T&T Clark, 2007), 147–69, esp. 157.

psalm: "For you are on high forever, *I AM!*" (Ps. 92:8). The proclamation "*I AM* is King/reigns" informs the entire psalm. Recall that the king was invested with supreme authority by virtue of his ability to lead, especially in war and in the administration of justice, and that the king is a builder (see p. 4). Psalm 93 praises Israel's King as a warrior, judge, and builder, but it intersects these motifs and magnifies them. As a warrior, he is mightier even than the wild fury of the raging seas (vv. 3–4); as a judge, he decrees laws (v. 5); and as a builder, he established the earth-disc so firmly that it cannot be toppled (v. 1; cf. Ps. 24:1–2). Recall, too, that a king's ability to lead depends on his noble qualities: strength, justice, majesty, and longevity (see p. 4). *I AM* possesses these virtues in an incomparable way. He may be compared to a human king, but no human king compares to him (cf. Jer. 10:6). Psalm 93 lauds both *I AM's* majesty, which is redefined as strength (vv. 1, 3–4), and his justice (v. 5). As for longevity, he is from the "eternal" past (v. 2) to "endless days" (v. 5).

A Canaanite Myth: Baal versus Yamm

Psalm 93 praises *I AM's* superlative employments and sublime qualities using the imagery, not the theology, of the Ugaritic myth "Baal versus Yamm ['Sea']." As Milton and Bunyan used the imagery of Greek mythology to dethrone the pagan gods, Psalm 93 uses the imagery of ancient Near Eastern combat myths involving a struggle against chaos (German *Chaoskampf*) to dethrone Canaanite deities. In chaoskampf myths, a heroic deity establishes his kingship by defeating a deified dragon or the Sea. In the Akkadian myth *Enuma Elish*, Marduk—the patron deity of Babylon—vanquishes the dragon Tiamat. In the Ugaritic myth, Baal—the Canaanite god of fertility/life—and his consort Anat defeat Yamm (Sea)/Nahar (River)/Mot (Death) and the seven-headed Serpent, deities who oppose life.[5] Anat boasts:

> Surely I fought Yamm, the Beloved of El,
> Surely I finished off River, the great god,
> Surely I bound Tunan and destroyed (?) him.
> I fought the Twisty Serpent,
> The Potentate with seven heads.[6]

5. The Ugaritic/Canaanite myth(s) was written down in the fourteenth century BCE but probably originated a few centuries earlier (cf. Michael David Coogan, *Stories from Ancient Canaan* [Philadelphia: Westminster, 1978], 1).

6. Simon Parker, ed., *Ugaritic Narrative Poetry*, trans. Mark S. Smith (Atlanta: Scholars, 1997), 111. Cf. Ps. 74:13–14; Isa. 27:1.

In Marduk's struggle to vanquish Tiamat—whose name is cognate to the Hebrew *tᵉhōm* ("ocean depths," Gen. 1:2)—the other gods proclaim: "Marduk is king."[7] After Baal defeats Yamm, it is proclaimed: "Yamm is indeed dead! Baal shall be king!"[8] The Ugaritic myth continues with an extended story about the building of Baal's palatial temple of cedar, gold, silver, and precious gems on the heights of Zaphon (cf. Ps. 48:2), where he sits enthroned.[9] The similarities between Psalm 93 and the Ugaritic myth are striking. In both, as J. Levenson notes, "creation [?], kingship, and temple . . . form an indissoluble triad."[10] Sarna argues that the use of the Ugaritic combat myth in Isa. 17:12–14; 21:14; Ps. 74:13–15; 89:9–10[10–11]; 92:10[11]; Job 26:12–13; 38:8–11 (cf. Hab 3:8, 15) entitles us to think that Psalm 93 is based on this "well-established, consistent, and widespread exegetical tradition."[11] But the myth's dissimilarities to Psalm 93 are also striking. There is no real combat in the psalm, and the sea is demythologized. God does not become king by conquering the sea; he conquers the sea because he is the eternal King (v. 2).

The Inclusio: Established and Trustworthy

H. Wildberger says, "In many respects *kûn* ['established,' v. 1] is surprisingly close to the root *'mn* ['to be proved firm,' v. 5] semantically."[12] This inclusio of the stability of the earth and of God's law is the psalm's sum and substance: *I AM* is sovereign over creation and over history (cf. Ps. 92:8), however unruly they may seem. This is so because of his majestic strength (vv. 1, 4). "With God things never get out of hand."[13] Also, the stability of the earth-disc brought about by *I AM's* rule over the rampaging sea generates confidence that his law and temple will not fail (cf. Matt. 5:17–18).[14] This is a King worth pledging allegiance to and to be feared if offended (cf. Ps. 97:12). When the Western world lost confidence that the God of the Bible was the Creator, it also ceased to take the Ten Commandments seriously. Creation theology and absolute ethics are inseparable.

7. *Enuma Elish* 4.25–30, trans. Benjamin R. Foster (COS 1.111:397).

8. Human, "Yahweh Robed in Majesty," 158.

9. See Dennis Pardee, "The Ba'lu Myth" (*COS* 1.86:241–86).

10. Jon Levenson, *Sinai and Zion: An Entry into the Jewish Bible* (New York: HarperCollins, 1985), 108f.

11. N. M. Sarna, "The Psalm for the Sabbath Day," *JBL* 81 (1962): 155–168, esp. 161.

12. H. Wildberger, *TLOT*, 1:136 s.v. *'mn*.

13. H. C. Leupold, *Exposition of the Psalms* (Columbus: Wartburg, 1959), 665.

14. Cf. John H. Eaton, *Psalms: Introduction and Commentary* (London: SCM, 1967), 229.

Form

Typically, form criticism is concerned with a composition's literary genre and with how it functioned in a society.

Genre

Psalm 93 is *poetry* (see p. 23–25). More specifically, it is a *hymn* (see p. 5). Psalm 93, like only a few other hymns, omits both an introduction that calls worshipers to praise and a conclusion that commonly renews the call (e.g., "Hallelujah!").[15] Psalm 93 does not mention the poet nor the worshipers nor their music; it focuses exclusively on *I AM*. The poet, speaking for true Israel, expresses his enthusiasm for *I AM* by repeating God's name five times in five verses. This hymn also combines proclamation to the congregation (v. 1) and direct address to *I AM* (vv. 2–5; see p. 98n1). "Being more personal, second person more forcefully expresses the direct piety."[16]

Setting

Hymns were composed for temple worship. The change of addressees from the congregation (v. 1) to *I AM* (vv. 2–5) suggests a liturgical setting, as does also the reference to the temple in verse 5. The LXX superscription informs that Psalm 93 was "for the day before the Sabbath, when the land was *first* inhabited"—the sixth day of the week (see n. 1). The Babylonian Talmud explains, "On [the sixth day] God completed his work and reigned over all creation in full glory" (b. Roš Haš. 31a). This use is also most appropriate, for it assures the covenant community that the earth-disc, the source of their life and the stage for their sacred history, is firmly established; it will never be toppled. Mishna Tamid 7:4 adds that it was sung by the Levites. These notices may have originated in the First or Second Temple periods. For a refutation of the theory alleging the psalm was used in an annual enthronement festival in which Yahweh became king, see pp. 19–22.

---

15. 11QPs opens this praise psalm with "Hallelujah," but it lacks other characteristics of an introduction to a hymn (see H. Gunkel and J. Begrich, *Introduction to the Psalms: The Genres of the Religious Lyric of Israel*, trans. James D. Nogalski [Macon, GA: Mercer University Press, 1998], 23–29).

16. Gunkel and Begrich, *Introduction to the Psalms*, 33.

II. Exegesis

Stanza I (I AM *Reigns*): *The World and His Throne Stand Firm* 1–2

Strophe A: I AM *the Warrior and Builder Firmly Established the Earth-Disc* 1

The framing juxtaposition of the proclamation, "*I AM* reigns" (v. 1aα) with the assertion that the earth-disc is firmly established (1bβ) implies that the earth-disc's secure existence is due to God's reign. The back-to-back repetition of "he is clothed" in the verse's inner core (1aβ, 1bα) puts the logical connection between his reign and his creation beyond reasonable doubt. In 1aα–bα the King is pictured as a warrior; in 1bβ, he is depicted as a builder. These two images find their background in the ancient Near Eastern chaoskampf myths, which proclaim the nature deities of land and life becoming kings through their victories over the primordial chaotic waters.

1. Proclamation: *I AM* Reigns 1aα

In the New Testament, I AM fully reveals himself as a Trinity (see p. 2). All three persons of the Trinity played a role in the creation (cf. Gen. 1:1–2; John 1:1–3; Rom. 11:36; Col. 1:16; Heb. 1:2). *I AM reigns* (not "has become king" in an enthronement ritual; see pp. 19–22) is not a didactic statement; it "has the ring of proclamation"[17] (cf. Isa. 52:7). The claims in verse 2, "Your throne stands firm from of old" and "you are from eternity," are an implicit argument against the notion that *I AM* became King through a primordial battle. Brettler notes that they seem "to undercut the [combat] myth . . . and [are] saying God has always been king."[18]

2. *I AM* Is Clothed in Majesty and Armed with Strength 1aβ–bα

I AM metaphorically *is clothed* as a divine warrior, to judge from the verse's syntax and the predication *he girds himself* (*hit'azzār*), which means "prepares for battle" in its two occurrences (Isa. 8:9; cf. Ps. 18:39[40]). The Masoretic

---

17. Derek Kidner, *Psalms 73–150*, TOTC (Downers Grove, IL: IVP Academic, 2009), 170.

18. Marc Zvi Brettler, *God Is King: Understanding an Israelite Metaphor*, JSOTSup 76 (Sheffield: JSOT Press, 1989), 147.

cantillation firmly binds the second *is clothed* (*lābēš*) with "he girds himself [for battle]." Thus "he is clothed" in 1a is redefined as "he girds himself [for battle]" in 1b and "in majesty" is reformulated as *with strength*. *HALOT* defines *hit'azzār* "to gird oneself with the waistcloth." The verb is a denominative of *'ēzôr* (traditionally, "waistband").[19] "This standard garment of Israelite worker or soldier extended to the middle of the thigh."[20] It is probably a synecdoche for the panoply of the warrior's vestment. Military dress also fits the sea's hostility against *I AM*'s creation, the psalm's adaptation of the chaoskampf myth, and the description of *I AM* as *'addîrîm* (= "mighty" in power," v. 4). *Majesty* (*gē'ût*) glosses a derivative of the root *g'h* ("to be/become high"). The repetition of "is clothed" joins versets 1aβ and 1bα and rhetorically effects excitement and enthusiasm. The inapposite juxtaposition of the concrete verbs "clothed" and "girded" with abstract qualities "majesty" and "strength" signals that these qualities are metonymies for the warrior's vestments—a visual emblem of his majesty and strength, two of a king's noble qualities.

3. The World Is Firmly Established 1bβ

Indeed glosses the Hebrew conjunction *'ap*, which signifies "addition, esp. of something greater . . . a new thought."[21] Thus it segues the imagery of a warrior into that of a builder. *I AM* fought the deadly, chaotic sea to establish the life-sustaining, firm earth. His victory assures the earth's permanence. Philip Sumpter plausibly defines the poetic word *tēbēl* as "*earth-disc* . . . which is the *ground* [italics his] for the existence of its inhabitants."[22] Christopher J. H. Wright notes: "It is used frequently in contexts that associate it with Yahweh's creative act and that, as a result, express the stability or durability of the earth (1 Sam. 2:8; Pss. 89:11[12]; 93:1; 96:10). It is used when the whole population of the world is referred to (Pss. 24:1; 33:8; 98:7; Isa 18:3; 26:9; Nah 1:5)."[23] *Is estab-*

---

19. *HALOT*, 1:28, s.v. *'āzar*. The use of similar, not identical, language for Woman Wisdom in Prov. 31:17 does not undermine the thesis, for, as Al Wolters and Erika Moore argued, that poem also belongs to the genre of heroic praise; the domestic wife is painted as a valiant warrior (see Bruce K. Waltke, *Proverbs 15–31*, NICOT [Grand Rapids: Eerdmans, 2005], 516f.).

20. Mark F. Rooker, *NIDOTTE*, 1:344, s.v. *'āzar*.

21. BDB, p. 64, s.v. *'ap*.

22. Philip Sumpter, *The Substance of Psalm 24: An Attempt to Read Scripture after Brevard Childs* (London: Bloomsbury T&T Clark, 2015), 97.

23. Christopher J. H. Wright, *NIDOTTE*, 4:273, s.v. *tēbēl*.

lished (see Ps. 103:19) is a divine passive (*I AM* is the agent), underscored by *cannot be toppled* (lit. "to rock/shake off a base"). The Builder is an engineer so skillful that he builds his unshakeable stage for life and salvation history in unstable, threatening sea currents (see vv. 3–4). David assumes the phenomenal cosmology of his day to teach the unchanging theology that until the last day, the earth will exist to sustain life and be the stage for salvation history.

Strophe B: The Eternal's Throne Has Been Established from of Old 2

The shift to "you"/*your* (vv. 2, 5) and a vocative (*I AM*, v. 3) signals Israel's personal bond with the Divine Warrior (see p. 4, "when/where"). The poet's inspired eye of faith sees that God's throne in heaven *is established* (see v. 1), implying that "the world shares in the stability and the endurance of God's existence and rule."[24] Hebrew *kissē'* means "chair" (cf. 2 Kgs. 4:10) but becomes *throne* (see Ps. 103:19) when a king sits on it as a symbol of his supreme authority (Gen. 41:40; Jer. 1:15; 22:30; 43:10). *From of old* is relative to the context (cf. 2 Sam. 15:34; Isa 44:8; 45:21) and here may refer to when God established the earth-disc. The linkage of the throne in the outer frame of this chiastic parallelism with *you are from eternity* (see Ps. 100:5; cf. Prov. 8:22–23) implies his eternal sovereignty and polemicizes against the pagan combat myths. Jenni notes that "eternity is associated with the concept of inalterability, constancy, and continuity of existence,"[25] and so matches "established."

Stanza II: I AM *Is Mightier Than the Swelling Seas 3–4*

Catchwords and stair-like parallelism link together verses 3 and 4 as a couplet. The dramatic mythopoetic combat imagery now shifts from the protagonist (vv. 1–2) to the antagonist (vv. 3–4), but the myth is demythologized (see p. 134). There is no diminishing of the "surge's angry shock"[26] to assure that God is greater than any threat to his throne. The breaking waves of the ocean currents aggressively threaten the Warrior-Builder's life-sustaining earth-disc, but *I AM* on high is mightier.

24. Frank-Lothar Hossfeld and Erich Zenger, *Commentary on Psalms 51–100*, trans. Linda M. Maloney, Hermeneia (Minneapolis: Fortress, 2005), 488.

25. Jenni, *TLOT*, 2:858, s.v. *'ôlām*.

26. Kidner, *Psalms 73–150*, 371, quoting Samuel Johnson's hymn, "City of God, How Broad and Far."

Strophe A: The Floods Lift Up Their Loudly Crashing Waves 3

Usually, *nāhār* refers to a perennial river (Num. 24:6; Isa. 41:18 [pl.]), but here the plural *floods* refer to currents of the ocean (cf. Isa. 44:27; Jonah 2:4).[27] "Floods" is redefined in verse 4 as "vast waters" and "sea"—general terms for larger expanses of water that threaten to inundate and submerge the earth-disc; think of an oil rig in a tsunami. *Lifted up* focuses on the sea's movement in contrast to the stability of the life-sustaining earth-disc and connotes the sea's aggressive threat against the earth-disc, whose position is precarious. In the phenomenal cosmology of the biblical world, subterranean waters lie beneath the land. Goldingay comments, "In the description of the sea the biblical authors ask the question of whether the earth might 'be washed away.'"[28] The vocative *I AM* expresses angst about the felt threat. The floods' aggressive action is first represented as having begun in the past ("have lifted up," vv. 3aα, 3aβ) and then as a continuing threat (*lift up*, v. 3b). The echo of the primordial roaring sea is still heard in its pounding waves; the sea is restrained, not eliminated (cf. Job 38; Rev 21:1). Moderns know this phenomenal cosmology does not accord with a scientific cosmology, but they too live in angst: of global warming and rising sea levels, asteroids, superbugs, and nuclear warfare. The psalm, using the language of its day, assures us that Israel's covenant-keeping God is mightier than any natural threat to the earth's existence, but it does not reckon with human folly. Nevertheless, even human folly will not defeat God's covenant promises to bring all things under the rule of Jesus Christ.

Strophe B: I AM Is Mightier Than the Raging Floods 4

Verse 4 escalates verse 3, replacing the singular *qôl* ("voice/sound") by plural *qôlôt* (*thunder*); and *nᵉhārôt* ("ocean currents") by *mayim rabbîm* (*vast waters* [in extent and quantity]); and the singular *dᵒkî* ("pounding wave") by the plural *mišbᵉrê yām* (*breakers of the sea*). Concerning the verse's difficult syntax, Alter enthuses, "The entire line is a wonderful use of a periodic sentence: At first we are not sure what or who is 'more' than the sound of the majestic breakers, and at the end—YHWH is the last word of the line—we learn that it is

27. Mitchell Dahood, *Psalms II*, AB 17 (New York: Doubleday, 1968), 340; Luis I. J. Stadelmann, *The Hebrew Conception of the World: A Philological and Literary Study* (Rome: Pontifical Biblical Institute, 1970), 162.

28. John Goldingay, *Psalms*, vol. 1, BCOTWP (Grand Rapids: Baker Academic, 2006), 357f.

God."[29] *Mighty*[30]/"majestic"[31] (*'addîr*) connotes commanding respect through the excellence of power. In Nahum 2:5, *'addîr* functions as a metonymy for "warriors"; in Psalm 136:18, God kills *'addîrîm* ("mighty kings"). Thus it belongs to the same semantic domain as *gē'ût* ("exalted majesty") and *'ōz* ("strength") in verse 1. *On high* is a metonymy for the heavens[32] and concretely visualizes *I AM*'s supra-earthly governance (see v. 3; Ps. 92:8[9]). Similarly, the Lord Jesus Christ displayed his superior might to the winds and the waves that threatened to capsize his boat when they submitted to his command: "Quiet! Be Still!" (Mark 4:39).[33] In the trajectory of salvation history, the perfect obedience and sacrifice of Christ defeated and disarmed Satan and all powers arraigned against God (Luke 10:18–19; Rom. 8:38; 10:9–11; Eph. 6:10–18; Col. 1:15).

Stanza III: I AM's Law and Temple Endure Forever 5

God's superior cosmic might gives assurance that he will uphold his law and preserve his holy temple. *Your stipulations* refers broadly to God's "laws," more precisely to his "legal provisions"[34]; and, according to Hillers[35] and C. van Leeuwen,[36] even more precisely to the Israelites' obligation to maintain the covenant stipulations.[37] The Hebrew word glossed *trustworthy* means "to be permanent," "stand firm," "endure" (1 Sam. 25:8; 2 Sam. 7:16; Isa. 7:9; 33:6; 55:3; Jer. 15:18; Ps. 89:29[30]; 1 Chr. 7:23) and speaks of what is certain (Hos 5:9) and

29. Robert Alter, *The Book of Psalms: A Translation with Commentary* (New York: Norton, 2007), 329.

30. *HALOT*, 1:13, s.v. *'addîr*.

31. BDB, p. 12, s.v. *'addîr*.

32. BDB, p. 929, s.v. *mārôm*, §2; *HALOT*, 1:633, s.v. *mārôm*, #6.

33. Evocatively, when Jesus got out of the boat, he was met by a man possessed by the demon horde "Legion." Jesus exorcised the man's demons, and they went into a herd of pigs that rushed down the steep bank *into the sea* (*thalassa*) and were drowned (Mark 5:1–13).

34. *HALOT*, 1:791, s.v. *'ēdût*, #2.

35. Delbert Hillers, *Covenant: A History of a Biblical Idea* (Baltimore: Johns Hopkins University Press, 1969), 160–68.

36. C. van Leeuwen, *TLOT*, 2:846, s.v. *'ēd*.

37. According to D. J. Wiseman ("Vassal-Treaties of Esarhaddon," *Iraq* 20, no 1 [1958]: 3, 81), the Akkadian cognate *adê* denotes "terms of a law or commandment to which a sovereign ceremoniously subjects a vassal or people in the presence of divine witnesses."

can be counted on (Deut. 7:9; Isa. 1:21; Prov. 11:13; Ps. 78:8, 37) and of what is proved reliable and true and so established (Gen. 42:20; 1 Kgs. 8:26). *Totally* underscores the permanence and reliability of the Ten Commandments, which undergirds the structure of the Book of the Law.[38] The physical association of the ark of the covenant and temple leads naturally to their association in verse 5. According to both Rudolph Otto[39] and H.-P Müller,[40] *holiness* (*qōdeš*) (see p. 176) indicates a fundamental conception of numinous quality sui generis. C. S. Lewis explains that the numinous experience of the presence of the divine is the dread of the uncanny, as of a believed-in ghost, not simply fear of danger, as of a tiger; and that experience of a ghost would also stir up a feeling of wonder and a certain shrinking, a sense of inadequacy to cope.[41] This power of the divine presence is seen in 1 Samuel 6:20: "Who can stand in the presence of . . . this holy God?" But Walther Eichrodt and Jackie Naudé infer from other uses of *qdš* that it fundamentally means "to be set apart from the profane and/or impure."[42] Leviticus 10:10 offers a textbook example of this notion: The priest must distinguish "between the holy and the common, between the unclean and the clean." The two notions—of a numinous experience and of purity—are combined in Isaiah's experience. In the presence of the seraphs calling to one another, "Holy, holy, holy is *I AM* Almighty," Isaiah cried "Woe is me! I am ruined! For I am a man of unclean lips, and live among a people of unclean lips" (Isa. 6:5). The root *qdš* is often associated with ethical purity: "Be holy because I, *I AM* your God, am holy" (Lev. 19:2). His holiness is defined by his stipulations, not by human reflection apart from them. Also, as Jackie Naudé notes, "Because God is holy by nature and separate from moral imperfection, he can be trusted to be faithful to his promises (Ps. 105:42)," and, by the same reasoning, faithful to uphold his law. The inapposite juxtaposition of the concrete image of *adorns your house* with the abstract notion "holiness" implies both that holiness is a metonymy for the temple's precious building material and that the building material visualizes his holiness. Moreover, if holiness is a spiritual quality, it is appropriate for a person, not a house, and

---

38. Bruce K. Waltke, "A Janus Decalogue of Laws from Homicide to Sexuality: Deuteronomy 22:1–12," *For the World: Essays in Honor of Richard L. Pratt Jr.,* ed. Justin S. Holcomb and Glenn Lucke (Phillipsburg, NJ; P&R, 2014), 3–19.

39. Rudolph Otto, *The Idea of the Holy* (Oxford: Oxford University Press, 1923).

40. H.-P Müller, *TLOT*, 3:1103, s.v. *qdš*.

41. C. S. Lewis, *The Problem of Pain* (Grand Rapids: Zondervan, 2001), 5–6.

42. Jackie Naudé, *NIDOTTE*, 3:877–886, s.v. *qdš*; cf. Walther Eichrodt, *Theology of the Old Testament*, I (Philadelphia: Westminster John Knox, 1967), 270–72.

so the implied building material symbolizes the Covenant Keeper within the temple and his covenant keepers without. In the trajectory of salvation history, the temple on Mount Zion finds its fulfillment in Jesus Christ (John 2:18–22) and his church, both individually (1 Cor. 6:19) and collectively (1 Cor. 3:16f.). Their spiritual "material" of love, joy, peace, and purity visualizes God's holiness. With no impurity to make it decay, God's temple exists *for endless days* (see Psalm 91:16). Torah and Temple will never pass away. Count on it.

PART III. VOICE OF THE CHURCH IN RESPONSE

I. Augustine of Hippo (354–430)

The LXX inscription heavily informs Augustine's homily on Psalm 93 [= LXX 92] (see n. 1). "These words," he comments, "recall the six days during which God created all things and set them in order, from the first day to the sixth; because He sanctified the seventh, and rested on that day from all the exceedingly good work He had been doing" (see Gen. 1:1–24).[43] A short psalm, it expresses what is unknowable other than in praise. "Robed in majesty," God's raiment is "beauty and strength" according to Augustine. Yet Jesus in his humility "girded himself with a towel" to serve as a slave! Likewise, God's throne is in humble hearts—dwelling in the temple, but also "dwelling in our hearts by faith."[44] Here Augustine applies the psalm pastorally rather than giving an exegesis of the text. He identifies "the sixth day" with the incarnation, and he sees the "sea" as this world in opposition to God's reign, weakening the real thrust of the psalm as a polemic against the mystery of anti-creational forces that "the sea" is in the mythopoetic genre.[45]

II. E. W. Hengstenberg (1802–1869)

E. W. Hengstenberg, a German Evangelical Lutheran, was well prepared to counter, with fearless daring, the growing liberalism of the German enlightenment. He was skilled in philology, Arabic, and Hebrew and in philosophy.

---

43. Augustine, *Exposition of Psalm 92* 1, in *Expositions on the Psalms*, trans. Maria Boulding, O.S.B., vol. 4 (Hyde Park, NY: New City, 2002), 362.
44. Augustine, *Exposition of Psalm 92* 2, 5 (Boulding, 362–64).
45. Augustine, *Exposition of Psalm 92* 1, 6 (Boulding, 362–64).

"The might of the world," he says, "roars like the tumultuous sea, but the Lord on high is more glorious than the sea with its swelling waves" (vv. 3–4). He found the summary of this short psalm in verse 5: "The Lord's promises are to be depended upon, He will always protect His house."[46] He continues, "In room of the *first* house destroyed by the Chaldeans, there arose the *second,* and the second was not destroyed till it had become a mere shell without a kernel, and a glorious new erection of the house of God had come into life in the Christian Church. . . . It is therefore the preservation of the *Church* that lies near the Psalmist's heart."[47]

PART IV. CONCLUSION

Book IV is God's inspired answer to the failed House of David and its exile in Babylon and to the crushing of his temple under the heel of Marduk, the patron deity of Babylon. God's reign transcends the House of David in space ("on high," Ps. 92:8[9]) and time ("forever," Ps. 90:1). Psalm 93 supports the good confession, "*I AM* reigns," by pointing back to the creation narrative, to when God first manifested his kingship (Gen. 1:2–12) using the mythic imagery of "chaoskampf."[48] God created and established the earth-disc with its life amid the primordial waters hostile to life. All agree that the poet has in mind more than a rampaging sea and also that the flood waters are used as an emblem of hostility to God's rule. Many think they are a metaphor of the hostile nations that menace the kingdom of God (cf. Ps. 46:3[4], 6[7]; Isa. 17:12f.; 51:9f.).[49] But Psalm 93 refers only to the cosmic realities. Moreover, the

46. E. W. Hengstenberg, *Commentary on the Psalms*, vol. 3 (London: T&T Clark, 1864; repr. Eugene, OR: Wipf & Stock, 2005), 148.

47. Hengstenberg, *Commentary on the Psalms*, 153.

48. For the exegesis of Genesis 1:1–3, see Bruce K. Waltke, *Genesis: A Commentary* (Grand Rapids: Zondervan, 2001), 58–60.

49. A. F. Kirkpatrick, *The Book of Psalms* (1902; repr., Grand Rapids: Baker Books, 1986), 565. Robert B. Chisholm, Jr. ("Suppressing Myth: Yahweh and the Sea in the Praise Psalms," in *The Psalms: Language for All Seasons of the Soul,* ed. Andrew J. Schmutzer and David M. Howard, Jr. [Chicago: Moody, 2013], 83f.) in an otherwise profitable essay, defends the political interpretation by appealing to "great waters" in v. 4 and in Pss. 18:16[17]; 29:3; 77:19[20] and to the placement of the psalm between 92:9–11[10–12] and 94:1–3. The first argument commits the lexical fallacy of "the illegitimate totality transfer," and the second argument wrongly gives priority to secondary placement of the psalm over the psalm's own context.

political interpretation is too simplistic. The boisterous sea that menaces the land is a metonymy and symbol of the deep, empirical reality that is alienated from God and that finds historical expression in the defeat of the good; namely, in disaster, disease, and death (cf. 1 Kings 8:30–39). The origin of this alienation is inexplicable and indeterminable. Eckhart Otto calls the sea, "The deep dimension of an empirical experience of alienation. . . . The experience of the failure of life is not a superficial empirical reality, but has a meta-empirical depth dimension."[50] In the trajectory of revelation, that deep reality alienated from God is unmasked as Satan.

But the Trinity (see v. 1) is mightier than this deep reality. Otto adds: "In [the creation] therefore the powers of the chaos are tamed, all empirical negative experiences are transcended in principle."[51] Sumpter comments, "That which happened in principle must be realized in history,"[52] and it happens in connection with covenant fidelity to *I AM*. And so each generation of the faithful experiences the pounding waves as Christ continues to build his church.

The Creator of the earth-disc also created and established Israel with its holy laws amid rampant evil. Those laws are just as trustworthy. As the earth-disc cannot be moved, so Christ's laws cannot be abolished. So let us take courage, for the future will happen just as the Ruler of All told us (cf. Acts 27:25).

50. "Tiefendimension von empirischer Entfremdungserfahrung . . .: Die Erfahrung des Scheiterns von Leben ist nicht Oberfläche empirischer Wirklichkeit, sondern hat metaempirische Tiefendimension" (Eckhart Otto, "Kultus und Ethos in Jerusalemer Theologie: Ein Beitrag zur Begründung der Ethik im Alten Testament," *ZAW* 98 [1986]: 161–79, esp. 174f.).

51. "In [der Schöpfung] also sind die Krafte des Chaos gebändigt, all empirischen negativerfahrungen prinzipiell transzendiert" (Otto, "Kultus and Ethos," 176).

52. Sumpter, *The Substance of Psalm 24*, 139n354.

CHAPTER 6

Psalm 95: Venite

Part I. Voice of the Psalmist: Translation

A song of praise, by David.[1]

1   Come, let us shout for joy to *I AM*;
      let us shout aloud to the Rock of our Salvation.
2   Let us meet him with an offering of grateful praise;
      with songs of praise we will shout aloud to him;
3   because *I AM* is a great God,
      and a great King above all gods,
4   in whose hands are the depths of the earth,
      and the peaks of the mountain heights are his.
5   His is the sea, for he made it;
      and his hands formed the dry land.
6   Enter; let us prostrate ourselves and kneel;
      let us get on our knees before *I AM*, our Maker;
7   because he is our God,
      and we are the people he tends, the flock of his hand.

      Oh, that today you would listen to his voice:

8   "Do not harden your hearts as at Meribah ["Quarreling"],
      as in the day of Massah ["Testing"] in the wilderness;
9   where[2] your fathers tested me;
      they put me to the test, though they had seen my deeds.

1. So LXX; MT lacks a superscript.
2. Or "when."

145

10   For forty years[3] I loathed that generation;
       and I said: 'They are a people of wayward hearts,
       and they do not know my ways';
11   against whom I swore in my anger,
       'They will not enter into my rest.'"

PART II. COMMENTARY

I. Introduction

Author

The Septuagint (LXX) and Hebrews 4:7 attribute the psalm to David (see pp. 13–15).[4] G. Henton Davies argues for the psalm's preexilic date based on "the polytheistic reference in v 3, the cultic value of 'today,' and the use of the Massah-Meribah illustration."[5] If the psalm is preexilic, why should we not ascribe it to David?

Form, Structure, and Rhetoric

The psalm consists of a hymnist's song of praise (vv. 1–7a) and a prophet's warning from *I AM* (7b–11). The first stanza has two strophes: calls to come to the temple with a grateful praise offering and songs of praise (1–5) and to enter the temple reverently, bowing prostrate before Israel's God and King (6–7). Each of these strophes has the typical motifs of a hymn (see p. 7): calls to worship (1–2, 6) and cause for worship (3–5, 7a). The causal clause (3) pertains to *I AM*'s sublime being ("a great God . . . above all gods") and to his sublime

---

3. Heb. 3:9–10 connects the "forty years" with "they saw my works," but Heb. 3:17 follows MT.

4. "In David" in Hebrews 4:7 probably means "through David," perhaps referring to the Book of Psalms.

5. G. Henton Davies, "Psalm 95," *ZAW* 85 (1973): 195. For a history of research on Psalm 95, see W. S. Prinsloo, "Psalm 95: Only You Will Listen to His Voice?" in *The Bible in Human Society: Essays in Honour of John Rogerson*, ed. J. Rogerson, M. D. Carroll, David J. A. Clines, and Philip R. Davies, JSOTSup 200 (Sheffield: JSOT, 1996), 393–410, esp. 393–97.

office ("a great King above all gods"). The two relative clauses of verses 4 and 5 defend this assessment by citing his great deed of creating the earth. In the second strophe (6–7), Israel personalizes these truths: "he made *it* [the sea]" (5) becomes "*our* Maker" (6); "*a great God . . . above all gods*" (3) becomes "*our* God" (7); and "his hands formed *the dry land*" (5) becomes "*we are . . .* the flock of his hand" (7).

Hymns occasionally have *a prophetic warning speech* (cf. 1 Sam. 2:5; Ps. 75:4–5[5–6]; 76:12[13]). Psalms 81 and 95 begin with hymns that end with a warning speech in the form of a petition (81:8[9]; 95:7b). Verse 7b segues praise to the monitory discourse (cf. 50:7–23; 81:8–16[9–17]).

The prophetic oracle exhibits the characteristic form of a judgment speech: the announcement that the messenger understands himself to be delivering God's word, which must be heard (v. 7b), followed by accusation and a sentence of judgment.[6] But Psalm 95 modifies the form. The accusation is delivered in a personal address by *I AM* and nuanced as a warning, and the judicial sentence is nuanced as a threat and based on "I loathed that generation" (10). In national judgment speeches, the accusation is typically developed as in verse 9, and a formula such as "I swore" introduces the judgment (cf. 11a; Amos 4:2).[7]

In Psalm 95:8–11, God does not accuse or sentence the pilgrims, but, using the refractory exodus generation as a type, warns them against hardening their hearts and cautions them about the threat of failing to enter God's rest.

Based on its form and rhetoric and on semantics, here is a rough outline of the psalm's structure:

Stanza I (Hymn): The Psalmist Speaks	1–7
Strophe A: Call and Cause to Worship *I AM*,	
Creator of the Earth	1–5
1. Call to Worship *I AM* with Offering and Grateful Praise	1–2
2. Cause for Praise: Great God and King, Creator of Earth	3–5
Strophe B: Call and Cause to Praise *I AM*, the Maker	
and Owner of Israel	6–7
1. Call: Bow Down to Israel's Maker	6
2. Cause: He Is Israel's God	7a
Transition (Warning): Hear God's Word Today	7b

---

6. Claus Westermann, *Basic Forms of Prophetic Speech*, trans. H. C. White (Louisville: Westminster John Knox, 1991), 93.

7. Westermann, *Basic Forms of Prophetic Speech*, 169.

Stanza II (Prophetic Warning): *I AM* Speaks	8–11
Strophe A (Warning): Hear God's Word Today	8–9
1. Do Not Harden Hearts	8
2. Explained as Quarreling and Testing *I AM*'s Worth	9
Strophe B (Threat): Judicial Sentence of No Rest	10–11
1. *I AM* Loathed the Wilderness Generation	10
2. *I AM* Swore They Would Not Enter His Rest	11

Apart from verse 3, the center line of the first strophe, the psalm is composed of couplets. K. Schaefer notes that the hymn (vv. 1–7a) consists of seven verses—the number signifying divine totality.[8] C. Riding[9] notes the stanza's chiastic structure:

> Our *Savior* (1–2)
>   *Creator* of everything (3–5)
>   Our *Maker* (6)
> Our *Savior* (7a)

Setting

According to A. Weiser, the Mishnah situated Psalm 95 in the New Year festival (Sukkoth),[10] the fall festival that recalled that *I AM* made Israel dwell in booths when he brought them out of Egypt. Sukkoth occurred at the end of the agricultural year, when the grapes and olives were harvested. At this festival, Israel was commanded to rejoice, to offer food offerings to YHWH, and to offer grateful praise in song and sacrifice to him (Lev. 23:33–43).[11] Originally, "today" (v. 7) referred to a cultic actuality (cf. Isa. 30:29).[12] Probably, the psalm was composed for a drought. Now "today" refers to any day when the psalm is used, as in Hebrews 4:6–7.

The first call to praise envisions a scenario outside the temple (vv. 1–2); the second, a scenario in the temple courtyard (6). After their movement into the courtyard, the pilgrims heard the prophetic warning not to lose heart.

---

8. Konrad Schaefer, *Psalms*, Berit Olam (Collegeville, MN: Liturgical Press, 2001), 236.

9. Charles Bruce Riding, "Psalm 95:1–7c as a Large Chiasm," *ZAW* 88 (1976): 418.

10. Artur Weiser, *The Psalms*, OTL (Philadelphia: Westminster, 1962), 625.

11. For the use of the psalms in various Jewish liturgies, see Amos Ḥakham, *Psalms with the Jerusalem Commentary*, trans. Israel V. Berman, vol. 2 (Jerusalem: Mosad Harav Kook, 2003), 403.

12. J. Finkel, "Some Problems Relating to Psalm 95," *AJSL* 50 (1933): 37.

II. Exegesis

Superscript

The LXX reads literally "the praise of a song by David," identifying the psalm's genre as a hymn and its author as David (see "Author" above).

Stanza I (Hymn): The Psalmist Speaks 1–7

Strophe A: Call and Cause to Worship I AM, *Creator of the Earth 1–5*

1. Call to Worship *I AM* with Offering and Grateful Praise 1–2

The poet expresses the fervency of his call to praise *I AM* with lavish use of terse poetry synonyms. "Tepid praise," says H. C. Leupold, "defeats its own purpose."[13] The call implies that the pilgrims had not yet hardened their hearts against God; if they had, he would have hidden his face from them and loathed them instead of inviting them into his presence (cf. Deut. 31:17–18; 32:20).

a) Worship without Restraint 1

The three verbs of motion energize the pilgrims to move from the profane sphere at the base of the Temple Mount into the holy presence of *I AM* on top of Mount Zion (cf. Ps. 92:13[14]): *come* (lit. "walk"), "meet him" (lit. "his face," v. 2), and "enter" (v. 6). This scenic depiction matches their spiritual movement from potential doubt and despair to faith and hope in God. *Let us shout aloud* (*rnn*; see Ps. 100:2) here signifies "loud, enthusiastic, and joyful shouts"[14] and may include articulate words (cf. Prov. 1:20; 8:3).[15] *The Rock* (see Ps. 92:15[16]) likens God to a haven and a refuge in trouble (Ps. 62:6–8[7–9]). D. M. Howard[16] thinks that the epithet "Rock" plays with the incident at Meribah (v. 8), where God quenched Israel's thirst by providing water from the rock (Exod. 17:1–7; Num. 20:2–13; cf. 1 Cor. 10:4, 6). *Salvation* signifies deliverance because it is just (see Psalm 92:15[16]).

13. H. C. Leupold, *Exposition of the Psalms* (Columbus: Wartburg, 1959), 676.
14. Tremper Longman III, *NIDOTTE*, 3:1127, s.v. *rnn*.
15. R. Ficker, *TLOT*, 3:1240, s.v. *rnn*.
16. David M. Howard, Jr., *The Structure of Psalms 93–100*, BJSUCSD 5 (Winona Lake, IN: Eisenbrauns, 1997), 54.

b) Worship Him with Offering and Songs of Grateful Praise 2

With an offering of grateful praise (*tôdâ*, see p. 5). The sacrifice is accompanied by *songs of praise* (*zᵉmīrôt*, see p. 25) Today, praise itself is the sacrifice (Heb. 13:15). The mood shifts from the imperative to the indicative of fact: *we will shout* (*rûaʿ* Hiphil). The loudness and strong emotion of the shout can be inferred from its use for an anticipatory victory shout in battle (cf. Josh. 6:10, 16; 1 Sam. 17:52).

2. Cause for Praise: Great God and King, Creator of Earth 3–5

a) He Is a Great God and King above All Gods 3

God (Ps. 90:2) denotes the quintessence of power. He is *great* both in rank and influence. *King* (see p. 4) *above all gods* (cf. Exod. 18:11; Pss. 29:1; 82:1) tacitly acknowledges that depraved people worship other gods, not a belief in henotheism (cf. Ps. 96:5; 1 Cor. 8:5).

b) Who Created Every Aspect of the Earth 4–5

Verses 4–5 are woven together by the initial "who," by merisms (i.e., depths/peaks; sea/dry land), and by the chiasm framed by "his hands" (v. 4a, 5b). The two merisms expresses the totality of the earth's geography. Figuratively, the merisms of spatial opposites symbolize spiritual inverses. The *depths of the earth*[17] and *the sea* symbolize death and alienation from God (cf. Psalm 93); the mountain *peaks* and *dry land* symbolize closeness to God and life (cf. Ps. 139:8–9). The *hand* extends from the elbow to the fingertips (cf. Ezek. 23:42) and symbolizes power and strength (Exod. 3:19–20), authority, control, and possession (Gen. 9:6; Num. 33:1; Judg. 4:24).[18] Paul expands the catalog of things that *are his* to "things . . . in heaven and on earth" (Col. 1:16) and to "principalities . . . powers . . . height . . . depth" (Rom. 8:38–39). As Derek Kidner notes, those things "which were created through and for the Son of God . . . in the end must bow to him [and], meanwhile, can do nothing to separate us from his love."[19] Though the sea's origin is "inexplicable

---

17. A reference to unexplored depths (*HALOT*, 1:571, s.v. *mᵉḥāqār*).

18. Leland Ryken, James C. Wilhoit, and Tremper Longman III, eds., *Dictionary of Biblical Imagery* (Downers Grove, IL: IVP Academic, 1998), 362.

19. Derek Kidner, *Psalms 73–150*, TOTC (Downers Grove, IL: IVP Academic, 2009), 176.

and indeterminate,"[20] it nevertheless *is his* (see v. 4; cf. Psalm 93:3). More than that, *he*—stated emphatically by the tautological pronoun—*made it* (see Ps. 100:3). Its opposite, *the dry land*, brought forth every kind of vegetation and animal (Gen. 1:11–12, 24) and from it God made humankind (Gen. 2:7); it is the place where they find their provision (Gen. 1:29–30). *Formed* points to God's craftsmanship.

*Strophe B: Call and Cause to Praise I AM,
the Maker and Owner of Israel 6–7*

The Sovereign who created, owns, and governs every aspect of the earth adopted Israel as his family.

1. Call: Bow Down to Israel's Maker 6

"Come" followed by three verbs for giving voice to praise—"shout for joy," and "shout" twice—is now advanced by *enter* followed by three synonyms for bowing down: *let us prostrate ourselves* (i.e., hands, forehead, knees, and toes to the ground), *kneel*, and *get on our knees*. Profiled against the terseness of Hebrew poetry, the poet's extravagant expenditure of synonyms for bowing in worship signifies the extreme reverence of the creature for the Creator, of the mortal for the Immortal, of the powerless for the All-Powerful (see vv. 1–2).

2. Cause: He Is Israel's God 7a

People ("relatives"; see Ps. 100:3; cf. Song 2:16) *he tends* reprises the covenant formula: "I will be their God, and they shall be my people" (Lev. 26:12; Jer. 31:33; cf. Exod. 19:5; 2 Sam. 7:24; Ezek. 14:11). In the biblical world, kings were known as shepherds of their people (cf. Jer. 23:1–4; Ezek. 34:1–10), and so, says J. Clinton McCann, "it is fitting that this metaphor [i.e., *flock*] appears in a psalm that celebrates God's kingship."[21] The Lord Jesus Christ is the good (John 10:11), great (Heb. 13:20), and chief (1 Pet. 5:4) Shepherd. "The shepherd that feeds, rules, and leads the sheep does so with *his hand*, which manages the rod and staff (Ps. 23:4)," says the eloquent Spurgeon.[22]

---

20. Dirk J. Human, "Psalm 93: Yahweh Robed in Majesty and Mightier than the Great Waters," in *Psalms and Mythology*, ed. Dirk J. Human, LHBOTS 462 (London: T&T Clark, 2007), 147–69.

21. J. Clinton McCann, Jr., *Psalms*, NIB 4 (Nashville: Abingdon, 1996), 1062.

22. Charles Spurgeon, *The Treasury of David*, ed. Roy H. Clarke (Nashville: Thomas Nelson, 1997), 846n.

Transition (Warning): Hear God's Word Today 7b

The essence of true religion is both enthusiastic, deferential worship and ethical obedience of God. The poet shifts from identifying himself with Israel, using "we/us," to distancing himself from them by addressing them as *you*. *Listen to his voice* means "obey"[23] and has an intertextual connection with Israel's disobedience at Kadesh (Num. 14:22). The logic of the confession, "He is the great King above all gods," demands obedience to him (cf. Luke 6:46–49; John 13:13–16). *Today* "presses for immediate attention."[24] It stands in contrast to "the day of Massah" (v. 8). Originally, it probably referred to a cultic setting—perhaps the New Year festival (see "Setting" above).

Stanza II (Prophetic Warning): I AM *Speaks 8–11*

The judgment speech is united by its form and by the consonance of initial *alephs* in every verse: *'al* (8), *'ăšer* (9, 11), and *'arbā'îm* (10).

Strophe A (Warning): Hear God's Word Today 8–9

1. Do Not Harden Hearts 8

A. S. van der Woude says of *harden* that its verbal and nominal forms "always have a figurative meaning and refer either to the severity of a matter that people perceive as oppressive or to the harshness that someone displays in interactions with others."[25] The latter meaning expresses itself in being "stubborn-minded."[26] A hard heart does not respond to an admonition from a superior (cf. Ps. 81:8[9]). *Your hearts* denotes their inner disposition—the religious affections that prompt behavior.[27] Israel grumbled for water at *Meribah* ("Place of Quarreling") in both the first year after the exodus (Exod. 17:1–7; Deut. 6:16; 9:22; 33:8; cf. Ps. 81:7[8]) and the fortieth year after the exodus (Num. 20:1–13; Ps. 106:32). G. Braulik notes that these two incidents form an

---

23. BDB, p. 1034, s.v. *šāma'*, §1m.
24. Spurgeon, *The Treasury of David*, 846.
25. A. S. van der Woude, *TLOT*, 3:997–99, s.v. *qšh*.
26. J. I. Durham, *Exodus*, WBC 3 (Waco: Word, 1987), 84.
27. Bruce K. Waltke, *Proverbs 1–15*, NICOT (Grand Rapids: Eerdmans, 2005), 90–92.

inclusio of Israel "in the wilderness" and sketch that generation's sinful history of putting God to the test and complaining against him from the beginning to the end. Though *I AM* opened that long march through the wilderness with his "deeds" (9) of wonders pertaining to water at the Red Sea, they put him to the test to give them water.[28] *Massah* ("Place of Testing") refers to the first incident but was added to show the nature of their sin, not to specify the place of Meribah. *On the day of Massah* epitomizes Israel's obstinate putting of God to the test, even as "the day of Jerusalem" in Psalm 137:7 epitomizes Jerusalem's catastrophe in 587 BCE.

2. Explained as Quarreling and Testing *I AM's* Worth 9

Your refers to the "today" generation of Israel (see 7b–8) and *fathers* refers to the refractory wilderness generation. The fathers trusted and praised *I AM* during the exodus (Exod. 14:31–15:21; cf. Ps. 22:4[5]) and experienced many of his spiritual blessings, but later they hardened their hearts against him. The cloud over them augured their destination of salvation, but they hankered after sin and never fulfilled that destiny. *Tested* with a personal object has its basic meaning to assay another to determine their worth (cf. 1 Kgs. 10:1–7; 2 Chr. 9:1–6; cf. Dan 1:12, 14).[29] The fathers wanted a miracle to prove whether God was among them (Exod. 17:2, 7; Num. 14:22; Deut. 6:16 bis; cf. Isa. 7:12; Pss. 78:18, 41, 56; 106:14). The law forbids this unbelief (Deut. 6:16; 9:22; 33:8). Jesus judges his generation as evil and adulterous because they looked for miraculous signs (Matt. 16:4). Paul says "Jews demand signs" and warns the church not to put Christ to the test (1 Cor. 1:22; 10:9).

Strophe B (Threat): Judicial Sentence of No Rest 10–11

The judicial sentence has two parts: God's emotional response of loathing and his oath that the loathed would not enter his rest. There are two reasons for his loathing: Their hearts are wayward and they do not resonate with his ways of grace.

28. G. Braulik, "Gottes Ruhe—Das Land oder der Tempel? Zu Psalm 95,11," in *Freude an der Weisung des Herrn: Beiträge zur Theologie der Psalmen*, ed. E. Haag and F.-L. Hossfeld (Stuttgart: Katholisches Bibelwerk, 1987), 37.

29. G. Gerleman, *TLOT*, 2:741, s.v. *nsh* Piel.

1. *I AM* Loathed the Wilderness Generation 10

The numeral *forty* with *years* (see Num. 14) or days is, as the church fathers observed, "most often associated with hardship, affliction and punishment" (see Gen. 7:4; Exod. 24:18; Judg. 13:1; Ezek. 4:6; Jonah 3:4; Luke 4:1–2).[30] The tense[31] of *I loathed* ('āqûṭ; cf. Ezek. 6:9) signifies that Israel's covenant-keeping God was time and again (Num. 14:22 mentions ten times) provoked to loathing by their continued acts of rebellion. Psalm 78 rehearses Israel's tragic history of repeated rebellions in spite of God's signs and wonders among them. The Jewish leaders said no to the Messiah Jesus, and if the days of Jerusalem's fall to Rome in 70 CE had not been cut short, none would have survived (Matt. 24:22). The verb denotes "to feel disgust, to reject in hostility"—the way God felt toward the practices of Canaanites that resulted in his driving them out of the good land (Lev. 20:23). *Generation* often denotes a person's lifetime from birth until the birth of offspring (Deut. 23:2[3]; 23:8[9]), but it also commonly denotes one group—as opposed to a single person—related to one another by natural descent (Job 42:16; Judg. 2:10) and often labels a generation in terms of an assessment of its moral qualities (Pss. 12:8; 14:5; 112:2; Prov. 30:11–14; Isa. 53:8; Jer. 7:29; cf. "baby boomers," "Gen X," and "millennials"). God's self-speech (*and I said*) is necessary because only God could judge their hearts and explain why he detested the whole generation. *Wayward* means "to leave a point of proper orientation," such as a right path (Exod. 23:4) or "to stagger in intoxication" and so become disoriented (Isa. 28:7). Figuratively, it may denote "to go astray from precepts" (Ps. 119:110; cf. Prov. 21:16) and/or, as here, from God himself. *And they do not know* denotes a lack of personal knowledge and intimate experience with a person's reality—to wit, *my ways* (see Ps. 103:7; cf. Exod. 34:6).

2. *I AM* Swore They Would Not Enter His Rest 11

I swore with an irrevocable oath is an intertextual reference to Deut. 1:35. God changes his prophecies when circumstances change (see Jer. 18:5–10), but he never changes his oaths (Heb. 6:13–17).[32] *In my anger* (lit. "in my nostrils") points

---

30. Ryken, Wilhoit, and Longman, *Dictionary of Biblical Imagery*, 305.

31. A customary imperfect (*IBHS*, §§31.2a, b).

32. R. L. Pratt, Jr., "Historical Contingencies and Biblical Predications," in *The Way of Wisdom: Essays in Honor of Bruce K. Waltke*, ed J. I. Packer and Sven K. Soderlund (Grand Rapids: Zondervan, 2000), 180–203; Robert B. Chisholm, "When Prophecy Appears to Fail, Check your Hermeneutic," *JETS* 53 (2010): 561–77; Matthew H. Patton,

to the physically visible state of excitement of an individual breathing heavily as a consequence of anger—an obvious anthropomorphism. *My rest* may denote either a "place of rest" (Gen. 49:15; Mic 2:10; Zech. 9:1) or a "state of being at rest" (2 Sam. 14:17; 1 Kgs. 8:56; Jer. 45:3). The former entails the latter. Here it functions as a metonymy for the temple.[33] Some think it refers exclusively to Canaan (cf. Num. 14:30).[34] Braulik observes that the expression "to come into [*enter*] rest" is found only in Deuteronomy 12:9 and Psalm 95:11. In Deuteronomy 12, "rest" refers to both the land of Canaan *and* the temple, and it implies the promise that Israel will worship there. Solomon's prayer in 1 Kings 8:56 regards the completion of the temple as the fulfillment of that promise.[35] Psalm 132:14 and Isaiah 66:1 equate "my resting place" with Zion, the site of the temple. Quitters do not enter and dwell forever in the temple of the living God (cf. Ps. 23:6) and so enjoy the eternal kind of rest God enjoyed when he finished the work of creation and ceased from his work. In the trajectory of revelation, the earthly temple finds its fulfillment in Christ and in the new Jerusalem, the heavenly city where the Lord God Almighty and the Lamb are the temple (Rev. 21–22).

A. Cohen approves Oesterley's explanation of the psalm's abrupt ending: "The abrupt ending of the Psalm with the words *I swore in My wrath, that they would not enter My rest* sets in relief the stern warning directed, by implication, against those who were now standing at the entrance to the Temple."[36]

PART III. VOICE OF THE CHURCH IN RESPONSE

In tracing the reception of Psalm 95, we shall contrast three reformers of the church—Augustine, John Calvin, and Robert Bellarmine—in their very different contexts. As we have seen in the exposition, the psalm combines the

---

Hope for a Tender Spirit: Jehoiachin in Biblical Theology, BBRSup16 (Winona Lake, IN: Eisenbrauns, 2017), 202–205.

33. Tg. translates "my sanctuary"; cf. 1 Chr. 28:2.

34. NET makes Canaan the referent of "my rest," glossing v. 11, "the resting place I had set aside for them [i.e., my sheep; see v. 7]"; cf. NIRV, "the rest I planned for them." Accordingly, the pronominal suffix is construed as a genitive of authorship (cf. 2 Chr. 24:6). But the text lacks the necessary disambiguating accusative "for them," which both translations must add for clarity. More probably, it is a genitive of inalienable possession (*IBHS*, §9.5.1g).

35. Braulik, "Gottes Ruhe," 41.

36. A. Cohen, *The Psalms*, The Soncino Books of the Bible (London: Soncino, 1992), 314.

voices both of praise and worship (vv. 1–7) and of prophecy and judgment (vv. 8–11). Yet only Calvin takes seriously the concluding section of judgment.

I. Augustine of Hippo (354–430)

Augustine preached on Psalm 95 [= LXX 94] early in his pastoral ministry, when he was still very innocent of church life. It was possibly on the odd occasion when he was invited to preach by Aurelius, bishop of Carthage, before he was ordained. When he equates praise with a cheerful heart and praise with devotion, he reveals that he is still not a very deep Christian! But he does realize that "anyone who praises God can be wholly free from anxiety, because there is no possibility that we shall ever be ashamed of the one we have praised."[37] We are being invited to a great banquet of joy, "exceedingly great" because it comes from *I AM*. "Come" (v. 1) suggests the guests live far away, whereas God is always near to us (Ps. 139:7–8). The distance is not geographic but moral, so we are drawn near morally. He invites us to live in harmony with our likeness to God as the *imago Dei*, just as a coin bears Caesar's image.[38]

"Shouting for joy" (v. 1) refers to times when our joy is inexpressible in words, for heavenly joy cannot be spelled out in words.[39] The refrain is repeated because God is the mighty God over all gods and because he will not reject his people.[40] Moreover, he made the heavens, which are inaccessible to demons, and he is "the great King above all gods" (v. 3). Here Augustine plays with the term "gods," understanding it to refer to creatures. God has also created humans to be "gods." But God himself, as the Eternal Maker, is not made.[41]

Then Augustine wanders off course—it's as if he were interpreting another psalm! His interpretation of "mountains" and "sea" (vv. 4–5) is not what the psalmist is disclosing: For Augustine, the "sea" is the chaotic condition of the world. God reduces us down to size, and he will not allow us to wreak havoc with what he has planted, "for his hands laid down the dry land."[42]

---

37. Augustine, *Exposition of Psalm 94* 1, in *Expositions on the Psalms*, trans. Maria Boulding, O.S.B., vol. 4 (Hyde Park, NY: New City, 2002), 409.

38. Augustine, *Exposition of Psalm 94* 2 (Boulding, 410–11).

39. Augustine, *Exposition of Psalm 94* 3 (Boulding, 411).

40. Augustine, *Exposition of Psalm 94* 5 (Boulding, 413).

41. Augustine, *Exposition of Psalm 94* 5 (Boulding, 415).

42. Augustine, *Exposition of Psalm 94* 7 (Boulding, 418).

Three times to this point, God has commanded us "to come": to sing (v. 1), to give thanks (v. 2), and to worship (v. 6). Now, says Augustine, we are called to confession (vv. 7b, 8). Now we are to weep in God's presence. The weeping Augustine finds in the text seems more rhetorical than exegetical, but it is effective preaching! Having made us "gods," Augustine now sees us as sheep—the "sheep of His pasture" (v. 7)—and he creatively describes our life in that state.[43]

In the last section, more solemnly, Augustine exhorts the congregation to hear God's voice once more. "Long ago, you heard his voice through Moses, and you hardened your hearts. He spoke again through his herald and you hardened your hearts. Now at last, when he speaks with his own lips, let your hearts become tender" (see v. 8).[44]

Augustine translates verse 10: "*For forty years I stayed very close to this generation, but I said, they are always astray in their hearts.*" He interprets "forty" to mean "always," as in Matthew 28:20: "*Lo, I am with you throughout all days, even to the end of the ages.*"[45] Yet God's people keep on provoking the patience of God. "Always astray in their hearts," they are angry with God, and the judgmental consequence is that "they shall never enter my rest." So Augustine notes, "We began the psalm with intense joy, yet it closes on a note of sheer terror: to them I have sworn in my anger, they shall never enter my rest." Yet the last word is "the Lord will not reject his people."[46]

The purpose of using such a receptive text is to encourage every novice preacher that, weak as we may be—as even the great Augustine started—God in his grace uses us all effectively to encourage, warn, and transform other people's lives with the proclamation of his word!

II. John Calvin (1509–1564)

John Calvin was a mature scholar when he published his *Commentary on the Psalms* in 1557 at forty-eight years old. He never formally studied theology, but from 1553 he had a Hebrew text and consulted other ancient versions—occasionally the Vulgate, but most frequently the LXX. He was familiar with con-

43. Augustine, *Exposition of Psalm 94* 9 (Boulding, 418).
44. Augustine, *Exposition of Psalm 94* 10 (Boulding, 419).
45. Augustine, *Exposition of Psalm 94* 12 (Boulding, 421).
46. Augustine, *Exposition of Psalm 94* 13 (Boulding, 422).

temporary commentaries, so his exegesis was scholarly.[47] For his commentary on Psalm 95, he also consulted the Ethiopic, Arabic, and Syriac versions. Based on Hebrews 4:7, he ascribed the psalm to David. In contrast to Augustine, his emphasis is on the second, judgmental stanza of the psalm (vv. 8–11). Calvin was more concerned about the hypocrisy of the worshipers than about their praises of God, though of course that has an appropriate place. It is this that makes him a great Reformer of the church.

"The joyful noise" (the "shout for joy to *I AM*," v. 1) is "the mingled din of voices and various instruments, in the temple-service."[48] Now a tool of the church, the joyful noise is useful for the Sabbath in the public, not a private, service.[49] We are "called to worship" because of our natural indifference to giving God thanks. This is intensified by the calling of worshipers "*to come before God's face.*" We have "abundant grounds" for praising God: First, because of God's greatness, above the many gods in our lives. (1 Cor. 8:5), which are "mere fictions of our brains." Second, Calvin observes that if the "angels themselves must yield before the majesty of the one God," how much more should mere mortals? Third, God "has clearly shown forth his glory in the creation of the world, and will have us daily recognize him in the government of it."[50]

Commenting on verses 6 and 7, Calvin exhorts us to have gratitude for our paternal favor inwardly as well as outwardly in sacrificial acts of godliness and such deportment as kneeling in his presence.[51] Like the children of Israel, the church should recall we are "the flock of his hand" (v. 7), not only made but also governed by his hand. But the warning, "today," signifies the continual daily obedience God requires of us. As this made Israel visibly distinct to the other nations, so this should make Christians visibly distinct at all times.[52] Likewise, we are continually "hearing God's voice," as the writer to the Hebrews reminds us when he quotes this verse (Heb. 4:7).

In "Do not harden your hearts as at Meribah" (v. 8), Calvin identifies the history contained in Exod. 17:2–7 (cf. Deut. 6:16; 9:22; 33:8; Num. 20:13, 24). He interprets "hardness" as contempt for the word of God, or even just

---

47. Wulfert de Greef, "Calvin as a Commentator of the Psalms," in *Calvin and the Bible*, ed. Donald K. McKim (Cambridge: Cambridge University Press, 2006), 91.

48. John Calvin, *Commentary on the Book of Psalms*, trans. James Anderson, vol. 4 (Grand Rapids: Baker Books, 1996), 31.

49. Calvin, *Commentary on the Book of Psalms*, 33.

50. Calvin, *Commentary on the Book of Psalms*, 34.

51. Calvin, *Commentary on the Book of Psalms*, 34–35.

52. Calvin, *Commentary on the Book of Psalms*, 36–37.

its neglect.[53] For Calvin, "your fathers tested me" (v. 9) represents habitual disbelief in God and the perception of his irrelevance in our lives in spite of the abundant evidence of his daily presence.[54] The conclusion of verse 11 is that if we do not cultivate God's presence, we will not be able to find our rest in God. Referring again to Hebrews 4:1–11, Calvin identifies our promised land not as a geographical reality, as the Zionist movement still believes, but as the moral rest of being "God's own people," dwelling in Him. "God has not ceased to speak; He has revealed His Son, and is daily inviting us to come unto Him; and undoubtedly, it is our incumbent duty, under such an opportunity, to obey His voice."[55]

III. Robert Bellarmine (1542–1621)

We conclude with the sacramental voice of Robert Bellarmine, which is a fresh one for evangelical Christians today. Bellarmine, who would be archbishop of Capua in the last twenty years of his life, was very prominent in his day and even consulted by contemporary leaders of the Reformation. He profoundly influenced three popes at Rome, especially Paul V. The scholarship of his mature work *Commentary on the Books of the Psalms* is as lucid and sound as any contemporary commentary. He was also an outstanding linguist and wrote a Hebrew grammar. At the same time, he truly lived the life of a saint, expressed in two ascetical treatises, "The Sighs of the Doves" and "The Elevation of the Mind to God."[56] He is regarded as one of the most distinguished members of the Jesuit Order. John Milton recognized his scholarship, and he incorporated Bellarmine's earlier exposition of Psalm 92 into his own rendition of the psalm within *Paradise Lost*. But today Bellarmine is largely unknown and scarcely ever mentioned by scholars!

Bellarmine's explanation of Psalm 95 is that it is simply "an invitation to adore and serve God, and to hear His voice." He writes:

> The word "come" contains an exhortation, exciting them to join heart and lips in praising God; just as the word is used in Genesis, where the people

53. Calvin, *Commentary on the Book of Psalms*, 39–41.
54. Calvin, *Commentary on the Book of Psalms*, 41–44.
55. Calvin, *Commentary on the Book of Psalms*, 46–47.
56. Saint Robert Bellarmine, *A Commentary on the Books of Psalms*, trans. John O'Sullivan (Dublin: Aeterna, 2015), 5f.

are excited and encouraging each other, say, "Come let us make bricks";
and "Come, let us make a city and a tower"; and in the same chapter, *I
AM* says, "Come let us go down, and there confound their tongue." He
invites them first to exult in the spirit, and then to compress their joy
into song; for song is of little value unless the mind be previously raised
up to God in interior joy and admiration. Hence it is written of the Lord
himself that "He rejoiced in the Holy Ghost, and said, I give thanks to
Thee O Father"; and the Mother of the Lord said, "My soul doth magnify
the Lord, and my spirit had rejoiced."[57]

Likewise, the psalmist calls us to be united in rejoicing.

Bellarmine interprets verse 2 in two ways: First, we should, first of all,
conduct our daily business with God before we are involved in the claims of
others. Second, we should all be united in the avowal of our need for God's
mercies anew every morning.[58]

In verses 3–7, the psalmist cites five reasons why God should be praised.
First, because God is above all gods, the King above all kings. Second, God's
power is over all the cosmos, over all created things to "the ends of the earth,"
indicating his power and presence over all imaginable reality and more. Third,
as Lord of land and sea, creation and chaos, he is Lord of all. Fourth, as our
Creator, though we daily offend him, he accepts our daily repentance and
adoration. Fifth, like a shepherd he governs us uniquely, a theme on which
Bellarmine cites Augustine's homily on this psalm. This theme, he notes, is
described in Ezekiel 34.[59]

David is exhorting his people, states Bellarmine,

> to praise God, not only by word of mouth, but also by their works. Now
> the most agreeable sacrifice we can offer to God is the observance of
> his commandments, according to 1 Kings 15, "Doth the Lord desire ho-
> locausts. . . ?" . . . For it is God himself who puts the question; so also
> the Holy Ghost in this passage says, "Today, if you will hear my voice,
> who am your Lord, harden not your hearts." The word "today" means at
> present; and as the Apostle in Hebrews 3 explains, holds good or stands
> "whilst today is named"; that is, during the whole time of this life, for
> after this life, time will be no longer, it will be eternity. The word "if"

57. Bellarmine, *A Commentary on the Books of Psalms*, 447.
58. Bellarmine, *A Commentary on the Books of Psalms*, 447.
59. Bellarmine, *A Commentary on the Books of Psalms*, 448.

seems to mean that God does not speak to us every moment, but he advises in fitting time and place, either through his preachers, or through the reading of the Scriptures, or in some other mode to make his will known to us. The expression "harden not your hearts," signifies that the hearing of the voice of *I AM* is of very little value unless it penetrates the very inmost recesses of our hearts.[60]

Bellarmine searches the Old Testament for the theme of "hardening of heart." Then, linking the relevant passages with the description of what the deceitfulness of sin does in Acts 7, he understands being hardened as resisting and rejecting God and so sinning against the Holy Spirit.[61]

The Israelites wandered for forty years in the wilderness, as verse 10 reminds us. According to Bellarmine, verse 11 explains "why they should have erred in their heart, 'because they have not known my ways,' my laws which are the straight path, and anyone walking therein, cannot possibly go astray; and when they say they have not known his laws, he means knowing them so as to observe them."[62] They were condemned, then, not to enter God's rest, which Bellarmine defines as "in a higher sense . . . that heavenly country, where alone is perfect rest and peace."[63] Like few other commentators, Bellarmine thus binds the linguistic knowledge and the theological meanings of the Scriptures with devotion and pastoral godliness. He is a fresh voice for us today!

Part IV. Conclusion

I. Canonical Context

Psalm 95, like the other hymns, summons Israel to praise *I AM* as Creator and Savior, but it uniquely warns Israel not to murmur against God amid trials. That warning has a sharp edge in Book IV of the Psalter, the book that responds to the failed House of David, the fall of Jerusalem, and Israel's exile in Babylon (see pp. 15–16). Today, the Trinity wants to be honored in the name of God's Son, the Lord Jesus Christ (see p. 3).

60. Bellarmine, *A Commentary on the Books of Psalms*, 449.
61. Bellarmine, *A Commentary on the Books of Psalms*, 449.
62. Bellarmine, *A Commentary on the Books of Psalms*, 449–50.
63. Bellarmine, *A Commentary on the Books of Psalms*, 450.

David Howard argues that Psalms 95 and 100 form a frame around Psalms 96–99, the core of the psalms that praise God as King. Both psalms begin with a call for "shouts" of joy using both *rûaʿ* and *rnn*, both liturgies first call the worshipers "to come and then to enter" (95:1a; 6a; 100:2a, 4a), both mention that *I AM* has made us (95:6a-7; 100:3); and the noun "grateful praise" occurs only in these two psalms.[64]

J. Clinton McCann notes strong affinities between Psalms 95 and 24. Both celebrate "God's role as creator (cf. 24:1–2 with 95:4–5) in the context of hailing God as King (cf. 24:7–10 with 95:3) and could easily have originated or been used as a liturgy for entrance into the Temple (but see p. 21)." McCann also notes the liturgical movement from praise to hearing God's word in Psalms 50 and 81.[65]

II. Message

The hymn of Psalm 95 (vv. 1–7a) is an extended call to worship. It is often called the *Venite* ("O Come") in Christian liturgy.[66] Enthusiastic praise of *I AM* entails unequivocal faith in him. The oracle "do not harden your hearts [in unbelief]" helps shape this fundamental religious affection, and so do repetitions of that exhortation among believers (Hebrew 3:13). In sum, both the hymn and the monition—the one positive ("come") and the other negative ("do not")—exhort congregants to praise enthusiastically and to obey him scrupulously day and night, in health and in sickness, in joy and in sorrow.

But the psalm's message is more than a call to praise God in all circumstances. It is a sober warning about the necessity in adversity to persevere in praise and faith (see 1 Cor. 10:1–13; Heb. 3:7–4:13). Each "today" generation must by faith enthusiastically confess, even in the symbolic wilderness, its faith in the Creator and Redeemer. Derek Kidner comments: "The 'today' of which it speaks is this very moment; the 'you' is none other than ourselves, and the promised 'rest' is not Canaan but salvation."[67]

---

64. David M. Howard, Jr., *The Structure of Psalms 93–100*, BJSUCSD 5 (Winona Lake, IN: Eisenbrauns, 1997), 176.

65. McCann, *Psalms*, 1061.

66. Marvin E. Tate, *Psalms 51–100*, WBC 20 (Dallas: Word, 1990), 503. The title is appropriate to the entire psalm. This is so because the monition "do not harden your hearts" entails not refusing to sing the hymn.

67. Kidner, *Psalms 73–150*, 376.

I AM has given sufficient reason to trust and praise him to be a savior in crises. Creation bears universal witness to his power and sovereignty (vv. 5–6; see Pss. 19:1–6[2–7]; 93:1–4; Rom. 1:18–33), and, as for his saving deeds, the wilderness generation saw them with its own eyes (v. 9).

The unfaithful refuse to trust God in crises. They put him to the test in each new crisis, demanding he save them with a miracle as a sign of his presence and worth. In response to the wilderness generation's grumbling, God had miraculously healed the waters at Marah (Exod. 15:22–27) and with signs and wonders satisfied their hunger with manna and quail in the Wilderness of Sin (Exod. 16). He did this so that they might know that *I AM* brought them out of Egypt (16:6). They were to put some manna in a jar to remind them and future generations of that heavenly bread (16:33). Nevertheless, when they left that wilderness and camped at Meribah (aka Rephidim, Massah), they again grumbled for their lack of water. There, they demanded a new sign of his presence with them. Ironically, after Jesus miraculously fed the five thousand, the Jews asked him to perform the sign of manna in the wilderness (John 6:1–14, 25–34). In other words, unbelievers demand uninterrupted signs and miracles before they believe God is worthy of their trust and worship. This is so because of the disposition of their wayward hearts for evil things (1 Cor. 10:6): "Contention and 'testing' [are] more congenial to [sinners] than [are] obedience and faith."[68] The truth is, "All those the Father gives me [the Son] come to me" (John 6:37). When faithful pilgrims hunger and thirst "today," they trust *I AM* with all their hearts and praise him with full lungs and voice, for they eat the true Bread from Heaven that gives life to the world.

Today "the gospel" refers both to Christ's saving death, burial, and resurrection *and* to the testimony of the apostles and many others of the resurrected Christ's appearances to *them* (1 Cor. 15:2–8), not to everyone (Acts 10:40–41). Those God chooses to be his people do not demand that they see the events of the gospel repeated. By faith, the elect receive the message of those to whom the resurrected Christ appeared. That testimony is in the elect's mouth and heart (Rom. 10:6). This is so because the faithful church, in conjunction with the convincing power of the Holy Spirit, has preached that gospel from generation to generation (Rom. 10:7–17; 1 Cor. 2:1–16). As the jar of manna reminded Israel of the heavenly bread God gave Israel's first generation, the Lord's Supper reminds those whom the Father has given to Christ of the true Bread from Heaven (Luke 22:14–20; John 6:30–58; 1 Cor. 11:23–26).

68. Tate, *Psalms 51–100*, 503.

God invites us to trust and obey; he does not exercise his sovereignty by coercion. "The consequences of disobedience," says McCann, "are severe, but God refuses to be an enforcer."[69] Our decision to trust him finds expression in our coming to the temple to worship and in our resting in the Lord Jesus Christ.

69. McCann, *Psalms*, 1063.

CHAPTER 7

Psalm 96: The King Comes to Establish Justice

PART I. VOICE OF THE PSALMIST: TRANSLATION

A song by David.[1]

1 Sing to *I AM* a new song;
    sing to *I AM*, all the earth.

2 Sing to *I AM*; bless his name;
    proclaim from day to day the good news of his salvation.

3 Recount among the nations his glory,
    among all peoples his wonders.

4 For *I AM* is great and to be praised exceedingly;
    he is to be feared above all gods.

5 For all the gods of the peoples are worthless idols,
    but *I AM* made the heavens.

6 Splendor and majesty are before him;
    strength and beauty are in his sanctuary.

7 Ascribe to *I AM*, all you clans of nations,
    ascribe to *I AM* glory and strength.

8 Ascribe to *I AM* the glory due his name;
    bring a tribute offering and come into his courts.

---

1. MT lacks a superscript. The LXX has the chronologically anomalous super-script: "When the house was built after the captivity. A song of David." The Briggs explain the anomaly: "The historical reference to the erection of the second temple probably came from a later hand than the reference to David. It is bracketed in the Psalterium Gallicanum, and the order of the statements varies" (Charles Augustus Briggs and Emilie Grace Briggs, *A Critical and Exegetical Commentary on the Book of Psalms*, vol. 2, ICC [1907; repr. Edinburgh: T&T Clark, 1976], 299).

9 Prostrate yourselves before *I AM* in holy majesty[2];
   tremble before him, all the earth.

10 Say among the nations, "*I AM* reigns."[3]
   Indeed, the world is established[4]; it cannot be moved.
   He judges the peoples with equity.

11 Let the heavens rejoice; let the earth be glad;
   let the sea roar and all that is in it.

12 Let the fields be jubilant and everything in them;
   let[5] all the trees of the forest sing joyfully

13 before *I AM*. For he comes,[6] for he comes to govern the earth;
   he will govern the world in righteousness
   and the peoples in his faithfulness.[7]

2. Instead of *hadrat qōdeš*, LXX (Syr.) reads *aulē hagia autou* (= *haṣrat qodšô*, "his holy court"). But elsewhere, *ḥṣr* is always plural (*ḥaṣrôt*). As for the meaning of *hādrâ/hadrat*, in one Ugaritic text (*Keret* l, iii:155, CML [Edinburgh: T. & T. Clark, 1977], 86), *hdrh* is parallel with "dream," suggesting it means "vision" (so Dennis Pardee, "The Kirta Epic," in *COS* 1 [Leiden: Brill, 2003], 335) and so in the semantic domain of "theophany/revelation" (= "Prostrate yourselves when *I AM* appears"; see A. A. Anderson, *The Book of Psalms 73–150*, New Century Bible Commentary [Grand Rapids: Eerdmans, 1972], 684; and Marvin E. Tate, *Psalms 51–100*, WBC 20 [Dallas: Word, 1990], 511). The appeal to Ugaritic for the meaning of *hdrh* is unnecessary, textually and philologically questionable, and followed in no English version.

3. A few MSS and 1 Chr. 16:31 transpose "say among the nations, '*I AM* reigns'" to after v. 11a. The *Psalterium Romanum* reads "Dominus regnavit a lingo" ("The Lord reigns from a tree"). Many Latin fathers from Tertullian onward refer to this as a prophecy of Christ's triumph through death (see p. 180), but no Hebrew MS or ancient version outside of the OL and some Greek texts dependent on it has this reading (see Alfred Rahlfs, *Septuaginta* [Stuttgart: privileg. Württ. Bibelanstalt, 1952], vii).

4. Other ancient versions (LXX, Symmachus, Syr., Tg., Vulg.) reflect *tikkēn* Piel, from *tkn* ("to regulate").

5. Hebrew adds *'āz*, traditionally glossed "then." But the poetic *then* throws "emphasis on a particular feature of the description" (BDB, p. 23, s.v. *'āz*, §c). Since English "then" expresses a sequential or logical sequence, not emphasis, it is better left untranslated (so NIV, NLT).

6. Construing *bā'* as a gnomic/characteristic perfective. It can also be glossed "has come," signifying a past situation that persists into the present (*IBHS*, §31.5.1). Or it could be a participle, signifying "he is coming" either as a present or future situation (*IBHS*, §§37.6e, f). See "Message" below.

7. Verset 13b is missing in 1 Chr. 16:33.

PART II. COMMENTARY

I. Introduction

Author

As with many psalms in Book IV of the Psalter, the Septuagint (LXX) attributes Psalm 96 to David, but the Masoretic Text lacks a superscript. There is no reason to doubt the attribution of the LXX (see pp. 13–15). When David appointed the Levites to minister before the ark of the covenant in the tent he had pitched, the Levites sang the hymn recorded in 1 Chronicles 16:8–34.[8] That hymn, or an earlier version of it, was later adapted into two hymns: 1 Chronicles 16:8–22 (= Psalm 105:1–15) and 1 Chronicles 16:23–33 (= Psalm 96:1–13).[9] Gunkel, though he rejects the Chronicler's credibility, says that at the time of the Chronicler (in his opinion c. 300 BCE) "Pss. 96 and 105 were already considered immeasurably old."[10] Also, though Psalm 96 may contain verses from other psalms,[11] its form and rhetoric reveal its unity.

---

8. Variation between Ps. 96 and its synoptic hymn in 1 Chr. 16:23–33 include: *leyôm* (Ps. 96:2, "today") versus *'el-yôm* (1 Chr. 16:23, with no difference in meaning); *kebôdô* (3, "his glory") versus *'et-kebôdô* (24, with no difference in meaning); *nôrâ* (4, "to be feared") versus *wenôrâ* (25, "and to be feared"); *wetip'eret bemiqdāšô* (6, "and beauty in his sanctuary") versus *wehedwâ bimqōmô* (27, "and joy in his place [a more general word for 'sanctuary']"); *lehaṣrôtāyw* (8, "to his courts") versus *lepānāyw* (29, "before him); *mippānāyw* (9, "before him") versus *millepānāyw* (30, with no difference in meaning); *'imrû* (10, "say") versus *weyō'merû* (31, "and let them say"); *yādîn 'ammîm bemêšārîm* (10, "he judges the world with equity"), omitted in 31; *ya'ālōz* (12, "be jubilant") versus *ya'ālōṣ* (32, with no difference in meaning); *śādeh* (12, "fields") versus *haśśādeh* (32, "the fields); *kol* (12, "all"), omitted in 33; *lipnê* (13, "before") versus *millipnê* (33, with no difference in meaning); *kî bā'* (13, second "for he comes"), omitted in 33; *hā'āreṣ* (13, "the earth") versus *'et hā'āreṣ* (33, with no difference in meaning).

9. Jörg Jeremias (*Das Königtum Gottes in den Psalmen: Israels Begegnung mit dem kanaanäische Mythos in den Jahwe-König-Psalmen*, FRLANT [Göttingen: Vandenhoeck & Ruprecht, 1987], 122f.] thinks the psalm is only two or three centuries older than the final redaction in the Chronicles.

10. H. Gunkel and J. Begrich, *Introduction to the Psalms: The Genres of the Religious Lyric of Israel*, trans. James D. Nogalski (Macon, GA: Mercer University Press, 1998), 64.

11. Citing McCullough's grouping, H. C. Leupold (*Exposition of the Psalms* [Columbus: Wartburg, 1959], 682) notes, "With v. 1, cf. Pss. 33:3; 40:3; 98:1; with v. 3, cf. Pss. 9:11; 105:1; with v. 4, cf. Pss. 48:1; 95:3; with vv. 7–9, cf. Ps. 29:1, 2; with v. 13, cf. Pss. 9:8;

Form and Rhetoric

Poetry

The psalms are sacred poems set to music (see pp. 25, 107). Psalm 96 relishes stair-like parallelism in which initial words are repeated and then developed still further (cf. vv. 1, 2, "sing to *I AM*"; vv. 4, 5, 13, "for"; vv. 7, 8, "ascribe to *I AM*"). "This exceptional build up," says Derek Kidner, "gives the psalm an insistent vigour . . . and contributes to the air of almost irrepressible excitement at the prospect of God's coming."[12]

Rhetoric and Structure

Hymns typically consist of calls to praise followed by reasons to praise; "because/for" (cf. 95:3) often introduces the latter (see p. 20-22). More narrowly, this is the second psalm that proclaims, "*I AM* reigns" (v. 10, see p. 7). The alternating repetition of calls for praise (vv. 1-3, 7-9, 11-12) followed by reasons for praise (4-6, 10, 13) divides the psalm into three stanzas (1-6, 7-10, 11-13).[13] Their initial couplets feature stair-like parallelism, followed by an expansion in the third verse (1-3, 7-9, 11-13). The first stanza displays this same structure in verses 4-6 and so is best analyzed as having two strophes of three verses each: the call to praise (vv. 1-3) and the reasons for praise (vv. 4-6). Thus, apart from verse 10, the hymn has four sections of three verses each (1-3, 4-6, 7-9, 11-13).

The first two stanzas begin with threefold calls to praise ("sing" twice and "recount" in vv. 1-3; "ascribe" twice and "prostrate yourselves" in 7-9). The formally distinguished calls to praise and reason for praise are blended at the seams to form a unified hymn. The reason for praise in verse 4 begins with "*I AM* is worthy of praise," looking back to the praise of 1-3. And the call "ascribe to *I AM* glory

---

98:9. Besides this, on v. 2, cf. Isa. 52:7; on v. 3, Isa. 60:6; 66:18, 19; on v. 11, Isa. 44:23, 24; 46:5-7; 44:7. Going back to v. 5, cf. Isa. 40:19ff.; 41:23, 24; 46:5-7; 44:9ff." Because of its intertextuality with Second Isaiah, many commentators (e. g., Kirkpatrick, Leupold, Cohen) date the psalm to the postexilic period, but as A. A. Anderson (*Psalms 73-150*, 681) notes, "one could also argue that the author(s) of Isaiah 40-66 is dependent upon the cultic language of the pre-Exilic period."

12. Derek Kidner, *Psalms 73-150*, TOTC (Downers Grove, IL: IVP Academic, 2009), 379.

13. For similar internal structures, cf. Pss. 66:5, 8; 95:6; 96:7; 98:4; 100:4; 139:14; 145:4, 10; 147:7, 12; 148:7; 149:5 (see Gunkel and Begrich, *Introduction to the Psalms*, 39).

and strength" (7) reprises the reason "strength and beauty are in his sanctuary" (6). The catchword "glory," a key word of the psalm, unites the first two calls for praise (3, 7). Verse 10 functions as a bridge uniting the second and third stanzas. It provides the reason for the praise in 7–9, and 10b ("he judges the people's with equity") is reprised by 13b ("he will govern . . . the peoples in his faithfulness").[14]

The several uses of the number seven and its multiples also unify the hymn and signify *I AM*'s perfection. Konrad Schaefer notes:

> Fourteen imperatives invite the assembly to worship (vv. 1–10), and the use of the synonyms "peoples" and "nations" (*'ammîm* and *gôyîm*) totals seven. After the proclamation "The LORD is king" (v. 10), the effects of this reign are described in seven facets, which encompass the world's stability, fair government, heavenly and earthly rejoicing, and echoes through sea, field, and forest. The word *kôl*, "all," resounds seven times— all the earth, peoples, gods, trees, and all that fills the sea and field.[15]

Based on form, rhetoric and semantics, here is an outline of the psalm's structure:

Stanza I: All the Earth to Sing a New Song to *I AM*
    for He Is Above All Gods   1–6
  Strophe A: All the Earth Called to Sing   1–3
    1. Sing a New Song of Salvation   1–2
    2. Recount His Saving Acts among the Nations   3
  Strophe B: Cause for Praise   4–6
    1. He Is Greater Than All Other Gods for
      He Made the Heavens   4–5
    2. Splendor and Beauty Fill His Sanctuary   6
Stanza II: All Clans to Worship *I AM* For He Is King   7–10
  Strophe A: All Clans to Worship *I AM*   7–9
    1. To Bring Him Verbal Gifts and a Tribute Sacrifice   7–8
    2. To Prostrate Themselves and Tremble before His Majesty   9
  Strophe B: Reason/Janus   10
Stanza III: All Creation to Praise Because *I AM* Comes to Govern   11–13
  Strophe A: All Creation Called to Rejoice Before Him   11–13aαα

14. So also David M. Howard, Jr., *The Structure of Psalms 93–100*, BJSUCSD 5 (Winona Lake, IN: Eisenbrauns, 1997), 65.

15. Konrad Schaefer, *Psalms*, Berit Olam (Collegeville, MN: Liturgical Press), 239.

Setting

The Levites sang this hymn as part of the Jerusalem temple liturgy. The Chronicler (1 Chr. 16:7) labels the psalm a song of grateful praise. Such songs were used as a libretto to the sacrifice of grateful praise (see p. 5). The psalm admonishes the nations to sing this song, to bring a tribute (*minḥâ*, "offering," v. 8), and to enter the temple's external courts. But how can all the earth sing and sacrifice in the Jerusalem temple? Psalm 47:9 suggests the answer: "The nobles of the nations assemble [at the temple] as the people of the God of Abraham." These foreign nobles, upon their returns to their own countries, are to spread the good news of God's reign "among the nations" (vv. 3, 10). One can understand Israel singing this song when David planted *I AM*'s flag in Jerusalem, in the heart of the Canaanites, but what amazing faith on the part of those who returned from the Babylonian captivity (see pp. 15–16) to admonish the nations to sing that *I AM* is King!

II. Exegesis

Superscript

A song of David (see "Author," above).

Stanza I: All the Earth to Sing a New Song to I AM for He Is above All Gods 1–6

  Strophe A: All the Earth Called to Sing 1–3

    1. Sing a New Song of Salvation 1–2

1 *Sing* and *song* in the Psalter refer "to the musical performance of address to God formulated in fixed language, usually of praise."[16] Dennis McCorkle

---

16. R. Ficker, *TLOT*, 3:1320, s.v. *šîr*.

Psalm 96: The King Comes to Establish Justice

notes that other musical terms refer to the instruments, but "song" refers to the human voice.[17] *To* I AM (see p. 1–3). *New* refers to this psalm—the very song being sung.[18] From Isaiah 42:10 it can be inferred that "a new song" corresponds to God's new saving act. Westermann says: "The song called for here is not 'new' because a new text is to replace the old or a new melody the old; this notion is thoroughly foreign to these psalms. The song is 'new' because God has brought about something new."[19] Kirkpatrick comments: "Fresh mercies demand fresh expressions of thanksgiving."[20] *All the earth* (see "Message" below).

2 *Bless his name* (see Psalm 100:4). *Proclaim . . . the good news* stands in apposition to "bless his name," identifying God as the originator of the good news. The Hebrew word glossed "proclaim good news" can mean simply "to bring news" (2 Sam. 18:19, 20) or even "bad news" (e.g., the loss of the ark, 1 Sam. 4:17), but usually it means "to bring good news" that gladdens the heart (Jer. 20:15; 1 Sam. 18:26; Ps. 68:11[12]). It is used of heralds of glad tidings (Nah. 1:15; Isa. 40:9; 41:27; 52:7) and of the messianic servant who brings good news to the afflicted (Isa. 61:1; see "Early Christian Use of the Psalm," below). "The key way one praises God," says Goldingay, "is by narrating what God has done, and it this that the nations need to hear."[21] What God has done is *his salvation* (cf. Ps. 40:9[10]). The universal praise from "all the earth" (v. 1) and "among all the nations" (v. 3) is balanced by the continuous temporal perspective of *from day to day*. Marvin Tate adds "until all people and nations know about his glory."[22] Today, the church is fulfilling its mission to tell everywhere and every day the good news that Jesus Christ has died for our sins, was buried, and was raised on the third day (Rom. 10:14–15; 1 Cor. 15:4). In this way, the church blesses God.

---

17. Dennis McCorkle, *The Davidic Cipher: Unlocking the Hidden Music of the Psalms* (Denver: Outskirts, 2010), 18.

18. John Goldingay, *Psalms*, vol. 3, BCOTWP (Grand Rapids: Baker Academic, 2008), 103.

19. C. Westermann, *TLOT,* 1:397, s.v. *ḥādāš.*

20. A. F. Kirkpatrick, *The Book of Psalms* (1902; repr., Grand Rapids: Baker Books, 1986), 576.

21. Goldingay, *Psalms,* 103, citing Jeremias, *Königtum,* 125.

22. Tate, *Psalms 51–100,* 512.

171

2. Recount His Saving Acts among the Nations 3

Recount . . . his glory—that is to say, his value and worth (i.e., honor).[23] Daniel Wu rightly recognizes that there are "substantive" and "responsive" aspects to glory. The former refers to "the actual properties of the object—irrespective of the perception of others" and the latter to "the action or disposition of a party in response to the object."[24] He also rightly distinguishes between the "Public Court of Reputation" and the "Divine Court of Reputation."[25] But one cannot recount an abstraction such as "honor." In that juxtaposition "honor/glory" is a metonymy for his person (e.g., his strength) and work (e.g., "he made the heavens"). A *people* refers to any organized community of people, often larger than a clan, who are related and unified in such ways as blood, history, memory, and culture. It differs from *nations* in that it refers to the subjective and personal instead of to the objective and impersonal.[26] Concerning *his wonders*, Albertz says,

> In the large, major category of its usage, the root *pl'/plh* indicates an event that a person, judging by the customary and expected, finds extraordinary, impossible, even wonderful. *Pele'* never hinges on the phenomenon as such but includes both the unexpected event and one's astonished reaction. Consequently, the language of *pele'* is the language of joyous reaction (praise).[27]

Strophe B: Cause for Praise 4–6

1. He Is Greater Than All the Gods for He Made the Heavens 4–5

4   In the outer frame of 4, "great" matches "above all the gods"; and in its core, "to be exceedingly praised" pairs with "to be feared." *Great* refers to rank and influence and implies a comparison, so it is part of the conceptual sphere of "glory/honor." So is *to be praised*, which signifies public proclamation bestowing social honor on someone or something (cf. Gen. 12:15; 2 Sam. 14:25; Ezek. 26:17). *Exceedingly* means more than normally (see Pss. 92:5[6]; 93:5). *He is to*

23. Daniel Y. Wu, *Honor, Shame, and Guilt: Social-Scientific Approaches to the Book of Ezekiel*, BBRSup 14 (Winona Lake, IN: Eisenbrauns, 2016), 58.
24. Wu, *Honor, Shame, and Guilt*, 64.
25. Wu, *Honor, Shame, and Guilt*, 59.
26. E. A. Speiser, " 'People' and 'Nation' of Israel," *JBL* 79 (1960): 157–66.
27. R. Albertz, *TLOT*, 2:982, s.v. *pl'* Niphil.

be feared may emphasize *emotional fear*, as when Israel saw the mighty hand of *I AM* displayed against the Egyptians at the Red Sea (Exod. 14:31); *cognitive awe and reverence*, as when the psalmist asks for an undivided heart that he may "fear/revere" God's name (Pss. 86:11; 112:1); or to *worship in awe and adoration*, as when those who fear *I AM* are equated with the congregation of Israel that honors *I AM* in worship (Ps. 22:22–23[23–24]).[28] These three aspects of fear should not be too sharply distinguished; they are opalescent—like the merging colors of an opal stone or of an oil slick. In the development of the next stanza, "tremble" suggests the emotion of fear is included here. This fear is a response to God's great deeds (Exod. 14:31; Josh. 4:23–24; 1 Sam. 4:7–9) and expresses itself subjectively in awe and adoration and objectively in obedience to his law (Deut. 10:12–13; cf. Ps. 112:1; 119:63). Samuel preached: "Be sure to fear *I AM* and serve him faithfully with all your heart; consider what great things he has done for you" (1 Sam. 12:24).

5 Lest one think "above all the gods" (v. 4; see 95:3) entails the existence of other gods, the poet immediately adds, *all the gods of the people are worthless idols*.[29] Cohen comments, "The prophet used the weapon of irony to prove this"—that is to say, he punned by pairing *'elîlîm* ("worthless idols") with *'elōhê hā'ammîm* ("gods of the people").[30] God's people are not politically correct. Goldingay comments: "As is usual in the Bible, the psalm does not reckon we should be respectful of other people's religions."[31] Objects of worship other than God have no worth or value but rather are deadly; they deserve social shame. *But* I AM *made the heavens* (i.e., the domelike sky). Heaven is a real place from which Christ came, to which he returned, and where he is preparing a place for his people (John 14:2–3). But when the biblical writers speak of God and of heaven, of necessity they must use imagery. God is spirit—a mystery beyond human experience and so beyond comprehension—and heaven is inhabited by spiritual beings (cf. 1 Kgs. 8:27).

---

28. The term sometimes refers to purely formal worship, as when the syncretists in the northern kingdom "feared *I AM*" with respect to cultic worship while not "fearing *I AM*" with respect to righteous obedience (cf. Isa. 29:13). In truth, the syncretists "do not fear *I AM*" at all (2 Kgs. 17:23–34).

29. *'elîlîm* is used as an idiomatic, derogatory metonymy for "idols" (Lev. 19:4; 26:1; Isa. 2:8; passim).

30. Other puns include: *'elîlîm 'illᵉmîm* ("mute idols," Hab. 2:18) and *'elîlîm kālîl* ("the idols totally . . . ," Isa. 2:18).

31. Goldingay, *Psalms*, 104.

2. Splendor and Beauty Fill His Sanctuary 6

The focus remains on the heavens, on *I AM*'s sanctuary. In Psalm 68:33–35[34–36], *I AM* is pictured as riding in the heavens and residing in his heavenly sanctuary. *Splendor and majesty* (*hôd wᵉhādār*—note the assonance) connote royalty (Pss. 21:5[6]; 45:3[4]; 145:5; cf. 96:10) and belong to the conceptual field of honor. *Hôd* ("splendor") designates a regal, lofty, stately magnificence or pomp.[32] *Hādār* ("majesty") adds eminence (see Lev. 23:40 [cf. Isa. 35:2]; Deut. 33:17; Prov. 14:28 [cf. Isa. 5:14]). Several times, it is used metaphorically of being arrayed in a magnificence that sets one apart and above others (Ps. 104:1; Prov. 31:25; Ezek. 16:14). *Strength* denotes having prevailing power as of the Leviathan (Job 41:14), or solid, protective strength as of a city (Prov. 18:19). *Beauty* refers to everything that causes people to rejoice and to be proud: "adornment, splendor, brilliance, beauty" (cf. Judg. 4:9; Esth. 1:4; Jer. 13:18; Isa. 28:1; 62:3; Ezek. 16:12, 17); it too is an aspect of "glory." Maclaren comments:

> 'Strength and beauty,' are often separated in a disordered world, and each is maimed thereby, but, in their perfection, they are indissolubly blended. . . . The archetypes of both excellences are in the Holy Place, and any strength which has not its roots there is weakness, and any beauty which is not a reflection from 'the beauty of the Lord our God' is but a mask concealing ugliness.[33]

The inapposite juxtaposition of abstract, royal terms with the local preposition *before him* and the parallel *in his sanctuary* jar the audience into realizing that "splendor and majesty," "strength and beauty" are divine attributes personified as throne attendants (cf. Ps. 78:61).

Stanza II: All Clans to Worship I AM For He Is King 7–10

The calls to worship in verses 7–9 are blended into the confession that gives the reason for worship by another imperative ("say," v. 10).

32. D. Vetter, *TLOT*, 1:356, s.v. *hôd*.
33. A. Maclaren, *The Psalms*, vol. 3, Expositor's Bible (New York: George H. Doran, n.d.), 57.

Strophe A: All Clans to Worship I AM 7–9

1. To Bring Him Verbal Gifts and a Tribute Sacrifice 7–8

7   In addition to its stair-like parallelism, the couplet is linked by the key word *kābôd* ("glory/honor"). *Ascribe* means literally "give!" *Glory* (see v. 3) *and strength* are a hendiadys: God uses his strength in a way that gives him glory. The collocation "give God glory" means to publicly acknowledge his glory—to wit, his strength. *Ascribe* captures the thought "to recognize" (NLT), "to acknowledge" (NET; cf. Deut. 32:3) his substantive worth and to do so publicly. As for *you clans of* [foreign] *nations,*[34] in the biblical world, the king was over the nation, the patriarch over the clan, and the father over the family. The clan was a person's address; it designates a person's corporate identity.

8   *His name* (see v. 2; Ps. 100:4). *Bring* (woodenly, "lift up") means "to present" with "a gift/offering" (*minḥâ*).[35] In profane contexts, a *minḥâ* denotes either a "gift" between people (cf. Gen. 32:20–21[21–22]; 33:10) or, as a specialized term, a tribute to a superior (Judg. 3:15, 17, 18). In cultic contexts, it refers to a gift-sacrifice to God (Gen. 4:3–5) or serves as a specialized term for a grain offering (i.e., an offering from crops rather than flocks/herds; see Lev. 2). Robert Alter says, "A pun is surely intended here: as a king (cf. v. 10) he expects 'tribute' (cf. Pss. 68:30; 72:10); as God he appoints his cultic sacrifices."[36] Whether the gift is gold, incense, animals, or crops, it must be of such quantity and quality that it honors and pleases the beneficiary. *And come into his courts* (see Ps. 100:2, 4; cf. Isa. 2:2-4; Mic. 4:1–4; Hag. 2:7–9). The command finds fulfillment in the Gentiles' coming to Jesus Christ, the true temple of God (John 2:21), and to the heavenly Jerusalem (Heb. 12:22–23). Other texts show they will be cleansed from their sin by the gospel of Jesus Christ, for in their unclean state they would not be welcome (Isa. 52:1).

---

34. The parallel Ps. 29:1–2 differs from Ps. 96:7–8 only in whom it addresses: "heavenly beings."

35. *HALOT*, 1:726, s.v. *nāśāʾ*, #16.

36. Robert Alter, *The Book of Psalms: A Translation with Commentary* (New York: Norton, 2007), 339.

2. To Prostrate Themselves and Tremble before His Majesty 9

As for *prostrate yourselves before* I AM, the sequence in the performance of praise reprises the sequence in Psalm 95:1, 6. The worshipers bend their knees *in holy majesty* (*bᵉhadrat qōdeš*). *Hadrat* (always construct) signifies magnificent and eminent splendor (see v. 6), and *qōdeš* (see p. 141) characterizes it as the dread of the preternatural and the supernatural and associates it with the demand for righteous behavior (see Ps. 93:5).[37] God's presence suffuses the scene of the prostrate worshipers with numinous dread. The notions of holiness, dread and ethical behavior match "trembling [in fear]" (v. 9b) and God's coming to judge the earth with equity (10). *All the earth* repeats verse 1. With *tremble* (*ḥîlû*) we arrive at the polar opposite of joyous singing in true worship. *Ḥîl* is associated with physical movements of a woman writhing in labor (Isa. 13:18; 26:17f.) and with the earth's tremors (Pss. 97:4; 114:7; Hab. 3:10). Here it is used metaphorically of deep emotional awe generated *from his presence*.

Strophe B: Reason/Janus 10

The nearest antecedent of the imperative *say* is "families of the nations," the addressees in verses 7–9; thus it links verse 10 with the calls to praise, which are addressed to them. "Say," in contrast to other verbs of speaking, refers to the content of what is spoken—here, a public confession of faith *among the nations* who give glory to no-gods and no glory to the true God. The confession I AM *reigns/*"is King" (see p. 4) is developed in two directions: He reigns as Creator, and he reigns as Lord of history. *Indeed* (*'ap*; see 93:1bβ) emphatically connects the confession with the permanent establishment of the earth-disc: *the world is established; it cannot be moved* (see 93:1–2). According to Psalm 93, *I AM* established the earth-disc by triumphing over the sea, which symbolizes the inexplicable and indeterminate deep empirical reality that is alienated from the living God, who is righteous and just. His permanent and universal rule over the creation gives assurance that as Lord of history, *he judges* or "will judge" (*yādîn*) *the peoples* (see v. 3) who alienate themselves from him and temporarily triumph over the righteous. *Dîn* ("judges") means "to issue just verdicts." Botterweck agrees with Liedke, who argues that the predominant meaning of *dîn* is the "authoritative, binding decision in a lawsuit," and that its synonym *šāpaṭ* ("judges," see v. 13) denotes "the action that restores the disturbed *sha-*

---

37. In Ps. 110:3, the masc. pl. (in contrast to the abstract fem. sing. of Ps. 96:9) is a metonymy for the garments of the army in worship.

lom (peace) of a community. . . .For the one who suffers under the disrupted order, *šāpaṭ* means 'to deliver, to aid in bringing about justice.' . . . For the one who is the cause of the disruption, the *šāpaṭ*-action is judgment that brings about exclusion and destruction."[38] Thus *dînû mišpaṭ* in Jeremiah 21:12 means "carry out the legal decision." God judges the nations (Gen. 15:14; 1 Sam. 2:10; Pss. 7:8[9]; 96:10; 110:6; Job 36:31), and he never judges unjustly. *With equity* (*bᵉmêšārîm*) derives from the Hebrew lexeme *yāšār* (see 92:15; p. 119).

Stanza III: All Creation to Praise Because I AM Comes to Govern 11–13

Strophe A: All Creation Called to Rejoice before Him 11–13aα

In response to the King coming to judge the whole world in righteousness, the poet enjoins the whole creation to rejoice in praise before *I AM* (cf. Isa. 35:1–3; 65:12–13). Two merisms (heaven and earth, v. 11; field and forest, v. 12), the repetition of "all," and its synonym "fullness" show that the cited aspects of creation are synecdoches for every part of it.

1. The Cosmic Elements to Rejoice 11

Let the heavens (see v. 5) *rejoice* (*yiśmᵉḥû*; see the nominal form *śimḥâ* in Ps. 100:2). *Gîl*, the lexeme of *let . . . be glad* (*wᵉtāgēl*), is frequently a parallel to and a synonym of "rejoice" (v. 11a), "exult" (12a), and "shout for joy" (12b). These verbs differ from "to sing" (v. 1) because they either denote manifestations of joy without words or they are spontaneous expressions of joy rather than planned ones.[39] The synonyms are difficult to distinguish from one another because the contexts are not specific; the LXX renders most of them by the same words, and Israel's vocabulary for her liturgical celebration is far richer than ours. Standing in parallel and yet in contrast with "sea," *the earth* refers to "the dry ground/land," as in Genesis 1:10. In the biblical cosmology, *the sea* (see Ps. 93:4; p. 139) refers to the waters that encircle the earth-disc and that are under it. The *roar* of the raging sea is heard as loud rejoicing, not as a menacing threat. The translation of *ûmᵉlō'ô* (LXX = *to plērōma autēs*; Vulg. = *et plenitude eius*) by "its fullness" in KJV, ASV, and ERV is ambiguous.

38. Botterweck, *TDOT*, 3:188, s.v. *dîn*.
39. Michael A. Grisanti, *NIDOTTE*, 1:855, s.v. *gîl*.

That translation could refer to its waves (cf. Ps. 93:3). Rather, *ûməlō'ô* refers to "everything in it" (NLT, NET) or *all that is in it* (NIV), such as fish and the monster Leviathan (see Pss. 8:8[9]; 74:13–14; Isa. 27:1).[40] If it be objected that "roar" is inappropriate with fish, it should be noted that that verb is also used with "the world and all who live in it" (Ps. 98:7). If it is considered a zeugma, "to rejoice" can readily be supplied from verse 11a.

2. Fields and Forests to Rejoice 12–13aα

The verb translated *let . . . be jubilant* occurs sixteen times, always in poetry and usually in connection with such other words denoting "to rejoice" as *gîl* (v. 11; see Hab. 3:18), *śmḥ* (2 Sam. 1:20), and *rnn* (Ps. 149:5). It is also used in parallel with *rûaʻ* Hiphil ("shout for joy") and in connection with merry-makers (Jer. 15:17) and being merry or tipsy when drunk (Jer. 51:39). *Fields* denotes open fields unfrequented by people, in contrast to a city or village (cf. Gen. 4:8; 24:63; Deut. 22:25). *And everything in them* includes all sorts of vegetation (Deut. 32:13; Isa. 55:12), herds and flocks (Gen. 29:2; Deut. 11:15), game animals (Gen. 25:29; Jer. 14:5), and other wild animals (Exod. 23:29; Lev. 26:22; 2 Sam. 17:8; Hos. 2:12; Hos. 13:8). *Let . . . shout for joy* (*yᵉranᵉnû* see Ps. 92:4). *All the trees* includes the high and the low, the green and the dry (Ezek. 17:24), and *of the forest* underscores their innumerability (cf. Josh. 17:15; Deut. 19:5). The personified creation is pictured as celebrating in the temple, and thus their rejoicing is in spontaneous praise *before* I AM.

Strophe B: I AM Comes to Judge the Earth in Righteousness 13aβ–b

He is coming refers to an epiphany for the sake of judgment: "*I AM* came from Sinai. . . ; he shone forth from Mount Paran" (Deut. 33:2); and "God came from Teman, the Holy One from Mount Paran" (Hab. 3:3). Presumably, *I AM* comes from his heavenly temple, and in its earthly counterpart his people meditate on and rejoice in his righteous judgments upon all the earth (cf. Ps. 48:9–10[11–12]). The anadiplosis *for he comes* leads expectantly to a climax— namely, *to govern* (*lišpōṭ*; cf. v. 10) *the earth* (see v. 1). Indeed, *he will govern* (*yišpōṭ*). The *špṭ* ("to govern") act transpires in a "triangular relationship":

40. Cf. the use of *mᵉlō'ô* with "city" (Amos 6:8), "land" (Ezek. 30:12), "earth-disc" (Ps. 50:12); its use in Ezek. 12:19 ("its land will be stripped of all it contains"); and its parallel "all who live in it/them" (Pss. 24:1; 98:7; Isa. 42:10).

One party oppresses another, and the third party restores a state of peace by eliminating the oppressor and delivering the oppressed. To this, G. Liedke adds: "The restoration of community order should be understood not only as a one-time act but also as a continuous activity, as a constant preservation of the *šālôm* ["peace"], thus the meaning 'to govern, rule' results."[41] He governs *the world* (*tēbel*, i.e., "earth-disc"; see 93:1) *in righteousness* (*bᵉṣedeq*), not in vindictiveness. *Ṣedeq* refers to the moral quality that informs right order from which ensue morally qualified acts (Deut. 33:21; Ps. 48:10–11[11–12]; Isa. 59:9, 11). "To judge in righteousness" means "not [to] show partiality to the poor or favoritism to the great" (Lev. 19:15), to "hear both small and great alike" (Deut. 1:17) and implicitly to enforce his verdicts. God established his throne on righteousness and justice (Ps. 97:2), and for this purpose he sits enthroned (Ps. 9:7[8]). *And the peoples* (see v. 3) *in his faithfulness* (see Ps. 100:5). God will judge the world fairly. Count on it.

PART III. VOICE OF THE CHURCH IN RESPONSE

I. Early Use of the Psalm in Temple Liturgy

This praise psalm was originally sung when the ark of the covenant was relocated to Jerusalem after being in storage in Kiriath-Jearim for twenty years during the reign of Saul (1 Chr. 15:1–16:37). It reflects a long story; for early on in his reign over Judah and Israel David tried and failed to relocate the ark (2 Sam. 6:1–19; 1 Chr. 13:1–14). He succeeded the second time, and the ark was firmly established in a tent within the city. There it remained until Solomon completed the First Temple as described in 1 Kings 8:1–9.

The psalm's superscription in the LXX—"When the House was built after the captivity, a song of David"—would date the redaction of the original work by David (c. 1000 BCE) into the Psalter after the Decree of Cyrus in 539 BCE. Because this psalm was associated with the bringing of the ark into the tent David had pitched for it, it might also have been chosen for the service of the dedication of the Second Temple mentioned in Ezra 6:15–22. In that new context, David's call to the nations to praise Israel's God as the Creator of all and as the one who comes to judge the earth takes on a new and deeper meaning.

41. G. Liedke, *TLOT*, 3:1393–94, s.v. *špṭ*.

II. Early Christian Use of the Psalm

Hippolytus of Rome (170–235), an important theologian in the diocese of Rome, uses the psalm as a manifesto for missionary evangelism. He comments on the words of Psalm 96:11:

> By these words it is signified that the preaching of the Gospel will be spread abroad over the seas and the islands in the ocean, and among the peoples dwelling therein, who are here called "the fullness thereof." And that word has been made good. For the churches of Christ fill all the islands, and are being multiplied every day, and the teaching of the Word of salvation is gaining successions.[42]

Other apologists used it against the prevalent idolatry of their times, including Justin Martyr (110–165), who echoes the words, "let all the trees of the forest sing for joy" (96:12b) and the Christian gloss added to text, "The Lord has reigned from the tree." He understood this to mean the cross (see 166n3).[43] This theme of "the tree" is repeated by Tertullian (c. 155–240) in *An Answer to the Jews*, where he wrote: "Come, now, if you have read in the utterance of the prophet in the Psalms, 'God hath reigned *from the tree*,' I wait to hear what you understand thereby; for fear you may perhaps think some carpenter-king is signified, and not Christ, who has reigned from that time onward when he overcame the death from His passion of 'the tree.' "[44]

III. Musical Psalmody among the Early Fathers

Since Psalm 96 calls for singing "a new song," it is appropriate to recall from our previous commentaries how universal was the role of music among the early Christians.[45] The Greek Pythagoreans had used music philosophically,

42. Hippolytus of Rome, "Fragments from Commentaries on Various Books of Scripture," in *Fathers of the Third Century: Hippolytus, Cyprian, Novatian*, ed. A. Roberts, J. Donaldson, and A. C. Coxe, vol. 5 (Buffalo, NY: Christian Literature Company, 1886), 203.

43. Justin Martyr, *The First Apology of Justin* 41 (ANF 1:176; PG 6:391).

44. Tertullian, *An Answer to the Jews* 10 (ANF 6:166). Tertullian connects this with the query of the Jews about whether Jesus is "the carpenter's son" (Matt. 13:55; Luke 4:22).

45. See Bruce K. Waltke and James M. Houston with Erika Moore, *The Psalms as*

as "a musical way of life."[46] The Greek orator, philosopher, and historian Dio Chrysostom (c. 40–115 AD) addressed the citizens of Alexandria:

> Music is believed to have been invented by human beings for the healing of their passions, and especially for transforming souls which are in harsh and savage state. That is why even some philosophers attune themselves to the lyre at dawn, thereby striving to quell the confusion caused by their dreams. And it is with song that we sacrifice to the gods, for the purpose of insuring order and stability in ourselves.[47]

When Origen (c. 185–254), an early Christian scholar, ascetic, and theologian, took refuge from all the calumny heaped upon him by his enemies in Caesarea, he must have been deeply comforted in composing his great commentary on the Psalms. Alas, it is extant in very fragmentary form, and we have no fragment of commentary on Psalm 96. But, as Ronald E. Heine has observed, for Origen the whole Psalter is a song upon a lyre! According to Heine, one fragment asserts that

> David is the only prophet . . . to have prophesied with the instrument the Greeks call the psaltery and the Hebrews the *nabla* [= "lute"/"harp"]. This instrument, the fragment continues, is unique in that it has no curve but is straight and in that the sound comes from the upper part of the instrument. The harp is then compared with the body of Christ and his saints, which the instrument alone has maintained *tēn euthutēta*, which means "straightness" in relation to the harp but also "righteousness" in relation to people. This harmonious, melodious, in-tune instrument, which has received no human discord, has maintained harmony with the Father in all things.[48]

Christian Worship: A Historical Commentary (Grand Rapids: Eerdmans, 2010), 39–40, 485–87.

46. John Dillon and Jackson Hershbell, *On the Pythagorean Way of Life: Texts, Translations, and Notes* (Atlanta: Scholars, 1991), 89.

47. Quoted by Paul R. Kolbert, "Athanasius, the Psalms, and the Reformation of the Self," in *The Harp of Prophecy, Early Christian Interpretation of the Psalms,* ed. Brian E. Daley and Paul R. Kolbert (Notre Dame, IN: University of Notre Dame Press, 2015), 96.

48. Ronald E. Heine, "Restringing Origen's Broken Harp: Some Suggestions Concerning the Prologue to the Caesarean Commentary on the Psalms," in *The Harp of Prophecy*, 60–61.

With "the usefulness" of the lyre, Origen is suggesting, we are being pointed to Christ! In a larger fragment, *De Orginis prologis* 13–14, Origen focuses on Psalms 89–99 [= Heb. 90–100?], to suggest they were all Mosaic psalms.[49]

An influential theologian in the late fourth century, the monk and ascetic Evagrius Ponticus (345–399), wrote his longest extant *scolia*, or marginal annotation in the Bible, on the Psalms.[50] At the end of the fourth century, the Psalter was becoming increasingly prominent in Christian life and worship. As J. McKinnon has stated about this trend, "it was an unprecedented wave of enthusiasm for the singing of the Psalms that swept from east to west through the Christian population of the closing decades of the fourth century."[51] In another essay he writes, "Nothing quite like it has been observed either before or after in the history of Christianity or Judaism."[52] Having said that, we do not appear to have a *scolia* on Psalm 96. Evagrius fell under the same ecclesial condemnation as his master Origen, causing many of his texts to be lost until very recently. But, like Athanasius of Alexandria (c. 293–373), Evagrius sees the curative properties of reciting a particular psalm, as well as the contemplative benefit of absorbing it into one's soul. He also sees the practical ascetical value of the psalm texts as a battlefield for the cultivation of virtue over vice, as expressed by Psalm 144:1, "Blessed be *I AM* my rock, who teaches my hands to fight and my fingers to do battle." He makes full use of the military metaphors of the psalms as well as their agricultural imagery of fruitfulness. He explores the strong theme of abandonment, with its cries of anguish and pleas for divine presence and assistance. Yet he also explores the cosmic dimensions of the psalms: of the demonic, the angelic, and the human in between. But his most frequent comment in his *scolia* is the preeminence of Christ in the Psalter, which Augustine would later capitalize on so strongly in pursuing the theme of the *toto Christi*, identifying the "the Lord" sayings of the gospels with *I AM* in the Old Testament.

49. Heine, "Restringing Origen's Broken Harp," 64.

50. Luke Dysinger, "Evagrius Ponticus: The Psalter as a Handbook for the Christian Contemplative," in *The Harp of Prophecy*, 97.

51. J. McKinnon, "Desert Monasticism and the Later Fourth-Century Psalmodic Movement," *Music and Letters* 75 (1994): 506.

52. J. McKinnon, "The Fourth Century Origin of the Gradual," *Early Church History* 7 (1987): 98.

IV. The Second Great Church Period of Hymnody

The Tudor period saw a revival of popular hymnody, but it developed more seriously with Isaac Watts (1674–1748), culminating in the Wesleys and their associates. William Law (1686–1761) chose Psalm 96 as his favorite morning hymn, and in his classic *A Serious Call to a Holy Living*, he devotes his most eloquent chapter to calling Christians to practice what they preach, saying, "Do but so live, that your heart may truly rejoice in God, that it may feel so affected with the praises of God, that it may feel itself affected with the praises of God, and then you will find, that this state of your heart will neither want a voice, nor ear to find a tune for a psalm."[53] The Wesley brothers, John (1703–1791) and Charles (1707–1788), were preaching and singing from the Psalms in all their ministry, but strangely, I (Houston) have not found any reference to Psalm 96.

Charles Spurgeon (1834–1892) reiterates the same message of missionary evangelism as the first commentators of the second century (such as Hippolytus), which was happening again on "islands" in the Caribbean, Hawaii, Tonga, Fiji, and so on.[54] Spurgeon weaves in his teaching about the salvific work of God with the mystery of his exaltation above all gods. Treating the psalm as an evangelistic text, Spurgeon exults in the gospel being spread throughout the earth and purifying Christians to live holy lives—for one day God will fill the world with both holiness and joy.[55]

More recently, Dietrich Bonhoeffer (1906–1945), recognized Psalm 96, along with Psalms 97, 98, 110, and 148–150, as "psalms of the final victory of God."[56] In a prison camp, awaiting his execution and daily contemplating the psalms, psalms such as 96 helped him celebrate "the time when the redeemed people of God will reign with him eternally, when the powers of evil will fall and God alone will rule."[57]

Shrewdly, the remarkable scientist Stanley Jaki (1924–2009), in his devotional commentary on the Psalms, comments on Psalm 96: "The profundity

53. Quoted by Rowland E. Prothero, *The Psalms in Human Life* (New York: E. P. Dutton, 1903), 303.

54. Charles Spurgeon, *Psalms*, ed. Alister McGrath and J. I. Packer, vol. 2 (Wheaton, IL.: Crossway, 1993), 51.

55. Spurgeon, *Psalms*, 52.

56. Dietrich Bonhoeffer, *Psalms: the Prayer Book of the Bible* (Minneapolis: Augsburg, 1970), 6.

57. Bonhoeffer, *Psalms*, 62.

of the psalm's call for a new song is still to be mined." He adds, "There is such density of meaning in Psalm 96 that much more needs to be explored."[58]

PART IV. CONCLUSION

I. Canonical Context

Psalm 96 belongs to the impressive collection of seven Psalms that proclaim or confess "*I AM* is King" (see pp. 4, 19–22; cf. v. 10 with 93:1; vv. 10–12 with 93:3–4; v. 13 with 98:9). This collection is strategically placed in the Psalter as a response to the Babylonian exile (see pp. 15–16). At the heart of this collection, the "new song" of Psalm 96 evokes an alternative, eternal reality: Israel's strong and righteous God, who created the heavens, is coming to judge the whole earth with equity just as surely as he established the earth that cannot be moved. There are a number of intertextual connections between the "good news" of Psalm 96 and Isaiah 40–55, but as McCann notes, "It is not clear which text originated first or even whether one text directly influenced the other."[59]

II. Message

About 70 percent of Psalm 96 is formally dedicated to "the call to praise" and 30 percent to reasons for praise (see p. 7). The two motifs function in unison to give glory to God. The psalm's unified message is summed up in the confession of all peoples: "*I AM* is King/reigns"[60] and so rules over all creation, all gods, and all peoples. Psalm 96 is the second psalm in Book IV that proclaims, "*I AM* is King/reigns" (cf. 93:1; 96:10; see p. xi). The so-called "enthronement psalms" are all about this proclamation, this confession, not about an annual enthronement of *I AM* (see pp. 19–22).

Psalm 96 calls all the earth to praise *I AM* both in word and gestures. "Verses 1–3," says Hossfeld, "contain imperatives with verbs of speaking (praise, proclaim, tell), followed in vv. 7–9 by imperatives with verbs of cultic worship

---

58. Stanley L. Jaki, *Praying the Psalms: A Commentary* (Grand Rapids: Eerdmans, 2001), 175.

59. J. Clinton McCann, Jr., *Psalms*, NIB 4 (Nashville: Abingdon, 1996), 1065.

60. For significance of being "king," see p. 4.

(bring, come, fall down, tremble)."[61] The repetition of imperatives is a sign of overwhelming enthusiasm.[62] Praise should be fervent (1–3), not slovenly; thoughtful ("ascribe to *I AM*," 8–9), not superficial; and suffused with holy trembling and obedience (10), not sinful. God desires everyone and everything to praise him: "all the earth" (1, 9) "all you clans of the nations" (7) and all creation (11–12).[63]

The reasons for praise are gradually unpacked in a way that holds the audience in suspense. The first verse unites call and reason in a comprehensive way: All the earth is called upon to praise *I AM*, and the reason for praise is bundled up in the object of singing—to wit, a new song that implies an act of salvation. What is this salvation that is so glorious and wonderful that its good news must be recounted daily among the nations (vv. 2–3); that prompts people to praise God's glory, beauty, strength and majesty (4–6); and to bow in holy awe and total submission to him? Our suspense is not relieved until the bridge (10): he judges or will judge the earth in equity. Finally, in a climactic, pithy line, the salvation is fully revealed; he is coming to judge all the earth in righteousness.

But the poet does not specify when or where or how this epiphany and the oxymoron of his judgment that saves occurs.[64] In Biblical Hebrew, the verbal forms indicate aspect (i.e., complete or incomplete action), not tense. David may have composed this hymn for the triumphal entry of the ark into Jerusalem, the stronghold of the Jebusites. Kidner says of that entry: "The symbolism of the march, in which God crowned his victories by planting his throne in the

---

61. Frank-Lothar Hossfeld and Erich Zenger, *Commentary on Psalms 51–100*, trans. Linda M. Maloney, Hermeneia (Minneapolis: Fortress, 2005), 464.

62. Gunkel and Begrich, *Introduction to the Psalms*, 25.

63. Cf. P. J. Botha, "The 'Enthronement Psalms': A Claim to the World-Wide Honour of Yahweh," *OTE* 11, no. 1 (1998): 25.

64. Perhaps it is assumed that it occurs in connection with holy war. Tremper Longman III ("Psalm 98," *JETS* 27 [1984], 269; "The Divine Warrior: The New Testament Use of an Old Testament Motif," *WTJ* 44 [1982], 290–307, esp. 300–302) argues that each of the seven occurrences of "new song" (Pss. 33:3; 40:3[4]; 96:1; 98:1; 144:9; 149:1; Isa. 42:10; plus Rev. 5:9; 14:3) celebrate a military victory. Though Longman ("The Divine Warrior") says, "A . . . connection between new song and Holy War can be clearly recognized in . . . 96:1," no other commentator to my knowledge has made that connection. Longman may be right, but there is danger here of committing the philological fallacy of total transference. Isaiah 2:2–4 and Micah 4:1–4 envision Mount Zion established as the highest mountain and nations going up to the temple where God will judge between them and settle their disputes.

enemy's former citadel, is matched by the theme of the psalm."[65] But this hymn was also minted for any occasion when the King judges the nations to exclude and punish tyrants and elevate the righteous. Tremper Longman III notes "a tendency that runs through much of the Psalter: the subduing of reference to specific historical events in order to preserve the immediate relevance of the poem to the cult."[66] The LXX glossator interpreted it as intended for when the Second Temple was built after the captivity (see n. 1).

This liturgical use segues into transforming the psalm into a prophecy, as David, a prophet, fully intended. The praise of the Gentile world is scarcely audible in the old dispensation; that dispensation ended with tyrants ruling a dark world, not with salvation. Then Jesus Christ came and inaugurated a new dispensation. "The people walking in darkness have seen a great light; on those living in the land of deep darkness a light has dawned" (Isa. 9:2). Magi from the east worshiped the child, Christ Jesus, presenting him with their treasures and so proclaiming him king of the Gentiles (Matt. 2:11; cf. Ps. 96:9). The Greeks came to Philip, asking to see Jesus. When he and Andrew told Jesus, Jesus replied, "The hour has come for the Son of Man to be glorified" (John 12:23)—that is to say, his hour had come to be lifted up in glory, to offer himself as the Lamb of God who takes away the sin of the word (John 1:29; 12:23). On the first Palm Sunday, "the whole crowd of disciples began joyfully to praise God in loud voices for all the miracles they had seen: 'Blessed is the king who comes in the name of the Lord!' " (Luke 19:37–38). Today, the God of Israel is praised through his Son on every continent and in every nation (Matt. 28:16–20). Jews and Gentiles daily sing of his glory, beauty, and strength. What strength and beauty Jesus Christ displayed in his career! "The blind receive sight, the lame walk, those who have leprosy are cleansed, the deaf hear, the dead are raised, and the good news is proclaimed to the poor" (Matt. 11:5). What strength and beauty shone forth from him on the mount of transfiguration (Matt. 17:2)! What glory must be ascribed to the crucified and risen Christ (John 12:16)! His apostles turned the world upside down; Gentiles burn their idols; his teachings impact kings.

But the psalm looks beyond today to the time when every knee will bow and every tongue acknowledge that Jesus Christ is Lord (Phil. 2:9–11) and when the whole creation will rejoice. Today, the church is persecuted, and the creation still looks forward to the time when it "will be liberated from its bondage to decay and brought into the freedom and glory of the children of God"

65. Kidner, *Psalms 73–150*, 379.
66. Longman, "Psalm 98," 272.

(Rom. 8:19–22). The psalm's motif of judgment in righteousness also finds fulfillment in the final judgment, when Jesus will judge the world in justice. God has given proof that he appointed Jesus to "judge the world with justice" by raising him from the dead (Acts 17:31). On that set day, the Lord Jesus will be revealed from heaven in blazing fire with his powerful angels (2 Thess. 1:7–10). John saw his coming in judgment in a vision: "I saw heaven standing open and there before me was a white horse, whose rider is called Faithful and True. With justice he judges and wages war. His eyes are like blazing fire, and on his head are many crowns" (Rev. 19:11–12). In sum, the ambiguous Hebrew tenses may describe both earlier epiphanies of God's righteous judgments on the peoples and the final, future judgment by Jesus Christ.

CHAPTER 8

Psalm 97: His Chariots of Wrath
the Deep Thunderclouds Form

PART I. VOICE OF THE PSALMIST: TRANSLATION

By David, when his land is established.[1]

1   *I AM* reigns;
    let the earth be glad;
    let the distant shores rejoice!
2   Clouds[2] and thick darkness are all around him;
    righteousness and justice are the base of his throne.
3   Fire goes before him
    and sets ablaze his foes all around.
4   His lightning bolts lit up[3] the earth-disc;
    the earth saw and writhed.
5   The mountains melted like wax from before *I AM*,
    from before the Lord of all the earth.
6   The heavens proclaimed his righteousness,
    and all the peoples saw[4] his glory.

1. So LXX. MT lacks superscript.
2. Clouds and fog are an extended, opaque mask (E. Jenni, *TLOT*, 2:799, s.v. *'ānān*).
3. The interpretation of the perfective conjugation in vv. 4–6 is disputed. Zenger (Frank-Lothar Hossfeld and Erich Zenger, *Commentary on Psalms 51-100*, trans. Linda M. Maloney, Hermeneia [Minneapolis: Fortress, 2005], 469) interprets it as prophetic, "describing an event yet to come, already determined by God, and now beginning." He supports this interpretation by the parallel *wᵉrā'û* (v. 6b), which he argues must be future (= "and so they will see," see n. 4). In 4b, however, the perfective conjugation is followed by *wattāḥēl* ("and trembled"), the past tense narrative form. This same construction occurs in 8.
4. While it is true that in its twelve other occurrences, *wᵉrā'û* is a *waw*-consecutive construction, the equivalent of an imperfect (i.e., future) conjugation, it could be a *waw*

188

7   All who serve images are put[5] to shame,[6]
        who make their boast in worthless idols;
        all the gods[7] prostrated themselves[8] to him.
8   Zion heard and rejoiced; the daughters of Judah were glad
        on account of your judgments, *I AM*.
9   For[9] you, *I AM*, are high over all the earth;
        you are exalted far above all the gods.
10 You who love *I AM*, hate evil!
        He guards the lives of his faithful;[10]

copulative with past tense (*IBHS*, §32.3). The tense is clearly past in vv. 8–9, which also begins with the suffix (i.e., perfective) conjugation, and probably also in 4. In these verses the perfective conjugation is followed by narrative *waw* (i.e., past tense).

5. Or "Let . . . be put"; or "will be put."

6. Or "are disappointed" (cf. Jer. 51:17); "dismayed, disillusioned, and despairing" (cf. Jer. 49:33); or "frustrated" (cf. Ps. 14:6).

7. The Briggs defend LXX *hoi angeloi* ("the angels"), "for he [the psalmist] would not in one breath call them 'nothings,' and in the next call upon them as exalted persons to worship the supreme God" (Charles Augustus Briggs and Emilie Grace Briggs, *A Critical and Exegetical Commentary on the Book of Psalms*, vol. 2, ICC [1907; repr. Edinburgh: T&T Clark, 1976], 306). But the Briggs fail to understand that "nothingness" refers to their ontological (i.e., actual, as God knows) existence and "worship" refers to their epistemological (i.e., as humans know) existence (see p. 8).

8. Or "Prostrate yourselves . . . all you gods"; or "all the gods will prostrate themselves." Construing the perfective conjugation as past tense (see *IBHS*, §§31.1.d–h), David M. Howard, Jr. (*The Structure of Psalms 93–100*, BJSUCSD 5 [Winona Lake, IN: Eisenbrauns, 1997], 70) explains, "The understanding here is that the statements in 7a–b are dependent on 7c: precisely because all the gods have worshiped (or do worship) YHWH (v. 7c), anyone who puts his trust in worthless idols or images is put to shame, doomed (vv. 7 and 7b)." The indicative mood matches the strophe of vv. 4–9. Also, the inclusio "all the gods" frames 7–9. In 9 "all the gods" is used with the perfective conjugation (*na'ǎlêtā*, "you are exalted"). It is better to interpret the ambiguous *hištaḥǎwû* by this unambiguous parallel than by the ambiguous parallel *yēbōšû*. (The NLT gloss, "for every god must bow to him," is grammatically indefensible.)

9. Or "surely," introducing a quotation: "Surely you . . . far above all gods" (*IBHS*, §39.3.4d).

10. MT is commonly emended to read, "*I AM* loves those who hate evil; he preserves the lives of his faithful ones." Aside from the general preference for MT, the received text is the more difficult reading and cannot be explained away. MT also finds support from the parallels between the first and last lines of the last stanza (vv. 10a and

from the hand of the wicked he delivers them.
11   Light is sown for the righteous,
        and for the upright of heart joy [is sown].
12   Rejoice in *I AM*, you righteous,
        and give grateful praise to his holy name!

Part II. Commentary

I. Introduction

Author

The author is both a temple leader whose hymn admonishes the righteous to "rejoice" (v. 12) and a prophet who admonishes them to "hate evil" (10). He is also a dramaturge who stages a theophany based on a true lightning storm in an unidentified battle. He does so to proclaim that *I AM* is King over heaven and earth. He presents the drama in poetic verse, and at the climax of his poem's parts, he proclaims truths about the King (see "Message" below). The faithful community recognized his hymn as inspired and preserved it as part of holy Scripture.

The Septuagint (LXX) attributes the psalm to David, and there is no reason to deny it (see pp. 13–15). Today, scholars recognize the psalm is based on the imagery of a Baal myth that antedates David by centuries (see pp. 112n64, 133–34). Reflection on those old myths also gives insights into the poet's mind. His hymn depicts *I AM* as a warrior routing his foes, who aim to set up a rival kingdom (v. 3), and this depiction resembles the pattern of the divine warrior motif in the Baal cycles (c. 1400 BC) and other mythologies in the West Semitic world,[11] including "the march of the warrior, the convulsing of nature; the return of the divine warrior to his holy mountain and the assumption of kingship."[12] Similarly, Psalm 97 proclaims "*I AM* reigns" (1a) in conjunction

---

12a; see "Rhetoric" below): Both contain imperatives addressed to those committed to *I AM* and mention him by name (so the ancient versions and most English versions).

11. West Semitic is a term for a language family of which Hebrew is a member. The cultures in which these languages were spoken are related. True Israel borrowed the imagery of these cultures, but not their theology.

12. Richard Hess, *Israelite Religions: An Archaeological and Biblical Survey* (Grand Rapids: Baker Academic, 2007), 160.

with his riding into battle in a storm cloud and routing his enemies (2–3); the earth "quakes" and its mountains "melt" (i.e., erode, v. 5). He returns to his holy mountain and temple where his worshipers praise him (8–9).

In Psalm 97, however, the myth is historicized. The theophany happened in history and serves as an exemplar of the second advent of the Lord Jesus Christ (see "Canonical Context" below). The historical context for its composition, according to the LXX, was "when the land is established" (cf. 2 Sam. 7:8–11a). In other words, King David praises *I AM* for his coming in a storm theophany that enabled David to give Israel a restful homeland in fulfillment of the Abrahamic covenant. This battle is not recorded in the historical books, but see David's war annals in 2 Samuel 8, which describe the fulfillment of the Davidic Covenant.

Form

Poetry

All psalms are poetry, which entails figurative language (see p. 23). K. Lawson Younger argues that the war stories in the book of Joshua wear the garb of ancient Near East military reports, and he documents that these stories commonly use hyperbole.[13] If the prosaic historian uses hyperbole in military reports, how much more likely is a poet to use hyperbole in a poetic account of the Divine Warrior. His hyperboles of the storm enable us to feel its brute force; scientific descriptions would distance us from it.

Proclaiming I AM *as King in Grateful Praise*

Psalm 97 is the third psalm proclaiming "*I AM* reigns/is King" (see 93:1; 96:10). Its typical introductory call to rejoice in conjunction with that proclamation (v. 1), which is followed by supporting evidence (2–9), marks the psalm as a hymn (see p. 7). Typically, the hymn closes with renewed call to praise (12).[14] But whereas the introductory call addresses the Gentile world, the concluding call addresses those "who love *I AM*." The final call, "to give grateful praise," identifies the psalm as a "grateful praise" hymn (see p. 5). As such, it reports

13. K. L. Younger Jr., *Ancient Conquest Accounts: A Study in Ancient Near Eastern and Biblical Writing*, JSOTSup 98 (Sheffield: Sheffield Academic, 1990), 209.

14. H. Gunkel and J. Begrich, *Introduction to the Psalms: The Genres of the Religious Lyric of Israel*, trans. James D. Nogalski (Macon, GA: Mercer University Press, 1998), 40.

God's saving deed. The theophany cannot be harnessed into the scholarly invention of an annual ritual of God's enthronement.

Setting

The theophany occurs on the battlefield. After the battle, the psalmist proclaims "*I AM* is King" at Zion's temple, where God is directly addressed as "you" (vv. 8–9; see pp. 292n4, 296). This victory has been used by God's covenant people for over three millennia and finds its fulfillment in the resurrection of Jesus Christ and its consummation in his Parousia. No topic for the theophany is given, so that the psalm can be used generically. At the time of composition, the distant nations praised God through their nobles in Jerusalem (see Ps. 96). Today, the church, by faith, ascends to heavenly Mount Zion where the song is heard (Heb. 12:22–24).

Rhetoric

On the basis of semantics, form, and rhetoric, Psalm 97 is usually recognized to have four parts of three verses each (1–3, 4–6, 7–9, 10–12). Each of these triplets consists of a single line and a couplet: 1, 2–3; 4–5, 6; 7, 8–9; 10, 11–12. By the same criteria, these verses can be grouped into stanzas, strophes, and units. The imperatives, "hate evil" (10) and "rejoice" (12), markedly separate verses 10–12 as a stanza from 1–9, which, written in the indicative, focus on *I AM*'s theophany in a storm cloud and constitute the first stanza. The first stanza consists of two strophes: a description of the storm (1–6) and varied responses to it (7–9). The first strophe (1–6) consists of two units that are marked by the shift of tense from present tense (1–3) to past (4–6) and by the inclusion of introductory materials in verse 1 beside the eminent description of the theophany in verses 2–3, which are in contrast to the report and reflection on the theophany verses 4–6. The psalm as a whole (1–12), its first stanza (1–9), the first strophe (1–6) and the first unit (1–3) are proportionately reduced. The psalm of twelve verses consists of four parts. Its two stanzas proportionately are verses 1–9 (¾ of the 12) and 10–12 (¼ of the 12). The first stanza (1–9) is divided into two strophes: 1–6 (⅔ of the 9) and 7–9 (⅓ of the 9). The first strophe is divided into two units: 1–3 and 4–6 (each ½ of the 6). Thus, both the numerators and denominators of the fractions are successively reduced by one going from stanza to strophe to unit: the numerators from 3 to 1; the denominators from 4 to 2. So the psalm is a literary artifice that exhibits an exquisite design and balance. Furthermore—as will be noted in the exegesis below—catchwords and associations skillfully unify the psalm's stanzas, strophes, and units.

In this introduction that considers the psalm holistically, we note only the inclusio of God's name ("*I AM*" and "his holy name," its first and last words) and "rejoice." Note, too, the repetition of "righteousness/righteous" (vv. 2, 12). Finally recall that the poet is a dramaturge who brings each of the four parts to a climactic conclusion. The inspired pen of our poet wrote a psalm worthy of the King.

Here is an outline of the psalm's structure:

II. Exegesis

Superscript

See note 1 and "Author" above.

Stanza 1: The Theophany 1–9

Verses 8 and 9 are an indivisible couplet. The chiastically structured catchwords "glad" and "rejoice" thus frame the stanza (vv. 1, 8).

Strophe A: The Theophany and Its Significance 1–6

The synonyms "distant shores" (v. 1) and "all the peoples" (6) and the catchword "righteousness" (2, 6) frame this strophe.

1. Introduction to the Hymn's Motifs 1–3

The chiastic association of "reigns" at the beginning of verse 1 and "throne" at the end of verse 2 unifies verses 1 and 2. Verses 2 and 3 are a couplet (see below).

a) I AM *Is King and Distant Shores Admonished to Rejoice 1*

I AM *reigns*/"is King" (see p. 20). *I AM*, who today wants to be known through his Son (see p. 2), is the eternal King. He first manifested his kingship at creation when he subdued the sea (see Psalm 93). He subsequently manifested his kingship in holy wars, such as in this theophany (see "Canonical Context" below). The Masoretic accents closely link the proclamation "*I AM* reigns" with "let the earth be glad," reinforcing the implication that *I AM*'s rule is the reason the earth should rejoice. The rest of the stanza takes us step by step to the recognition of his glory. *The earth* probably refers to the physical land as well as its inhabitant (cf. Ps. 96:1, 11). *Let . . . be glad* (see 96:11; p. 177). *Distant shores*, a literary gloss for "many coastlands," refers to the many islands and coastlines of the nations bordering the Mediterranean Sea, a synecdoche for the world as Israel knew it.

b) Depiction of Theophany 2-3

This couplet is united by the association of dark clouds (v. 2a) with fire (v. 3a), as when God appeared at Sinai with his law (Exod. 19:16–20; Deut. 4:11; 5:22; cf. Exod. 24:16, 18; 34:5). The divine Lawgiver now enforces his law.

i. *I AM* in Dark Clouds on a Throne of Righteousness and Justice 2

In the biblical world, *clouds* are the domain of divine existence and activity. They are God's veil (Lam. 3:44) and the dust at his feet (Nah. 1:3). So, paradoxically, the storm clouds *all around him* both hide *I AM* and mark his appearance, as when he led Israel in a cloud (Exod. 13:21; 34:5). Sometimes, as in Psalm 97:2, he appears as a warrior in a cloud: "See," says Isaiah, "*I AM* rides on a swift cloud and is coming to Egypt. The idols of Egypt tremble before him" (19:1–2). To the poet, clouds are *I AM*'s war chariot (Pss. 18:11; 68:4; 104:3; Dan. 7:13; Nah. 1:3). *And thick darkness* marks his presence as ominous; he is coming to punish his foes who fight to depose him (cf. Ezek. 34:12; Joel 2:2). The association of the theophany with judgment is confirmed by the parallel *righteousness and justice* (see 96:13). Zenger says that this frequent collocation can be called "saving judicial action: the divine judge judges in order to save, or he saves by judging—and judging according to righteousness and law."[15] The *base* (*məkôn*) denotes a fixed, established place, as in "he set the earth on its foundation (*məkôn*); it can never be moved" (Ps. 104:5; cf. 93:1).

Of his throne (see Ps. 93:2) is the symbol of the Sovereign's rule as warrior, judge, and builder (see p. 4; cf. Ps. 89:14[15]; Prov. 16:12; 20:28). The Egyptologist Helmut Brunner noted that the side view of the Egyptian divine or royal throne became the model for the hieroglyphic character that originally meant "throne base" and then became the Egyptian *ma'at* ("righteousness, truth, right order").[16] Craig Broyles argues that the dark storm clouds and throne reprise, with modification, the holy of holies. At the dedication of the temple, Broyles notes, after the ark had entered the holy of holies, clouds filled the temple and Solomon quoted *I AM* as saying that "he would dwell in thick darkness" (1 Kgs. 8:6–12). Also, Broyles thinks the outer wings of the cherubim provided the mobility and their inner wings formed the throne of *I AM*. He calls attention to Psalm 18:9–14:

15. Hossfeld and Zenger, *A Commentary on Psalms 51–100*, 474.
16. H. Brunner, "Gerechtigkeit als Fundament des Thrones," *VT* 8 (1958): 426–28.

9 He parted the heavens and came down; dark clouds were under his
feet.

10 He mounted the cherubim and flew; he soared on the wings of the
wind.

11 He made darkness his covering, his canopy around him—the dark
rain clouds of the sky.

12 Out of the brightness of his presence clouds advanced, with hail-
stones and bolts of lightning.

13 *I AM* thundered from heaven; the voice of the Most High
resounded.

14 He shot his arrows and scattered the enemy, with great bolts of
lightning he routed them.[17]

ii. Fire Precedes Him and Sets His Foes Ablaze 3

Fire also represents God's presence, as when he passed between the animal
pieces as a blazing torch (Gen. 15:17). He appeared to Moses in a burning bush
(Exod. 3:2), and he led Israel as a pillar of fire to give them light (13:21). He
baptizes in fire (Matt. 3:11), and the Spirit descended in flaming tongues (Acts
2:3). In a number of passages, he uses fire as the instrument of his judicial
punishment of the wicked, often in association with his anger: Burning sulfur
rained down on Sodom and Gomorrah (Gen. 19:24); fire came out from his
presence and consumed Nadab and Abihu (Lev. 10:1-2; Ps. 106:18); his fire
consumed the grumblers (Num. 11:1) and Ahaziah's captains (2 Kgs. 1:10; cf.
Ps. 11:6; Isa. 30:30; Jer. 21:14; Ezek. 20:47[21:3]; Amos 7:4; Matt. 3:11; 18:9, Heb.
10:27). The Lord Jesus will be revealed "from heaven with his mighty angels in
flaming fire" (2 Thess. 1:7; cf. 2 Pet. 3:7; Rev. 8:7, 8). *Goes* [lit. "walks"] *before him*
possibly connotes that the fire serves him, as when it is said, "David walked
before *I AM* in faithfulness" (1 Kgs. 3:6). *And sets ablaze* (cf. Deut. 33:22; Ps.
83:14[15]; Isa. 42:25; Job 41:21[13]; Mal. 4:1[3:19]) is a metonymy for "burns up."
All around describes a scorched-earth policy (cf. Joel 1:19). *His foes* (ṣārāyw)
is generally a designation for "enemy, adversary" which, with the exception
of Esther 7:6, is used for groups, not individuals. Its root (ṣrr) deals with the
harassment and torment engendered by those who oppose *I AM's* kingdom—
both his anointed king and his subjects, to supplant it with a rival kingdom.
Since *I AM* is righteous, these adversaries are the wicked. In short, a righteous
system of ethics demands the elimination of the wicked, who, as a group, seek

17. Craig C. Broyles, *Psalms*, NIBCOT (Peabody, MA: Hendrickson, 1999), 378.

to establish a kingdom not based on *I AM*s character and law. Their defeat is reason to rejoice.

2. Report and Significance of Historical Theophany 4–6

This unit is subtly unified by the switch to the perfect tense, in contrast to the imperfect tense in verses 3 and 7; by the consonance of initial *hes* in 4a, 5a, and 6a (*hē'îrû, hārîm, higgîdû*); and by the inclusio "the earth saw" and "the peoples saw" in 4b and 6b. The unit consists of a couplet that describes the theophany (4–5) and a verse reflecting on its significance (6). The tense switch shifts the focus from a description of what is habitual in war theophany (2–3) to a specific historic theophany in battle. This second unit of the first strophe is linked with the first unit (1–3) by "*I AM*" (1), the antecedent of "his [lightning]" (4); the catch-phrase "before him" (3a) and "from before *I AM*" (5b); and the association of fire and lightning in a storm theophany. "Lightning is fire on a supernatural scale with a supernatural purpose."[18] The sutures are so subtle that the strophe (1–6) almost appears seamless.

a) Report of Theophany and I AM's Sovereignty 4–5

i. Lightning and Earthquakes 4

His lightning bolts bears witness to both the Creator's direct involvement with his creation and his power and control over nature. Moreover, "in several biblical accounts lightning is the divine tool of choice because it is swift, precise, [and] unambiguous" and creates panic.[19] Elsewhere, King David petitions God: "Send forth lightning and scatter the enemy; shoot your arrows and rout them" (Ps. 144:6; cf. Pss. 18:14[15]; 77:17[18]). The lightning storm is so intense and expansive that the bolts of lightning *lit up the earth-disc* (see Ps. 93:1). The scene reprises the crossing of the Red Sea: "Your thunder was heard in the whirlwind, your lightning [bolts] lit up the world; the earth trembled and quaked" (Ps. 77:18). *The earth* in parallel with "the earth-disc" probably refers to what we would call the planet earth. The personified earth *saw* a lightning storm so intense that it *writhed* in the pangs of an earthquake.[20] If the earth

18. Leland Ryken, James C. Wilhoit, and Tremper Longman III, eds., *Dictionary of Biblical Imagery* (Downers Grove, IL: IVP Academic, 1998), 512.

19. Ryken, Wilhoit, and Longman, *Dictionary of Biblical Imagery*, 513.

20. Construed as a past definite perfect. "Writhing in pain" may denote mental

itself trembled in fear before the Warrior riding on the storm, how much more will mortals?

ii. Mountains Melted Away before the Lord of the Earth 5

From before I AM signals the continuation of the theophany. *The mountains* are remote, rugged, immense, inaccessible and thought of as ancient and everlasting. They are the standard of ancient existence (Deut. 33:15), against which God's everlasting existence is compared (Ps. 90:2). "The most striking images of destructiveness of nature in the Psalms are the shaking of mountains in earthquakes (Ps. 46:2-3) or volcanic eruptions (Ps. 104:32)."[21] The figure *melted like wax* probably refers to erosion from heavy rains. The repetition *from before* adds the reflection that one so powerful that the earth quakes and mountains melt before him is indeed *the Lord of all the earth*.

b) Significance of Theophany 6

i. The Heavens Proclaimed His Righteousness 6a

Tyrants abuse their sovereign power, but the Lord of all—over all gods and human rulers—uses his omnipotence to establish righteousness. Our dramaturge brings his depiction of the theophany to a climactic conclusion with the heavens proclaiming his righteousness and all people seeing his glory. *The heavens*, like the "earth," refers to the physical heavens. *Proclaimed* refers to *the vitally important message* of *his righteousness* (see v. 2). The heavens, from where God descended on wings of the dark clouds and from which he shoots his lightning bolts, are heralds of the hidden God's revelation of his righteousness through the salvific storm. The next strophe of this drama (vv. 7-9) presents the response of all the earth to the heralds' proclamation.

ii. All Peoples Saw *I AM's* Glory 6b

All the peoples (see v. 10) refers to the foreign nations who *saw* (see v. 4) the theophany. Perhaps the foes consisted of mercenaries from many nations, like

---

anguish in witness of God's judgments (Isa. 23:5; Ezek. 30:4; Joel 2:6; Mic. 4:10) and/or writhing or trembling in terror (Pss. 77:16[17]; 96:9; 114:7; Jer. 5:22).

21. Ryken, Wilhoit, and Longman, *Dictionary of Biblical Imagery*, 573, s.v. "mountain."

Assyria's imperial army that besieged Jerusalem (cf. Mic. 4:11).[22] *His glory* (see p. 186) is a metonymy for the events of the theophany (vv. 2–5), and the response of all people to it is to give *I AM* glory.

Strophe B: Responses to Theophany 7–9

"All the gods," the last words of verses 7 and 9, frame this strophe. The strophe, composed of three tricola, describes the different theological effects the theophany has upon idolaters and Judah: shame on the one hand, praise on the other. The idolaters are embarrassed because their nature deities prostrated themselves before *I AM*, who is Lord of all. Verses 8 and 9 are a couplet bound together grammatically by medial "because/for" (cf. n. 9) and rhetorically by the unique direct address to *I AM* in these two verses: "your judgments, *I AM*," the last words of verse 8, and "you, *I AM*," the first words of 9.

The second strophe (vv. 7–9) is linked to verses 4–6 by the antithesis of "glory," the last word of 6, and "shame," the first word of 7, in connection with their associated subjects, "all peoples" and "all idolaters." The catchword "all the earth" (5 and 9) also binds them. "The heavens proclaimed" (6) can be associated with "Zion heard" (8). The strophe is connected with vv. 1–3 by the catchwords "justice" and "judgment" (2 and 8) in addition to the stanza's framing words "rejoice" and "be glad."

1. All the Gods Worship *I AM* and Their Worshipers Put to Shame 7

All who serve are slaves (see Ps. 100:2). The poet probably chose this nomenclature to condemn them for serving worthless images and not the true "Lord of all the earth" (v. 5). *Images* were objects of worship in preexilic Israel (2 Kgs. 17:41; 2 Chr. 33:22; Mic. 5:13). They were carved or cast and in various shapes (Deut. 4:16f.). Apostate Israelites made images of *I AM*, as at Dan (cf. Judg. 17–18), and even with his consort Asherah, as found in the caravansary at Kuntillet Ajrud.[23] Idols could be sculpted from various materials, such as wood and stone, or cast from metal into various shapes (Deut. 4:16f.). They were sometimes overlaid with gold or silver (Deut. 7:25). Nevertheless, the image, such as Aaron's golden calf, was regarded as being made divine in heaven.[24] In

22. Bruce K, Waltke, *A Commentary on Micah* (Grand Rapids: Eerdmans, 2007), 250, 258.

23. Hess, *Israelite Religions*, 284.

24. Hess, *Israelite Religions*, 156.

preexilic Israel and today, these nature deities give way to anything a person depends upon for life, security, or significance (cf. Ps. 49:6[7]), be it wealth, self, pleasure, or renown. Calvin noted: "We all invent idols in infinite number."[25] Daniel Wu notes that when people *are put to shame*, "it is often difficult to distinguish between anthropological and psychological shame." He suggests, "'Embarrassment' may helpfully capture the span of meaning across emotional and social categories." Finally, he notes, "Shame—whether social, psychological, or both—can be seen to fall under the wider umbrella of disappointment."[26] To intensify their embarrassment, the idolaters are further characterized as those *who make their boast*. They talked with excessive pride and self-satisfaction about their possessions; to wit, they boast *in their worthless idols* (see 96:5)! *All the gods*, who are like the worthless money of a Monopoly game, *prostrated themselves* (see n. 8; Ps. 96:9) *to him*. The bowing of the nature deities of heaven and earth, who ontologically have no existence but who existentially are worshiped by depraved humans, symbolizes their recognition and acceptance of *I AM* as their Lord (v. 5) and King (v. 1) after his coming in the lightning storm and the convulsions of the earth and mountains.

2. Judah Rejoices 8–9

The dramaturge brings his drama to a climax by citing a hymn of Zion (v. 9).

a) I AM's Judgments 8

In the Psalter, *I AM's* city on earth, representing his heavenly city, is often called *Zion*. The name is probably of pre-Israelite origin, but its etymology is uncertain. Originally, it was the name of the Jebusite hill or fortress on the southeast hill of Jerusalem (2 Sam. 5:7ff.). After David had placed the ark on the northeast hill of the city, the southern hill came to be known as the City of David, or the "Ophel," and Zion came to designate the hill where the ark and temple were located (Ps. 132:13; Isa. 10:12; Mic. 4:2) or by synecdoche the whole city (Isa. 10:24; Jer. 3:14; Amos 6:1) and/or by metonymy its inhabitants (Isa. 1:27; 33:5). In Psalm 97:8, it refers to the worshipers on the temple mountain. *Heard* gaps the object of the report—namely, the awesome theophany. Thus,

25. John Calvin, *Sermons on the Ten Commandments*, ed. Benjamin W. Farley (Grand Rapids: Baker, 1980), 66.
26. Daniel Y. Wu, *Honor, Shame, and Guilt: Social-Scientific Approaches to the Book of Ezekiel*, BBRSup 14 (Winona Lake, IN: Eisenbrauns, 2016), 103.

the temple city *rejoiced* (see v. 1; 96:11), and she did so in connection with her boasting about *I AM*, as verse 9 shows. She rejoiced because her God is greater than all gods, and so the gates of Hades cannot prevail against her. There will be an end to tyranny and injustice. *The daughters of Judah* is a personification of the other towns and cities in the royal tribe of Judah, such as those enumerated in Micah 1:10–16, including heavily fortified Lachish.[27] *Were glad* (see v. 1; 96:11) is another synonym connected with praise. Westermann, commenting on *hll* Piel ("to praise"), says, "The many parallel verbs of celebration and rejoicing (*gîl, rnn, śmḥ*) demonstrate that this praise of God can take place only in joy. . . . One cannot, therefore, hear the call to praise God in the Old Testament without hearing the encompassed call to joy."[28] Conversely, one cannot hear of temple joy and gladness without hearing the associated call to praise. Zion's and Judah's celebratory joy and gladness are not jingoistic but *on account of your* righteous *judgments* (see 97:2), which I AM accomplished by routing his wicked foes (see v. 3).

> b) I AM *Is Exalted above All Gods* 9

Over all the earth reprises "Lord of all the earth" (v. 5b) and its parallel polar opposite, *above all the gods*, reprises "all the gods worship him" (7b). *For* (see n. 9) expresses the cause more distinctly and forcibly than its synonym "on account of" (v. 8). In the clause *you, I AM, are high over all, 'elyôn* functions as an adjective (cf. Deut. 26:19), not a name for God ("the Most High"; cf. Pss. 91:1; 92:1[2]). This adjective was chosen for the phrase (*'elyôn 'al kol*) over other synonyms, such as *mārôm* (see Ps. 92:8), for the pun with the parallel *na'ªlêtā 'al kol* (*you are exalted . . . above all*). The scalar adverb "very" (see 92:5[6]; 93:5; 96:4), glossed *far* [above] to accommodate the English idiom, is appropriate in reference to "gods," who were regarded as heavenly deities above the earth.

Stanza II: Admonitions to Faithful to Hate Evil and Rejoice 10–12

The final stanza brings the psalm to its climactic conclusion. The theophany (vv. 1–9) added substance to faith. The concluding imperatives add ardor to

27. In Hebrew, all nouns are inflected: either marked as feminine or unmarked. "Since the Hebrew word for city is inflected as feminine, poets were led to personify cities as females" (e.g. "daughters"; *IBHS*, §§6.4.1c,d).
28. C. Westermann, *TLOT*, 1:372, s.v. *hll* Piel.

virtue and embolden those who love *I AM* to fidelity. David adorns the covenant community with accolades: "those who love *I AM*," "the faithful," "the righteous," and "the upright of heart." In other words, they are those who fulfill the basic covenant command "to love *I AM*" (Deut. 6:5), who by persevering in hating evil prove that they are faithful. So, they are those who salt the earth with righteousness. The prophet emboldens them to fidelity by assuring them of their deliverance from the wicked (v. 10b); of their bright future (11a) and "joy" (11b). The references to "love" (10a) and "heart" (11b) show that what is at stake is personhood, not merely performance; disposition rather than mere deeds; character behind and beyond conduct; love, not legalism. The catchword "rejoice" (the first word of v. 12), its nominal derivative "joy" (the last word of 11), and the catchword "righteous" (11a, 12a) unite verses 11–12 into a couplet.

Strophe A: Admonition to Hate Evil; I AM Delivers Godly from Wicked 10

Although not grammatically linked by a logical particle, verse 10b ("*I AM* watches over the faithful") functions as the reason to heed the admonition "hate evil."[29] *You who love* designates those with emotional feelings of strong desire for I AM that flow out of their perceptions and so cause them to go after (Jer. 2:25b), seek (Prov. 8:17), run after (Isa. 1:23), cleave to (Deut. 11:22; 30:20; Prov. 18:24), and continue to be faithful to their beloved. They have a passionate desire to follow *I AM*. *Hate*, by contrast, expresses a feeling of passionate dislike or hostility toward someone or something and so causes the people who hate to distance themselves from the hated person or thing. On the surface, the command is tautological, for lovers of *I AM* by nature hate evil. However, it is "an encouraging admonition to fidelity"[30] and may imply that there is temptation to apostatize to preserve one's life. A popular Christian hymn captures the truth that mortals are "Prone to wander, Lord I feel it; prone to leave the God I love." *Evil* here means moral behavior that injures others (Ps. 15:3; cf. 91:10). Stoebe says, in connection with its antonym "good," it basically means "what harms life, not what benefits it."[31] Righteous is here defined not by positive virtues but by the negative of rejecting destruc-

29. NIV adds the logical particle "for he guards."
30. F. Delitzsch, *Psalms,* trans. Francis Bolton, Keil and Delitzsch Commentary on the Old Testament 5 (London: T&T Clark, 1866–91; repr., Peabody, MA: Hendrickson, 1996), 627.
31. Stoebe, *TLOT,* 2:491, s.v. *ṭôb.*

tive attitudes and action. *He guards* (see 91:11) *the lives* (*npš*; see Ps. 103:1) *of his faithful* (*ḥᵃsîdāyw*). The root *ḥsd* has two concomitant ideas: loyalty to a person or a group and love for them. The *ḥāsîd* is one who is "faithful" to God (2 Sam. 22:26; Ps. 89:19[20]) and "devoted" to him (Ps. 86:2); in the plural they are equated with "those who made a covenant with me." In other words, it is a synonym for "those who love *I AM*" and so returns to the positive attitudes and actions of the righteous. *From the hand* (see 95:4) *of the wicked* (see 91:8) *he delivers them* (see 91:3).

Strophe B: Admonition to Righteous to Rejoice 11–12

1. Righteous Rewarded with Light and Joy 11

Light here refers to physical light. It is not figurative of goodness in contrast to evil (Job 24:13; 2 Cor. 4:6), but it symbolizes blessings.[32] *Is sown* is a di-

32. Without trying to be exhaustive, light symbolizes manifold blessings: (a) *God's hidden presence*: God creates light (Gen. 1:3; Ps. 74:16) and covers himself "with light as with a garment" (Ps. 104:2). (b) *Life*: Job laments that he was born and curses his birthday and the morning stars with darkness (Job 3); it is said "the light of a lamp will never shine in you again" (Rev. 18:23); and death is described as "the land of gloom and chaos; where light is as darkness" (Job 10:22). (c) *Overcoming chaos*: God created light and separated it from the primeval darkness (Gen. 1:4). (d) *Safety*: Job pictures deposed rulers who "grope in the dark without light" (Job 12:25), and, when an angel rescues Peter from prison, a light shines in the cell (Acts 12:7). (e) *Guidance*: The star guided the magi to the house where Jesus was born (Matt 2:9f.). (f) *Knowledge of Jesus*: "For God, who said, 'Let light shine out of darkness,' made his light shine in our hearts to give us the light of the knowledge of God's glory displayed in the face of Christ" (2 Cor. 4:6); and, "In him was life, and that life was the light of all mankind. The light shines in the darkness, and the darkness has not overcome it" (John 1:4f.). (g) *Blessing*: The Egyptians were enshrouded in darkness while Israel had light where they dwelt (Exod. 10:23). (h) *Renewed hope*: Light dawned when Jacob arose from wrestling with the angel at night (Gen. 32:31) and when Jesus arose from the dead. (i) *Joy, sweetness, pleasure*: The Preacher says: "Light is sweet, and it pleases the eyes to see the sun" (Eccl. 11:7); Elihu says: "I shall live to enjoy the light of life" (Job 33:28); Ps. 97:11 sets "light" parallel to "joy." (j) *Salvation*: "Giving joyful thanks to the Father, who has qualified you to share in the inheritance of his holy people in the kingdom of light. For he has rescued us from the dominion of darkness and brought us into the kingdom of the Son he loves" (Col. 1:12f.). (k) *Righteousness*: "The light of the righteous shines brightly, but the lamp of the wicked is snuffed out" (Prov. 13:9; cf. Matt. 6:22f.).

vine passive. Robert Alter comments: "The delicate agricultural image of light sown—presumably to bear refulgent fruit—is an elegant counterpart of the fierce fire that burns up God's enemies and to the lightning that makes the earth shake."[33] Moreover, that refulgent fruit is pregnant with fulfillment. *For the righteous* (see v. 2). *And for the upright* (see Ps. 92:15[16]) *of heart* (see Ps. 95:8) *joy* (*śimḥâ*; see Ps. 100:2) is sown.

2. Admonition to Rejoice and Give Grateful Praise 12

The righteous are now to enter by faith into the joy of their destiny (cf. Ps. 95). *Rejoice* (see v. 1) *you righteous* (see vv. 2, 11). *In* I AM is shorthand for his extraordinary deeds in creation and salvation history and for his qualities of strength with righteousness and justice (see v. 2). When married, strength and righteousness are sublime; when divorced, righteousness is weak and strength is hideous. *And give grateful praise* (see Ps. 92:1[2]) *to his holy name* (*zēker*, usually "memory"). *Zēker* seems to be equivalent to *šēm* ("name") as in Hos 12:5[6]: "*I AM* God Almighty, *I AM* is his name [*zikrô*]!" But in Exodus 3:15, it is differentiated from *šēm*: "This is my name [*šᵉmî*]. . . and this is my memory [*zikrî*]." The full meaning seems to be "the name by which *I AM* is remembered." In Proverbs 10:7, the two nouns are used in parallel: "The memory of the righteous is used in blessings, but the name of the wicked is blotted out." Denial of a person's name is denial of a person's fame. God's holy memorial name denotes the active cognitive occupation of retaining and reviving impressions of his preternatural and supernatural attributes and deeds. By using God's name, worshipers show their identification with Israel's God. Today, God wants to be known and remembered by the name of his Son, Jesus Christ. The name of the Conqueror of sin and death will be remembered forever.

PART III. VOICE OF THE CHURCH IN RESPONSE

I. Robert Bellarmine (1542–1621)

Robert Bellarmine draws out the sacramental and liturgical roles of the Psalms. He begins his explanation of Psalm 97 by echoing its two basic themes:

---

33. Robert Alter, *The Book of Psalms: A Translation with Commentary* (New York: Norton, 2007), 343.

This psalm admits of two literal explanations. Some refer it to the kingdom of God absolutely; others to the kingdom of Christ after his resurrection. Read according to the first, the meaning of this verse is, "The Lord hath reigned." The Lord God is the true and supreme King, and all other kings are but his servants; therefore "let the earth rejoice; let many islands be glad." . . . In the second sense, the meaning is, Christ our Lord, who at one time humbly appeared before the kings of this world, for judgment, "hath reigned," for "all power on earth and in heaven hath been given unto Him," so that He is subject to no one, nor can anyone claim any authority over Him, but, on the contrary, He governs all as "Prince of the kings of the earth, as King of kings, and Lord of lords"; and therefore "let the earth rejoice, let many islands be glad," because the Lord, who has got possession of His Kingdom, has let Himself down to be our brother, though He is our God, by having created us, and our Lord, by having redeemed us."[34]

Bellarmine has clearly and plainly explained the first verse of Psalm 97.

With respect to the next six verses, Bellarmine continues to distinguish these two basic themes. His inference in verse 7 is that all worshipers of idols should be confounded and ashamed. For the angels adore the supreme God, and the prophets prove why idols should be forbidden. The word "again" applies to Christ's second coming. Verses 8 and 9 thus explain the cause for rejoicing, and the conclusion beginning in verse 10 is the exhortation for God's people to live a holy life. So Bellarmine concludes simply with two Scriptures: "It is God's will that you should be sanctified" (1 Thess. 4:3); and "Be holy, for I am holy" (Lev. 11:44; 1 Peter 1:16).[35]

II. Jonathan Edwards (1703–1758)

Jonathan Edwards interprets the imagery of Psalm 97 as expressive of "the uncontainable God"; his goodness surpasses all our imagination. He links verse 2 ("Clouds and thick darkness are all around him; righteousness and justice are the base of his throne") to Psalm 18:11: "He made darkness his secret place; his canopy around Him was dark waters and thick clouds of the skies." As Edwards

34. Saint Robert Bellarmine, *A Commentary on the Books of Psalms*, trans. John O'Sullivan (Dublin: Aeterna, 2015), 455.

35. Robert Bellarmine, *A Commentary on the Books of Psalms*, 458–60.

explains, "God is so great, that He is infinitely above all comprehension; and therefore it is unreasonable of us to quarrel with his dispensations, because they are so mysterious . . . for it is fit that God should dwell in thick darkness, or in the light which no man can approach, which no man has seen or can see."[36] But "quarreling with his dispensations" is precisely what John Nelson Darby and the followers of the Romantic-movement "Dispensationalism" would do in the mid-nineteenth century.

Bridging the generation between Edwards and the Darby was the sanity of the Scots theologians, such as Andrew A. Bonar, following a worthy Presbyterian heritage of Scots theologians such as John Boston, Murray McCheyne and Matthew Henry. With Edwards, they all shared an animating optimism about cosmic redemption linked with the restoration of the Jews as the people of God to the Promised Land. Edwards's immensely influential 1774 tract *An Humble Attempt* was the basis for the later Scottish revival movements as well as for what Nathan Hatch calls "civil millennialism" in America during the French and Indian War.[37]

III. Andrew A. Bonar (1758–1821)

Andrew Bonar focuses on the theme of Christ and the church in the Psalms. He begins by affirming the Messiah "*has come* in glory; he is not merely expected and anticipated." Psalm 97 is thus a song about "the effects of his coming in the ruin of his foes and idols."[38]

> From age to age, the heavens seemed silently to hear, as if almost indifferent to the cry of sin; but not so any longer. . . . Angels who were present, and who adore Him at Bethlehem, at his first Coming, are again adoring. . . . But specially his saints, who have long prayed and waited, now find they have not waited in vain; and hence the exhortation in verse 10, and the promise in verse 11. . . .

36. Jonathan Edwards quoted in David P. Barshinger, *Jonathan Edwards and the Psalms: A Redemptive-Historical Vision of Scripture* (Oxford: Oxford University Press, 2014), 102.

37. Nathan O. Hatch, "The Origins of Civil Millennialism in America: New England Clergymen, War with France, and the Revolution," *William and Mary Quarterly*, 3rd ser., 31 (1974): 408f.; see Barshinger, *Jonathan Edwards and the Psalms*, 135.

38. Andrew A. Bonar, *Christ and the Church in the Book of Psalms* (New York: Robert Carter & Brothers, 1860), 290.

Into the furrows made by the plough of affliction and temptation, God casts the seeds of after-joy. Christ, "the Righteous One," is first partaker of this harvest of joy, as abundant as were his tears, his woes, his sorrows—and joy is synonymous with "*light*," because of light's cheerfulness, and because the rich flood of rays from the sun may be emblematic of the gifts and blessings to be poured on the Righteous One and his members. . . .

All this blessedness, as the very hour of judgment comes on idols and idolaters, may well call forth the rejoicing with which our psalm begins and ends. And the "*holiness*" of verse 12 may remind us that all this joy is the result of Jehovah having at length introduced his own holiness into a fallen world. It is a blessed song concerning

The Advent of the Messiah, and its results to earth.[39]

Bonar is very skilled at communicating and sharing the exuberance he has for divine joy.

IV. John Nelson Darby (1800–1882)

How sharp a contrast to Bonar is the spirit of John Nelson Darby! Darby was the founder of one branch of the Plymouth Brethren, an evangelical reform movement of the Church of England that began in the 1830s. He was the Irish exponent of dispensationalism, doing exactly what Edwards had said could not be done: "quarreling with God's dispensations" in all their mystery. In his *Practical Reflections on the Psalms,* Darby eliminates all commentary on Psalms 95 to 102. He writes, "[These] psalms . . . I do not dwell upon, because they are the actual coming of the Lord in judgment, not the exercise of the heart in awaiting it." That is, they belong to a "different dispensation" from what we are living in and hence have no relevance to us as Christians. It is in a future dispensation that "He [God] will actually come in clouds from heaven, as Ps. 97 predicts, but that is not now!"[40] This approach to Scripture skews all of Darby's biblical interpretation—perhaps more than any other serious expositor in reception hermeneutics! As a contemporary Greek scholar, he was well educated, but

---

39. Bonar, *Christ and the Church*, 291–92.

40. John Nelson Darby, *Practical Reflections on the Psalms* (London: Robert L. Allan, 1870), 253–54.

his approach illustrates how Romanticism was gaining influence in both the nineteenth and twentieth centuries and is a prime example of how we are all influenced by the prevailing culture we live under—like "a sacred canopy" according to the sociologist Peter Berger.[41]

V. The Modern French Existentialists

In contrast to Darby are the modern French Christian existential scholars such as Paul Beauchamp (1924–2001), who sharpens the contrast between "night and day" in his commentary on the Psalms,[42] and André Chouraqui (1917–2007), whose sweep of the Living Word of God over all cosmogonies is a context with no horizons.[43] As Chouraqui puts it, "As a celebration of the light at the dawn of day, so the psalmist celebrates at the dawn of creation, the work of its Creator."[44] Both translate Psalm 97 as an eschatological hymn describing an ancient theophany with God as Judge. Both scholars interpret theophanies as a genre promoted by the postexilic period and associated with the Assyrian, Persian and later invasions of Israel. Verses 7–9 describe the joy of Israel in the face of the destruction of idols. The last section (vv. 10–12) describes the revelation of divine light, which illumines the joy of the just.

The earth is exalted, as in Psalm 96:11, because it is viewed as a living force of God's creative acts (v. 12). Psalm 97:2 is an allusion to the epiphany of Moses within the pillar of cloud (Exod. 33:7–11). That same "cloud" which had guided Israel through the wilderness still continues to guide His people. But compared to Psalm 18:7–15[8–16] and Habakkuk 3:2–15, the epiphany of Psalm 97 is much shorter. The bare message of the Psalm is sufficient to declare that God is Master of all nature and, by extension, over all the affairs of humanity. The fire that burnt up Gog and Magog still destroys all idols and all God's foes (v. 3). The light that illumined the Exile still continues to light the way of God's people (v. 4). The mountains in verse 5, which are a metaphor for human stability, are not so with God since they "melted like wax before him." The resonant praise of the "Elohims" is echoed by the glory given to God by

41. Peter Berger, *The Sacred Canopy* (Garden City: Doubleday, 1967).

42. Paul Beauchamp, *Psaumes Nuit et Jour* (Paris: Editions du Seuil, 1980).

43. I have consulted the Portuguese translation of André Chouraqui, *A Biblia Livores, Salmos,* trans. Paulo Neves, vol. 2 (Rio de Janeiro: Imago, 1998).

44. Chouraqui, *Salmos,* 187.

all mankind in verse 6. There is a comprehensiveness to the "images" or idols of verse 7, whether they be of gold and silver, or are sex or violence or anything that would pollute the universe. In verse 8, "Zion" refers to all the cities of Judah and all their village populations, who also rejoice. For *I AM* reigns over all. He is exalted above all "Elohims." The implacable hatred of evil is basic to the love of God (v. 10); indeed, the qualification of the messianic servant was to "hate iniquity and love righteousness." For love, joy, and righteousness are all on the same continuum—much more than we usually think (v. 11). Finally, to "praise his holy name" is to dwell in the sanctuary of *I AM*, as Moses did, who was bidden to act as one of His messengers (v. 12; see Exod. 3:15).

Part IV. Conclusion

I. Literary Context

In Psalm 96, the nations were commanded to confess *I AM* as King and so glorify him (96:7–10); in Psalm 97 the idols of the nations worship him. Psalm 96 left off with "let the earth be glad" and with the promise that *I AM* the King is coming to judge the world in righteousness (13); Psalm 97 begins with "let the earth be glad" and reports that *I AM* comes in a storm.

II. Message

Though a hymn, the psalm contains four imperatives: (a) The nations are to rejoice (v. 1), and (b) the righteous are to rejoice (v. 12). The latter should also (c) hate evil (v. 10a) and (d) give grateful praise (v. 12b). In essence, there are two kinds of admonition. Three of the imperatives pertain to the liturgy ("rejoice in grateful praise") and one pertains to ethics ("hate evil"). The rest of the hymn gives reasons for these admonitions: in a nutshell, "*I AM* is King," the bold proclamation that opens the psalm. The rest of the psalm unpacks that proclamation in the poet's dramaturgy of a theophany. The presentation of *I AM* as the Divine Warrior follows the pattern of ancient West Semitic myths (see "Author" above).

The dramaturge brings the depictions of the theophany to climactic conclusions. The first unit closes in verse 3 with *I AM* incinerating the foes who would supplant his laws with their own, such as Islam's sharia or the secular rulings of the US Supreme Court.

The first strophe closes in verse 6 with the heavens declaring that the Warrior is righteous and all the peoples seeing his glory. The theme of his righteousness pervades the hymn. Metaphorically enthroned on righteousness and justice (v. 2a), *I AM* descends on the wings of the cherubim and in the dark cloud to deliver the righteous from the wicked. He disempowers their worthless gods (7) but rewards the righteous with life (10) and light (11). In sum, the God of Zion is also the God of Sinai, as Jon Levenson cogently argues.[45] Because he judges according to Sinai, Zion rejoices (8).

The first stanza is drawn to its conclusion in verse 9 with Zion's confession that *I AM* is exalted over all the earth and far above all gods. The motif of his sovereignty also permeates the psalm. Lightning bolts from the dark cloud lit up the earth, and the heavens declared his righteousness; on earth the ancient mountains melted "before the Lord of all the earth" (v. 5) and all peoples saw his glory. In sum, *I AM* extends his judgments to the ends of the earth and so also extends the boundaries of his righteous kingdom.

Paradoxically, the cloud and fire reveal the transcendent One's immanence on earth while the blackness of the cloud preserves his mystery. He acts according to the good pleasure of his will.

III. Canonical Context

Prior to this theophany, albeit apart from a theophany, fire rained down on Sodom, and fire consumed the apostate priests Nadab and Abihu, for offering unauthorized fire before *I AM*.[46]

This theophany, like others, describes God's sudden appearance and his act of leading his people to military victory (cf. Deut. 33:2; Judg. 5:4-5; Hab. 3:3-4). There is also an eschatological dimension to this theophany. *I AM* is staged as ruling over all the earth: *All* the peoples see his glory (v. 6), *all* those who serve idols are put to shame (7a), and *all* the gods worship him (7b). But we do not yet see him ruling all people, as the psalm tacitly acknowledges by its promise of deliverance and by its admonition to the righteous to persevere

---

45. Jon D. Levenson, *Sinai and Zion: An Entry into the Jewish Bible* (New York: HarperCollins, 1987).

46. Hess (*Israelite Religions*, 113) suggests based on a text of Emar in North Syria (c. 1350 BCE) that Nadab and Abihu were following a West Semitic ritual in which priestly figures used a torch on the final day of the installation, when they went to meet the god and live in the temple.

and hate evil (10). The report of and reflection on *I AM*'s universal rule is a prolepsis (see pp. 17–18).

This particular cloud and fire theophany that eliminates the paradoxically godless idolaters and triumphs over their rival kingdoms is a foreshadowing of God's coming in Christ. In Christ's first advent, he triumphed over Satan's kingdom by removing sin through his blood on the hard wood of the cross and by swallowing death in his resurrection. He began his church by descending in flaming tongues to depict that their testimony would triumph over pagan idolatry. Christ's final victory over all that is alienated from God will occur at his second advent. Then, as Paul taught the Thessalonians:

> God is just. He will pay back trouble to those who trouble you and give relief to you who are troubled, and to us as well. This will happen when the Lord Jesus is revealed from heaven in blazing fire with his powerful angels. He will punish those who do not know God and do not obey the gospel of our Lord Jesus. They will be punished with everlasting destruction and shut out from the presence of the Lord and from the glory of his might. (2 Thess. 1:6–9)

Then every knee will bow and every tongue confess that Jesus Christ is Lord (Phil 2:9f.), and God will completely crush Satan under the church's feet (Rom. 16:20).

John saw a third advent: "the Holy City, the new Jerusalem, coming down out of heaven from God." And God said to him: "It is done. I am the Alpha and the Omega, the Beginning and the End" (Rev. 21:2, 6). Will the Son of Man find a faithful preacher of Psalm 97 when he comes?

CHAPTER 9

Psalm 98: A Divine Warrior Victory Song

Part I. Voice of the Psalmist: Translation

A psalm by David.[1]

1 Sing to *I AM* a new song for the wonders *I AM*[2] has done!
     His right hand and his holy arm[3] have gotten him victory.[4]

2 *I AM* has made known his salvation;
     in the sight of the nations he has revealed his righteousness.

3 He remembered his love to Jacob[5]
     and his faithfulness to the house of Israel;
     all the ends of the earth have seen the salvation of our God.

4 Shout for joy to *I AM*, all the earth!
     Burst forth with rejoicing[6] and make music;

5 Make music to *I AM* with the lyre,
     with the lyre and the sound of music!

6 With trumpets and the sound of the ram's horn—
     shout for joy before the King, *I AM*!

7 Let the sea roar, and its fullness!

1. MT has the superscript "a psalm." LXX adds to it "by David."

2. Following LXX. MT probably omitted this second YHWH ("*I AM*") due to homoeoteleuton occasioned by the final *he* at the end of *ʿāśâ* (written consonantally as *ʿśh*, "has done").

3. *Arm* includes the shoulders (cf. BDB, p. 285, s.v. *zᵉrôaʿ*). By contrast, A. S. van der Woude (*TLOT*, 1:392, s.v. *zərôaʿ*), M. Dreytza (*NIDOTTE*, 1:146, s.v. *zᵉrôaʿ*) and *HALOT* (1:280, s.v. *zᵉrôaʿ*) define it as "forearm." Their citations, however, are not convincing, as the Heb. *yād* includes the forearm (see Ps. 95:4).

4. The same Heb. word is glossed "salvation" in vv. 2, 3.

5. LXX, not MT, adds "to Jacob," a common parallel to "house of Jacob/Israel" (cf. Isa. 46:3; Jer. 2:4; 5:15, 20; Mic. 1:5; 3:1).

6. Construing *piṣḥû wᵉrannᵉnû* as a hendiadys (*HALOT*, 2:953, s.v. *pṣḥ*).

Let the earth-disc [resound] and those dwelling in it!
8   Let the ocean currents clap their hands!
Let the mountains in unison rejoice
9   before *I AM*! For he comes[7] to judge the earth.
He will judge[8] the earth-disc in righteousness
and the peoples with equity.

PART II. COMMENTARY

I. Introduction

Author and Date

To Masoretic Text's superscript "a psalm," the Septuagint (LXX) adds "by David." The LXX is more credible in the light of its other superscripts in Book IV of the Psalter (see pp. 13–15). Psalm 98 has such striking resemblances to Psalm 96 that some think "they may even have come from the same hand" (see "Canonical Context" below).[9] If Psalm 96 is by David (see p. 167), so probably is Psalm 98. Many commentators, however, date these two psalms to the postexilic period because of their intertextualities with Second Isaiah (Isaiah 40–66), but as A. A. Anderson rightly comments, "This similarity could be explained in many different ways."[10] The psalmist refers to *I AM* as "our God" and so reckons himself a member of God's family and speaks on its behalf (see v. 3).

Form and Rhetoric

Poetry

The genre title, "a psalm," means a sacred poem set to music (see pp. 25, 107). As in Psalm 96, the poet favors both the personification of nature (v. 8) and

7. Or "is coming" (see Psalm 96:13; p. 166n6).
8. Or "he judges."
9. David M. Howard, Jr., *The Structure of Psalms 93–100*, BJSUCSD 5 (Winona Lake, IN: Eisenbrauns, 1997), 178.
10. A. A. Anderson, *The Book of Psalms 73–150*, New Century Bible Commentary (Grand Rapids: Eerdmans, 1972), 691.

anadiplosis ("make music" in vv. 4–5; "with the lyre" in vv. 5a, b; and "to judge the earth"/"he will judge the world" in vv. 9a, b).

Hymn

Psalm 98 displays the characteristics of a hymn: a summons to praise (v. 1a) followed by the reason to praise (vv. 1b–3), the latter of which is introduced by the benchmark "because" (see p. 7). Its fundamental mood is joy, signaled by verbs such as "sing" (v. 1) and "rejoice" (v. 4) and by verbs of performance (e.g., "make music with the lyre," v. 5) and movement (e.g., "clap their hands," v. 8).[11] The verbs summoning praise commonly occur in a series (e.g., vv. 4–5), "a sign of the overwhelming enthusiasm of the Hebrew poet."[12] The object of praise, *I AM* (see pp. 1–3), is mentioned by name seven times (1a, 1b [LXX], 2, 4, 5, 6, 9), and, as is normal in hymns, is extolled in the third person.[13] Thus, God overhears this most satisfying form of praise (see p. 105).

Rhetoric

The internal structure of a hymn's stanzas is marked by the repetition of verbs summoning praise. Verses 4–6, the second stanza, with its cluster of plural imperatives addressed to all people to make music, comes after the hymn's first stanza (vv. 1–3). Verses 7–9, the third stanza, using jussives, summons the cosmic elements to praise in 7–8 with cause for praise in 9. Presumably, the reasons all the people are summoned to make music are those of the first and third stanzas. In sum, Psalm 98 consists of three stanzas of three verses. Here is a sketch of its structure:

Superscript
Stanza I (Address to Israel): Sing a New Song — 1–3
  Strophe A (Summons): Sing a New Song to *I AM* — 1aα
  Strophe B (Reason): His Victory Made Nations Know
    His Righteousness — 1aβ–3
     1. Summary Statement: He Did Wonders — 1aβ
     2. Details of His Salvation — 1b–3

11. H. Gunkel and J. Begrich, *Introduction to the Psalms: The Genres of the Religious Lyric of Israel*, trans. James D. Nogalski (Macon, GA: Mercer University Press, 1998), 22, 25.
12. Gunkel, *Introduction to the Psalms*, 25.
13. Gunkel, *Introduction to the Psalms*, 32.

This sketch exposes the poet's rhetorical aim: to expand the praise in space, in volume, and in time. Tremper Longman notes, "As each stanza succeeds the other, the size of the worshiping community increases."[14] As the circles of praise expand, so does the intensity: from the human voices of Israel (vv. 1–3), to the whole earth making instrumental music (4–6), to the roaring of the sea and joyful shout of the earth-disc (7–8). The change of the grammatical tenses in each stanza advances the praise from the past to the present to the future.

The rhetoric of each stanza will be noted under "Exegesis" below. We note here only that "all the ends of the earth" (v. 3) segues naturally into "all the earth"(4), and that the title King (6) segues into the theme of his government over the whole creation (7; see Ps. 93). The second and third stanzas are connected by the catchwords "before *I AM*" and "rejoice" (6, 8–9). The first and last stanzas are connected by "the nations" (2) and its semantic equivalent "the peoples" (9). Hossfeld notes: "The nations are present throughout all three [stanzas]; in vv. 2 and 3 they are eyewitnesses; in vv. 4–7 they are the sole addressees; in v. 7 they are included among those who dwell on earth; and in v. 9 they are the addressees of the Judgment."[15]

14. Tremper Longman III, "Psalm 98: A Divine Warrior Victory Song," *JETS* 27 (1984): 267–74, esp. 271.

15. Frank-Lothar Hossfeld and Erich Zenger, *Commentary on Psalms 51-100*, trans. Linda M. Maloney, Hermeneia (Minneapolis: Fortress, 2005), 481.

A Divine Warrior Victory Song

Psalm 98 praises God as King, but instead of the proclamation, "*I AM* is King" (Pss. 93, 96, 97, 99), Psalm 98 uses the epithet "the King" (v. 6). The King is a warrior (see p. 4). All hymns proclaiming "*I AM* is King" praise him as a victorious warrior, though it is less clear in Psalm 99.[16] Thus:

- 47:3[4]: "He subdued nations under us, peoples under our feet."
- 93:1: "Clothed is *I AM*; with strength he girds himself [as a warrior]."
- 95:1: "Let us shout aloud to the Rock of our salvation."
- 96:2: "Proclaim from day to day the good news of his salvation."
- 97:3: "Fire goes before him and all around burns up his foes."
- 98:1-3: "His right hand and his holy arm have gotten him victory" (v. 1); "salvation" (i.e., victory over his foes, v. 2); "salvation of our God" (v. 3).
- 99:1: "*I AM* sits enthroned between the cherubim—the earth shakes."

Psalms proclaiming "*I AM* is King" belong to the larger genre of Divine Warrior victory songs. Tremper Longman's identification of Psalm 98 as a Divine Warrior victory song gives new and helpful insight into its interpretation.[17] Longman notes Divine Warrior imagery and language based on the lists by von Rad and P. D. Miller.[18] In Stanza I, "right hand" and "holy arm" (v. 1b) signify his warring activity[19]; "new song" occurs seven time in the Old Testament (Pss. 33:3[20]; 40:3[4]; 96:1; 98:1; 144:9; 149:1; Isa. 42:10) and twice in the New Testament (Rev. 5:9; 14:3), each time in the context of holy war; and "salvation" (vv. 1, 2, 3) has usually been taken as a reference to a military victory. In Stanza II,

16. On the basis of similarity of content, setting, motifs, and language, Longman ("Psalm 98: A Divine Warrior Victory Song," 273) also classifies as Divine Warrior victory songs Pss. 18, 21, 24, 29, 46, 47, 66, 68, 76, 93, 96, 97, 114, 118, 124, 125, and 136. Ps. 20 is less certain.

17. Longman, "Psalm 98: A Divine Warrior Victory Song," 269.

18. G. von Rad, *Der heilige Krieg im alten Israel* (Goettingen: Vandenhoeck und Ruprecht, 1951); P. D. Miller Jr., *The Divine Warrior in Early Israel* (Cambridge: Harvard University, 1973).

19. See J. Muilenburg, "A Liturgy on the Triumphs of Yahweh," in *Hearing and Speaking the Word: Selections from the Works of James Muilenburg*, ed. Thomas F. Best (Chico, CA: Scholars, 1984), 160, 242.

20. The identification of Ps. 33 as a victory song is questionable.

"*I AM*, the King," (v. 6b) is associated with his warring activity. Musical praise is given to the Divine Warrior:

> Simply stated, while the Divine Warrior wars, music languishes (Isa 24:8 ff. . . .), and when the Divine Warrior wins, music is taken up again in a paean of praise. This reflects historical custom, since we know that the human war leader and his army were greeted by instrumental music and victory songs upon their return (1 Sam. 18:6–7; Judg. 11:34). Indeed, a musical response to military victory was common in the ancient Near East.[21]

L. Greenspoon delineated the connection between the revitalization of nature and the Divine Warrior's victory, as in Stanza III.[22] Longman writes, "When the Divine Warrior wars, nature droops, withers, languishes (Isa. 24:4–13), but when the Divine Warrior wins, nature is revivified and participates in praising Yahweh."[23]

Setting

Hymns were sung in the Jerusalem temple, the earthly continuum of the heavenly temple. The summons to "sing a new song to *I AM*" (v. 1a) and the depiction of giving a shout before the King (v. 6) assume temple worship. Longman thinks the Divine Warrior victory hymn was sung upon "the return of Yahweh the commander of the heavenly hosts who is leading the Israelite army back home after waging victorious holy war."[24] He is on firmer historical ground when he speaks of the psalm's "dehistoricization." Psalm 98 does not specify the time and place of *I AM*'s victory "to preserve the immediate relevance of the poem in the cult."[25] This intentionality can be inferred by comparing the dehistoricized Divine Warrior victory songs in the Psalter with the historical victory songs in Exodus 15 and Judges 5.

---

21. Longman, "Psalm 98: A Divine Warrior Victory Song," 270.
22. L. Greenspoon, "The Origin of the Idea of Resurrection," in *Traditions in Transformation: Turning Points in Biblical Faith*, ed. B. Halpern and J. D. Levenson (Winona Lake, IN: Eisenbrauns, 1981), 247–322.
23. Longman, "Psalm 98: A Divine Warrior Victory Song," 271.
24. Longman, "Psalm 98: A Divine Warrior Victory Song," 268f.
25. Longman, "Psalm 98: A Divine Warrior Victory Song," 272.

II. Exegesis

Superscript

Psalm 98 uniquely does not qualify its superscript, *a psalm*, and so it is sometimes called an orphan psalm. The title "psalm" is most appropriate with a song that specifies the musical instruments that produce the melody (vv. 4–6; see p. 7).

Stanza I (Address to Israel): Sing a New Song 1–3

The possessive "our God" (v. 3) signals that a temple leader is addressing the house of Israel (see p. 13). The stanza unpacks "the wonders *I AM* has done" in a chiastic pattern, as noted by K. Schaefer[26]:

A. his victory (*yᵉšûʿâ*)
    B. in the sight of the nations
        C. he revealed
            D. his love and faithfulness to the house of Israel
        C'. have seen
    B'. all the ends of the earth
A'. his victory (*yᵉšûʿâ*)

The key word "salvation/victory" occurs in every verse of this integrated stanza, and the focus is on its international impact.

Strophe A (Summons): Sing a New Song to I AM 1aα

Sing . . . a song is addressed specifically to the Levitical choirs, the experts in music (see p. 15).

---

26. Konrad Schaefer, *Psalms*, Berit Olam (Collegeville, MN: Liturgical Press), 243.

Strophe B (Reason): His Victory Made All Nations Know
His Righteousness 1aβ–3

1. Summary Statement: He Did Wonders 1aβ

Wonders is a parallel to "glory" in 96:3. Because the victory was so unexpected and extraordinary, it astonished people.

2. Details of His Salvation 1b–3

In the chiastic construction of this stanza, "salvation in the sight of the nations" and "all the ends of the earth have seen [his] salvation" frame the core that celebrates his righteousness and his faithfulness for Israel.

a) His Strength to Save 1b

The anthropomorphisms *right hand* (see 91:7) and *arm* (see n. 3) speak of power (Exod. 15:6–12; Lam. 2:3) in connection with the warring activity of *I AM*.[27] The focus is on him, as can be seen in the repetition of the pronouns "his" and "him" in verset 1b. In a single-handed exploit, *I AM* won the victory, so all homage belongs to him (cf. Ps. 44:3[4]). Kidner says of *has gotten him victory*, "Its chief aspect is 'salvation,' as in the name 'Jesus'; so it looks at both friend (with salvation) and foe (with victory), and is big enough to combine the hard decisiveness of the latter with the compassion and construction of the former."[28] It belongs to both the military (cf. Judg. 12:2; 1 Sam. 11:3, 9) and the juridical (2 Sam. 14:4) spheres. It denotes military or physical intervention that is one's due or right. Sawyer notes that other words in the semantic domain of "deliverance," such as *nṣl*, stress the idea of violent action but not invariably intervention on behalf of justice.[29] Its parallel in verse 2 is "righteousness." *Holy* (see 93:5; 96:9).

27. J. Muilenburg, "A Liturgy on the Triumphs of Yahweh," 242.

28. Derek Kidner, *Psalms 73–150*, TOTC (Downers Grove, IL: IVP Academic, 2009), 385.

29. J. Sawyer, "What Was a *Mōšiaʿ*?" *VT* 15 (1965): 479. For a fuller discussion, see Bruce K. Waltke and James M. Houston with Erika Moore, *The Psalms as Christian Worship: A Historical Commentary* (Grand Rapids: Eerdmans, 2010), 199–200, 199n60.

b) His Salvation Revealed His Righteousness to the Nations 2

Had made known (see Ps. 90:9, 10, 12) denotes the mental and visceral experiencing of a reality. *In the sight of* (see "they saw," v. 3b) refers to an action, not to a verbal communication. *The nations* (see 96:3, 10). The sense of *revealed* (i.e., "to make uncovered"; cf. Mic 1:6[30]) is similar to Isaiah 40:5: "And the glory of God will be revealed"—that is to say, "will be recognizable, perceptible." One perceives, not literally sees, the abstraction *righteousness* (see 96:13). In other words, "The righteousness/glory of *I AM* will be recognizable in his act of deliverance of Israel,"[31] and correlatively in the justice meted out to her oppressors (cf. Deut. 33:21; Pss. 48:10–11[11–12]; 96:13; 97:2; 98:9; 99:4; Isa. 59:9, 11). In sum, the Divine Warrior's victory was so wondrous, unexpected, and astonishing, the nations knew it was a deed of Israel's God.

b') He Remembered His Loving-Kindness to Israel 3a

He remembered denotes not merely "to recall" but also to accept and to make the past effectual, to participate in the past in the present.[32] So *I AM* accepts and participates in *his love . . . and his faithfulness,* words commonly paired in the Psalter (see Pss. 36:5[6]; 88:11[12]; 89:1[2], 24[25], 33[34]; 92:2[3]; 100:5; see Exod. 34:6). They are metonymies for the covenants he made with *the house of Israel.*[33] In sum, when *I AM* remembers his covenant with Jacob, he puts into practice his covenant with the patriarchs.

---

30. Cf. *gālâ* Qal: "*I AM* uncovered the ear of Samuel" (1 Sam. 9:15).

31. C. Westermann/R. Albertz, *TLOT*, 1:319, s.v. *glh.*

32. Brevard Childs, *Memory and Tradition in Israel* (Naperville, IL: Allenson, 1962), 56; H. Eising, *TDOT*, 4:65, s.v. *zākar.*

33. Literally, "house" refers to an enclosed area where people live made of any material, usually in distinction from a "tent." By metonymy, the meaning shifts to the contents of the house and beyond that to the personal sphere of the household living in the house (classically in Josh. 24:15: "but I and my house will serve *I AM*") and so means "family" (Gen. 7:1). E. Jenni (*TLOT*, 1:235, s.v. *bayit*) says, "The entire tribal and national society could also be described as *bayit* according to the model of a family and tribe."

a') The Ends of the Earth Witnessed His Salvation 3b

In biblical times, *all the ends of the earth* extended from lands beyond the Euphrates in the east to the lands surrounding the Mediterranean Sea in the west, and from the Peloponnesian Islands in the north to Ethiopia in the south.

Stanza II (Address to All the Earth): Make Music before the King 4-6

All the earth (a metonymy for the earth's people; see 100:1), having seen the salvation of Israel by "our God," is now summoned to provide the orchestral accompaniment to Israel's victory song to her Divine Warrior. As the inclusio "salvation" framed the first stanza (vv. 1, 3), "shout for joy" (*harî'û*) frames the second (vv. 4a, 6b). The anadiplosis "make music" unites verses 4 and 5 and sounds the stanza's theme. Naming the musical instruments to be played and the repetition of "the sound of" (see 93:4) unite verses 5 and 6. The references to *I AM* in every verse further unify this tightly integrated stanza. "Before the King, *I AM*" brings the stanza to its climax. Verbs related to "praise" and the range of instruments performing the praise fill the stanza with fervent enthusiasm.

Strophe A (Summons): Make Music 4

The sound of a *shout* (see 100:1; 95:1, 2) *to* I AM (see 100:1) by *all the earth* (see 96:1, 9; 97:5, 9; 98:3) in God's temple is more deafening than the shout of a packed football stadium when the home team scores. For *and make music* (*zammērû*), see p. 105.

Strophe B: Musical Instruments 5-6

Poets prefer to develop the form of performance by naming the instruments.[34] The twang of the lyre and the blare of the trumpets are heard in the poet's inspired imagination. His imagined temple is wide enough to hold "all the ends of the earth," and he hears the sea roaring its praise and the mountains clapping before *I AM* in his Jerusalem temple, where Israel sings its new song.

34. Gunkel and Begrich, *Introduction to the Psalms*, 24.

1. Chordophones 5

The anadiplosis *play music* gives the command an insistent vigor. The same is true of the repeated *with the lyre* (see Ps. 92:3[4]). The addition of *and the sound of music* suggests the lyre is a synecdoche for chordophones (i.e., instruments that produce sound from the plucking or bowing of strings stretched over or into a sounding box).

2. Aerophones and Shofar 6

Trumpets are mentioned only here in the Psalms. They were probably made of silver (cf. Num. 10:2) or of gold (2 Kgs. 12:13) and may be a synecdoche for all aerophones (i.e., musical instruments that produce sound through the vibration of air in, through, or around them). "In Numbers and Ecclesiasticus, they are signs of divine favor."[35] The *ram's horn* (*šôpār*) is singled out because, as Jones explains, "the *šôpār* is linked with the *tərû'â* ['shout']" whose rich associations include "celebration of victory and blessing for the land." The *shofar* was also used at coronations (1 Kgs. 1:34, 39, 41; 2 Kgs. 9:13).[36] *Before the King* (see Ps. 93:1) assumes a temple setting.[37] The orchestration of all nations is probably a hyperbole of the poet's imagination, not an actual orchestra of musicians from the nations, just as the roar of the ocean before *I AM* in his Jerusalem temple (v. 9aα) cannot be literal (see v. 9aβ).

Stanza III (Address to Cosmos): Applaud I AM's Coming in Victory 7–9

The sound is now intensified to the highest decibel: to the roar of the whole creation. The stanza consists of a quatrain that summons the cosmic elements to shout with rejoicing (vv. 7–9aα) and a tricolon explaining that they do so because *I AM* comes to judge the whole creation and its creatures with righteousness (9aβ–b). The two summons and the reason for them are tightly linked by the enjambment "before *I AM*" in 9aα followed by the benchmark "because" in 9aβ.

35. Ivor H. Jones, "Music and Musical Instruments," *ABD* 4:936
36. Jones, "Music," 936.
37. So also Hossfeld and Zenger, *Commentary on Psalms 51-100*, 480.

Strophe A (Summons): Roar with Rejoicing before I AM *7–9aα*

Using the merism of "the [breadth of the] sea" and the "[width of the] earth-disc" (v. 7) to encompass the cosmic elements and their inhabitants on the horizontal axis and the merism of their more specific "ocean currents" and "mountains" (v. 8) to encompass the cosmic elements on the vertical axis, the poet summons the whole creation to roar (the first word in the Hebrew text of v. 7) with rejoicing (the last word of v. 8).

1. Cosmic Elements to Roar on Horizontal Axis 7

Verse 7 matches two merisms in synonymous parallel: "the sea" with "the earth-disc" and "its fullness" with "those who dwell in it." *Let the sea roar and its fullness* repeats Psalm 96:11. *The earth-disc* (see Pss. 93:1; 96:10) *and those who dwell in it* (see 91:1). The gapped "roar" is a zeugma, for it is inappropriate with "earth-disc" and so glossed *[resound]*.

2. Cosmic Elements to Rejoice on Vertical Axis 8–9aαα

N*e*hārôt can denote "rivers, streams" (cf. Isa. 41:18) or *ocean currents* (see Ps. 93:3; cf. 24:2). In Jonah 2:3[4], these ocean currents are associated with the ocean depths: "You hurled me into the depths, into the very heart of the seas, and the currents [*nāhār*] swirled about me; all your waves and breakers swept over me." Ocean currents form a merism with *mountains* (see 97:5) on the vertical axis. Upon reaching the shoreline, the rolling currents become crashing waves that, in the poet's ear, resemble applauding hands. In Psalm 93, the "floods" rebel against God's rule; in Psalm 98 they praise his coming kingdom. *Clap* occurs only three times and always in collocation with the obviously collective singular *kāp* (*hands*; lit. "palms"). The bodily movement expresses applause (see Ps. 47:1) and extreme joy, as seen in the parallel *let . . . rejoice* (i.e., to utter cries of jubilation; see v. 4; 90:14). When Joash was crowned king, the people clapped their palms/hands (2 Kgs. 11:12), and the poet probably associates the clapping waves with the recognition that Israel's God is King. They are to do so *in unison*: "together, all at once."[38] Obviously, the jubilant roar of the sea and the clapping of the mountains before *I AM* in his temple are heard in the poetic imagination.

---

38. *HALOT*, 1:405, s.v. *yaḥad*, #2.

Strophe B (Reason): He Comes to Judge with Righteousness 9aαβ–b

The reason they roar with jubilant cries essentially repeats Psalms 96:13 and 97:2. But 98:9 omits the anadiplosis "because he is coming" and reads *with equity* (see Ps. 96:10) instead of "in his faithfulness" (i.e., reliability). Though it is already filled with God's glory, the whole creation depends on humanity to fulfill its determined destiny of political righteousness and peace (Rom. 8:19–21).

PART III. VOICE OF THE CHURCH IN RESPONSE

I. New Testament

The New Testament interprets Psalm 98 with reference to the birth of the Lord Jesus Christ. For the evening prayer, *The Book of Common Prayer* interposes Psalm 98, known as *Cantate Domino* ["Sing to the Lord"], in the context of its New Testament fulfillment, between Mary's *Magnificat* (Luke 1:46–55) and Simeon's *Nunc Dimittis* (Luke 2:29–32). Mary magnifies the Lord in part because he showed strength with his arm and scattered the proud (Luke 1:51; cf. 98:1) and because he remembered his mercy for his servant Israel (Luke 1:54; cf. 98:3). Simeon is ready to depart the earth in peace because his eyes have seen God's salvation that God prepared "in the sight of all the nations" (Luke 2:30f.; cf. 98:2).

II. Augustine of Hippo (354–430)

Augustine reads Psalm 98 in light of the incarnation—in light of the wonderful deeds Christ performed to heal both bodies and souls. The deeds the psalmist rejoices in have been performed by *I AM*'s "right hand and his holy arm" (v. 1)—an echo of Isaiah 53:1: "Who has believed our message and to whom has the arm of *I AM* been revealed?" He interprets "his right arm" as Christ himself in his salvific ministry, revealing our salvation.[39] When the psalmist says, "He has remembered his love to Jacob and his faithfulness to the house of Israel" (v. 3) he is not talking about the Jews

---

39. Augustine, *Exposition of Psalm 97 1–2*, in *Expositions on the Psalms*, trans. Maria Boulding, O.S.B., vol. 4 (Hyde Park, NY: New City, 2002), 459–60.

but about those who see God. All the ends of the earth, in turn, will see the salvation of *I AM*.[40]

In verse 4, the psalmist makes the imperative "shout for joy," which, comments Augustine, we do when words fail us. Yet the whole earth hears it.[41] Drawing on his musical expertise, Augustine interprets the various musical instruments used in verse 5–6. He identifies them as kingly instruments—the kind that would be used for a coronation.[42]

Those instruments are loud because other kingdoms of the earth hear and rise up in wrath. Yes, argues the psalm in verse 7, "let the sea roar" as the crowd may roar, from whom we can expect persecution. But "the mountains," as notable Christians, "will leap for joy," and the "rivers," as ordinary Christians who have drunk "the living water," all rejoice![43] In contrast, at Christ's coming, "the wicked," as Psalm 1:4–6 depicts, will be judged (v. 9). "Take thought then," Augustine challenges his audience, "what kind of person you are. If you say, you are a Christian, then you live by the Lord's prayer, asking, 'Thy Kingdom come, thy will be done.' . . . Correct yourself, so that you no longer pray against yourself."[44]

III. John Calvin (1509–1564)

John Calvin belongs to a very different world than Augustine and had different training, as a lawyer engaging in the evolving discipline of theology. He might have described himself as a medical diagnostician since he described the Psalms "as the anatomy of all parts of the soul." As Sinclair Ferguson appraises him, "He had an uncanny knack of seeing the real issue—an unlearnable combination of understanding, logic, sensitivity, and illumination."[45] Yet like Augustine, he was a truly humble man, describing himself as "just a mere novice, and tyro!"[46] Clearly influenced by Augustine, who saw the psalms as expressive of "the Body of Christ," Calvin was gripped by the conviction that

40. Augustine, *Exposition of Psalm 97* 3 (Boulding, 460–61).

41. Augustine, *Exposition of Psalm 97* 4 (Boulding, 461).

42. Augustine, *Exposition of Psalm 97* 5–6 (Boulding, 463–4).

43. Augustine, *Exposition of Psalm 97* 7–8 (Boulding, 465).

44. Augustine, *Exposition of Psalm 97* 8 (Boulding, 465).

45. Sinclair B. Ferguson, *John Calvin: Heart Aflame, Daily Readings from Calvin on the Psalms* (Phillipsburg, NJ: P&R, 1999), v.

46. Quoted in Ferguson, *John Calvin*, vi.

the whole Bible was Christocentric. He preaches to expound the word of Christ within the text of the Bible.

Calvin notes the similarity of this psalm with Psalm 96, with its great scope of spreading the glory of God worldwide. To sing a new song unto *I AM* "denotes an extraordinary, not a common ascription of praise. For God had manifested his salvation in a singular and incredible manner. God had procured salvation *with his own right hand;* that is, not by human means, nor in an ordinary way, but by delivering his Church in an unprecedented manner."[47] Like Augustine, Calvin focuses on verses 3 and 4 as the motive for the whole composition.

In both Psalm 98:1 and in Isaiah 49:16, observes Calvin, "the arm of *I AM*" indicates his unique power, used in unexpected places of darkness to demonstrate his salvation and righteousness to all the peoples of the earth. The psalm is therefore described as "a new song," not as any ordinary form of celebration. In verse 2, "salvation" is mentioned first, but in reverse order, since it is "righteousness" which is the cause. For, adds Calvin, "the righteousness of God, which is the source of salvation, does not consist in his recompensing men according to their works, but it is just the illustration of his mercy, grace, and faithfulness."[48]

In verse 3, Calvin turns his focus to God giving and exhibiting that glory to his own people, the children of Abraham. "As Christ said, 'Salvation is of the Jews' " (John 4:22). The psalmist therefore very properly observes that "God in redeeming the world *remembered his truth*, which he had given to Israel, his people— . . . which implies that he was influenced by no other motive than that of faithfully performing what he had promised."[49] "Remembered" is used antithetically to mankind's forgetfulness about God so that the nations formerly immersed in delusions and superstitious would now participate in it.

Calvin doesn't bother describing the various musical instruments in verses 5–6 but interprets them in light of verse 4 ("Shout for joy to *I AM*, all the earth!"). He suggests that the range and variety of musical instruments are the best efforts humanity can make to praise *I AM*; but they fall far short, as the ceremonies of the law also did, of giving God adequate praise.[50]

---

47. John Calvin, *Commentary on the Book of Psalms*, trans. James Anderson, vol. 4 (Grand Rapids: Baker Books, 1996), 69–70.

48. Calvin, *Commentary on the Book of Psalms*, 70.

49. Calvin, *Commentary on the Book of Psalms*, 71.

50. Calvin, *Commentary on the Book of Psalms*, 73.

As Robert Davidson has reminded us, "No psalm more neatly or suc-cinctly lays bare the heart of genuine worship. In worship God's people join with the whole creation in celebrating the wonderful deeds of the one who is King and Creator of all."[51] But in such worship, we also open ourselves up to the future the New Testament reveals. The church sings to proclaim, "Jesus is Lord" (1 Cor. 12:3). Calvin states in his *Institutes* that singing is the way to "exercise the mind in thinking of God and keep it attentive." Singing allows believers to glorify God together, and allows "all men mutually, each from his brother [to] receive the confession of faith and be invited and prompted by his example."[52]

We draw our section on the Christian response to Psalm 98 to a conclu-sion by noting that most Christians are unwittingly familiar with this psalm and its themes through Isaac Watts's hymn "Joy to the World."

PART IV. CONCLUSION

I. Canonical Context

Psalms 93 and 96–99 all refer to *I AM* as King and are Divine Warrior vic-tory songs (see "Divine Warrior Victory Song" above). The themes of Psalm 97 and 98 are chiastically structured, as David Howard observes: "Psalm 97 opens with attention to the world and closes by focusing on Israel; Psalm 98 opens with an eye to Israel and closes by emphasizing the world."[53] Psalms 98 and 96 echo one another (cf. "let the sea roar, and its fullness" in 96:11b and 98:7a). Both are called "a new song" in their first verses; both have an internal structure of multiple three-verse stanzas demarcated by volitional forms. Their concluding stanzas (96:11–13; 98:7–9), using jussives, call upon creation to join the celebration and give the same reason for celebration in almost identical concluding verses. Both use the not-so-common poetic tools of anadiplosis and personification.

For the New Testament context, see "New Testament" above.

---

51. Robert Davidson, *The Vitality of Worship: A Commentary on the Book of Psalms* (Grand Rapids: Eerdmans, 1998), 323.

52. John Calvin, *Institutes of the Christian Religion*, ed. John T. McNeill, vol. 1 (Louisville: Westminster, 1960), 3.20.21.

53. Howard, *The Structure of Psalms 93–100*, 178; cf. 157.

II. Message

The message of Psalm 98 is to sing a new song—a victory song celebrating the noble qualities and astonishing salvation of *I AM*, Israel's God, King, and Divine Warrior. Psalm 98 exudes enthusiastic praise for him. In expanding horizons and escalating volume, the psalmist calls upon Israel to sing a new song and to shout with joy, upon the nations to add accompanying music, and upon the entire creation to roar with applause. If the seraphim's calling to one another, "Holy, Holy, Holy," made the doorposts and threshold of the Jerusalem temple shake (cf. Isa 6:4), one can imagine that the joyful shout of the whole creation and all that is in it would be so loud as to shake the heavenly palace.

All rejoice because *I AM* did what was right by the house of Israel, the nation he adopted as his family. The Divine Warrior's victory on behalf of Jacob's heirs was so great and his exploits without human help so extraordinary that all nations took note of it and knew Israel's Divine Warrior did it. Through his victory, he made known his noble qualities: strength, justice, majesty, and longevity (see p. 4).[54] His strength is symbolized by "his right hand and his holy arm" (v. 1b); his righteousness is revealed by his saving Israel (2); and his majesty can be inferred from his universal homage (4, 7–8). The eternal King's longevity extends in salvation history from his past saving deeds (1b–3), including the creation (Ps. 93), to the end of history, when he will govern the whole earth with equity (9). To these noble attributes, Psalm 98 adds his reliable loving-kindness to the house of Israel (3).

The psalm is dehistoricized so that it can be used in Israel's hymnbook on any occasion of God's victory and indeed at any time as a reminder of all of his victories, such as when he plundered Egypt at Israel's beginning and Babylon after its exile, while delivering his family from bondage (Exod. 12:17–51; Isa. 45; Ezra 1).

But all of God's victories in the Old Testament were only a rehearsal of his real victory: the victory of his Son, the Lord Jesus Christ, over Satan, sin, and death. That victory has been celebrated weekly by Christians for over two millennia. Through their witness, God has made known his righteousness in Christ on every continent and in almost every language (Ps. 22, esp. vv. 27–31[28–32]).

The Divine Warrior's past victories are a guarantee of his ultimate victory, when he comes and judges all peoples with equity (vv. 7–9). At that time, the

54. Marc Zvi Brettler, *God Is King: Understanding an Israelite Metaphor*, JSOTSup 76 (Sheffield: JSOT Press, 1989), 51–75.

creation will rejoice, for it will be liberated from its bondage to decay and brought into the freedom and glory of the children of God.

The psalmist's supreme concern is that all peoples join in Israel's victory song. He mentions the nations in every stanza. One can understand readily why Israel would sing this victory song, but why do all nations? Is not Israel's victory their defeat? In truth, the psalm assumes not all Gentiles praise Israel's God. According to the psalm's conclusion, the Divine Warrior is yet to come and judge all peoples. But the focus of Psalm 98 is on those in all the earth who do praise him. They join the song because they know both mentally and viscerally that Israel's God is a Warrior who has the will and power to do what is right, that he keeps faith with those who trust him, and that he wants all to know his salvation.

All peoples today who praise God for raising Jesus Christ from the dead and seating him at his right hand confess their faith in him as their Lord. And so, out of faith, they reorient their lives in conformity with the Son's righteous rule. Indeed, the psalmist portrays the Gentiles becoming with Israel a kingdom of priests, as indicated by their playing temple instruments. In the Old Testament, only the priestly tribe of Levi played music in the temple (see 1 Chr. 16:42; 2 Chr. 5:12). But the psalmist summons the nations to play the holy trumpets and even the ram's horn, which was used by Israel's captains and priests, both in war and in liturgy (cf. Lev. 23:24; 25:9; 2 Sam. 2:28; Judg. 6:34; 1 Kgs. 1:41).

CHAPTER 10

Psalm 99: Holy Is He

PART I. VOICE OF THE PSALMIST: TRANSLATION

A psalm by David.[1]

1   *I AM* reigns—the peoples tremble;[2]
       who sits enthroned[3] between[4] the cherubim—the earth shakes.[5]
2   *I AM* is great in Zion;[6]
       and he is exalted over all the peoples.[7]
3   Let them give grateful praise[8] to your great[9] and fearsome name—
       he is holy.
4   And the King is mighty, he loves justice;

1. So LXX; MT lacks a superscript.

2. Although the verb may be jussive ("let . . . tremble"), the indicative is favored because (a) the parallel verb *tānûṭ* is indicative, not jussive (see n. 5), and (b) the psalm's rhetoric demands it (see below).

3. For this specific meaning of *yšb* see BDB, p. 442, s.v. *yšb*, §1c; *HALOT*, 1:444, s.v. *yšb*, #3a.

4. See "between the two cherubim" (Exod. 25:22; 37:7-9; Num. 7:89).

5. *Nûṭ* is a hapax legomenon—probably the Hebrew cognate of Ugaritic *nṭṭ* "to wobble" (Cyrus H. Gordon, *Ugaritic Textbook*, AnOr 38 [Rome: Pontificium Institutum Biblicum, 1965], 443, #1961).

6. MT accents forbid the gloss "*I AM* in Zion is great."

7. A few Hebrew MSS, with some weak support in the ancient versions, read "gods" (cf. Pss. 95:3; 96:4; 97:9). But Zenger (Franz-Lothar Hossfeld and Erich Zenger, *Commentary on Psalms 51-100*, trans. Linda M. Maloney, Hermeneia [Minneapolis: Fortress, 2005], 483) notes that the theme of the gods is absent from Ps. 99, while the perspective of the nations dominates vv. 1-3.

8. The verb form could be indicative ("they praise"), but jussive is preferred by "an almost universal consensus" (Hossfeld and Zenger, *Commentary on Psalms 51-100*, 482) and best fits the psalm's rhetoric (see below).

9. For omission of the article, see GKC, 126z.

you have established equity;

justice and righteousness you have promoted in Jacob.

5   Exalt *I AM* our God

and prostrate yourselves at[10] his footstool—

he is holy.

6   Moses and Aaron among his priests

and Samuel among those who called on his name—

they were calling out to *I AM*, and he would answer them.

7   In a column of a cloud he would speak to them;

they kept his stipulations and the decrees he gave them.

8   *I AM*, our God, you answered them;

you were a forgiving God to them

and an avenger of[11] the wrongs done to them.[12]

---

10. Or "toward" (so also v. 9).

11. For the use of *'al*, see BDB, p. 754, s.v. *'l*, §1f (*b*).

12. The unanimous interpretation of the English versions that the pronominal suffix of *'alîlôtām* as agentive (= "the wrongs done by them") demands an extended defense of interpreting the suffix as an objective genitive. The agentive interpretation finds support in (a) Exod. 34:7, where, in the same breath, God says he forgives wickedness and does not leave the guilty unpunished; (b) the psalm's emphasis on God's holiness (vv. 3, 5, 9); and (c) the historical fact that God punished Aaron and Moses (Num. 20:24). Nevertheless, this interpretation is not probable for at least three reasons:

First, in this series of psalms that celebrate God as Israel's Warrior-King (92–93, 95–100), his punishment of Israel would strike a sour note. To be sure, "forgiveness" in 8b also strikes a new note in these psalms, but forgiveness expresses mercy and favor toward Israel and so, unlike punishment, is consistent with the tenor of these psalms. So authorities on these kingship psalms have sought to bring Psalm 99:8bβ into harmony with the others in various ways. David M. Howard (*The Structure of Psalms 93–100*, BJSUCSD 5 [Winona Lake, IN: Eisenbrauns, 1997], 86f.) glosses *nqm* by "vindication" and, on the basis of two texts (Job 10:7; 34:6), translates *'al* by "despite" (= "and One who vindicates [them] despite their evil deeds"). This strained interpretation is possible but seems less plausible than "wrongs done to them." Others emend the text. Sigmund Mowinckel (*The Psalms in Israel's Worship*, trans. D. R. Ap-Thomas, vol. 1 [Nashville: Abingdon, 1967], 156n138) inserts *lô'* (= "did not avenge"). C. F. Whitley ("Psalm 99:8," *ZAW* 85 [1973]: 227–30), whose amendment is accepted by *HALOT* (1:720, s.v. *nqh*; and 1:721, s.v. *nqm*) repoints *nqm* as *nōqām* (Qal ptcp. of *nqh* with 3 masc. pl. suffix) and, on the sole biblical basis of Ps. 16:2, questionably translates *'al* with "from" (= "who cleanses them from their wrongs"). However, *nqh* occurs in Niphal and Piel, not in Qal (the *binyan* here) apart from its use as an infinitive absolute modifying a verb in Niphal.

Second, the notion that God took revenge on those who effectually called upon

9   Exalt *I AM* our God and prostrate yourselves at his holy mountain.
     Surely, *I AM* our God is holy.

---

him is not compatible with the parallel, "you answered them." The '*olewᵉyored* separates
8a from 8b, and the *'athnaḥ* separates 8bα from 8bβ:

> (8a) *I AM* our God, you answered them:
> (8bα) You were to them a God who forgives,
> (8bβ) and an avenger of their wrongs.

According to the normal interpretation of this accentuation pattern, both "you are
a God who forgives," and "an avenger of their wrongs" expand "you answered them."
In other words, "an avenger of their wrongs" is not an antithetical parallel to 8bα ("a
God who forgives") but an explanation of 8a (see Pss. 90:17; 93:1; 96:13; 97:9 [= 98:3];
100:3; see also Pss. 1:1, 3; 2:6; 5:10). Surely, the poet does not intend that God answered
the prayers of Moses and Samuel (cf. Jer. 15:1) by taking vengeance against them.

Third, *nqm* refers to punishing someone outside of one's *imperium*. According
to F. Horst ("Recht und Religion im Bereich des AT," *EvT* 6 [1956]: 49–75; cited ap-
provingly by G. Sauer, *TLOT*, 2:768, s.v. *nqm*), the concept of vengeance refers to "private penalty that properly pertains to persons located *outside* [italics mine] one's own
jurisdiction and authority." This is in contrast to *pqd*, "the official inspection carried
out in one's own sphere of authority . . . which holds those concerned responsible for
negligence and error and intervenes against them" (W. Schottroff, *TLOT*, 2:1027, s.v.
pqd; cf. Exod. 34:7). Surely, forgiven covenant-keepers (v. 7) and effectual pray-ers (6b;
8a; 8bα) are members of God's jurisdiction, not outsiders. R. N. Whybray ("'Their
Wrongdoing' in Psalm 99:8," *ZAW* 81 [1969]: 237–43, esp. 238) notes,

> The brutal words *nāqam*, 'take vengeance,' and its cognates *nāqām* and *nᵉqamâ*
> are only very occasionally used in O.T. of Yahweh's actions against Israel, [both]
> in prophetic denunciations [see Isa. 1:24; Ezek. 24:8; esp. Jer. 5:9 = 9:9, where
> Israel is called a *gôy*, a word normally reserved for people other than Israel] and
> in a curse (Lev. 26:25), where the situation envisaged is that the covenant is at an
> end and Yahweh has become Israel's enemy. On the other hand, they are used
> on innumerable occasions of Yahweh's taking vengeance on Israelites' *enemies*
> [italics his]; these passages include two psalm passages, Psalms 94:1 and 149:7.

In other words, "punish" (NIV) is too imprecise: It does not distinguish between
nōqēm (Ps. 99:8) and *pōqēd* (Exod. 34:7).

Independently from R. N. Whybray and others, I (Bruce) drew the conclusion that the
genitive of the suffix was the genitive of the mediated object ("objective"; see *IBHS*, §9.5.2d;
Jouon-Muraoka, 129e; GKC, 128h, 135m) for several reasons: (a) It does not involve emend-
ing the text or a strained reading. (b) The objective genitive is well known (see *bᵉqōrᵉ'ê
šᵉmô*, v. 6), esp. with a pronominal suffix (see GKC, 135m). (c) This was the interpretation
of Symmachus and Kimchi (cited by Delitzsch, although he inconsistently disagrees). (d)
'Al to govern the accusative of *nqm* would be unique. With an objective genitive, *'l* has its
normal meaning: "on account of/in return for [the wrongs done to them]."

PART II. COMMENTARY

I. Introduction

Author

The Septuagint (LXX) and one Qumran manuscript (4QPsk) attribute this psalm proclaiming "God is King" (cf. Psalms 93, 97, 98) to David. There is no reason to deny that attribution (see p. 13). Its reference to the cherubim throne (v. 1) implies a composition during the First, not the Second, Temple period (see pp. 15–16, 78n66).

Though a director of music is not mentioned, the hymn is handed over for temple worship, for it speaks of *I AM* as "our God" (vv. 5, 9). The music leader summons Israel to worship.

Form and Rhetoric

A Psalm Proclaiming the Kingship of I AM

This terse poem (see p. 23) uses—more than most other psalms—the figure of parataxis (note the relatively numerous dashes in the translation) in what Kraus calls "staccato-like cultic cries."[13] The poem's content of summons to praise with reasons mark it as a hymn, but it reverses the normal sequence (see p. 5).[14] Aside from possibly verset 9b,[15] however, the psalm lacks the benchmark "because" to segue into reasons to praise. Nevertheless, the whole psalm gives reasons, and so substance, to praise. The poet summons both foreigners (v. 3) and Israel (5, 9) to praise *I AM* for his sublimities (1–2, 4, 7–8). The cycle of reason and summons is repeated three times (1–3, 4–5, 6–9), but the summons to foreigners is in the grammatical form of a wish (1–3) and functions as the reason why Israel should worship (v. 5; see "structure" below). As often happens in hymns, verses 3 and 6 use "name" as a surrogate

13. Hans-Joachim Kraus, *Theology of the Psalms*, trans. Keith Crim (Minneapolis: Augsburg, 1979), 268.

14. H. Gunkel and J. Begrich, *Introduction to the Psalms: The Genres of the Religious Lyric of Israel*, trans. James D. Nogalski (Macon, GA: Mercer University Press, 1998), 24.

15. *Kî* in v. 9 is better construed to mean "surely," not "because," though the two notions overlap.

for YHWH.[16] Also, as in many hymns, the poet addresses the worshipers, referencing God in the third person (i.e. "he"), or addresses *I AM* directly, in the second person (i.e., "you"). The latter, "being more personal . . . more forcefully expresses the direct piety."[17] The former, where God overhears his praise, may bless God's heart and expand his kingdom more than praise addressed directly to him. The initial proclamation specifies the hymn as a psalm proclaiming "*I AM* is King."

Aside from the grammatically ambiguous *yhwh mālāk* (v. 1)—a call for homage, not a cry of enthronement—nothing else in the psalm suggests God is being installed in a ritual of enthronement at the New Year festival (see pp. 19–22).[18]

Structure

Gunkel notes that, "here and there," conclusions to a poem's sections are "expressly accented by refrains" and cites Psalm 99:5, 9 as an example.[19] Thus the almost identical long refrain that summons Israel to "exalt" and to "bow down to" *I AM* demarcates the psalm into two stanzas of about equal length: six lines[20] of forty-two words (vv. 1–5) and forty-one words (vv. 6–9). The first stanza uses abstractions to celebrate God's justice, equity, righteousness (v. 4). The second stanza gives specific examples of these sublimities drawn from the likes of Moses and Samuel: He answered the prayers of those who kept covenant.

The short refrain "he is holy" (vv. 3b, 5b)—escalated climactically to "surely, *I AM* our God is holy" (v. 9b)—further divides the first stanza into two strophes (vv. 1–3, 4–5).[21] In addition to other similarities (see "Exegesis" below), both

16. Gunkel and Begrich, *Introduction to the Psalms*, 28. This may be due to the factor of *sogetto cavato*—the letters of a name signifying notes (see Dennis McCorkle, *The Davidic Cipher: Unlocking the Hidden Music of the Psalms* [Denver: Outskirts, 2010], 23–25, 31–33).

17. Gunkel and Begrich, *Introduction to the Psalms*, 24.

18. *Pace* Richard J. Clifford, "Psalms of the Temple," in *Oxford Handbook of the Psalms*, ed. William P. Brown (Oxford: Oxford University Press, 2014), 333.

19. Gunkel and Begrich, *Introduction to the Psalms*, 40.

20. Vv. 4, 6, and 8 are tricola that make two lines (see format of *BHS*).

21. F. Delitzsch (*Psalms*, trans. Francis Bolton, Keil and Delitzsch Commentary on the Old Testament 5 [London: T&T Clark, 1866–91; repr., Peabody, MA: Hendrickson, 1996], 631) hears in the threefold "he is holy" (vv. 3, 5, 9—the third "more full-toned") "the earthly echo of the trisagion of the seraphs" (Isa. 6:3). But Kraus (*Theology of the Psalms*, 269) hears in Isaiah's seraphic trisagion an echo of Ps. 99. A true echo of the

strophes shift from objectifying praise about God (vv. 1–2, 4a) to direct address and praise to God (vv. 3, 4b). The same shift in the second stanza, signaled by an emphatic *'attâ* ("you," vv. 4b, 8), also divides it into two strophes (vv. 6–7, 8–9). Formally, the repeated command that Israel praise "*I AM*, our God," (vv. 5a, 9a) should be combined with the reason to praise of the two stanzas' second strophes (vv. 4, 8). The chiastically structured instances of "*I AM* our God" (vv. 8aα and 9bβ) supports this analysis. The result is four strophes, each consisting of three lines and about the same number of words: verses 1–3 (22 words), 4–5 (20 words), 6–7 (20 words), and 8–9 (21 words). Other rhetorical features unifying the stanzas and strophes will be observed below under "Exegesis."

Viewing the psalm holistically, YHWH (*I AM*) is the psalm's alpha and omega—its first and last word. The divine name occurs seven times, and so do its pronouns ("he" four times and "you" three times; see p. 1).

Here is a sketch of the psalm's unified structure:

Superscript	
Stanza I: Praise of *I AM* as the Strong and Righteous King	1–5
Strophe A: Let the Peoples Praise *I AM*,	
the Fearsome King over Them	1–3
1. *I AM* Is King over All Peoples	1–2
a. Proclamation: *I AM* Reigns—Peoples Tremble	1
b. *I AM* Is the Sole Majesty over All People	2
2. Let Peoples Praise *I AM*—He Is Holy	3
Strophe B: Exalt *I AM*, the Strong and Just King in Jacob	4–5
1. *I AM* Is Strong and Just	4
2. Exalt *I AM*—He Is Holy	5
Stanza II: Praise of *I AM* for Answering Prayers	
of Covenant Keepers	6–9
Strophe A: Answered the Prayers of His Faithful People	6–7
1. Answered Prayers of Those Who Cried Out to Him	6
a. Moses, Aaron, and Samuel among	
Those Who Prayed	6a
b. He Answered Them	6b

---

seraphs' trisagion is heard in Rev. 4:8. More probably, the triple repetition is not an echo but a common feature of hymns (e.g., "sing," Ps. 96:1–2; "ascribe," 96:7–9; "praise," 103:20–22; 135:1; "let say," 118:2–4; "give thanks," 136:1–3). Laws are also arranged in groups of three (Lyle Eslinger, "Drafting Technique in Some Deuteronomic Laws," *VT* 30 [1980]: 251–252).

II. Exegesis

Superscript

See "Author" above.

Stanza I: Praise of I AM *as the Strong and Righteous King 1–5*

The cherubim above the ark (v. 1) and the footstool beneath it (5) are essential parts of the King's throne and so frame this stanza that proclaims *I AM* as King. The stanza's two strophes each begin by referencing *I AM* as King (*mālāk*, "reigns," v. 1; *melek*, "King," v. 4). Both strophes shift from objectifying speech about God (1–2, 4a) to direct address to him (3a, 4b); both are drawn to a conclusion with volitional forms (vv. 3, 5), followed by the staccato-like "he is holy." The two strophes are exceptionally linked by the conjunction "and." The catchwords "in Zion" (2a) and "in Jacob" (4b) decisively distinguish Israel and their God from the nations. The first strophe pertains to his kingship over all peoples and so implies his sovereign strength. The implication segues into his stated attribute: "total strength." *I AM*'s strength empowers him to exercise justice (4) in answer to prayer (6–8). In sum, *I AM* is holy—that is to say, a just and righteous God to be feared and praised in worship.

Strophe A: Let the Peoples Praise I AM, *the Fearsome King over Them 1–3*

The introductory proclamation, "*I AM* reigns," will be expounded in the rest of the psalm and locates the worship of *I AM* at the temple, where he sits enthroned between the cherubim above the ark. That "the peoples tremble" and "the earth shakes" (v. 1) gives visual evidence that he is "fearsome" and "holy" (3). The catchword "great" links verses 2 and 3. Its repetition strongly implies his superiority over all contenders, an implication certified by the claim "he is exalted above all the peoples." The reality that he reigns and is exalted over all gives reason why the nations should join Israel in praise of the Hero of her salvation history (v. 3) and why Israel should exalt him.

1. *I AM* Is King over All Peoples 1–2

The couplet (vv. 1–2) is linked by (a) initial *I AM*; (b) the chiastically structured catchword "peoples" in 1aα, escalated to "all the peoples" in 2bβ; and (c) the co-referential places "between the cherubim" (v. 1b) and "in Zion" (v. 2a). *I AM* actualizes his universal rule from Mount Zion, where he sits invisibly on his cherubim throne.

a) Proclamation: I AM *Reigns—Peoples Tremble* 1

I AM's rule is underived and was in force before the creation, but it manifests itself in the people's trembling and the earth's shaking (see p. 134), as happened during the exodus from Egypt (Exod. 15:15 and the conquest of Canaan (Deut. 2:25). The parataxis of the clauses in verse 1a, I AM *reigns* (93:1; 97:1) and *the peoples* [of foreign nations] (see 96:3) tremble, forces the audience to form a logical connection of cause and effect: The peoples' trepidation is caused by *I AM*'s holy rule. The same syntax and significance also holds for verse 1b: *The earth* (*hā'āreṣ*; see 96:11; 97:1) *shakes* (cf. Isa. 64:3[2]) because he "who sits enthroned between the cherubim" (see p. 78n66) is holy. As for "tremble," *rāgaz* signifies "to shake physically" and connotes trembling *in dread.* Perhaps the wish that the nations rejoice is subsequent to their trembling, but more probably the contrary emotions complement, not contradict, one another, as in "rejoice with trembling" (Ps. 2:11). True worship entails awed obedience and joy (cf. 2 Samuel 6). *Enthroned* visually depicts *I AM*'s transcendent rule. As for *the cherubim*, God spoke to Israel from between the two cherubim that overshadowed the ark-throne. Within the tabernacle's holy of holies, two golden cherubim with wings extended toward one another formed part of the ark's cover.[22] In the Jerusalem temple, two enormous olive-wood cherubim,

---

22. Cherubim were also expertly woven into the fabric of the curtains that surrounded the tabernacle and into the veil that separated the holy of holies from the rest of the tabernacle (Exod. 25:18–22; 37:7–9). On the inner cedar-board panels that lined Solomon's temple and on the doors separating its inner chambers, cherubim were carved and overlaid with gold. The temple also had cherubim carved into the panels that formed the base and part of the top of the stands for the lavers (1 Kgs. 6:29; cf. 2 Chr. 3:7; Ezek. 41:18–20, 25; 1 Kgs. 7:29, 36).

overlaid with gold, virtually filled the inner chamber as a covering for the ark (1 Kgs. 6:23–28). The Old Testament does not clearly describe the appearance of the cherubim other than that they had wings. Most scholars today associate the cherubim with ancient images of winged lion-sphinxes with human heads.[23] If this is the case, cherubim symbolized the highest creaturely powers ("strength, swiftness, sharpness of intellect"[24]). They represented both protection of God's sanctity, the numinous holiness of his being, and the temple on the one hand and God's swift mobility on the other.

b) I AM *Is the Sole Majesty over All Peoples 2*

"Verse 2," notes Zenger, "underscores this dialectic of particularism ['in Zion,' v. 2a] and universalism ['all peoples,' v. 2b]."[25] *Great* refers to the King's rank and influence and implies the comparison of v. 2b. Of all the mountains of the earth, God chose to dwell *in* Mount *Zion* (see 97:8), making it the capital of his earthly kingdom, the place for his royal house and for the ark of the covenant as his throne (Ps. 99:2) and so the seat of *I AM*'s universal rule. From Zion, God's laws

23. Ivory panels unearthed at Samaria depict a composite figure with a human face, an animal body with four legs, and two elaborate and conspicuous wings. Excavations at Byblos revealed a carved representation of two similar figures that appear to be cherubim supporting the throne of Hiram (c. 1000 BCE). Zenger (Hossfeld and Zenger, *Commentary on Psalms 51-100*, 487; see plate 1) comments, "In ancient Near Eastern iconography they symbolized a multiplication of creaturely powers (strength, swiftness, sharpness of intellect)." He says that these sphinxes had two functions: "the *watcher* or *protector function* (sphinx at the tree of life) and *the bearer function* (sphinx as bearer of the deity)" (italics his). These two functions are also encountered in the Old Testament. As for the former, in Gen. 3:24, flaming cherubim prevent sinners from grasping for immortality; and in a mythological allusion to Gen., the king of Tyre is represented as a guardian cherub (Ezek. 28:14). As for the latter, David metaphorically pictures God riding upon the wings of the cherubim, which are equated with the wind in a lightning storm (Ps. 18:10[11]; cf. 80:1–2[2–3]), and Ezekiel sees God's mobile chariot-throne borne by cherubim. Zenger also notes that in the iconography of the Late Bronze (1500–1200 BCE) and Early Iron (1200–1000 BCE) periods in Palestine/Israel and its Canaanite-Phoenician environment, "winged lion-sphinxes are also found in the context of depictions of thrones . . . each of them bearing a throne on which the king or god-king is seated. As a symbol of all-encompassing regal competence . . . intended to convey sovereignty . . . the sphinx throne indicates the numinous rank of the one seated upon it."

24. Hossfeld and Zenger, *Commentary on Psalms 51-100*, 487, plate 1.

25. Hossfeld and Zenger, *Commentary on Psalms 51-100*, 488.

are promulgated and universal peace prevails (Mic. 4:1–4). It was an extension of the heavenly reality where Christians come to worship the Trinity (Heb. 12:22). In reference to God, *exalted* describes his "sole sovereign majesty" (Pss. 46:10[11]; 99:2; 113:4; 138:6).[26] This significance is reinforced by *above all the peoples* (see Pss. 96:10; 98:9). "Is great" (cf. 95:3; 96:4) and "is exalted" (92:8; 93:4; cf. Isa. 6:1) speak of his power and influence and connote his victory over nations (Pss. 46–48).[27]

2. Let Peoples Praise *I AM*—He Is Holy 3

Let them give grateful praise refers in the liturgy to joyful and spontaneous praise of *I AM* for his saving deeds in conjunction with peace offerings (see p. 5). *To your . . . name* (see Ps. 100:4; cf. 111:9) is the means by which the divine, transcendent reality is made present and can be experienced. The psalmist wishes that all people will enter into a personal relationship with Israel's covenant-keeping God by adoring his name. *Fearsome name* (cf. Deut. 7:21) is the passive equivalent of the collocation "to fear *I AM*."[28] The collocation refers to both the rational aspect of understanding the revelation of his moral will and the nonrational, emotional aspect of responding to his person and revelation in fear, love, and trust.[29] Deuteronomy 10:17 associates "great and fearsome" with his justice. The poet hopes for the universal acknowledgment of God's righteous kingdom. The abrupt juxtaposition of *he is holy* with the preceding clause assumes, as in verse 1, a logical connection of effect and cause. The peoples are to praise his name because *I AM* is to be dreaded for his preternatural and supernatural deeds that are associated with his righteousness (see Ps. 93:5). As in 96:9, the notions of holiness, dread, and ethical behavior are fitting for his fearsome name. Zenger writes, "There is no intent merely to emphasize the transcendence of YHWH as the Wholly Other, but rather his judicial, that is, law-establishing and law-restoring, royal power" (see the so-called Holiness Code in Leviticus 17–26).[30]

---

26. H.-P. Stähl, *TLOT*, 3:1225, s.v. *rûm*.

27. In Ps. 76, the God of Jacob deprives nations of their power, breaking their instruments of war (v. 3[4]), and is alone to be feared (7[8]); his wrath against humankind brings him praise (10[11]).

28. *HALOT* (1:433, s.v. *yr'* Niphal, #2) classifies "name" as an equivalent of YHWH.

29. Bruce Waltke, "The Fear of the LORD," in J. I. Packer and I. Wilkinson, eds., *"Alive to God": Essays in Honour of James D. Houston* (Downers Grove, IL: InterVarsity, 1992), 17–33.

30. Hossfeld and Zenger, *Commentary on Psalms 51-100*, 488.

Strophe B: Exalt I AM, *the Strong and Just King in Jacob 4–5*

Although the addressees shift from *I AM* (v. 4) to the people (5), the psalm's structure (see "structure" above) suggests verses 4–5 link the reason to praise (4) with the command to worship him (5; similarly, 8–9).

1. *I AM* Is Strong and Just 4

And unites *I AM*'s reign over the nations (vv. 1–3) with his reign in Jacob (4–5). The King's holiness manifests itself to the nations in his dreadful strength; it manifests itself in Israel in his revealed righteous laws. These laws originate in his very being. Humans experience both aspects of his holiness as they bow low at his footstool. *King* is a metaphorical epithet of *I AM*—not a title of a human king—in this psalm that proclaims *I AM* as King.[31] By parataxis, the poet tightly binds the amoral *mighty* (4aα) with moral justice (4aβ). Pascal wrote, "Justice without might is helpless; might without justice is tyrannical. . . . Being unable to make what is just strong, we have made what is strong just."[32] *He loves* (see 97:10) *justice* (see 97:2) expresses God's strong desire to deliver the oppressed and punish the oppressor—eye for eye and tooth for tooth—and so by precise compensation to restore the moral order that conforms to his nature and laws. Emphatic *you* signals the return to adoring *I AM* in direct address. As the King placed the unmovable earth-disc in the midst of the surging sea, so also he has *established* ("to make firm, fixed"), amid depraved social chaos, *equity* (see Ps. 96:10) both in word (i.e., in Torah) and in deed (i.e., in salvation history). *Justice and righteousness* (see Ps. 97:2) are also metonymies for words and deeds. Most English versions gloss *'attâ 'āśîtā* by "you have executed/done" and so put emphasis on performance (i.e., saving deeds; see 2 Sam. 8:15; 1 Chr. 18:14; 1 Kgs. 10:9; Isa. 16:5). However, it may also entail the production of the Law and decisions based on it (see Ps. 98:1). NET combines word and deed successfully with *promoted*. Perhaps the poet identifies God's chosen people by *in Jacob* ("heel grabber," see 98:3; Deut. 4:8) to signify their radical transformation from taking advantage of others to their doing what is right, just, and fair. By transforming Jacob, God brought heaven to earth (Matt. 6:10).

31. *Pace* H. C. Leupold, *Exposition of the Psalms* (Columbus: Wartburg, 1959), 697.
32. Blaise Pascal, *Pensées* 298 (New York: Dutton, 1958), 85.

2. Exalt *I AM*—He Is Holy 5

The reality "he is exalted" (v. 2) lays the foundation for the command *exalt I AM*. *Rûm* Polel means "to raise to a considerable height above the base level," a metaphor here for social status and authority (cf. "Ascribe to *I AM* ... glory" in Ps. 96:7, 8). The poet and the singers of Psalm 99 regard themselves within the dynamics of a community that orders its life by faith in *our God* (see Pss. 98:3; 100:3). By default, the antecedent of "our" in Israel's sacred texts is Israel (see p. 13). *And* complements the command to exalt God in thought, word, and deed with a command about posture: *prostrate yourselves* (see Ps. 95:6) *at his footstool*. The royal footstool, a part of the throne (2 Chr. 9:18), symbolizes power and authority.[33] Here it functions as a synecdoche for the sanctuary and/or Zion (see v. 9; Ps. 132:7; Lam. 2:1). Isaiah (66:1) uses "my footstool" as a metaphor for the whole earth, but here the framing with "sits enthroned on the cherubim" (v. 1) argues against this meaning. *He is holy* (see v. 3).

Stanza II: Praise of I AM for Answering Prayers of Covenant Keepers 6–9

The second stanza illustrates from sacred history God's righteousness: He answered the prayers of covenant keepers—the likes of Moses and Samuel—to be forgiven and to be avenged for the wrongs done against them. (Serendipitously, through their prayers God advances his kingdom on earth.) To the King's strength and justice, the stanza adds that he is a sin-bearing-away God and an avenger. The chiastically structured "answered them" (vv. 6b, 8a) frames the parenthesis qualifying why their prayers were answered (v. 7): They kept God's revealed law. In the first stanza, the nations confess his name; in the second stanza, Israel prays in that name.

---

33. When a victor makes his enemies his footstool, he depicts his complete power and authority over them (cf. Josh. 10:24; 1 Kgs. 5:3). On the Tutankhamun footstool are representations of foreign captives, prostrate, with their hands behind their backs, symbolically depicting the pharaoh's enemies as bound and under his feet. The picture connotes the disdain and judgment of the victor and the shame and humiliation of the victims.

Strophe A: Answered the Prayers of His Faithful People 6–7

1. Answered the Prayers of Those Who Cried Out to Him 6

a) Moses, Aaron, and Samuel among Those Who Prayed 6a

Moses and Aaron were the first priests and so both represent the whole priesthood and function as a microcosm of Israel, a kingdom of priests. Although Moses was never consecrated as a priest, he was—in Delitzsch's term—a "proto-priest."[34] In view here is the role of the priests to mediate and intercede between God and the people (see the defeat of Amalek, Exod. 17:11f.; the sin of the golden calf, Exod. 32:11–14, 30–32; cf. Deut. 9:18, 25–29; the healing of Miriam, Num. 12:13; Aaron stopping the plague, Num. 16:47[17:12]f.). *Among his priests* extends the intercessory power of Moses and Aaron to their successors.[35] Jeremiah, like Psalm 99, lists *Samuel* with Moses as an effectual pray-er (Jer. 15:1).[36] Samuel "cried out [*wayyizʿaq*] to *I AM*, and God delivered Israel" (1 Sam. 7:9; cf. 12:16). Although *zʿq* specifically means "to cry for help," here *qrʾ* is its semantic equivalent, as indicated by the parallel "he answered them" (v. 6bβ; see Deut. 15:9; 24:15; Judg. 15:18; Pss. 28:1; 30:8).[37] For Samuel, to cease

---

34. Delitzsch, *Psalms*, 633. Moses sprinkled the blood on the altar that ratified the covenant at Sinai (Exod. 24); he consecrated Aaron, setting a model for the consecration of the priesthood (Lev. 8); and he performed the services of the sanctuary prior to Aaron's consecration (Exod. 40:22–27).

35. It would be difficult to overstress the role of the priest in Israel's religion. The temple's highest official, called *hakkōhēn* ("the priest"; i.e., the high/chief priest) actualizes God's presence in Israel. He and other priests protect the sanctity of God's house and perform the activities proper to it: offering sacrifices, singing, and conducting other acts of worship (Lev. 1–27; Num. 1:53; 3:28, 32). He also dispenses oracles (1 Sam. 14:36f.; 23:2; 30:7f.; cf. Jdg. 18:5) and with all the Levites is involved in teaching torah (Deut. 31:9f.; 2 Chr. 17:8f.; Ezek. 44:23; Hag 2:11ff.; Mal 2:7). Closely related to teaching is his role in jurisprudence. In lawsuits, the priest joined the judge to arrive at a ruling (Deut. 17:8-13; 21:5). The high priest, bearing the names of the twelve tribes on his breastplate, represents the entire nation before God.

36. Samuel is another pivotal hero in salvation history. After Israel's founding generation, Israel grew ever blacker spiritually and politically during the dark age of the warlords (Judg. 2). At the time of Samson, a generation before Samuel, the royal tribe of Judah rebuked Samson for not realizing the Philistines ruled them (Judg. 15:11).

37. *Qārāʾ* broadly denotes "to draw someone's attention with the sound of the voice in order to establish contact" (see Ps. 91:15), and the collocation "to call on *I AM*," as

praying for Israel would have been to sin against *I AM* (1 Sam. 12:23). But these three heroic pray-ers are merely *among those who called on his name* (cf. Heb. 11:30–32)—from Moses to Samuel. In answer to Joshua, *I AM* made the sun stand still (Josh. 10:12–14). Samson first prayed for life (Judg. 15:18) and then for death (Judg. 16:28), and *I AM* answered both prayers.

b) He Answered Them 6b

They were calling out to I AM, *and he would answer them.* This broad group does not include unholy Levites such as Korah and his rebels, whose censers *I AM* did not respect; instead, he caused the earth to swallow them alive into Sheol (Num. 16). Nor does it include the "loathsome" Israelites—as God called them—who at Meribah hardened their hearts in unbelief, grumbled against *I AM* and Moses, did not repent of their unbelief, did not pray to or praise *I AM*, and so, unfit for the Promised Land, died in the wilderness (Ps. 95:8–10; 1 Cor. 10:5–12; Heb. 3:7–12; 4:2–5).

2. God Spoke to Pray-ers, and They Kept His Law 7

a) He Spoke to Those Whose Prayers He Answered 7a

In a column (or "pillar") *of a cloud* that descended to the tent of meeting, *I AM* dramatically depicted the heavenly origin of his words to his chosen people. Paradoxically, the cloud hid God from the presumptuous glances of humankind and so separated him from them while at the same time assuring them of his presence and his fellowship with them.[38] *He would speak to them* (i.e., the pray-ers, vv. 6bβ, 8; cf. Exod. 33:9–10).

b) They Kept His Law 7b

Delitzsch says: "V. 7bc, is[,] virtually at least, a relative clause, declaring the prerequisite of a prayer that may be granted."[39] *They kept* signifies "to pay careful attention to."[40] *His stipulations* (see 93:5). The concrete meaning of *decree*

Labuschagne (*TLOT*, 3:1163, s.v. *qr'*) notes, "has varied connotations—to praise, thank, lament, cry, *call for help*" (italics mine).

38. So Artur Weiser, *The Psalms* (OTL; Philadelphia: Westminster, 1962), 643.

39. Delitzsch, *Psalms*, 633.

40. Keith Schoville, *NIDOTTE*, 3:182–84, s.v. *šmr*.

is a boundary line, a prescribed limit. A related, but non-graphic, notion is "established order." The singular in 99:7 may refer to the prescribed law viewed holistically. *He gave (nātan)*, along with "set" (*śîm*) and "make" (*'śh*), is characteristically used with "decree" and indicates the establishment of authority. Thus, the divine decree must not be transgressed.[41]

Strophe B: Exalt I AM, Who Answered Prayers of the Faithful 8–9

Although verse 8 is addressed to *I AM* and 9 to the people, the catchwords, "*I AM* our God" at the beginning of 8a and 9a and at the end of 9b unite the verses as a couplet, linking reason for praise (v. 8) with the command to praise (9a).

1. Answered Prayers of Faithful: Forgave and Avenged Them 8

I AM, *our God* (see v. 5), *you answered them* (see v. 6). *You were a forgiving* signifies literally "taking away." Sometimes the object, such as sin, guilt or transgression, is stated (cf. Gen. 50:17; Exod. 32:32; 34:7), but not always (Gen. 18:24; Hos 1:6; Isa. 2:9; Ps. 99:8).[42] God "has an unlimited abundance of power and a presence that overcomes the barriers of time," comments Weiser.[43] *And* the forgiving God of covenant people is an *avenger (nōqēm)* (see n. 12).[44] G. Sauer says that the original meaning of the *nqm* may have been legal: "Punishment rectifies and thus cancels an injustice." He also notes, "Emotionally laden action often assumes the foreground and largely determines the meaning of *nqm* as can be seen with special clarity in Prov. 6:34 (the merciless vengeance of a jealous husband: but [see] Lev. 19:18)."[45] But "vengeance" is more than "justice"; it signifies that "a ruler secures his sovereignty and keeps his community whole by delivering his wronged subjects and slaying their guilty slayers who do not respect his rule."[46] G. E. Mendenhall writes: "The root NQM designates what we have termed 'defensive vindication.'" He adds, "In over two thirds of

41. G. Liedke, *TLOT*, 2:472, s.v. *ḥqq*.

42. BDB, p. 671, s.v. *nāśā'*, §3c.

43. Weiser, *The Psalms*, 597.

44. John Goldingay (*Psalms*, vol. 3, BCOTWP [Grand Rapids: Baker Academic, 2008], 131) suggests a subtle change from negative *nkh* ("to not be acquitted") in Exod. 34:7 to *nqm* ("to take vengeance").

45. G. Sauer, *TLOT*, 2:768, s.v. *nqm*.

46. Bruce K. Waltke, *Micah: A Commentary* (Grand Rapids: Eerdmans, 2007), 329.

the total occurrences [fifty-one] the root designates the exercise of the divine *imperium* either directly or indirectly."[47]

2. Exalt *I AM* For He Is Holy 9

Exalt I AM *our God and prostrate yourselves* repeats verse 5. The change from "at his footstool" to *at his holy mountain* (i.e., Mount Zion; see Pss. 2:6; 99:2) suggests the latter is a synecdoche of the genus for the species, the whole for one of its parts.[48] *I AM*'s presence, symbolized by the Glory Cloud, made Zion "holy" (see v. 3). The poet, in his hymn's conclusion, makes the trisagion full-toned: *surely,* I AM *our God is holy* (see 9aα).

Part III: Voice of the Church in Response

This is the third psalm that opens with the same thrilling declaration, "*I AM* is King" (Pss. 93:1; 97:1; 99:1). We consider this a psalm of David and not contemporaneous with the later Assyrian invasions, as many scholars do. In this regard, we agree with Luther's interpretation, and not with Calvin—a cleavage that still exists among scholars.

I. Augustine of Hippo (354–430)

Augustine preached on this psalm (= LXX Ps. 98) in Carthage, possibly late in 411. It is one of his mature homilies, as is evident from its more paradoxical contemplation of God. Reflecting upon the incarnation, Augustine writes,

> The Judge of all the earth, appeared as a baby. Since He is so august a judge, many heralds preceded Him, even before His first coming in humility. When He was still to be born of the Virgin Mary, still destined to be an infant suckling judge, many heralds preceded Him, even before His first coming in humility, even then destined to be an infant sucking milk, even then with a succession of heralds going ahead of Him. Many a herald went in advance of the Word of God, the Word through whom

47. G. E. Mendenhall, *The Tenth Generation: The Origins of the Biblical Tradition* (Baltimore: Johns Hopkins University Press, 1973), 82f.
48. E. W. Bullinger, *Figures of Speech* (Grand Rapids: Baker Books, 1968), 614.

all things were made, who yet was to be an infant [Lat. *infantem*] herald. They spoke in such a way as to conceal their meaning under certain figurative signs.[49]

Augustine doesn't call his congregation to sing the psalm but to *listen* to it, to seek Christ's presence in it.[50] They are to do so "in Zion," which means "a look-out place" in the city of God, God's holy church. Augustine relates a "look-out place" with the acts of vision and contemplation. "Every city is held together by some law, and the law of this city is charity [Lat. *caritas*]." But God Himself is this "charity" (1 John 4:8). We make Zion our home, where God will never be far from us. "Then you, God will be *most high over all the peoples*—over those who are still angry, and over those who used to be angry in earlier days."[51] Augustine is not making, as the text does, the distinction between Zion and the temple, the dominion of *I AM* over all peoples and over His own people.

But Augustine does explore the fear we should all have in confessing "God's great Name . . . because it is terrible and holy."[52] All religions have the deep sense of "the ominous," but true biblical fear has manifold expressions. Augustine elaborates on the ethical consequences of obedience to verse 3. It demands avoidance of presumption, of pride. It demands dealing justly and with equity:

> But who deals justly? Who practices justice? A sinful human being, an unjust person, a perverted man or woman, one turned away from the light of truth? Let us rather turn to God so that He may form this fairness in us, for of ourselves we cannot form it, but only deform it. . . . The psalm sets out to persuade men and women to give themselves to God, that he may form them in justice . . . since [we] have no capacity for justice within [ourselves].[53]

But Augustine misses the key statement: "Justice and righteousness you have promoted in Jacob" (v. 4)—that is, only in God's people, formerly Israel and now the church, is justice possible.

49. Augustine, *Expositions of Psalm 98* 1, trans. Maria Boulding, vol. 4 (Hyde Park, NY: New City, 2002), 466.
50. Augustine, *Expositions of Psalm 98* 1 (Boulding, 466).
51. Augustine, *Expositions of Psalm 98* 4 (Boulding, 470).
52. Augustine, *Expositions of Psalm 98* 6 (Boulding, 473).
53. Augustine, *Expositions of Psalm 98* 6 (Boulding, 473).

Augustine wrestles with the meaning of "worship at his footstool" in verse 5. Quoting Isa. 66:1, "Heaven is my throne, the earth is my footstool," he asks rhetorically whether we are to worship the earth. He turns this thought to Christ, who, as "earth," came from Mary's womb, and who commanded us "to eat my flesh and drink my blood" (John 6:56). Yet we are to understand this in a spiritual way (John 6:54, 64).[54]

Augustine reflects on the "holy people"—Moses and Aaron as priests and Samuel as a prophet (v. 6)—to whom God spoke "from the pillar of cloud" (v. 7). "What does this *pillar of cloud* signify? It means that God used to speak to them in figures [i.e. in metaphors]. . . . He who of old used to speak in a pillar of cloud, has spoken to us now from his footstool, for he is holy."[55] But as a holy God, He punished the misdeeds of His people (v. 8b). Augustine then elaborates that the misdeeds of Moses, Aaron, and Samuel represent all the misdeeds of the people of Israel. They were punished, but God was "propitious" unto them, implying punishment and forgiveness. This propitious punishment prepares them and us for the life to come.[56]

In the concluding verse, Augustine rightly sees that the worshiper, having worshiped at "His footstool," now does so at "His Holy mountain." He elaborates on the metaphor of Daniel 2:35—"the rock that grew into a lofty mountain which filled the whole earth." That rock is Christ (Ps. 118:22; Acts 4:11).[57] Perhaps Augustine is celebrating the overthrow of another "rock," the goddess Caelestis, that previously had been worshiped in Carthage. But now, Augustine implies, "the worship of the Lord in His holy mountain" has smashed all the pagan idolatry of the Roman Empire.

II. Bonaventure (1217–1274)

Bonaventure, the early Franciscan who was known as "the Devout Teacher," then later as "the Seraphic Doctor," was the best exponent of Augustine in the Middle Ages. Unfortunately, we have no commentary by Bonaventure on any of the Psalms, probably because he sees the Psalms as texts for meditation and contemplation, not for commentary. (In his various works, Bonaventure cites

---

54. Augustine, *Expositions of Psalm 98* 8 (Boulding, 474–75).
55. Augustine, *Expositions of Psalm 98* 9 (Boulding, 477).
56. Augustine, *Expositions of Psalm 98* 10 (Boulding, 477–81).
57. Augustine, *Expositions of Psalm 98* 11 (Boulding, 481–82).

Pss. 91:5–6; 92:5; 94:2; and 96:3; but not Ps. 99.[58]) He focuses on "the Soul's Journey to God" (as one of his works is titled).

If this psalm is to be "heard" rather than "sung," then Bonaventure was right to emphasize using the psalm contemplatively. Francis of Assisi, before him, had a vision of the six-winged seraph, but later, Bonaventure spent much of his life meditating on the six-winged seraph as an image of contemplation, with the six wings representing "the six levels of illumination."[59] In other words, the seraphim are the archetype of the Christian's contemplative life. Without commentary, Bonaventure exemplifies how we should contemplate Psalm 99.

III. William Romaine (1714–1795)

Significantly, Robert Bellarmine (1542–1621), the sacramental commentator, is in contemplative tune with Bonaventure as he exclaims, "Nothing tends so much to stir up that devotion suited to the house of God as an attentive consideration of God's greatness and his gifts."[60] Bellarmine's voice is consistent with later the voice of William Romaine, who argued that evangelical activism was losing the art of contemplation during the rise of the Romantic movement and Christian Zionism. Evangelicalism was eclipsing the sacramental contemplative life with a new emphasis upon hymnody.

Because he was a Hebrew scholar, the new hymnody of the Wesleyan movement strongly upset Romaine. Born a French Huguenot, he became an Anglican priest in central London after a short career as an astronomer. He was also one of the very few Hebraic scholars of his day, understanding the Psalms like few others. No wonder he was a prominent, scholarly preacher! Using the text of 1 Chronicles 16:8–9 ("Sing unto Him, *sing psalms* unto Him") he produced a blistering attack upon the new movement of hymnody. He noted the psalms were prominent in the Anglican prayer book, so why not in the worship? For our dignity as human creatures is solely to glorify God.[61] He wrote a

---

58. See Ewert Cousins, trans., *Bonaventure*, The Classics of Western Spirituality (New York: Paulist, 1978).

59. See Bonaventure, *The Soul's Journey into God* prologue, 5.2, 7.3 (Cousins, 54–55, 61, 112).

60. Saint Robert Bellarmine, *A Commentary on the Books of Psalms*, trans. John O'Sullivan (Dublin: Aeterna, 2015), 468.

61. William Romaine, *An Essay on Psalmody* (London: s.n., 1775), iii–iv.

manifesto against the new cultural trend toward hymnody in 1775 entitled *An Essay on Psalmody*. Following Augustine, he sees that "the testimony of Jesus is the spirit of prophecy," and the Psalms thus speak with the voice of Christ.[62]

In Romaine's second chapter, he notes the three Hebrew words used in the psalms. "Hymns" (*tehilim*) signify rays of light; hence the response is *praise*. Such are the psalms, intended to manifest the glory of God.[63] The Hebrew word *zemer* is "psalm" as a noun, but it refers to tree pruning in its verb form, which Romaine relates to Zechariah 6:12–13 and Christ the God-man—"the branch" who will rebuild the temple.[64] The word *sher* refers to a song, signifying the rule and government of the Prince of Peace.[65] Thus "these three names take in the subject of the whole book [of Psalms]—the *hymns* contain the praises of Immanuel. . .—the *psalms* treat of his taking our nature. . .—the *songs* celebrate the glories of his kingdom, both in earth and heaven, in time and eternity."[66]

For Romaine, all this richness of worship is being lost in the new "hymnody"! In his third and fourth chapters, he shows how Scriptures commanding psalm-singing are being ignored.[67] Then, in his fifth chapter, he shows how "the rules laid down in Scripture for singing them aright" are also lost.[68] Bitingly, Romaine argues the motive for the new hymnody is selfish and displeases God: "Their music is hateful to him. . . . They sing to please themselves, and to please God is not in their thoughts."[69] In his final chapter, Romaine seeks a remedy for his contemporary church, tactfully avoiding the name of John Wesley, who, after all, was preaching in the fields, not in the Anglican churches! He vigorously resents Isaac Watts for apparently having started the retrogression of biblical worship, but he does not tell us so outright!

We close with Romaine's interpretation of Psalm 99:

> This psalm describes the kingdom of Christ, and extols him for vouchsafing his gracious presence to his church, his dwelling place, dwelling visibly in the cherubim to protect it by his love, and to oppose its enemies

---

62. Romaine, *An Essay on Psalmody*, 7–8.
63. Romaine, *An Essay on Psalmody*, 22–23.
64. Romaine, *An Essay on Psalmody*, 24–25.
65. Romaine, *An Essay on Psalmody*, 27.
66. Romaine, *An Essay on Psalmody*, 30–31.
67. Romaine, *An Essay on Psalmody*, 30–60.
68. Romaine, *An Essay on Psalmody*, 60.
69. Romaine, *An Essay on Psalmody*, 85.

by his greatness and holiness: Therefore his people are called upon to worship at his footstool, and to exalt him as their forefathers had done, whose petitions he graciously heard and answered.

The subjects of this most blessed king may rejoice in him at all times. Every sentence in this psalm affords them joy and praise. . . . May the Spirit of the Father and the Son help us to receive all the profit from singing this hymn, which he intended it should be the means of bringing to the people of God in every age.[70]

Romaine composes his own metric rendering of Psalm 99:

I.
The Lord doth reign, altho' at it
    the people rage full sore,
He on the cherubim doth sit
    tho' all the world do roar.

II.
The Lord that in his church doth dwell
    is high and wondrous great,
Above all folk he doth excel,
    and he aloft is set.

III.
The princely pow'r of our great king
    doth love judgment and right;
Thou justly rulest ev'ry thing
    in right'ousness and might.

IV.
To praise the Lord our God devise,
    and honor to him shew,
And at his footstool worship him
    who holy is and true.[71]

70. Romaine, *An Essay on Psalmody*, 170.
71. Romaine, *An Essay on Psalmody*, 170–71.

Part IV. Conclusion

I. Changing Canonical Contexts

See pp. 12–17.

II. Message

Psalm 99 summons Israel to exalt *I AM*, their King, because he is holy, answers prayer, and rules universally. Let us reflect upon the four essentials of this encapsulation of its message.

Exalt Our God and King

The complementary commands in the repeated refrain, to "exalt *I AM* our God" and to "prostrate yourselves" (vv. 5, 9), state the aim of the psalm: to do homage to our God and King, Jesus Christ. In light of Christ's de facto reign over all peoples, and so over their gods (see v. 2), it is right and fitting to exalt him in thought, word, and deed and to bow down in a symbolic gesture of self-lowering in his presence. Though these commands pertain to temple worship in their social context, they should be the Christian's quotidian practices. Because Jesus Christ humbled himself on the cross, "God exalted him to the highest place and gave him the name that is above every name, that at the name of Jesus every knee should bow, in heaven and on earth and under the earth, and every tongue acknowledge that Jesus Christ is Lord, to the glory of God the Father" (Phil. 2:9–11).

Our God Is Holy

The psalm's opening proclamation "*I AM* reigns" (v. 1) is qualified by the thrice repeated "he is holy" (vv. 3, 5, 9). "This psalm," says Maclaren, "grasps the eternal central principle of that rule—namely, holiness. The same thought has been touched upon in other psalms [e.g., 97:12; 98:1], but here it is the single subject of praise."[72] The trisagion, says Weiser, "tunes the whole hymn to a uniform

---

72. A. Maclaren, *The Psalms*, vol. 3, Expositor's Bible (New York: George H. Doran, n.d.), 72.

key note to which the various thoughts continually return."[73] Holiness refers to God's numinous power (vv. 1–3) and his moral perfection (4–5). The disciples experienced holy terror when Jesus calmed a furious storm (Mark 4:39–41), an equivalent to the earth shaking in battle (v. 1). Peter's response, when he saw Christ orchestrate the miraculous catch of fish, captures the union of Christ's terrifying power and his purity: "He fell at Jesus' knees and said, 'Go away from me, Lord; I am a sinful man!' " (Luke 5:4–11). Paradoxically, Gentiles and the creation respond to his holy reign both in rejoicing (97:1) and in quaking (99:1). Both are aspects of worship (Ps. 2:11). Christ reigns according to the covenant stipulations (v. 7; cf. Matthew 5–6), not according to unjust "social justice." He answers the prayers of his people; he does not engineer oppressive laws that deny human freedom.

God Answers Prayer

God illustrates his righteousness by answering the prayers of those who call out to him in faith and who by faith keep his law. "There is commerce of desire and bestowal between the holy Jehovah and us," says Maclaren.[74] The venerable heroes of prayer, Moses and Samuel, called upon God's name, YHWH ("*I AM*," see pp. 1–3). Today, the church calls upon the name of the Lord Jesus Christ. They prayed for forgiveness and to be avenged. The church prays for forgiveness for themselves and others, knowing that they will be avenged at the final judgment (Rev. 6:9–11).

Forgiveness is necessary for the continuation of God's presence. Without forgiveness, people would despair; and without hope, they would not persevere. "Forgiveness," says Maclaren, "is something far better than escape from penalties."[75] This is so because forgiveness kindles a warm spiritual, not merely a cold judicially satisfied, relationship between the wronged and the forgiven. Psalm 99 speaks of our God as "lifting up sin" from off of us; Christ bore them on the cross as he made atonement for us.[76]

73. Weiser, *The Psalms*, 641.
74. Maclaren, *The Psalms*, 75.
75. Maclaren, *The Psalms*, 76.
76. Weiser, *The Psalms*, 644.

Our God's Kingdom Is Universal and Particular

Finally, the psalm presumes the paradox of universalism and particularism. Zion and Israel are "the funnels of God's benefactions to the whole world," says Schaefer.[77] God chose Israel not to exclude the nations but to include them by their identifying themselves both with Israel's God and with his people (cf. Ps. 100:3). *I AM* universally rules all nations from Mount Zion, not from Gerizim or Mecca (vv. 1–2; cf. Isa. 48:1–3). He rules all nations through "Jacob," not Ishmael (v. 4). Both Zion and Jacob are types of the true reality. Christ sits at the right hand of God in the heavenly Mount Zion and sends forth his mighty scepter of word and Spirit (Heb. 12:22–24). "Jacob" finds his true identity and fulfills his mission in the Lord Jesus Christ; and Jesus Christ is fulfilled in his anointed church, the members of his body on earth. She is a royal priesthood (1 Pet. 2:9), the true successor of Moses and Aaron, whose prayers her Lord answers (John 14:13f.).

---

77. Konrad Schaefer, *Psalms*, Berit Olam (Collegeville, MN: Liturgical Press, 2001), 245.

CHAPTER 11

Psalm 100: Jubilate Deo

PART I. VOICE OF THE PSALMIST: TRANSLATION

A psalm for giving grateful praise.[1]

1   Shout to *I AM*, all the earth!

     2   Serve *I AM* with rejoicing!
        Come before him with a joyful shout!

3   Know that *I AM,* he is God!
        He himself has made us;
     indeed, we are his people[2]
     and the flock he shepherds.[3]

4   Enter his gates with grateful praise,
          his courts with praise!
     Give him grateful praise!
        Bless his name!

5   For[4] *I AM* is good;
     his unfailing love [endures] forever,
     his reliability throughout generations.

---

1. Or "for the sacrifice of grateful praise."

2. *Kethiv* reads (and LXX reflects) *welō' 'ănaḥnû 'ammô* (= "and not we ourselves; [we are] his people"), but *Qere* (so also Aquila, Tg., Jerome) reads *welô* (= "and we are his, his people"). More probably *l'* is emphatic; see C. F. Whitley, "Some Remarks on *lu* and *lo*," *ZAW* 87 (1975): 202–204.

3. Or "flock of his pasture" (see *IBHS*, §5.6b).

4. Or "surely."

PART II. COMMENTARY

I. Introduction

Form, Structure, and Rhetoric

The psalmist rivets our praise on *I AM* by mentioning him in sixteen out of about forty words.[5] To adorn his subject, he interlaces an alternating and a chiastic structure. The psalm's two stanzas alternatively call for praise and give cause for praise. Thus:

Superscript	
Stanza I	1–3
Strophe A: Call to Praise (Resolve)	1–2
Strophe B: Cause for/Content of Praise (Reason)	3
Stanza II	4–5
Strophe A: Call to Praise (Resolve)	4
Strophe B: Cause for/Content of Praise (Reason)	5

Besides this alternating pattern, the poet arranges his seven (the number of divine perfection) imperatives in a chiastic structure. Thus:

A. Shout to *I AM*
    B. Serve him
        C. Come (*bō'û*) before him
            X. Know
        C'. Enter (*bō'û*) his courts
    B'. Give him grateful praise
A'. Bless his name

"His name" is referenced in A/A'; possibly, the joyful shout blesses his name. "Serve him" is clarified by the liturgical commands: "enter his gates/courts" and "give him grateful praise" in B/B'. This is reinforced by "come"/"enter" (*bō'û*), chiastically repeated as the last and the first words calling for praise in C/C'. In a chiastic structure—like throwing a rock into a pond with mirroring ripples—the poet focuses attention on the pivot (X): "Know that *I AM* is God and he has made us [Israel; see p. 13]." Both notions are introduced with an

5. *I AM* (4×), name (1×), pronoun (11×).

emphatic "he" (*hû'*). As in all Hebrew poetry, verset b expands or intensifies verset a (see pp. 23–25). Thus Psalm 100:3a is expanded in 3b, and 3b is intensified by matching α and β versets:

> (3a) Know that *I AM,* he is God!
>> (3bα) He himself has made us;
>>> (3bβα) indeed we are his people
>>> (bββ) and the flock he shepherds.

Beat Weber notes that the psalm begins with universal space ("all the earth," v. 1) and ends with eternal time ("throughout all generations," v. 5), forming a type of inclusio.[6]

II. Exegesis

Superscript

The anonymous author includes himself in the "we" (i.e., Israel) of verse 3. This psalm has striking similarities to Psalm 95. Both praise psalms begin with a call for "shouts" of joy, using both *rua'* and *rinnâ*. In both liturgies, the worshipers are called "to come/enter" (95:6a; 100:2a, 4a), and both say that *I AM* has made us (95:6a–7; 100:3).[7] A *psalm* is a sacred song set to music (see 92:1; p. 25). In this psalm, the nations ("all the earth," v. 1) confess that *I AM* is God and that he shepherds Israel. Probably, the psalm serves as a libretto to a grateful praise sacrifice (see p. 5). If so, the Gentiles, who are reckoned as clean, share in eating the grateful praise sacrifice with Israel while telling of God's wonderful deeds (cf. Ps. 107:21–22). This sacrifice was highly esteemed in later Judaism: "In the time to come, all sacrifices will cease, but the sacrifice of thanksgiving will not cease."[8] The sacrifice of praise continues in the church, which is composed of some Jews and mostly Gentiles: "Through Jesus, therefore, let us continually offer to

---

6. Beat Weber, "Psalm 100," *BN* 91 (1998): 90–97, esp. 93.

7. For a detailed argument that Psalms 95 and 100 form an inclusio around the "*I AM* is King" group in Psalms 96–99 see David M. Howard, Jr., *The Structure of Psalms 93–100*, BJSUCSD 5 (Winona Lake, IN: Eisenbrauns, 1997), 138–141, 175f.

8. Quoted in Jack R. Lundbom, *Jeremiah 21–36*, AB (New York: Doubleday, 2004), 536.

God a sacrifice of praise, the fruit of lips that openly profess his name"
(Heb. 13:15).

Stanza I 1-3

Strophe A: Call to Praise (Resolve) 1-2

1 The loudness and strong emotion of *shout* (*hārî'û* = *rûa'* Hiphil) can be
inferred from other uses of *rua'*. For example, battle orders rise to a dramatic
climax, with the command that the attacking army give an anticipatory victory
shout (*rua'*, cf. Josh. 6:10, 16; 1 Sam. 17:52; Amos 1:14; Isa. 42:13; Jer. 50:15). Shouts
also accompany blasts on a trumpet to sound an alarm, causing people to tremble before impending doom. Here the verb occurs as an inclusio with the noun
"joyful shout" (*renānâ*). Worship should not be like a funeral. The plural refers to
all the individuals of the earth (see below). *To* I AM (see pp. 1-3). To judge from
the similar call to praise in Psalm 98:4-9, *the earth* refers to the planet, though it
may denote specifically the "land [of Israel]." The seven plural imperatives show
that the earth is a metonymy for its human inhabitants, to wit, "the Gentiles" (see
Gen. 12:1-3), though it may also be a personification for terrestrial objects (cf.
Ps. 98:4-8). *All*, a synecdoche of the whole for the parts, excludes none. Perhaps
Gentile officials at the Jerusalem temple represent the nations.

2 *Serve* I AM fundamentally means to be in subjection to or in a subordinate position to him as Master. "To serve *I AM*" may be an ethical,
comprehensive notion of regarding one's whole life to be in his service, as
in Joshua's famous confession: "As for me and my household, we will serve *I
AM*" (Josh. 24:15; cf. 1 Kgs. 8:23). That meaning *a fortiori* entails the Psalter's
narrower liturgical notion: to serve him in the temple ritual, as "enter his
gates/court" (v. 4) suggests. The six imperatives calling for praise ("shout,"
"serve," "come/enter," "give grateful praise," "bless") are nuanced by the audience: They admonish non-worshipers (cf. Psalm 2:11) but encourage worshipers—like the commands of a cheerleader. As admonitions, they function
to deliver the nations and the unregenerate from their idols (see p. 9). In
other words, "to serve *I AM* entails a change of masters."[9] *With rejoicing*
(*śimḥâ*) denotes gladness and joy with the whole disposition, as indicated

9. David Daube, *The Exodus Pattern in the Bible*, All Souls Studies (London: Faber
and Faber, 1963).

by its association with the heart (cf. Exod. 4:14; Pss. 19:8[9]; 97:11; 104:15; 105:3) and *nepeš* (trad. "soul"; i.e., desire and appetites; see p. 268n1). This is not a restrained, inactive disposition of the psyche, but joy expressing itself spontaneously in an elementary way: in joyful leaping (Jer. 50:11), stamping of the feet and hand clapping (Isa. 55:12), dance, music, and joyful shouts (1 Sam. 18:6; 2 Sam. 6:12, 14).[10] *Come before him* as a liturgical term means substantially "enter the sanctuary," [11] where the ubiquitous God is uniquely present above the ark of the covenant to bless (cf. Ps. 139:7–12). None can escape his ubiquitous presence, but none can enter God's unique presence lightly or as a matter of right (cf. Ps. 15). Gentiles may come before him because they praise *I AM* for his benevolences to Israel and so bless Abraham's mediatorial people (see v. 3; cf. Gen. 12:3). Today, Christians come without doubting to God's throne of grace through the priesthood of Jesus Christ (Heb. 4:16). *With joyful shouts* (*birnānâ*; see 90:14) means primarily a loud expression and so shares the semantic domain of *rûaʿ* ("shout"; see v. 1; cf. Ps. 47:1).

Strophe B: Cause for / Content of Praise (Reason) 3

Know that (see 90:11) entails making a decision to trust Israel's testimony that their God is the living God and that they are his people, a confession that "simultaneously expresses pride and humility, awe and trust."[12] Their confession "dethrones and nullifies every other claimant."[13] I AM is emphatic: something like "*I AM* himself."[14] *God* (*ʾelōhîm*) signifies the quintessence of his divine nature and his eternal power (Rom. 1:20) in contrast to mortals. In Israel's bold confession to the world, *he himself has made us*, the "he" is emphatic, and "us" (as always in Israel's hymnbook) refers to the children of Israel. "Made" refers to the production of the nation through its founder, Moses. *And indeed we are his people*—that is to say, his family whom he adopted as his sons (Exod. 4:22,

10. Ruprecht, *TLOT*, 3:1274, s.v. *śmḥ*. Such "Dionysian exuberance" is found at marriages (Song 3:11; Jer. 7:34; 25:10), the wine harvest (Isa. 9:3[2]; 16:10), the reception of victors (1 Sam. 18:6), the coronation of a king (1 Sam. 11:15; 1 Kgs. 1:40, 45), and on holy days (Num. 10:10).

11. A. S. van der Woude, *TLOT*, 2:1012, s.v. *pānîm*.

12. Artur Weiser, *The Psalms*, OTL (Philadelphia: Westminster, 1962), 647.

13. Walter Brueggemann, "Psalm 100," *Int* 39 (1985): 66.

14. With the addition of *hûʾ*, the subject is expressly resumed and therefore strengthened (GKC, 141g).

23; Rom. 9:4). *De jure*, Israel is his people; *de facto*, they enjoy the benefits of that relationship conditionally upon obedience to his covenant. *The flock he shepherds* (see 95:7a).

Stanza II 4–5

Strophe A: Call to Praise (Resolve) 4

All nations are now invited to *enter* (see v. 2) *his gates*—the sanctuary's holy precincts. The temple, God's house, was viewed as a palace, with walls, gates, courtyards, and the palace itself. *His courts* refers to both the outer courtyard and the inner courtyard, where the priests offered sacrifices. *With praise* denotes the Gentile's verbal expression of sincere and deep approval and admiration of Israel's God. God adopted Israel as his family that they might proclaim his praise (Isa. 43:20; 1 Pet. 2:10). Paradoxically, the psalmist calls upon people to volitionally laud *I AM*, but to be true praise, it must be spontaneous and joyful (see v. 1). The content of the psalm provides the fuel for praise, and the call to praise provides the match that ignites it. By exalting God's glory, worshipers align themselves with God's ways: his character and his purpose to establish his kingdom, where his will is done *ex animo* on earth as it is in heaven. The Gentiles entered *I AM*'s courts to *give him grateful praise* (see superscript) and are now called upon to execute that worship. The future vocation of the redeemed in glory is to sing praise to God and the Lamb (Rev. 4:11; 5:12–14; 7:12). *Bless* differs from other words in the semantic domain of "praise" by proclaiming that God bestows blessings (e.g., life and success). J. N. Oswalt writes:

> [Blessing's] major function seems to have been to confer abundant and effective life upon something (Gen. 2:3; 1 Sam. 9:13; Isa. 66:3) or someone (Gen. 27:27f; Gen. 49). . . . The verbal blessings . . . could be descriptive, an acknowledgement that the person addressed was possessed of this power for abundant and effective living (Gen. 14:19; 1 Sam. 26:25). This address becomes a formalized means of expressing thanks and praise to this person because he has given out of the abundance of his life.[15]

---

15. John N. Oswalt, *TWOT*, 1:132, s.v. *berek. Knee*. Oswalt questionably thinks the verb "to bless" (*bārak*) is a denominative of *berek* ("kneel").

C. A. Keller essentially agrees: "to bless God" means to "declare him *bārûk* ['blessed'],"[16] and "the one designated as *bārûk* is the originator of a healthful situation and therefore the object of praise and thanks."[17] *His name* describes his nature and character and anticipates its full meaning in further revelation (see pp. 1–2). Moreover, as William Sanford LaSor says, "To learn a person's name is to enter into a relationship with his very being."[18] Today, God's people enter and enjoy relationship with him through the name of the Lord Jesus Christ (see "Message" below; also p. 3).

Strophe B: Cause for / Content of Praise (Reason) 5

Good (*ṭôb*) frequently introduces the liturgical list of God's praiseworthy attributes (see Jer. 33:11; Pss. 106:1; 107:1; 118:1, 29; Ezra 3:11; 1 Chr. 16:34; 2 Chr. 5:13; 7:3). It signifies being ethically moral (i.e., beneficial[19]) and being pleasing (i.e., delightful[20]) and so connotes desirability. Its Latin equivalents are *util* (useful, beneficial, helpful) and *frui* (enjoyable, pleasurable, delightful). "The sun is *util*; the sunset *frui*."[21] The cherries of a cherry tree are *util*; its blossoms are *frui*. The two notions often become attenuated as in "a good [i.e. cheerful] heart" (Prov. 15:15). So it signifies what benefits and enriches life and is also attractive, with an emphasis more or less on one or the other but never in contradiction to one another, unlike the roughly put distinction in Greek between *kallos* (aesthetically good) and *agathos* (morally good). Weiser comments, "This shows to what a high degree the aesthetic and artistic and the ethical and religious aspects of the worshipping life are . . . comprehended as a unity."[22] The antonym of "good" is "evil"—what is baneful.

16. C. A. Keller, *TLOT*, 1:272, s.v. *brk* Piel.
17. C. A. Keller, *TLOT*, 1:269, s.v. *brk* Piel.
18. William Sanford LaSor, David A. Hubbard, and Frederick Bush, *Old Testament Survey: The Message, Form and Background of the Old Testament* (Grand Rapids: Eerdmans, 1992), 134.
19. Used of a just, virtuous man (Prov. 14:14), and of a kind and helpful person (1 Sam. 25:15).
20. Used of a good-looking woman (Gen. 24:16; cf. Zech. 9:17), of well-fed cattle (Gen. 41:26), of a quality mantle (Josh. 7:21), and of a favorable promise (Jer. 33:14) or news (2 Sam. 18:27).
21. James Bryan Smith, *The Magnificent Story* (Downers Grove, IL: InterVarsity, 2017), 66.
22. Weiser, *The Psalms*, 615.

But what is the basis of goodness? Plato, in the dialogue *Euthyphro*, posed a moral problem in its classic form: "Is what is morally good commanded by God because it is morally good, or is it morally good because it is commanded by God?" On the one hand, if there are moral standards independent of God's will, then God is not sovereign over the standard but himself subject to a higher eternal standard independent from him. On the other hand, if something is good simply because God commanded it, then what he commands could be arbitrary, capricious, despotic and tyrannical. There would be no meaningful distinction between good and bad, and morality would no longer be based on reason and on conscience. The confession that God is "good" cuts through the nonsense. The basis of goodness is God himself. God does what is in the best interest of others because that is his inherent nature, not because he must conform to a standard independent of himself. And because he is "good," he does not command what is detrimental to another; he wills only what is beneficial. The confession that God is good, however, is a judgment by the faithful. Who has not been disturbed by the catastrophes of war and the excesses of humanity? But the faithful recognize their limitations. We can only decide whether a matter is good or bad when we see it holistically and thus clearly. No one has ascended to heaven and has seen the whole picture. The psalmist's foot of faith almost slipped off the path of godliness when he saw the prosperity of the wicked and the plight of the pious. His perplexity lasted "till I entered the sanctuary of God; then I understood [the wicked's] final destiny" (Ps. 73:17). What he saw in the sanctuary were symbols to live by faith in God's benevolence; e.g., the altars and the mercy seat where atonement was made; the table of "showbread" (KJV, lit. "bread of the face/presence") that spoke of his sustenance for those who live in his presence, and the lampstand that provides light in darkness. All of these prefigure Jesus Christ, who is the same yesterday and today and forever (Heb. 13:8). The wicked, who do not participate by faith in these means of grace, die. Finally, "good," like all of God's communicable attributes, entails community. Love, fidelity, grace, and goodness have no existence apart from their being exercised toward another. God himself is Being in Community. The three Persons of the Trinity benefit one another with no taint of damaging self-interest. So also is God's community with humankind: His thoughts, words, and deeds always benefit people.

The ten liturgical lists cited above (p. 260) supplement God's goodness with his *unfailing love* (*ḥesed*). *Ḥesed* entails a relationship between two parties, one of whom meets the need of the other for deliverance or protection. The stronger party does so out of the intrinsic motivation of his or her nature that is characterized by loyalty, fidelity, love, and kindness; not out of an extrinsic, self-serving motivation. When the time drew near for Jacob to die, he called for his son Joseph and said to him, "Show me *ḥesed.* Do not bury me in Egypt, but when I rest with my fathers, carry me out of Egypt and bury me where they are buried" (Gen. 47:29f.). Obviously, Jacob could not bury himself; he had to depend on his son's kindness to him. Moreover, Jacob does not threaten Joseph or offer to reward him for his "responsible keeping of faith."[23] Joseph fulfills his promise to his father out of his godly nature, his *ḥesed.* God's *ḥesed* assumes his covenant with Abraham, Isaac, and Jacob and includes forgiving his people when they repent and renounce their sin (Prov. 28:13), as David did when he committed adultery with Bathsheba (Ps. 51:1[3]). *Forever* (*'ôlām*), says Jenni, "with the exception of a few later passages in Koheleth, has the meaning 'the most distant time,'"[24] and that is within some historical framework. With the prepositions "from" and "to," it refers to the remote past and to a final, distant time respectively. But with reference to God, who transcends time, it has the theological and philosophical notion of eternity ("forever, ever, always"; cf. Pss. 90:2; 92:8[9]; 102:12[13]; 103:17). The Hebrew word glossed *reliability* (*'emūnâ*) derives from *'mn,* whose root meaning is "to be firm." This fundamental sense of firmness occurs literally in Exodus 17:12: "When Moses' hands grew tired . . . Aaron and Hur held his hands up . . . so that his hands remained (*'emūnâ*) till sunset." From this is derived the figurative meaning "dependable, faithful, reliable." But, as Jepsen says, "'*emunah* is not so much an abstract quality, 'reliability,' but a way of acting which grows out of inner stability, 'conscientiousness.' Whereas *'emeth* is always used in relationship to something (or someone) [such as words] on which (or whom) one can rely, *'emunah* seems more to emphasize one's own inner attitude and the conduct it produces."[25] With *throughout generations* ("until generation and generation"), the static *'ôlām* ("forever") is broken down into dynamic, successive generations.

23. K. D. Sakenfeld, *The Meaning of Ḥesed in the Hebrew Bible*, Harvard Semitic Museum 17 (Missoula, MT: Scholars, 1978), 233.

24. E. Jenni, *TLOT*, 2:853, s.v. *'ôlām.*

25. Jepsen, *TDOT*, 1:317, s.v. *'āman.*

Part III. Voice of the Church in Response

I. Augustine of Hippo (354–430)

Augustine preached on Psalm 100 (= LXX 99) in late 403 or early 404. His method of exegesis was always to follow the words carefully, so scholars who exaggerate the contrast between the Antiochene and Alexandrian schools should note that Augustine uses both approaches as the text requires. Trained as he was as a rhetorician, he is careful to use the tools appropriate to the genre. For Augustine, Psalm 100 is both universal praise and personal confession.

Michael Cameron points out that Augustine, in his interpretation of the Psalms, was

> less concerned with passages whose meaning was obvious, or, as he put it, "needed only a reader and a hearer," than with those that demanded an expositor because the meaning was obscure. . . . His custom was not to focus on "the letter," or the literal sense, of the psalm . . . , but to reach "through" the letter, as it were, to search out the mysteries within. . . . The dialectic between the parts of the Bible that were open or closed to the understanding was like the constant opening and closing of "God's eyelids" (Ps. 10:5), either encouraging or challenging the interpreter of Scripture (10:8. . .). . . . The Scriptures were full of "secrets," "enigmas," and "shadows" that were plainly "mystical," "pregnant," and "veiled."[26]

Augustine exhorts his audience to contemplate God in the glories of creation, which is why "we shout for joy." We contemplate them when we ask, "Who made all these things? Who created them? Who created you, my soul, as one among them all? What are the things you are contemplating? And what are you, who contemplate? Who is he, who made both the things you contemplate and you, who contemplate them? Who is he?"[27] Augustine then exhorts us to "draw near to God by recovering his likeness." He writes, "Think about him, then, before you speak of him, and in order to think about him, draw near to him . . . to get a good view."[28] This requires us

---

26. Michael Cameron, *"Enarrationes in Psalmos,"* in *Augustine Through the Ages,* ed. Allan D. Fitzgerald, O.S.A. (Grand Rapids: Eerdmans, 1999), 291.

27. Augustine, *Exposition of Psalm 99* 5, in *Expositions on the Psalms,* trans. Maria Boulding, vol. 5 (Hyde Park, NY: New City, 2002), 15.

28. Augustine, *Exposition of Psalm 99* 5 (Boulding, 16).

to have purity of heart, as Jesus taught in the Beatitudes. "Be like him, then, in tender dutifulness, and love him with your power of thought, because God's invisible reality is contemplated through things which are created."[29]

Christians should "serve the Lord with cheerfulness" because there is freedom in serving God with spontaneity and joy.[30] "Yet there is no escape from tiresome neighbors," so we need Paul's exhortation "to bear with each other in love" (Eph. 4:2).[31] As sheep of the Creator and Redeemer, we can never be proud but always full of thanksgiving. As "gates" are symbolic of a new entry, so we are invited to begin a new life with confession, indeed confessing with hymns, for "hymns are songs of praise."[32] Augustine concludes, "Never think that you will weary of praising him. Your songs of praise are like eating: the more you praise, the more strength you acquire, and the more delightful he becomes whom you are praising."[33]

II. Robert Bellarmine (1542–1621)

Robert Bellarmine has been our sacramental commentator throughout this volume, and again he refreshes us with his spirit. He begins his commentary on Psalm 100 by saying

> To sing joyfully means, as we have frequently repeated, to praise with loud and joyful voice and to serve with gladness means to be obedient through love, and not through fear. . . . All you worshippers of the true God, in whatever part of the world you may be cast, praise him. Good and bad are to be found all over the world: in the wheat there will be found the cockle, and thorns among the lilies.[34]

Likewise, in our own experiences—good or bad—the apostle Paul reminds us, "In all things God works for the good of those who love him" (Rom. 8:28). We serve *I AM* with gladness, by "obeying him freely, and not as if you were under

29. Augustine, *Exposition of Psalm 99* 6 (Boulding, 17).
30. Augustine, *Exposition of Psalm 99* 7 (Boulding, 18–19).
31. Augustine, *Exposition of Psalm 99* 9 (Boulding, 20).
32. Augustine, *Exposition of Psalm 99* 16 (Boulding, 27).
33. Augustine, *Exposition of Psalm 99* 17 (Boulding, 28).
34. Saint Robert Bellarmine, *A Commentary on the Books of Psalms*, trans. John O'Sullivan (Dublin: Aeterna, 2015), 467.

coercion—with joy as freemen, and not with the bitterness of slaves. For, as St. Augustine expresses it, Truth delivered us, but love has made us slaves; and he that is a slave from love is one with pleasure."[35] Nothing, he adds, so much incites us as devotion to God and consideration of who God is. As his people, we are the sheep of his pasture, in his divine providence over us.[36]

According to Bellarmine, the psalmist enumerates three divine attributes: sweetness, mercy, and veracity. Yet God's divine power can appear to be contradictory to these other attributes. He is "the Father of compassion and God of all comfort" (2 Cor. 1:3), and yet "it is a dreadful thing to fall into the hands of the living God" (Heb. 10:31). But this apparent contradiction is easily reconciled since "God is sweet to the upright in heart. . . ; he is rough and terrible to the crooked in heart."[37]

III. William Romaine (1714–1795)

William Romaine's (see p. 248n66) commentary and metric rendering of Psalm 100 is so valuable that I present it here in full:

> The whole church is here called upon to praise our God for his greatness, and goodness, and truth, and to praise him with joy, especially in the great congregation. Considering his relation to us, our shepherd, and our relation to him—his people; we ought to rejoice in him in every ordinance. Singing of psalms is appointed for the outward expression of our joy. He requires it. He accepts it. May we perform it today in a manner well pleasing to him, and may we sing to our mutual edification.

> I.
> All people that on earth do dwell,
> Sing to the Lord with cheerful voice,
> Him serve with fear, his praise forth tell,
> Come ye before him and rejoice.

> II.
> The Lord ye know is God indeed,
> Without our aid he did us make,

35. Bellarmine, *A Commentary on the Books of Psalms*, 467.
36. Bellarmine, *A Commentary on the Books of Psalms*, 468.
37. Bellarmine, *A Commentary on the Books of Psalms*, 468.

We are his flock, he doth us feed,
And for his sheep he doth us take.

III.
O enter then his gates with praise,
Approach with joy his courts unto,
Praise, thank, and bless his name always;
For it is seemly so to do.

IV.
Because the Lord our God is good,
His mercy is forever sure;
His truth at all times firmly stood,
And shall from age to age endure.[38]

PART IV. CONCLUSION

I. Literary Context

Psalms 95 and 100 form a frame around Psalms 96–99 (see pp. xi, 262).

II. Message

The psalmist calls all the earth to come before *I AM* in his temple and to bring him a sacrifice—a grateful offering—while enthusiastically singing his praise. Today, Abraham's natural descendants and the Gentiles are one people, fulfilling this summons in a new way. Brueggemann helpfully reflects: "When the community praises, it submits and reorders life. It is not only a moment of worship but also an embrace of a *doxological life*, which is organized differently [than a self-grounded life]"[39] (see p. 9). The doxological life is grounded in faith—faith in Israel's testimony that *I AM* is the living God, that he has made Israel, and that he is reliably good and kind.

38. William Romaine, *An Essay on Psalmody* (London: s.n., 1775), 296–97.
39. Brueggemann, "Psalm 100," 65.

In the old dispensation, God wanted to be known by his name, YHWH (see pp. 1–3). Today, he wants to be known by the name of his Son: the Lord Jesus Christ. Jesus said of himself, "Before Abraham was, *I AM*" (John 8:58). Whatever the church does, whether in word or deed, it does it all in the name of the Lord Jesus (Col. 3:17). It prays in his name (John 14:13f.) and preaches that "there is no other name under heaven given to mankind by which we must be saved" (Acts 4:12). Today, Christians, who praise the name of Jesus Christ, come from more nations and tribes than there are nations in the United Nations or that participate in the Olympic games. For over two millennia, the church has testified to the world: "Know that Jesus Christ is God's Son and we are the flock he shepherds" (see v. 3; John 10).

CHAPTER 12

Psalm 103: Praise, My Soul, the King of Heaven

Part I. Voice of the Psalmist: Translation

By David.

1   Bless *I AM*, my soul[1];
     all my inward parts, [bless] his holy name!

2   Bless *I AM*, my soul,
     and forget not all his deeds—

3   who forgives[2] all your iniquities,
     who heals all your infirmities;

4   who redeems your life from[3] the pit,
     who crowns you with unfailing love and compassion;

---

1. Possibly, *nepeš* has its more original meaning of "throat" (Travis J. Bott, "Praise and Metonymy in the Psalms," in *The Oxford Handbook of the Psalms*, ed. William P. Brown [Oxford: Oxford University Press, 2014], 137f.). Its traditional gloss, "soul," may mislead an English-speaking audience into thinking of *nepeš* as an equivalent of the Greek *psyche*, "the seat and center of life that transcends the earthly" (BAGD, 893). Hebrew *nepeš*, however, refers to the passionate drives and appetites of all breathing creatures, both animal and human. In the NT, a person *has* a "soul"; in the OT, a person *is* a *nepeš* (B. Waltke, *TWOT*, 2:387–91, s.v. *nephesh*).

2. The perfectives in vv. 12, 13, 19b are construed as gnomic (*IBHS*, §30.5.1c) as indicated by other predicates that pertain to a universal situation—participle ("works," v. 6), imperfectives ("renews," 5; "accuse," 9; "flourish," 15), statives ("towers," 11; "knows," 14), and nominal clauses (8, 17)—by the comprehensives "all" (3) and "forever" (9, 17); and by the gnomic situations (5, 11, 13, 15, 16, 19).

3. Perhaps "[from] going down to [the pit]" is elided (*IBHS*, §11.4.3d), but that notion could have been expressed clearly by "to keep/preserve from" (cf. Job 33:13; Isa. 38:17) or by using "from going down" (Job 33:24, 28; Ezek. 28:8; Pss. 30:9; 55:23[24]), "draw near to" (Job 33:22), "spare from going down to" (Job 33:24, 28), or "to turn back from" (Job 33:30).

268

5   who satisfies your desires[4] with good things—
      your youth renews itself like the eagle's.
6   *I AM* does righteousness
      and justice for all the oppressed.
7   He made known his ways to Moses,
      his mighty deeds to the children of Israel:
8   *I AM* is compassionate and gracious,
      slow to anger, abounding in unfailing love.
9   He does not accuse forever,
      nor does he harbor his anger forever;
10   he does not treat us as our sins deserve,
      nor repay us according to our iniquities.
11   For as the heavens are high above the earth,
      his unfailing love towers over those who fear him;
12   as far as the east is from the west,
      so far he removes our transgressions from us.
13   As a father has compassion on his children,
      so *I AM* has compassion on those who fear him;
14   for he himself knows how we are formed,
      mindful that we are dust.
15   As for mortals, they are like grass;
      as a flower of the field, so they flourish;
16   because[5] the wind blows over it and it is gone,
      and its place remembers it no more.
17   But the unfailing love of *I AM* is from everlasting to everlasting
      upon those who fear him,
      and his righteousness to their children's children—
18   to those who keep his covenant
      and remember to do his precepts.
19   *I AM* has set up his throne in heaven,
      and his kingdom rules over the whole [universe].
20   Bless *I AM*, you his angels,
      you mighty ones, who do his bidding,
      who obey his word.
21   Bless *I AM*, all his [heavenly] hosts;

4. Text uncertain. Reading LXX *tēn epithymian sou*, not MT ʿ*edyēk* ("your jewels"). Some emend the Heb. to ʿ*ōdēkî* (cf. ʿ*ôdî*, "my continuance," Ps. 104:33).

    5. Or "when."

you his servants who do his will.
22 Bless *I AM,* all his works
in all the places of his dominion.
Bless *I AM,* my soul.

PART II. COMMENTARY

I. Introduction

Author

The MT and the Septuagint (LXX) superscript identify King David as the author (see pp. 13–15), and there is no reason to think otherwise.[6] This psalm has several intertextualities with the prophets, but it is unclear who is citing whom.[7]

Genre

Psalm 103 is a hymn. It speaks of "all of *I AM*'s benefits" (v. 2f.), and its perspective is a universal present, not one looking back on a historical answer to prayer (see n. 2). The psalm contains the typical motifs of a hymn: call for praise, cause for praise, and renewed call for praise (see p. 191n14). The original setting is a worship service, presumably at the well-appointed house of *I AM,* where salvation history was remembered. *I AM* overhears the psalmist addressing expanding circles (vv. 1-6, 7–19, 20–22) in the psalmist's praise of him, and *I AM is* pleased (see p. 10).

6. Some debunk the LXX superscript because the rare fem. sing. suffix *ēkî* (see n. 4; GKC, 91e) corresponds to the Aramaic suffix. But Aramaisms do not prove a late date (*IBHS,* §§1.4.1e, 1.4.2c). Mitchell Dahood (*Psalms II,* AB 17 [New York: Doubleday, 1968], 24) thinks the form might be a Canaanite archaism (c. 1300 BCE).

7. Instructively, Hermann Gunkel (H. Gunkel and J. Begrich, *Introduction to the Psalms: The Genres of the Religious Lyric of Israel,* trans. James D. Nogalski [Macon, GA: Mercer University Press, 1998]) contradicts himself. On the one hand, he says that v. 9a relies upon Jer. 3:5, 12; that v. 9b relies on Isa. 57:6; and that vv. 15ff. rely on Isa. 40:6f. (p. 290). On the other hand, he says that Deutero-Isaiah cites Ps. 103 (p. 221). A similar ambiguity of dependence exists between v. 16b and Job 7:7.

Rhetoric

As is common, and so probably intentional, the psalm's twenty-two verses match the number of letters in the Hebrew alphabet. An inclusio, "Bless *I AM*, my soul" (vv. 1, 22), frames the psalm. By these two restraints, the poet feels the catharsis of having fully expressed his boundless enthusiasm. He widens the circle of praise from himself (vv. 1–5) to Israel (6–19) to everything (20–22), forming three stanzas. The first stanza consists of a call to praise (vv. 1–2) and a cause for praise (3–5), the second of only the cause, and the third of only the call. Verse 19 is a janus that segues the second stanza into the third stanza. Addressed to Israel, it belongs with the second stanza. But its references to God's throne in heaven—matching the (heavenly) host in verses 20–21 and the inclusio "rule" (*māšālâ*, v. 19) and "dominion" (*memšālâ*, v. 22), both from the Hebrew root *mšl*—link it with the third stanza.

Here is a sketch of its structure according to its form, semantics, grammar, and rhetoric:

Superscript
Stanza I: Address to Self 1–5
    Strophe A: Call to Praise 1–2
    Strophe B: Cause for Praise: Deliverance from the Pit 3–5
        1. Forgiveness and Healing 3
        2. Redemption and Honor 4
        3. Satiation with Good and Rejuvenation 5
Stanza II: Address to Israel 6–19
    Strophe A: *I AM*'s Righteousness 6
    Strophe B: *I AM*'s Unfailing Love and Mercy 7–18
        1. With Reference to Sin 7–12
          a. Confession of *I AM*'s Mercy and Unfailing Love ... 7–8
          b. *I AM*'s Anger Has Limits 9–10
          c. *I AM*'s Love Has No Limits 11–12
        2. With Reference to Time 13–18
          a. *I AM*'s Compassion for Mortals 13–14
          b. Brevity of Mortals 15–16
          c. *I AM*'s Love Is Everlasting 17–18
    Strophe C: *I AM*'s Sovereignty 19
Stanza III: Address to Everything 20–22
    Strophe A: To Angels Who Do His Will 20–21
    Strophe B: To Everything 22a
    Strophe C: To Self 22b

The second stanza is framed by "righteousness," "do/does," and "unfailing love" (vv. 6, 17f). Verse 6 stands apart from the six quatrains that follow. These quatrains unfold the beauty and fragrance of God's grace that informs his forgiveness, like the unfolding petals of a maturing rose. The first three pertain to sin, beginning with Israel's classic confession in connection with the golden calf incident (7–8). The last three quatrains pertain to time, contrasting the brevity of mortals (13–14, 15–16) with *I AM*'s everlasting love to the children of children (17–18). These three quatrains are framed by the inclusio, "children" and "those who fear him" (vv. 13, 17f.). In sum, the second stanza is framed by two single, transitional verses (6, 19) around a center of six quatrains that confess and amplify *I AM*'s mercy and unfailing love.[8] Thus, the second stanza consists of two sections of seven verses each: one (v. 6) and six (vv. 7–12) followed by six (vv. 13–18) and one (v. 19).

Transitional terms segue the changes within the structure: "benefits" (v. 2) into specific causes (3–5); "good deeds" (5) into the confession of *I AM*'s benefits (6–18); and a pun on *mšl* ("rule," 19; "dominion," 22). If the janus (v. 19) is numbered with vv. 20–22, the size of the first and last stanzas and their fourfold "all" balance each other.

Like a skillful upholsterer, the poet covers over his outline's seam in verses 12, 13 with the chiastic pun on the particle *k-*: "because"/"as" (vv. 11, 12) and "as"/"because" (vv. 13, 14).[9] The poem sparkles with escalations, inclusio, assonance (see n. 10), and memorable images. The poet's lavish gilding of the flowers (v. 15) contributes to making this three-thousand-year-old hymn, sung by the Son of God himself, one of the most familiar and beloved of all the psalms.

II. Exegesis

Superscript

By David (see "Author" above).

---

8. Note the initial (predicate) participle that links v. 6 with the initial (relative) participles in 3–5.

9. The assonance of initial palatal *k* and palatals *g* and *ḥ* also covers this seam: *kî kigbōah* (v. 11), *kirḥōq* (12), *kᵉraḥēm* (v. 13), *kî* (14). The assonance of *kî* in *bārᵃkî* (1, 2) with the rare poetic feminine suffix form in *ʿăwônēkî* ("your iniquities," GKC, 91l) binds the call to praise (1–2) with its cause (3).

Stanza I: Address to Self 1–5

The repetitions of "bless" in the call (vv. 1–2) and of relative clauses that substantiate the call ("[the one] who . . . ," vv. 3–5) unify this stanza and its strophes.

Strophe A: Call to Praise 1–2

1   In a soliloquy for the benefit of the congregation at the temple, the psalmist, through an abrupt threefold anaphora of *bless* (see 100:4) I AM (see 100:1), awakens himself from his apathy and lethargy to praise *I AM* (cf. 42:5–6). *My soul* (i.e., my vital forces and cravings, see n. 1) is enhanced by *and all my inward parts* (e.g., heart, liver, kidneys; cf. Isa. 26:9), which were thought to be the seat of disposition, thought, will, and emotion. A person's enthusiasm in praise is a measure of one's spiritual health. *His . . . name* (see pp. 1–3; 100:4) is a surrogate for God's person. To cut off the name is to destroy a person (cf. Deut. 7:24; 9:14; 1 Sam. 24:21). *Holy* (see Ps. 96:9) refers to preternatural and supernatural dread that lead to behavioral purity.

2   The litotes *and forget not* is a strong way of saying "remember." God does not repeat his saving acts, such as the exodus and the resurrection of Jesus Christ. Salvation comes by remembering (i.e., participating in, not "dismembering" from[10]) the ancestors' testimony (cf. Deut. 4:9; Judg. 2:10f.; Pss. 63:5; 77:11; Luke 24:19; Rom. 10:9). *All* God's deeds "would be too many to declare" (Ps. 40:5), and so "all" is relative to the deeds recounted in verses 3–5. *Deeds*— always intentional and ethical—may refer to evil and/or harmful actions (Isa. 3:11), but here it refers to beneficial acts (Judg. 9:16; 2 Chr. 32:25).

Strophe B: Cause for Praise: Deliverance from the Pit 3–5

The benefits of forgiveness (v. 3a) escalate to total healing (3b) to deliverance from the pit (4a) to being crowned (4b) and to total saturation with everything good (5a), even eternal life (5b).

1. Forgiveness and Healing 3

Forgives is the only nonfigurative term signifying "to stop feeling anger toward an offender and to forgo punishing them." I AM is always its subject,

---

10. W. Schottroff, *TLOT*, 3:1325, s.v. *škḥ*.

for only the Lawgiver can pardon breaking his law (cf. Ps. 51:4[6]; Mark 2:7). To confess God's forgiveness entails repentance and faith in God's grace. *Iniquities* (see Ps. 90:8) comprehensively encompasses religious and/or ethical crimes and also the resulting guilt.[11] *Heals* with the object *infirmities* refers to physical maladies.[12] *All* encompasses past, present, and future sins and healing (cf. vv. 11–12). Setting "forgives all your iniquities" parallel to "heals all your infirmities" implies the infirmities are due to sin (see Pss. 6, 38, 130; cf. 32:1–5) and that healing is entailed in forgiveness. But not all infirmities are due to sin (cf. Job and protest psalms; e.g., Ps. 44:22). Also, although forgiveness is immediate, healing may not be immediate. The healing of all infirmities looks beyond clinical death to the eschaton (cf. Isa. 33:24). The logic of the psalm demands this eschatological interpretation. All mortals die due to one form of infirmity or another (15–16), and so the healing of *all* infirmities must go beyond these terminal infirmities.[13] A saint dying of a terminal cancer once said: "There is no sickness that a good resurrection can't cure!"

2. Redemption and Honor 4

Redeems refers to the action of the legal protector of a family member who has fallen into distress at the hands of a stronger opponent (cf. Ps. 19:14[15]; Prov. 23:10f.; Jer. 50:34): for example, redeeming a family member from slavery. The living God obliges himself to redeem his family members from sin and death. The New Testament deepens this doctrine immeasurably (Rom. 3:22–26). *Life* refers to vital and functioning existence. *From* signifies separation. *Pit* denotes a hole large enough that a person or animal cannot escape from it: a trap (Ezek. 19:4; Pss. 7:15[16]; 35:7), a dungeon (Isa. 51:14), or, as here, a metaphor for Sheol/the Grave (Ps. 30:9; Job 33:24, 28). Had the poet intended salvation from a premature death, he could have expressed that notion clearly (see n. 3). Figuratively, *crowns* signifies placing on the honoree a wreath woven out of *I AM's unfailing love* (see Ps. 100:5) *and compassion.* "Compassion" denotes the tender yearnings of a superior for a helpless inferior, such as a mother

11. R. Knierim, *TLOT*, 2:862, s.v. ʿāwōn.
12. Diseases (Jer. 16:4), starvation (Jer. 14:18 NLT), destruction of land (Deut. 29:22f.), and Jehoram's bowels coming out (2 Chr. 21:19).
13. David's own son died (2 Sam. 12:13–14), and the New Testament provides a number of examples of sick believers whom the Lord did not will to heal: Paul (2 Cor. 12:7–10), Epaphroditus (Phil. 2:25–30), Timothy (1 Tim. 5:23); Trophimus (2 Tim. 4:20).

feels for her baby (cf. Gen. 43:30; 1 Kgs. 3:26). Its sense may be evoked from its etymology: "womb."

3. Satiation with Good and Rejuvenation 5

Satisfies signifies to fill to the full measure of something's capacity. *Desires* (see n. 4) assumes righteous desires. The trusting psalmist would not desire anything gained unethically, and the holy God satisfies him *with good things* (lit. "good," *ṭôb*: what is beneficial and beautiful [see Ps. 100:5]), not evil things— what is detrimental to abundant life). The proverb "food for the stomach and the stomach for food" (1 Cor. 6:13) implies that God both creates the hunger and satisfies it; to create hunger without provision would be diabolical. Like Juan Ponce de León, who is said to have sought the fountain of youth, all desire *youth* that *renews itself like the eagle's.*[14] The eagle may have been chosen because it is the "strongest of the feathered race, most fearless, most majestic, and most soaring"[15] (cf. Isa. 40:31). Moreover, it has a much longer life span than other birds (c. 30 years compared to the average of two to five years). Adult birds molt at least once a year, "renewing" their appearance.

Stanza II: Address to Israel 6–19

Strophe A: I AM's Righteousness 6

I AM *does* (see 98:1) *righteousness* (i.e., establishes right order, see 98:2) *and justice* (i.e., restores right order; see 96:13; 97:2; 98:9; 99:4)—two metonymies for "deeds" (v. 2). He does this *for all the oppressed*—not just Israel. Note the shift from an individual to a collective. The oppressed are in a situation in which someone stronger takes from them, directly or indirectly, their produce and labor without giving anything in exchange.[16] Egypt, for example, unjustly robbed Israel of its wealth and gave nothing in return; but in the exodus, Israel plundered Egypt (Exod. 12:36).

---

14. *Nešer* may signify "eagle" or "vulture" (*HALOT*, 1:732, s.v. *nešer*).

15. Charles Spurgeon, *The Treasury of David*, ed. Roy H. Clarke (Nashville: Thomas Nelson, 1997), 910.

16. It may be by dishonest scales (Hos 12:7–8[8–9]), through the court system (see Mic. 2:2; 6:9–12; 7:1), or by withholding wages from a hired man who is poor and in need of them before sunset (Deut. 24:14).

Strophe B: I AM's *Unfailing Love and Mercy 7–18*

The second stanza continues on the theme of *I AM's* forgiveness. It commences by confessing *I AM's* benevolent attributes that inform his forgiveness and then developing them like the unfolding petals of a rose.

1. With Reference to Sin 7–12

  a) Confession of I AM's *Mercy and Unfailing Love 7–8*

Verse 8 stands in apposition to "ways" in verse 7.

7 *He made known* (see Ps. 98:2) *his ways to Moses* echoes Moses' prayer "show me your ways" (Exod. 33:13). Figuratively, "way" evokes the intertwined notions of character (cf. v. 8) and conduct. *The children*[17] *of Israel* are the patriarchs' organized offspring, who are united by their common blood, memory, and acceptance of God's covenant. *His mighty deeds*, with reference to God, refers to his mighty acts (cf. parallel "wonders" in 78:11), such as in the exodus and conquest (see Exod. 34:11).

8 David now recites the words of God's self-portrait in Exodus 34:6, what Moses called "your glory" and *I AM* called "my goodness" (Exod. 33:18, 19).[18] *Compassionate* (see v. 4) *and gracious* (i.e., "bestows a favor that cannot be claimed"). *Slow to anger* woodenly means "long of face" (i.e., a relaxed face), signifying patience. The patient person is relaxed when wronged and controls their emotions to think and act according to kindness and ethics. With God, this is a benevolence giving sinners an opportunity to repent (Jonah 4:2). *Abounding* shows that God's love exceeds that of people.

  b) I AM's *Anger Has Limits 9–10*

Verses 9–10 are united by their amplifying *I AM's* forgiveness and love through litotes.

9 *Accuse* (i.e., "to reclaim the right of") envisions a situation wherein an aggrieved party makes an oral complaint against the party held responsible for

---

17. The pl. form can mean children of both sexes (Haag, *TDOT*, 2:150, s.v. *bēn*).
18. The creed occurs in Exod. 34:6; Pss. 86:15; 103:8; 145:8; Joel 2:13; Jonah 4:2; Neh. 9:17.

the grievance. *Forever* (*neṣaḥ*, v. 9a) refers to perpetuity without limits; *forever* (*'ôlām*, v. 9b) refers to the most remote future. The root *nṭr*, glossed *harbor his anger*, occurs only four other times and belongs to the semantic domain of "to be angry" (cf. Lev. 19:18). The gloss "to bear a grudge" is questionable, for it is based on a probable homonym meaning "to guard, maintain" (cf. Song 1:6; 8:11–12).[19]

10 *Sin* (*ḥāṭâ*) woodenly means "to miss [the mark]" (cf. Judg. 20:16). With regard to ethical behavior, a sin is "a disqualifying error,"[20] specifically "against someone with whom one stands in an institutionalized community relationship."[21] *Repay* (cf. 2 Sam. 22:21) glosses a verb meaning to perform an act that affects someone favorably (cf. Prov. 31:30) or unfavorably (see Prov. 3:30).

c) I AM's Love Has No Limits 11–12

Two spatial similes link this quatrain. On the vertical axis, the love of God "over-towers" those who fear him (v. 11), and on the horizontal axis, it "over-distances" their transgressions from them (12).

11 *For* or "surely" introduces an analogical, not logical, argument. *Towers over* sometimes has the sense of "prevail over," but that sense is inappropriate with people who subject themselves to God's will. *Those who fear him* has a rational aspect: an objective revelation that can be taught and memorized (Ps. 34:11[12]ff.; cf. 19:7–9[8–10]). It also has an emotional aspect: people respond to God in fear and love, trusting that he will keep his threats and promises.[22] It narrows nominal Israel down to true Israel as the beneficiaries of God's grace.

12 Etymologically, *the east* means "the place of [sun's] rising/shining," and *the west* means "the place of [sun's] setting/evening." *Our transgressions* denotes "a willful, knowledgeable violation of a law or standard."[23]

19. In *The Concise Dictionary of Classical Hebrew* (ed. David Clines [Sheffield: Phoenix, 2009]), 271, s.v. *nṭr*, cf. entries #1 and #2.

20. M. Saebo, *TLOT*, 1:406–408, s.v. *ḥṭ'*.

21. K. Koch, *TDOT*, 4:311, s.v. *ḥāṭā'*.

22. Bruce K. Waltke, *Proverbs 1–15*, NICOT (Grand Rapids: Eerdmans, 2004), 100f.

23. Robin C. Cover, "Sin, Sinners (OT)," *ABD* 6:32.

2. With Reference to Time 13–18

a) I AM's Compassion for Mortals 13–14

13 *As a father . . . children* applies to many, but not all, fathers.[24]

14 The reason for mercy is much the same as God's reason not to decree another flood (Gen. 8:21)[25] and Moses' reason for God to forgive (Exod. 34:9): to wit, the limitations of human nature. *Mindful* (see 98:3) *that we are dust* refers to the loose dirt (Ezek. 24:7) on the surface of the ground and is an allusion to Genesis 2:7. Dust is associated with death and ignominy (Gen. 3:19; Ps. 22:29[30]; cf. Gen. 3:14; 1 Sam. 2:8; 1 Kgs. 16:2; Isa. 47:1; Pss. 7:5[6]; 22:15[16]; 44:25[26]; 119:25).

b) Brevity of Mortals 15–16

15 *As for mortals* glosses *'enôš* (i.e., humankind in its weakness; see Ps. 90:3). *Like grass* (cf. Ps. 90:5–6; Job 14:2; Isa 40:6; 51:12) is a powerful image that provokes pathos for the mortal's brief lifespan.

16 *Because* (or "when"). *The wind* connotes unpredictable and sudden adversity. *Passes through it* recalls when God passed through Egypt with death (Exod. 12:12–23). The personification, *and its place* where it once thrived *remembers it no more,*[26] calls to mind the disconsolate Preacher's reflections on death (see Eccl.).

c) I AM's Love Is Everlasting 17–18

Mortals cannot guarantee *I AM*'s unfailing love will endure from generation to generation, but the everlasting God can. Moreover, there is a reciprocity between *I AM*'s initiative and human response.

17 *Everlasting* (eternity past) *to everlasting* (eternity future; see Pss. 90:2; 100:5). *Their children's children* echoes *I AM*'s words following the golden calf

---

24. David pitied his children to a fault: Amnon (2 Sam. 13:2–19), Absalom (2 Sam. 18:5–33), and Adonijah (1 Kgs. 1:6).

25. F. Delitzsch, *Psalms,* trans. Francis Bolton, Keil and Delitzsch Commentary on the Old Testament 5 (London: T&T Clark, 1866–91; repr., Peabody, MA: Hendrickson, 1996), 648.

26. *HALOT*, 1:700, s.v. *nkr.*

incident (Exod. 34:7). There, the phrase refers specifically to the third and fourth generations of the unrepentant guilty, but here it refers to the thousands of generations of the forgiven who keep *I AM*'s covenant.

18 *To those who keep* (see 99:7; cf. Exod. 34:11). *His covenant* alludes to the Ten Commandments, which are housed in the sacred ark (cf. Exod. 34:28; Deut. 10:1–5).[27] The precise meaning of *regulations* (*piqqûdîm*) is uncertain because its three occurrences share the same context.

Strophe C: I AM*'s Sovereignty* 19

Established (see 93:1) here signifies "to set up on a firm basis."[28] *His throne* (Ps. 93:2) symbolizes the King's "authority, power, majesty and splendor"[29] as a warrior, administrator of justice and builder (see p. 4). *The heavens* denotes "the unchangeable realm above the rise and fall of things below."[30] *His kingdom* refers to the *I AM*'s universal kingdom, not to his particular kingdom, Israel.[31]

Stanza III: Address to Everything 20–22

The reference to *I AM*'s throne in the heavens and his rule over everything (v. 19b) segues into a call for the angels in heaven (19a; 20f.) and everything in

27. It found a fuller elaboration in the Book of the Covenant (Exod. 24:7) and its fullest amplification in the Book of the Law (see Bruce K. Waltke, "A Janus Decalogue of Laws from Homicide to Sexuality [Deuteronomy 22:1–12], in *For the World: Essays in Honor of Richard L. Pratt Jr.*, ed. Justin S. Holcomb and Glenn Lucke [Phillipsburg, NJ: P&R, 2014], 3–19).

28. Of *I AM*'s kingdom (1 Sam. 13:13; 2 Sam. 7:12; 1 Chr. 17:11), of his throne (Isa. 9:7), and of the world (Jer. 10:12).

29. Leland Ryken, James C. Wilhoit, and Tremper Longman III, eds., *Dictionary of Biblical Imagery* (Downers Grove, IL: IVP Academic, 1998), 868.

30. Delitzsch, *Psalms*, 648.

31. In his universal kingdom, *I AM* "rules over the whole [universe]" (i.e., exercises his will over everything everywhere, v. 19) without regard to human consent (cf. Dan. 4:3). In this kingdom, the Sovereign even assigns the nations their deities (Deut. 4:19; 29:26) and establishes all governing authorities (Rom. 13:1). In his particular kingdom, *I AM* exercises his will through human beings who subject themselves to his rule. The psalm does not attempt to resolve the mystery of human accountability within his sovereignty.

his dominion (19b; 21) to praise. The connection, strengthened by the pun on "rule" and "dominion" (see p. 272), suggests that *I AM* exercises his sovereignty through the angelic host.

Strophe A: To Angels Who Do His Will 20-21

"*I AM* presides from his throne, surrounded by all the host of heaven (1 Kgs. 22:19; 2 Chr. 18:18)."[32] "Heavenly hosts" (v. 21) qualifies "angels" (v. 20; cf. Ps. 148:2).

20 *Angels* means "messengers." These beings are frequently used as couriers (see p. 83n83). We can infer much about these messengers of *I AM* in his heavenly court from human messengers in the king's court on earth. Messengers had facility in languages and played a number of roles: diplomats, soldiers, royal agents, military governors, intelligence agents, postmen, chaperones, and agent-provocateurs. "The professional courier had to be courageous and bold and his training must have included the study of military strategy and tactics."[33] *Mighty ones* are elite military champions.[34] *Who do his bidding by obeying him* shows that the King exercises his sovereignty through these elite heavenly spirits (Heb. 1:14).

21 *Heavenly* is added to *hosts* in translation to distinguish the celestial armies from human armies (cf. 1 Sam. 17:45). The celestial hosts in the poet's imagination may be connected with the stars "by virtue of the stars' infinite number [cf. Isa. 40:26], their brilliant light, their strength and their identity with a specific ruler"[35] (cf. Ps. 33:6; Isa. 40:25-26; Neh. 9:6) The stars also do *I AM*'s bidding (Job 9:7), fight his battles (Judg. 5:20) and praise him (Job 38:7; Ps. 148:3). *His servants* (*mᵉšārtāyw*) denotes those in the heavenly court "who minister to or wait on another" (cf. Heb. 1:14). No hierarchical distinction is intended by the qualification "his ministering angels," but there may be an intentional dis-

---

32. Ryken, Wilhoit, and Longman, *Dictionary of Biblical Imagery*, 869.

33. A. D. Crown, "Tidings and Instructions: How News Traveled in the Ancient Near East," *JESHO* 17 (1974): 244-71, esp. 254-66; see A. D. Crown, "Messengers and Scribes," *VT* (1974): 366-70.

34. The Hebrew word for "mighty one" was used of Nimrod (Gen. 10:8), Goliath (1 Sam. 17:51), David's three mightiest soldiers (2 Sam. 23:9), the king (Ps. 45:3[4]), the Messiah (Isa. 9:5), and God (Deut. 10:17; Ps. 24:8; Isa. 10:21).

35. Ryken, Wilhoit, and Longman, *Dictionary of Biblical Imagery*, 372.

tinction between them and fallen angels (2 Pet. 2:4; Jude 6; Rev. 13:4). *Pleasure* also means "will."[36]

Strophe B: To Everything 22a

22 The Sovereign also accomplishes his will and pleasure through his works, such as wind and flames of fire (104:4). *All his works* (see Ps. 92:5) are his by virtue of the fact he made them. The poet personifies the praise that his works elicit from humankind (see p. 18–19). Everything everywhere (*in all the places*) functions according to his good pleasure, for it all belongs to *his dominion* (cf. "kingdom," v. 19).

Strophe C: To Self 22b

See v. 1.

Part III. Voice of the Church in Response

I. Introduction

Like Psalms 1 and 2, this psalm is one of the pivotal psalms of the whole Psalter, one of the great hymns of praise. The posture of Psalm 103 is the posture of all the great fathers of the church, from Augustine of Hippo to Martin Luther, John Calvin, and Robert Bellarmine. It is a failure of liberal scholarship today to have no "Christian emotions" aroused by Psalm 103—to describe merely physical posture, "praise from the throat," and other cognitive descriptions. The psalm's creational posture, showing that we were created to be the *imago Dei*—"praise before God"—is ignored. But previous generations of commentators rightly saw in it the centrality of praise as a hymn that David himself might have sung.

Psalm 103 begins as a soliloquy addressed twice over to "my soul" (vv. 1, 2). This phrase is repeated seven times between Psalms 103 and 104, indicating the freedom of the worshipers to explore their inner being before *I AM*. This repetition is meant to explore the five virtues of the soul: one's inner being, the exercise of the eyes, the *élan vital* of the body, the joy of *I AM*, and the deep recesses of the heart. These are recognized in the Talmud, whose scholars also distinguish three virtues of the soul: bodily, intellectual, and spiritual. This is

36. N. Walker, "The Renderings of *Rāṣôn*," *JBL* 81 (1962): 184.

all "my soul"—"my being." But the second cry of verse 2 acknowledges that the virtues of the soul identified in verse 1 still need divine forgiveness to recover their original innocence, for praise is addressed to "his holy name." Then, verse 3 applies two descriptions of the state of the soul: iniquity and sickness. The former needs retribution, the latter needs healing.

II. Augustine of Hippo (354–430)

Augustine preached on Psalm 103 [= LXX 102] in Carthage on the occasion of a martyr's festival around the year 411.[37] His audience was in a state of reverent grief and fear, but Augustine could comfort them that "the voice of the soul need never fall silent as it blesses the Lord." We bless *I AM* "for every gift he gives us, for every consolation he sends, for the forgiveness that stays the punishment . . . and for all his works [of creation]."[38] Augustine invites them to express gratitude, to explore God's kindness in spite of temptation to sloth or unbelief. The invitation is repeated so that we never forget "all His benefits." With such seriousness, urgency, and fullness of being, we can never respond enough.

What Is the Soul?

All is encapsulated in what we call "the soul." This is more than any organ of the body, more than the voice, bodily gestures, or even the mind or spirit. It is comprehensive of all our actions, as the apostle exhorts us: "Whether you eat or drink or whatever you do, do it all for the glory of God" (1 Cor. 10:31). Awake or sleeping, silent or vocal, we are called to be praising people.[39]

Augustine is preaching to an audience remembering the kinds of martyrs we rarely have today in the West and we rarely think about. Theirs was the praise of those who laid down their lives for their friends (1 John 3:16). No one can show greater love than to lay down their life for their friend. But can we repay God in any way, when all we are—our existence and gifts—are all "His benefits" to us? Even with regard to our being, it is God who has made us and made to be humans, not animals. Such then is our need for "humility,

37. Augustine, *Exposition of Psalm 102*, in *Expositions of the Psalms*, trans. Maria Boulding, vol. 5 (Hyde Park, NY: New City, 1990), 78n1.

38. Augustine, *Exposition of Psalm 102* 1 (Boulding, 78).

39. Augustine, *Exposition of Psalm 102* 2 (Boulding, 78–79).

... obedience, ... religious worship."[40] "Think then, my soul, about all the ways in which God has repaid you, but think about them in the context of all your evil deeds."[41]

How Can We Repay God?

Mindful of this, the martyrs looked for a gift they could offer God and almost despaired when they found none. They wondered, "What return shall I make to the Lord for all the repayment He has made to me?" They found no means of repayment, save one: "I will take in my hands the cup of salvation" (see Ps. 116:13). They could not give to God from their own resources, but only from his. Augustine says, "If you look to yourself to find the means of repayment, all you will give him is sin. The repayment he wants is not from your resources, but from his. . . . Make truth your repayment, and praise the Lord in truth."[42]

Our response might be to truly meditate on Jesus's prayer in the Garden of Gethsemane: "If it is possible, let this cup be taken from me" (Matt. 26:39). This is what the martyrs imitated in identifying with the sufferings of Christ. Yet Jesus challenged the disciples: "Can you drink the cup I am to drink?" (Matt. 20:22). Augustine exhorts: "Render your homage in full awareness that you received everything that you offer. Let your soul bless the Lord in such wise that you do not forget all the ways in which he has repaid you."[43]

Christ, the Omnipotent Healer

The psalm lists the ways God has repaid us. Sin is like a disease that corrupts everything. He heals that by forgiveness. It appears as one disease, but it is a complex of diseases. We have "weak flesh," susceptible to and battered by many temptations. " '[These diseases] are great,' you say; but the physician is greater. An omnipotent doctor is never confronted with an incurable disease. All you need to do is to allow yourself to be cured."[44] The psalmist assures us, *I AM*

---

40. Augustine, *Exposition of Psalm 102* 3 (Boulding, 80–81).
41. Augustine, *Exposition of Psalm 102* 4 (Boulding, 81).
42. Augustine, *Exposition of Psalm 102* 4 (Boulding, 81).
43. Augustine, *Exposition of Psalm 102* 4 (Boulding, 82).
44. Augustine, *Exposition of Psalm 102* 5 (Boulding, 83).

"will redeem your life from corruption," after he has "healed all our diseases." Will he who loves us not heal us wholly?[45]

I AM *"Crowns You" for the Victory He Has Won in You!*

As the compassionate, *I AM* crowns us with his pity and mercy (v. 8). "We were vanquished in ourselves, but victors in him." Such are some of the many paradoxes about God! The apostle could claim, "I worked harder than all of them—yet not I, but the grace of God that was with me" (1 Cor. 15:10); "I have finished the race, I have kept the faith" (2 Tim. 4:7). "There is no room for pride," only unceasing praise for the exceeding goodness of God. "God made all things exceedingly good in creation. . . . Words fail us, to express how good he is, so we shout for joy, to express inarticulately how good he is."[46]

Being Renewed like an Eagle

In Augustine's world, there was a myth that as the eagle grew old, its beak grew excessively, preventing it from being able to eat. To prevent this, the eagle would break its beak to renew its life. Augustine uses this illustration to express that Christians die in Christ while still alive, enabling them to live in the light of the resurrection.[47] A young couple recently told me their marriage was "dead." To their astonishment, I responded, "How wonderful, now you can make a new marriage 'in Christ.' " And that is what has happened: Their marriage has been "renewed like the eagle's"!

Augustine comments that only the triune God can "satisfy our longing with good things," for his fatherhood is not human fatherhood that may be wanting. It is divine. Nor does he sleep, unheeding of our cries. Expressing human desire, Philip asked Jesus, "Show us the Father, and that is enough for us." But Jesus told him that those who had seen him had seen the Father, and that the Holy Spirit would also communicate the Father to us (John 14:8–9, 26). Augustine, who had written a profound treatise on the Holy Trinity, in old age now confesses, "I have some notion of the Trinity. But

---

45. Augustine, *Exposition of Psalm 102* 6 (Boulding, 83).
46. Augustine, *Exposition of Psalm 102* 8 (Boulding, 87).
47. Augustine, *Exposition of Psalm 102* 9 (Boulding, 89–90).

it is like looking at a confused reflection in a mirror. . . . But when shall I be satisfied?"[48]

Demand Justice Only If There Is Nothing in You That Deserves Punishment

The God who exercises abundant mercy is the One who commands us to love our enemies! Augustine answers the natural response of his audience, "How can I do so?" First, he says, make sure you are not the offender in blaming him. Second, as in the incident of the adulterous woman, make sure you are not adulterous too in your thoughts (John 8:7)! Third, remember God's mercy is to everyone, even to the ravens, that in turn fed Elijah. Fourthly, realize that God gives gifts to those living an immoral life, so "If your enemy is hungry, feed him" (Rom. 12:20). He adds, "Do not let your compassionate instincts remain dormant because it is a sinner who accosts you . . . for we all bear two names, a human being, and a sinner!"[49]

Anyone then, who gives a cup of water in Jesus's name is acting as Jesus would (Matt. 10:41–42). The Christian life is all about showing mercy, giving mercy, and being merciful, because all we can express about God is compassion!

God's Mysterious Purpose in Giving the Law

"The law," says Augustine, "was given that the patient's sickness might be diagnosed, and that he might beg to have the doctor's aid."[50] For as the apostle Paul realized, "there was a war within himself," and longing for peace in the wretched state he was in, he cried out, "Who will rescue me from this body that is subject to death?" (Rom. 7:23–25). This deep mystery is shared with us, argues Augustine, "that as sin multiplied, proud people might be humbled, and being humbled might confess, and having confessed might be healed."[51]

---

48. Augustine, *Exposition of Psalm 102* 9 (Boulding, 90).
49. Augustine, *Exposition of Psalm 102* 12 (Boulding, 94).
50. Augustine, *Exposition of Psalm 102* 15 (Boulding, 97).
51. Augustine, *Exposition of Psalm 102* 15 (Boulding, 98).

God's Long Patience

Regarding verse 9 Augustine asks, "Could there ever be any greater instance of long-suffering patience than God had with His people?" But we must be careful that his wrath does not suddenly descend upon us! God is constant and not to be trifled with. As the apostle teaches, "Like the rest, we were by nature deserving of wrath" (Eph. 2:3). This "wrath" began in the Garden of Eden: "By the sweat of your brow you will eat your food until you return to the ground" (Gen. 3:19). But the psalm also comforts us that "He does not accuse forever, nor does he harbor his anger forever" (v. 9).[52] For we have not received what we deserved. "The Lord has consolidated his mercy over those who fear him: in what measure? In proportion to the height of heaven above the earth." It is as if Augustine knew the findings of modern atmospheric science: that there is an ozone layer that makes it possible for planet earth to be a human habitation! Yes, he argues, we are sometimes tempted to believe God has forsaken us, but this would "only be true if the sky was withdrawn from the earth."[53]

Why has God removed our sins from us? Because "as a father has compassion on his children, so *I AM* has compassion on those who fear him" (v. 13). *I AM* remembers we are as dust. Augustine again refers to the Genesis story, when God took and breathed into that dust to create man.[54] Our days, then, are as grass that springs up momentarily then dies and dries up. Human glory is, as Isaiah says, "like the flower of the grass. The grass is dried up, and its flower wilted, but the word of the Lord abides forever" (Isa. 40:6–8). "The wind will blow over them—in ruin and destruction—knowing the place no more," as indeed we can witness at the archaeological sites in the Middle East today. But Augustine marvels, "All flesh is but grass, yet the Word was made flesh!" (John 1:14).[55] Clearly there is no room for human pride!

In God's Ultimate Justice, Charity Fulfills the Law

God's saving justice is for the children's children. Here Augustine interprets "children" as human actions, and the rewards of those actions are "children's

---

52. Augustine, *Exposition of Psalm 102* 17 (Boulding, 99).
53. Augustine, *Exposition of Psalm 102* 18 (Boulding, 100).
54. Augustine, *Exposition of Psalm 102* 21 (Boulding, 102).
55. Augustine, *Exposition of Psalm 102* 22 (Boulding, 102–103).

children." By "memory"—that is, continual observance—we keep his covenant, not worrying about keeping all "the laws." The essential thing is to exercise constant love. "Hold on to whatever you have already, but above all hold onto charity, for the end of the commandment is charity" (1 Tim. 1:5). Verse 19 closes the stanza by declaring that he who descended and has ascended is now sovereign Lord of all and will be sovereign forever.[56]

Angelic Praise

Psalm 103 extends the sphere of God's rule within our own hearts and over Israel to be over the whole cosmos—to angels, archangels, and all the habitation of God. Angelic ministry is to be obedient to God's word, to carry it out, and to wholly do God's will. "All his works," praise their Creator God, the Sovereign of all. There is no place where his presence is not and where his will is not done. He blesses universally.[57]

Finally, as alpha and omega, the last verse ends as the first verse began: "Bless *I AM*, my soul."[58]

III. John Calvin (1509–1564)

Jean Cadier, a biographer of John Calvin, has called the Swiss reformer "the man God mastered."[59] Calvin had a horror of those who preached their own ideas in place of the gospel of the Scriptures.[60] In Augustinian reflection, Calvin recognizes that God is holy and that we are not. This is the meaning behind the "total depravity" of man before the majestic holiness of God. As he states in the *Institutes*: "True humility gives God alone the glory. . . . As our humility is his loftiness, so the confession of our humility has a ready remedy in his mercy."[61]

---

56. Augustine, *Exposition of Psalm 102* 23ff. (Boulding, 103ff.).

57. Augustine, *Exposition of Psalm 102* 28–29 (Boulding, 105).

58. Augustine, *Exposition of Psalm 102* 29 (Boulding, 106).

59. Jean Cadier, *Calvin: The Man God Mastered*, trans. O. R. Johnson (Grand Rapids: Eerdmans, 1960).

60. Burk Parsons, "The Humility of Calvin's Calvinism," in *John Calvin, A Heart for Devotion, Doctrine, & Doxology* (Orlando: Reformation Trust, 2008), 8.

61. John Calvin, *Institutes of the Christian Religion*, ed. John T. McNeill, vol. 1 (Louisville: Westminster, 1960), 2.2.11.

Calvin endorses the claim by John Chrysostom "that the foundation of our philosophy is humility." But he prefers the approach of Augustine: "When a certain rhetorician was asked what was the chief rule in eloquence, he replied 'Humility' ... the second rule, 'Humility' ... the third rule, 'Humility'; if you ask me concerning the precepts of the Christian religion, first, second, and third, and always, I would say, 'Humility.' "[62] By "humility" Augustine meant "freedom from self-consciousness." When a church worship leader exhibits self-consciousness, they are not leading true worship. The problem is worse when the congregation cheers the church choir for their good singing or when the congregation cheers itself; then worship becomes idolatrous. Yet sadly, this is a weekly event in many churches. According to Calvin, only the humble can praise God for all his benefits. These will praise him throughout the whole course of their lives. The Israelites constantly failed to do so, and only when we live "in Christ" will we not likewise fail. Christ benefits us in his humility toward us.

If the mystery of the Trinity undergirds the doctrinal basis for Augustine's exposition of Psalm 103, then for Calvin, it is the doctrine of justification by grace, through faith. But even before Calvin, the Franciscan reformers in Spain at the new university of Alcala, led by Cardinal Cisneros, Primate of Spain under Queen Isabella, were developing this basic doctrine. A young graduate of Alcala, Juan de Valdes (c. 1498–1541), wrote his thesis on the doctrine of justification in 1529. Suspected of heresy by the Dominicans, he fled to Italy to ignite an underground Calvinist reform movement called *Il Beneficio di Christo*—"the Benefit of Christ Movement"—and even persuaded Cardinal Contarini in the Vatican to summon a council of the later reformers to find agreement on the doctrine of justification.[63]

IV. William Swan Plumer (1802–1880)

The nineteenth-century American clergyman and theologian William Swan Plumer agrees with Matthew Henry's assessment that "this Psalm calls more for devotion than exposition."[64] He wisely observes, "He, who with a warm heart ... enters into its spirit in any version of it extant, is more enriched by it, and has

62. Quoted by Burk Parsons, "The Humility of Calvin's Calvinism," 11–12.
63. See Leon Morris, introduction to *The Benefit of Christ: Living Justified Because of Christ's Death*, ed. James M. Houston (Portland: Multnomah Press, 1984).
64. Matthew Henry quoted in William S. Plumer, *Studies in the Book of Psalms* (Philadelphia: J. B. Lippincott & Co., 1866), 913.

a better understanding of it, than he who with a cold heart can critically weigh every word in the original, and in each of the many translations given us by ripe scholars."[65] And thus Plumer can pray over the psalm at the conclusion of his commentary: " 'Whatever others do, let me do service to my God. Whatever others love, let me love my Redeemer. Whatever others glory, let me glory in the Lord.' This is my first, my greatest business. Bless the Lord, O My Soul."[66]

Reflecting on verse 22, Plumer concludes:

> As the Almighty is never at a loss for means, agents, or instruments to accomplish his holy will and effect his blessed purposes, so neither shall he ever be at a loss for those who shall pour benedictions on his name, vv. 20–22. There is the innumerable company of angels. Their voices are never silent. But if they should be dumb, redeemed men would praise him. And if all intelligent creation should keep silence, the very stones would cry out, and the planets and fixed stars would become vocal and fill the azure vault above us with unspeakable melody.[67]

Plumer wrote these words in the context of the Newtonian Age of astrophysics, when deism was beginning to silence the praise of God in the culture! In contrast to that cultural trajectory, which has only gained momentum in our time, our historical summary encourages us to take up Psalm 103 with a humble and sacrificial voice. Henry Lyte famously adapts the psalm to English hymnody:

> 1. Praise, my soul, the King of heaven;
> To His feet thy tribute bring.
> Ransomed, healed, restored, forgiven,
> Who like me His praise should sing? . . .
> Praise the everlasting King.
>
> 2. Praise Him for His grace and favor
> To our fathers in distress.
> Praise Him still the same forever,
> Slow to chide, and swift to bless. . . .
> Glorious in His faithfulness.

65. Plumer, *Studies in the Book of Psalms*, 913.
66. Plumer, *Studies in the Book of Psalms*, 919.
67. Plumer, *Studies in the Book of Psalms*, 919.

3. Frail as summer's flower we flourish;
Blows the wind and it is gone;
But while mortals rise and perish,
God endures unchanging on. . . .
Praise the high eternal One.

4. Fatherlike He tends and spares us;
Well our feeble frame He knows.
In His hands He gently bears us,
Rescues us from all our foes. . . .
Widely yet His mercy flows.

5. Angels, help us to adore Him;
Ye behold Him face to face;
Sun and moon, bow down before Him;
Dwellers all in time and space, . . .
Praise with us the God of grace.

PART IV. CONCLUSION

I. Canonical Context

The editors of the Psalter appended this hymn to the lament Psalm 102 because both reflect on human mortality—like withering grass (102:4[5]; 103:15) in contrast to God's everlasting being and his mercy (cf. 102:11–13[12–14], 24–28[25–29]; 103:15–19). But in other ways, they are as different from one another as the moping owl (102:6–7) is from the soaring eagle (103:5). Psalm 103 opens a group of associated praise psalms (Psalms 104–107). It ends with the theme of God's sovereignty over his creation, and Psalm 104 opens in the same way and carries on that theme.

Perhaps David's particular healing from a terminal infirmity provoked this praise song, but this is not a grateful song of praise celebrating an individual's historical deliverance (see p. 5). Rather, it is a hymn praising God for all his benefits, including the eternal life of the faithful saints and of the faithful nation. It is particularly apt in Book IV of the Psalter, the book that responds to the exile that came about because of Israel's sin (see pp. 14–15). In her distress, Israel finds hope in her eternal and heavenly King (cf. v. 17ff.) and finds courage in her history, beginning with Moses (cf. v. 7). By robustly remembering and praising God's forgiveness and everlasting, unfailing love in this reflective song, Israel adds substance to faith, ardor to virtue, and conviction to confession and is nerved to fidelity in testing.

II. Message

Psalm 103 reflects upon and praises God for his forgiveness (v. 3a) and for his sublime benefits beyond what we could ask or think (Eph. 3:20). In each stanza, the poet describes the immensity of those benefits, concluding with the eternal life of the psalmist (his youth is renewed like the eagle's, v. 5), and of Israel (his unfailing love for his people endures through generations, v. 17). These benefits are due to *I AM*'s ways made known to Moses: mercy, grace, patience and especially his unfailing love (vv. 7–8). They are due entirely to his grace, not Israel's merit (v. 10). The focus on forgiveness can be seen in what the poet left out of God's self-revelation to Moses: "He does not leave the guilty unpunished; he punishes the children . . . to the third and fourth generations" (Exod. 34:6–7).

God's elect people can count on these sublime benefits for several reasons. First, *I AM* displayed them to Israel after the incident of the golden calf, as can be inferred from the psalm's many intertextualities with that incident (cf. vv. 7–10; Exod. 32–34). Second, he is everlasting, unlike mortals (14–17). Finally, he is sovereign, working all things according to his good pleasure, even through his mighty angels (19–22).

In our time, God the Father wants to be known by the name of God the Son: the Lord Jesus Christ (see Matt. 18:20; John 14:13; Acts 3:6; 1 Cor. 1:2; Phil. 2:10; Heb. 13:15). Thus, Jesus Christ is the subject of Psalm 103's praise (see pp. 2–3). Through his incarnation as man, he became the true covenant keeper for those who trust him. His perfectly obedient life and his atoning death make God's unfailing love even more certain. Israel and the church's history through toil and tribulation for more than three millennia demonstrates that God's love for those who fear him is everlasting, to children's children until and beyond the time when Christ comes again.

CHAPTER 13

Psalm 104: A Very Great God

PART I. VOICE OF THE PSALMIST: TRANSLATION

By David.[1]

1 Bless *I AM*, my soul.
   I AM, my God, you are very great.
      You are clothed with splendor and majesty,
2 wrapping yourself in light as with a cloak,
      stretching out[2] the heavens like a tent.[3]
3 Who lays the rafters of his[4] upper chambers on their waters;
      who makes the clouds his chariot;
      who goes to and fro on the wings of the wind,
4 making winds his messengers,
      flames of fire his ministers.
5 He set the earth on its foundations;
      it will never be moved.
6 You covered it with the watery depths as a garment;
      the waters stood above the mountains.

1. So LXX and Qumran, not MT.

2. Note the assonance of *'ōṭeh* ("wrapping") and *nôṭeh* ("stretching out").

3. Lit. "curtain," but always (c. 50×) of a tent-curtain; 43× of the tabernacle curtains.

4. Ancient Near Eastern literature, as in the Tell Fekherye Inscription, shifts pronouns between first, second, and third persons without formally signaling the change of perspective (A. Abou-Assaf, P. Bordreuil, and Alan Millard, *La Statue de Tell Fekherye et Son Inscription Bilingue Assyr-Armenne*, Recherche sur les Civilisations 7 [Paris: ADPF, 1982]). An indicator of the stylistic freedom in the Tell Fekherye Inscription is the fact that the first change of person does not take place at exactly the same point in the Akkadian and Aramaic versions. The English idiom does not allow this personal shift without signaling the change.

7   But at your rebuke the waters fled,
         at the crash of your thunder they took to flight.
8   They went up over the mountains;
             they went down into the valleys,
         to the place that you assigned for them.
9   You set a boundary they cannot cross;
             never again will they cover the earth.
10   Who makes springs pour out water in the wadies;
             they flow between the mountains.
11   They give water to all the beasts of the field;
             the wild donkeys[5] quench their thirst.
12   The birds of the heavens reside by them;
             they give voice among the foliage.
13   Who waters the mountains from his upper chambers[6];
             the land is satisfied from the fruit of his work.
14   He makes grass grow for the animals
             and plants for humankind to cultivate,
         to bring forth food from the earth
             15 and wine that gladdens the heart of the mortal—
         to make their faces shine from olive oil—
             even [to bring forth] food that sustains the heart of the mortal.
16   The trees of *I AM* are well watered,[7]
             the cedars of Lebanon that he planted.
17   There the birds make their nests;
             the stork has its home in the junipers.
18   The high mountains belong to the ibex;[8]
             the crags are a refuge for the hyrax.[9]

5. "Wild ass, less probably zebra, of the steppe" (*The Concise Dictionary of Classical Hebrew* [Sheffield: Phoenix, 2009], 364, s.v. *prʾ*).

6. Note the assonance of the Hebrew consonant *mem: mašqeh hārîm mēʿăliyôtāyw mippᵉrî maʿᵃśêkā.*

7. *Yiśbᵉʿû* (lit. "are satisfied") in the context of the gift of water probably means "sated [with water]" (see v. 13).

8. Or "mountain goat." See John McClintock and James Strong, eds., *The Cyclopedia of Biblical, Theological, and Ecclesiastical Literature* (orig. New York: Harper and Brothers, 1894), s.v. "Wild Goat," http://www.biblicalcyclopedia.com/W/wild-goat.html.

9. This yellow and brown Syrian coney (*procavia syriacus*) lives among rocks from the Dead Sea valley to Mount Hermon. About the size of a hare and with small ears,

19   He made the moon to mark the seasons,
       and the sun knows when to go down.
20   You ordained[10] darkness and it became night;
       in it all the beasts of the forest prowl.
21   The lions[11] roar for their prey
       and to seek their food from God.
22   The sun rises, and they are taken away;
       they return and lie down in their dens.
23   Then humankind goes out to their work,
       to their labor until evening.
24   How many are your works, *I AM*!
       In wisdom you made them all;
       the earth is full of your creatures.[12]
25   There is the sea, vast and spacious,
       teeming with creatures beyond number
       —living things both large and small.
26   There the ships go to and fro,
       and Leviathan, which you formed to frolic in it.
27   All creatures look to you
       to give them their food at the proper time.
28   When you give [it] to them, they gather it up;
       when you open your hand, they are satisfied with good things.
29   When you hide your face, they are terrified;
       when you take away their breath, they expire
       and return to the dust.
30   When you send your breath, they are created,

---

it is admirably suited for its habitat. "It has no hoofs but broad nails. The toes, four on the forelegs and three on the back limbs, are connected with skin almost like a web. Under its feet it has pads like sucking-discs, which enable it to keep its footing on slippery rocks" (F. S. Bodenheimer, *Flora and Fauna in the Bible*, Helps for Translators 11 [London: United Bible Societies, 1972], 69–70).

     10. Short prefix conjugation to signify a preterit situation (*IBHS*, §§31.1.1d, e).

     11. Probably young lions that go out on their own in search of prey.

     12. Or "possessions, acquisitions." W. H. Schmidt notes that *qinyān* consistently means "possession, property" (*TLOT*, 3:1150, s.v. *qnh*) but thinks it means "creatures" in Ps. 104 (p. 1152). The same ambiguity exists in the verb *qnh*. The parallel "made"/ "work" favors the Greek translation *ktisis* ("creatures"). This is the meaning of the verb in Prov. 8:22, where it occurs, as here, in connection with "wisdom" (see Bruce K. Waltke, *Proverbs 1–15*, NICOT [Grand Rapids: Eerdmans, 2004], 408–9).

and you renew the face of the ground.
31 May the glory of *I AM* endure forever;
     may *I AM* rejoice in his works—
32 who looks at the earth, and it trembles;
     he touches the mountains, and they smoke.
33 I will sing to *I AM* as long as I live;
     I will sing praise to my God as long as I am.
34 May my meditation¹³ be pleasing¹⁴ to him,
     as I rejoice in *I AM*.
35 But may sinners vanish from the earth
     and the wicked be no more.
Bless *I AM*, my soul!
     Praise *I AM*!

PART II. COMMENTARY

I. Introduction

Author

Psalm 104 is anonymous in the Masoretic Text (MT), but "by David" in the Septuagint (LXX) and Qumran texts (see pp. 13–15). The author adores *I AM*. Twice he calls him "my God" (vv. 1, 33). The poet's pallet is colored with metaphors, similes, metonymies—all sorts of figures of speech. His eye finds the telling detail: The wild donkey slakes its thirst at a pond; birds chirp as they nest in the foliage; the lion roars at night; the rock badger hides in an inaccessible crag.

Some scholars connect the psalm to *The Great Hymn to the Aten*, which is attributed to Pharaoh Akhenaten (1352–1336 BCE). But the Aten, the sun-disc, rules over only the day, not the night "when earth is in darkness as if in death."¹⁵

---

13. Lexicographers dispute the meaning of *śîaḥ* in 1 Kgs. 18:27 and 2 Kgs. 9:11. Aside from Ps. 104:34, it occurs in a context of a person's grievance (1 Sam. 1:16; Job 7:13; 9:27; 10:1; 21:4; 23:2; Prov. 23:29; Pss. 55:2[3]; 64:1[2]; 102:superscription; 142:2[3].
14. The verb is used of sacrifice/offering (Jer. 6:20; Mal. 3:4), of sleep (Jer. 31:26; Prov. 3:24), of lovers (Ezek. 16:37), and of a fulfilled longing (Prov. 13:19).
15. *COS* 1:44–46.

Form

The author identifies his poem as a meditative hymn sung with musical accompaniment. The anaphora of "who" (e.g., v. 3) followed by *I AM*'s sublimities catches us up in his enthusiastic praise of the Creator and Sustainer of all things. He uses the past tense only for God as Creator: his making the earth (vv. 5, 24aβ), manipulating the flood (6–9), and making the moon and darkness (vv. 19–20). But he follows these up with the present tense for God as Sustainer. Unlike in most hymns, he focuses almost exclusively on God's creation, not on salvation history, though he draws his meditation to a conclusion with the prayer "may sinners vanish from the earth." They alone mar it.

Typical of hymns, calls to praise (vv. 1a, 35b) frame reasons for praise (1b–30). The inclusio "Bless *I AM*, my soul" occurs uniquely in 103:1, 22 and 104:1, 35. Instead of beginning his psalm with resolves (e.g., "I will sing" or "I will play") the psalmist uniquely includes them in a "contribution formula" (vv. 33–34).[16] His final call for others to "praise *I AM*" (35c) points to a liturgical setting.

The hymnist mixes direct address to God (e.g., vv. 1–2, 5–9) with proclamations about God (3–5) without signaling the change of perspective. This grammatical anomaly occurs elsewhere in Semitic literature, both in Babylonian and Aramaic (see n. 4) as well as, according to Gunkel, in Egyptian, Vedic and Mexican poetry.[17]

Rhetoric

Following the tripartite cosmology of the ancient world, the hymn reflects upon the heavens (vv. 1–4), the earth (vv. 5–23), and the sea (vv. 24–26). Semantically, and according to its form, the structure of the song can be broadly sketched as follows:

Superscript
Stanza I (Introduction): Call to Soul to Bless *I AM*   1a

---

16. H. Gunkel and J. Begrich, *Introduction to the Psalms: The Genres of the Religious Lyric of Israel*, trans. James D. Nogalski (Macon, GA: Mercer University Press, 1998), 26. Gunkel, whose citations are usually exhaustive, cites Ps. 104 as the only example of such a reversal (p. 28).

17. Gunkel and Begrich, *Introduction to the Psalms*, 33.

The psalm's structure roughly follows the sequence of the creation days in Genesis 1,[18] although it reverses the sequence of sea and land creatures to bring the psalmist's meditation on them to a dramatic climax. The people of the biblical world feared the sea above all things, and especially the mythological Leviathan (v. 26). But our poet climactically pictures ships sailing safely on its surface, and he demythologizes Leviathan to a creature that frolics in it.

The poet gilds his theme of *I AM*'s care for his earth with the divine number. "*I AM*"—apart from its three occurrences in the frame (vv. 1a, 35b)—appears seven times (vv. 1, 16, 24, 31 [2×], 33, 34), as does the "earth" (vv. 5, 9, 13, 14, 24, 32, 35).

The seven strophes of the cause for praise (vv. 1b–32) more or less begin with summary statements unpacked by quatrains (v. 1bα + 1bβ–2, 3–4; v. 5 + 6–7, 8–9; v. 10 + 11–12; v. 13 + 14–15; v. 16 + 17–18; v. 19 + 20–21, 22–23; v. 24 + 25–26, 27–28, 29–30). Similarly, generalizations are particularized by the telling exemplar: "beasts of the field" (11a) by "wild donkeys" (11b), "birds" (17a) by "the stork" (17b), and "beasts of the forest" (20b) by "the lions" (21a). A janus prayer that *I AM*'s glory endure forever and that *I AM* rejoice in his work (31–32) segues the cause for praise into the concluding calls for praise (33–35). The artistry of this exquisitely composed hymn itself brings glory and joy to *I AM*.

II. Exegesis

Superscript

By David (see n. 1 and "Author" above).

Stanza I (Introduction): Call to Soul to Bless I AM *1a*

Bless I AM, *my soul* (see 103:1).

18. Light (v. 2a; day 1); "firmament" (vv. 2b–4; day 2); land and water distinct (vv. 5–13; day 3); vegetation and trees (vv. 14–18; day 3); sun and moon as time keepers (vv. 19–24; day 4); sea creatures (vv. 25–26; day 5); land animals and man (vv. 21–24; day 6); provision of food for all (vv. 27–30; Gen. 1:28–29).

Stanza II (Body): Cause for Praise 1b–32

Strophe A: I AM *Is Great in the Heavens 1b–4*

1. *I AM* Is Great and Clothed in Stately Splendor 1b–2

a) I AM *Is Great 1bα*

You are . . . great ranks *I AM* above other gods (see 95:3). Indeed, he is exceedingly (*very*) so—that is to say, way above normal. In other words, no God even compares to him.

b) Clothed in Splendor: Wrapped in Light and Stretching Out the Heavens 1bβ–2

i. Clothed in Splendor 1bβ

His magnificent clothing sets him apart. *You are clothed* (see 93:1) is a metaphor for light and earth's domelike canopy, and *splendor and majesty* (see 96:6) are metonymies for his clothing. Whenever mortals speak of the divine realm, there is necessarily an "as if" quality.

ii. Wraps Himself in Light 2a

Wrapping yourself in light as with a cloak (śalmâ, i.e., a person's essential garment, a tunic; cf. Exod. 22:26; Deut. 24:12f). Intertextualities with Genesis 1 identify the light as the physical light of the first day of creation. Light connotes many blessings: order (overcoming chaos), life, salvation, safety, joy, sweetness, pleasure, and righteousness (Ps. 97:11; cf. Ps. 36:9). For this reason, on the Mount of Transfiguration, the face of the Lord Jesus shone like the sun and his clothes became dazzling white, bright as a flash of lightning (Matt. 17:1–8; Mark 9:2–13; Luke 9:28-36). The apostles liken him to "light" coming into the world (John 1:4–5; 2 Cor. 4:6).

iii. Stretches Out the Heavens 2b

Earth's dome is now pictured as a tent-top curtain. *Stretching out the heavens* (see Gen. 1:7) signifies that he extends the firmament—a crystal-clear dome by day and studded with stars at night—from one horizon to another (cf. Isa 40:22). *Like a tent* refers to a tent curtain (see n. 3).

2. He Built His Heavenly Temple on the Celestial Waters and Rides the Clouds 3–4

a) He Built His Heavenly Temple on the Celestial Waters 3a

The association of curtains with the tabernacle (cf. 1 Sam. 7:2; 1 Chr. 17:1) segues to the vivid imagery of likening *I AM* to a temple-builder *who lays the rafters of his upper chambers* or upper rooms on the roof of his temple, where the king had his private residence (Judg. 3:20; 2 Kgs. 1:2). This heavenly temple was imagined resting *on their* (i.e., the heavens') *waters.* The Egyptian sun god "sits enthroned in a bark in which he crosses the heavenly ocean."[19] A ninth-century BCE Assyrian icon shows the sun god Shamash seated on his throne. Beneath a canopy over his throne are symbols of the three celestial deities: Moon, Sun, and Venus. Under the throne are a number of wavy lines, representing the celestial ocean. The inscription reads that the stellar deities are situated "above the ocean." Beneath the heavenly ocean is a slab that divides the waters above from those beneath.[20] The upper chambers or storehouses above the firmament (Ps. 33:7) were imagined to hold the wind (135:7), snow and hail (Job 38:22), and rain, which were then released to fall upon the earth (see 104:13).

b) He Rides the Clouds and Makes the Wind and Lightning His Servants 3b–4

i. He Rides the Clouds Furiously 3b

In the poet's imagination, the Warrior-King transforms the swiftly flying storm clouds into his *chariot. Who makes* (or "transforms").[21] *Clouds* envisions dark

---

19. H. Bonnet, *Reallexikon der ägyptischen Religionsgeschichte* (Berlin: de Gruyter, 2000), 628; J. Spieggel, "Der Sonnengott in der Barke als Richter," *MDIA Abteilung Kairo* 8 (1939): 201–206.

20. Tryggve N. D. Mettinger, "YHWH SABAOTH—the Heavenly King on the Cherubim Throne," in *Studies in the Period of David and Solomon,* ed. T. Ishida (Tokyo: Yamakawa-Shuppansha), 119 (see the drawing on p. 120).

21. *The Concise Dictionary of Classical Hebrew* (Sheffield: Phoenix, 2009), 436, *śîm,* entry 6.

(1 Kgs. 18:45) storm clouds (Pss. 18:13[12]; 77:17[18]) swiftly flying on a horizontal plane (Isa. 60:8) accompanied with crashing thunder (Isa. 29:6) and bolts of lightning (Job 37:15). Though chariots were used for hunting, parade, and travel, we should probably think of a frightening war chariot. "In warfare, they were a mobile platform to shoot volleys of arrow to soften up enemy infantry."[22] *Who goes to and fro on the wings of the wind* clarifies and escalates the chariot imagery to portray the royal Charioteer's soaring speed, power, and supremacy in his use of the storm clouds. Jehu was legendary for his speed: "he drives like a maniac" (2 Kgs. 9:20; cf. Isa. 19:1).

ii. The Winds and Lightning Serve Him 4

The Charioteer uses the four *winds* (cf. Ezek. 37:9) as his official *messengers* (see 103:20). Hebrews 1:7 quotes this verse from the LXX, which translates "messengers" (*mal'ākîm*) as "angels." *Flames of fire* in this meteorological context is a metonymy for the bolts of lightning that are *his ministers* to destroy his enemies (see 97:3; 103:21; Joel 1:19).

Strophe B: I AM*'s Supremacy over the Earth 5–9*

Three inclusio capture *I AM*'s sovereignty and the reliability of the earth: (a) a pun on *yāsad* ("to found [the earth]," v. 5; "to fix [the seas]," v. 8); (b) "to cover the earth" (vv. 6, 9); and (c) the poetic negative *bal* ("not [moved]," v. 5; "not [return to cover]" v. 9).

1. He Firmly Established the Earth 5

The Builder (a royal function; see p. 4) *set* (or laid) *the foundations of the earth* (i.e., the dry ground) firmly.[23] "Founded" (*yāsad*) with the tautological object "foundation" (a derivative of *kûn*, "to be established") underscores the dry land's stability and permanence. And so *it will never*[24] *be moved*, toppled, or shaken off its base (see 93:1; 96:10). The stage for salvation history is fixed until the Parousia, when the Lord Jesus Christ will return before the general resurrection and before the new heaven and the new earth is created.

---

22. Leland Ryken, James C. Wilhoit, and Tremper Longman III, eds., *Dictionary of Biblical Imagery* (Downers Grove, IL: IVP Academic, 1998), 138.
23. Mosis, *TDOT,* 6:111, s.v. *yāsad.*
24. "Forever" (*'ôlām*; see 103:9) intensified by "and ever" (*wā'ed*, "and perpetuity").

2. He Removed the Abyss and Fixed the Sea 6–9

a) *The Triumph and Defeat of the Abyss in the Flood 6–7*

i. Its Rise in Triumph 6

You shifts the perspective from talking about God to addressing him directly (see pp. 98n1, 135). *Covered it* (the earth) could refer to the primeval abyss, and if so, the reference to the mountains would refer to submerged mountains that later appeared when he created the dry land (cf. Gen. 1:10). This would, however, be a unique reference to *I AM* directly causing the primeval, chaotic water apart from his creative word. To be sure, *the watery depths* (*tᵉhôm*) denotes the inexplicable and indeterminate primeval abyss (the *tᵉhôm* of Gen. 1:2, 9–10; cf. Ps. 93). But the assertion in verse 9 that the waters of the *tᵉhôm* would never again cover the earth must refer to the waters that broke forth from beneath the earth and brought on the great catastrophe of Noah's flood. This is so because the waters of the primeval abyss again covered the earth during Noah's flood (Gen. 7:11–20), but never thereafter (v. 9; cf. Gen. 8:2; 9:11b). Also, the reference to the waters covering the mountains finds explicit intertextuality with the flood story, not the creation story. In the flood *I AM* covered the earth, as when he overwhelmed the Egyptians in the Red Sea (Exod. 15:10; Pss. 78:53; 106:11; cf. Ezek. 26:19; Job 22:11).

I AM's triumph over the prevailing flood is presented in two battle scenes, personifying the waters as fleeing in fright at his rebuke. The first scene pictures their standing above the mountains (v. 6) and then their flight (7). The second reprises the first (8a) and then adds that *I AM* assigned them a place and restrains them forever within his set boundaries.[25] To *I AM*, however, they were nothing more than a *garment* (*lᵉbûš*), the most common Hebrew word for apparel/clothing (35:13; cf. 33:7). *The waters* of the abyss *stood* (i.e., took up their position[26]) and would have remained "upon" or *above the mountains* (Gen. 7:19–20)[27] had *I AM* not intervened.

---

25. In the biblical cosmology, the watery depths are thought of as under the earth (Gen. 49:25; Deut. 33:13; Pss. 77:16[17]; 78:15) and bounded as the oceans (Job 38:16; Ps. 107:26; Prov. 8:27; Jonah 2:5).

26. The preposition *ʿal* with *ʿāmad* possibly has the specialized meaning "to be in a position of authority" (cf. Num. 7:2; *The Concise Dictionary of Classical Hebrew* [Sheffield: Phoenix, 2009], 330, s.v. *ʿmd*, #2).

27. The lexeme *gābar* in Gen. 7:19, 20, though commonly translated by the neutral "rose," more literally means "to prevail" with a connotation of hostility.

ii. Its Flight in Defeat 7

At (i.e., "from," "by reason of") *your rebuke.* The fifteen uses of "rebuke" always occur in poetry and refer to a protest with moral indignation.[28] *The waters* (lit. "they") *fled* to remove themselves quickly from danger, as in battle.[29] The personification implies the hostility of the primeval sea to the creation. *I AM*'s rebuke, his voice, was heard as thunder. *At the crash* (lit. "voice," "sound") *of your thunder* is as in a whirlwind (cf. Ps. 77:18; Isa. 29:6), not a rainstorm; it speaks of power and hostility (Job 26:14). *They took to flight* continues to connote the hostility between the Creator and the primeval abyss. The Lord Jesus wielded the same authority when he rebuked the wind and commanded the sea (Mark 4:39).

b) *Their Fixed Boundaries 8–9*

i. Their Divinely Appointed Place 8

I AM did not rid the earth of the watery depths hostile to his creation; rather, he constrained them for his own sovereign purpose, and in that sense they are "good" (cf. Gen. 1:10). They will be eliminated entirely in the new heaven and new earth (Rev. 21:1).

ii. Their Fixed Boundaries 9

The repetition of verse 8 is emphatic.

Strophe C: I AM's *Gift of Life-Sustaining Waters 10–18*

The third strophe, about fructifying waters, consists of two units demarcated by the relative clause "[the one] who" (vv. 10, 13). These units cover the transformed waters from below (10–12) and rain from above (13–18). The second

28. Ten times, *I AM* is the Agent who expresses his moral indignation with devastating effects against his enemies: the fiendish power of nature (2 Sam. 22:16 = Ps. 18:15[16]; Job 26:11; Ps. 104:7; Isa. 50:2); nations (Ps. 76:7; Isa. 17:13; 66:15); his own people (Ps. 80:16; Isa. 51:20). Twice (Isa. 30:17 [2×]) Israel's enemies are agents who in the expression of their angry protests threaten utter effects. Three times, the wise threaten fools with devastating ruin (Prov. 13:1; 17:10; Eccl. 7:5).

29. S. Schwertner, *TLOT*, 2:725, s.v. *nûs.*

unit consists of two subunits of three verses: the water that provides the vegetation for mankind and domesticated animals (13–15) and the habitats of birds and vulnerable animals (16–18). Consequently, if the summary (13) is included with verses 14–15, the strophe is a triad of triadic verses, and a frame about beasts and birds (10–12, 16–18) is formed around mankind (13–15).

1. Of Water from Below 10–12

a) I AM *Makes the Fountains* 10

Springs denotes the places where the water from the subterranean depths springs up. As oceans, they destroyed the earth; as fountains, they nourish it (cf. Prov. 8:24). *The wadies* are sharply defined depressions of a valley or streambed, usually in desert areas, that are bone dry in summer but gulley washers in the rainy season (cf. Deut. 8:7; Isa. 35:6). *Their water* (lit., "they," a metonymy for the water that flows from the springs) *flows* (lit., "go") *between the mountains*. The great Sovereign rules the deadly seas and the fructifying springs, the dried-up brooks and the gulley washers.

b) *The Fountains Water Beasts and Birds* 11–12

i. The Beasts of the Field 11

The wild donkeys run freely and cannot be roped (Job 39:5), whether in a dry wilderness (Job 24:5; Jer. 2:24), on the barren heights (Jer. 14:6), or in the wastelands and salt flats (Job 39:6). Although they will not serve mankind, by *I AM*'s provision they *quench their thirst*.

ii. The Birds 12

The fountains also provide a habitat for *birds*. *They give voice* testifies to their thriving life, and *the foliage* is a metonymy for food and protection.

2. Of Water from Above 13–15

The catchword *śāba'* (= "satisfied," v. 13; "well watered," v. 16; see n. 7) marks off the units (vv. 13–15, 16–18). "Mountains" (13, 18) form an inclusio around the two units.

a) I AM *Provides the Heavenly Water* 13

Who waters (see v. 11) marks off a new unit (cf. v. 10). No distinction can be made in Hebrew between *mountains* and hills. Life-giving water, be it rain, dew, or snow, is pictured as coming from the *upper chambers* of *I AM*'s heavenly temple (v. 3). *From the fruit of his work* (see 90:17; 92:5; 103:22) refers to his laying the rafters of his upper chambers (v. 3). "Fruit"—probably a dead metaphor—is commonly used for the results of an action.[30] *The land* (*hā'āreṣ*, translated "earth" in vv. 5, 14) *is satisfied* (lit. "satiated," see 103:5). "Mountains/hills" and "earth" may be a merism for all arable land.

b) Vegetation for Humankind to Cultivate 14–15

Verses 14 and 15 are one sentence: a main clause ("he makes grass grow . . . for humankind to cultivate," v. 14a), followed by two purpose clauses (vv. 14b–15). The first of these ("to bring forth food and wine," vv. 14b–15a) is interrupted by the second purpose clause ("to make their faces shine from oil") in order to link wine and oil with the fall harvest. In any case, "even food" in 15bβ stands in a chiastic parallel with "to bring forth food" in 14b, and the two instances of "the heart of the mortal" stand as parallels in 15aα and 15bβ.

14 *Grass* refers to the "wild growth that comes up regularly and abundantly after the winter rains (Ps. 147:8). . . . As quickly as *ḥāṣîr* sprouts in the rain, it withers in draught (Isa. 15:6) or is found along streams at best (1 Kgs. 18:5)."[31] S. Amsler says of *grows*:

> [It] does not specifically concern the germ of the seed . . . or the bloom . . . but the entire dynamic phenomenon of the development and unfolding of the plant. . . . The author of this growth is the earth (*'ᵃdāmâ*, Gen. 3:18; 19:25) with its rich fertility (Job 8:19); but decisively significant is the water, especially the rain, which fertilizes the ground and causes it to produce plants (Gen. 2:5; Isa. 55:10; Job 38:27).[32]

30. *HALOT*, 2:968, s.v. *pᵉrî*, #3.
31. M. D. Futato, *NIDOTTE*, 2:246, s.v. *ḥāṣîr*.
32. S. Amsler, *TLOT*, 3:1085–86, s.v. *ṣmḥ*.

Animals may refer to both domestic and wild animals, but mostly to domestic.[33] *Plants* refers to plants in general, both for feed and food. *Humankind* (*'ādam*) is the broadest Hebrew term for human beings. *To cultivate* (*'ᵃbōdâ*) means "to work, labor" and recalls mankind's fundamental task as seen in the introduction to the creation of humankind ("There were not yet any people to cultivate the earth," Gen. 2:5), in their commission to cultivate and care for the ground (2:15), and in the repetition of this commission at the conclusion (3:23).[34] *To bring forth food* (*leḥem*) refers to all kinds of food, both animal and vegetable (cf. 1 Chr. 12:40[41]).

15 *The earth* refers to the ground (see v. 13). *And wine that gladdens* (*śāmēaḥ*; see 96:11; 97:1) *the heart* (see Pss. 95:10; 97:11) *of the mortal* (*'enōš*; see 103:15) shows that the Creator and Sustainer desires mankind to enjoy life, not to be workaholics. *To make their faces shine from olive oil* expands that notion. "In a climate where dry skin was a problem . . . anointing with oil was a refreshment."[35]

3. The Protective Habitat for Birds and Vulnerable Animals 16–18

This unit features the growth of trees planted directly by *I AM*, not by mankind, providing a place for birds to nest (vv. 16–17), and the notion of security segues into the mountain whose height protects the ibex and whose crags protect the hyrax (18).

a) Trees for Birds 16–17

16 Since the poet elsewhere moves from generalizations to the specific (e.g., v. 11), *the trees of* I AM probably refers to all the trees not planted and cared for by humankind, and *the cedars of Lebanon* (see 92:12) specifies the most majestic of these. If so, *he planted,* while grammatically modifying the "cedars," probably implies the other trees as well. In short, they are all "trees of *I AM*" because he planted them and they are *well watered* (see n. 7) by him.

17 Similarly, *there* modifies "the trees of *I AM*," not just "the cedars of Lebanon." *The birds* (*ṣipporîm*; perhaps "chirpers") is the generic term for commensal birds. *Make their nest* connotes security (cf. Jer. 22:23; Hab. 2:9). *The stork*

33. N. Kiuchi, *NIDOTTE*, 1:612, s.v. *bᵉhēmâ*.
34. C. Westermann, *TLOT*, 2:824–25, s.v. *'ebed*.
35. Ryken, Wilhoit, and Longman, *Dictionary of Biblical Imagery*, 603.

(*ḥᵃsîdâ*—related to *ḥesed*, "unfailing love"; see 103:17) exemplifies building a nest to protect its young. The *ḥᵃsîdâ* is so called because of its reputedly kind and loyal behavior to its mate and its young.[36]

b) The Mountains and Crags for the Ibex and Hyrax 18

The vulnerable *hyrax*, or rock badger, knows how to reside in security (see n. 9). The habitats of *high mountains* and *crags* in the Dead Sea rift may be a merism representing all protective habitats.

Strophe D: I AM *Made a Time for Everything 19–23*

In the fourth strophe, the night prowlers (vv. 20–21) expand upon the moon (19a), and day laborers (22–23) expands upon the sun (19b). The lion is lord of the night (21); mankind the lord of the day (23). As in the third strophe, the initial *creatio prima* (19a) is followed by *creatio continua* (19b–23). As in the other strophes, *I AM* controls the phenomena that both hinder and advance the interests of humankind.

1. The Moon and the Sun 19

This bicolon shifts from chronological monthly cycles marked by the moon (v. 19a) to the daily cycles marked by the sun (19b). "When *the moon* is mentioned alone (and not as part of the familiar triad of "sun, moon and stars"), the main purpose is to demarcate a time in the monthly cycle."[37] The personification, *the sun knows when to go down*, points to the ultimate rational Cause.

2. Darkness of Night for Predators 20–21

This unit neutralizes the danger that the night poses.

a) Summary Statement 20

If light provides human beings with life, safety, freedom, and success, then darkness deprives them of these blessings (cf. Pss. 6:6; 30:5; 42:3; 77:2). Never-

36. G. R. Driver, "Birds in the OT," *PEQ* 87 (1955): 5–20, esp. 17; Jack R. Lundbom, *Jeremiah 1–20*, AB 21A (New York: Doubleday, 1999), 510.

37. Ryken, Wilhoit, and Longman, *Dictionary of Biblical Imagery*, 565.

theless, *you ordained darkness and* [in conjunction with that] *it became night.* That is to say, *I AM* harnessed the inexplicable, primeval darkness to function as his timepiece to organize all life.[38] *The forest* refers to a dense collection of large trees and/or shrubs, herbs, and small vegetation with predators roaming in it. In biblical times, Israel's landscape was more densely forested than it is today (cf. Josh. 17:15, 18; 2 Sam. 18:6). "The forest is . . . used figuratively for danger (esp. wild animals in it threatening people)."[39] *Prowl* (lexeme *rmś*), of animals, normally means "to creep or crawl" (Gen. 7:8; Lev. 11:44; Deut. 4:18), but it can also denote more generally of land animals, as here, "to move about" (Gen. 1:28; 7:21).

b) I AM *Provides the Lion Its Prey* 21

The lions that *roar for their prey* epitomize the nighttime predator. "The Bible uses nearly a dozen words to designate lions of various ages and genders, but not all of these terms are securely defined. . . . Lion in the OT evokes ferocity, destructive power and irresistible strength."[40] As top predator, raider of live-stock (1 Sam. 17:34; Amos 3:12) and foe with legendary strength, the lion was feared, especially by pastoralists. The many references to its roar suggest that it was heard more often than seen, but even its voice, audible for miles, was a cause for concern: "The lion has roared; who will not fear?" (Amos 3:8). "When the lion is on the hunt, something is going to die," and "there is no way to pre-pare for its attack. It lurks secretly (Ps. 10:9), bursts from hiding, emerging from thicket (Jer. 49:19; 50:44; 25:38; Job 38:40) or forest (Jer. 5:6; 12:8). . . . Malicious in action, premediated in harm, ruthlessly efficient in killing, the lion meta-phorically embodies evil"[41] (cf. Ps. 7:2). Though the lion's roar terrifies its prey and humankind, God hears it as a prayer. *To seek* or to search for something missed implies a goal to fulfill or a plan to realize and connotes "to strive after something, be busy, be concerned." *Their food* (from the lexeme "to eat") can re-fer to cereal or flesh (Ps. 78:18, 30). It is also used for the prey of eagles (Job 9:26; 39:29) and ravens (Job 38:41). It is used uniquely here with wild animals. The psalmist, not the lion, knows it is seeking its food *from God*, who has an unlim-ited abundance of power and a presence that overcomes the barriers of time[42]

38. Ryken, Wilhoit, and Longman, *Dictionary of Biblical Imagery*, 594.
39. I. Cornelius, *NIDOTTE*, 2.492, s.v. *ya'ar*.
40. Ryken, Wilhoit, and Longman, *Dictionary of Biblical Imagery*, 514.
41. Ryken, Wilhoit, and Longman, *Dictionary of Biblical Imagery*, 30.
42. Artur Weiser, *The Psalms*, OTL (Philadelphia: Westminster, 1962), 597.

(Pss. 90:2; 95:3; 99:8). The personification again points to the ultimate Cause of the predator.

3. Daytime for Humankind to Work 22-23

a) At Sunrise, Animals Retreat to Their Dens 22

The catchword "sun" shows that *I AM* (v. 19) ordains the sun's rising and the removal of the dangerous night (v. 22). *The sun* (v. 19b) *rises* refers to the routine cycle of life: "an image of order in the Bible—a point of reference in a predictable universe."[43] The Preacher says, "Light is sweet, and it is pleasant for the eyes to see the sun" (Eccl. 11:7).

b) And People Go Out to Their Work until Evening 23

I AM provides beasts and mankind their habitats that assure life for both of them.

Strophe E: I AM *Made the Sea Creatures 24-26*

This strophe features all of God's works, with a focus on the sea and its creatures. After the introductory summary statement (v. 24), the stanza consists of two units, featuring the sea and its creatures (25-26) and the dependence of all creatures on the living God for their lives (27-30). The strophe ends with a wish that God's glory and joy—with reference to his works—will endure forever (31-32). "Your/his works" forms an inclusio around the strophe (24, 31).

1. Summary Statement 24

The exclamatory praise *how many are your works* (v. 24), I AM! shifts the focus from the activity of humankind, which is restricted by time, to *I AM's* unrestricted works. The tricolon's three parallels emphasize the large number and variety of God's creatures: "many," *them all* and *full of. In wisdom* adds their superb quality to their quantity. "Wisdom" generally means "masterful understanding," "skill," "expertise."[44] *You made* (see v. 4) is the verbal counter-

---

43. Ryken, Wilhoit, and Longman, *Dictionary of Biblical Imagery*, 826.

44. M. Saebo, *TLOT*, 2:420-22, s.v. ḥkm; Michael V. Fox, *Proverbs 1-9*, AB 18A (New York: Doubleday, 200), 32-34.

part to the noun "works" and matches the summary statement that *I AM* made the temporal habitats of his creatures (v. 19). As in the other strophes, the poet moves from God's creation to his sustenance. *The earth*, unlike its earlier uses with reference to the land, refers to what we would call "planet earth"; this is so because here it is also the topos of the sea creatures. *Your creatures* (see n. 12).

2. The Sea, Ships, and Leviathan 25–26

The unit on sea creatures consists of a summary statement about the vastness of the sea and its innumerable creatures (v. 25) and then describes humankind triumphantly sailing in ships on its surface while the dreaded Leviathan frolics (see Job 41) in its depths (v. 26).

a) The Vastness of the Sea and Its Innumerable Creatures 25

There is the sea, the remnant of the original inexplicable and indeterminate abyss that was hostile to life, that—in the flood—destroyed earth, and that still poses a threat to life (Pss. 93; 104:6–9). Though restricted within boundaries that it cannot transgress, it nevertheless is still *vast and spacious. Teeming with creatures* beyond number matches the geographic extent. *Living things* is the same word for the wild animals qualified as living on the plains (v. 11) and in forests (v. 20) and here is used of aquatic animals, which are not domesticated, living in their own habitat. The merism *both small and large* adds to the notion of innumerability and extensive variety.

b) Ships and Leviathan 26

As elsewhere, the poet shifts from generalizations to particular exemplars: ships and Leviathan. This unlikely coupling was in the realm of God's wisdom. *There the ships go to and fro* (see vv. 3, 10) is a metonymy for humankind's presence in, and perhaps relative mastery over, the vast sea. Isaiah 27:1 describes *Leviathan* as a twisting serpent, a dragon in the sea. This imagery, not theology, is taken from a Baal myth that refers to destroying *Litan* (*ltn*), the coiling serpent, the tyrant with seven heads. *Ltn* is probably a variant of Hebrew *lwytn* (Leviathan); they are cognate with *liwwah* ("wreath," "twisting one"). In the Ugaritic myth, the coiling serpent is also described as a dragon with seven heads. "The heads of Leviathan" in Psalm 74:13 reprise this dragon. Along with other monsters, Leviathan symbolizes the threat to the divine cosmic order. Psalm 104:26, however, reduces this hideous and threatening image to the divine cosmic order to nothing more than a rubber ducky playing in a tub. *Which you formed* points to God's sovereignty and craftsmanship. *To frolic* denotes generally "to make merry, to play." Here it has a positive sense expressing joyful vitality and favor in actions, involving dancing and making merry in general (1 Sam. 18:7; Jer. 15:17; cf. Prov. 26:19). *In it* transforms the dreaded sea into a habitat totally under God's control and to be enjoyed.

Strophe F: All Creatures Owe Their Existence to I AM *27–30*

All creatures depend upon God for their food (vv. 27–28) and for their very life (vv. 29–30).

1. Their Food 27–28

The catchword "give" (vv. 27b, 28a) binds 27 and 28 into a quatrain. Verse 27, personifying the animals, pictures the animals looking to God for their food, and verse 28, using anthropomorphism, pictures God giving food to the animals. The double perspective emphasizes the dependence of all animals on God for their food and his care for them.

a) *The Creatures Look to* I AM *for Food 27*

All [of them] reprises "them all" in verse 24 and so points to all "your works" (i.e., *creatures*) as the antecedent, not just the sea creatures of verse 26. *Look* signifies to hope for something (e.g., "salvation," Ps. 119:166; "faithfulness," Isa. 38:18) or to wait for something (e.g., "until they are grown," Ruth 1:13). Here they look *to you* (*I AM*)—as known by the psalmists, not by the animals—to *give them their food* (see v. 21). *At the appointed time* refers to a definite or fixed point in *I AM*'s calendar (e.g., when crops mature, birds migrate, etc.; see Ps. 1:3). Elsewhere, the psalmist says, "You open your hand; you satisfy the desire of every living thing" (145:15–16).

b) I AM *Tenderly Feeds Them 28*

The syntax making the animals' feeding conditional upon *I AM* giving them their food implies the close relationship between God and the animals. This is further underscored by the emblematic parallelism. The prosaic *when you give [it] to them* (see v. 27) is pictured in the parallel *when you open your hand*. God feeds them as human beings feed their pets. *They gather it up* slows the action down, picturing the animals picking up their food piece by piece. "Gather up" is used of collecting stones to make a heap (Gen. 31:46) and of the bread rained down from heaven (Exod. 16:4). *They are satiated* (*yiśbeʿûm*; see vv. 13, 16) shows that God supplies them with more than they need. An apple tree does not reproduce itself with one apple but with hundreds (see "Conclusion" below). In addition to its abundant quantity, its quality is signified by the metonymy *good* (see 100:5).

2. Their Breath 29–30

The catchword "breath" binds verses 29 and 30 into a quatrain. Now the close relationship between *I AM* and his creatures can be seen in linking "their breath" with "your [God's] breath." The conditional syntax of both verses further underscores this close relationship. Verse 29 features the taking away of this breath and the creatures' death, and verse 30 features his giving them breath and so creating each one, as he had done at the beginning of life on the fifth and sixth days of the Genesis creation account.

a) *Takes Away Their Breath and They Die* 29

The tricolon, like an expanding telescope, slowly unpacks the hard reality of the creatures' death: from "you hide your face" to "you take away their breath" to "they expire" (i.e., the act of dying) to "they return to dust" (i.e., their burial). *When you hide your face* signifies the end of a relationship. A. S. van der Woude comments, "Statements in which 'God's face' appears as the obj. of an action concern the bestowal of his grace or life-giving or disaster-bringing glance."[45] "To hide your face" signifies God's withdrawing his presence and benevolent guardianship. Wehmeier comments, "Just as turning the face toward someone signifies friendliness and favor, turning away or concealing the countenance expresses displeasure."[46] He adds, "God conceals his countenance from a person as an expression of wrath. Expressions that parallel and contrast with *str* Hiphil *pānîm* ['hide the face'] make this concept esp. clear" (e.g., "forget," "abandon," "smite," "be angry," "scorn," "abhor," "reject," "cast aside").[47] "A hidden face ignores requests for help (Pss. 13:1; 69:17) and refuses to answer

---

45. A. S. van der Woude, *TLOT*, 2:1006, *pānîm*.
46. G. Wehmeier, *TLOT*, 2:815, s.v. *str* Hiphil.
47. Wehmeier, *TLOT*, 2:817, s.v. *str* Hiphil.

(102:2)."[48] No wonder *they are terrified* (see Ps. 104:29). *Take away . . . breath* signifies "to cause to die."[49] *Rûaḥ* refers to "breath" as in "the breath of God is in my nostrils" (Job 27:3).[50] R. Albertz and C. Westermann comment, "The basic meaning of *rûaḥ* is both 'wind' and 'breath', but neither is understood as essence; rather it is the power encountered in the breath and wind, whose whence and whither remains mysterious." These authorities continue that the reference to breath "is not as a constant phenomenon but as a force expressed in respiration. . . . *Ruah* does not indicate 'normal' breathing, a component of human life . . . , but the particular process of breathing that expresses the human being's dynamic vitality."[51] Similarly, *gāwaʿ* ("expire") means "essentially to gasp for breath" and so "to pass away"[52]—the act of dying (Gen. 25:8; 49:33). *And they return* (Ps. 90:3) *to the dust* (Ps. 103:14), one of several collocations for death (cf. Job 34:15; Eccl. 3:20), recalls that mankind's body originates from the ground.

b) Sends His Breath and They Are Created 30

By contrast, every living creature owes its extraordinary creation to *I AM*'s sovereign, free grace, by which he gives them his breath of life; they are not merely the material of their begetter. *When you send* (i.e., "send out") *your breath* (see v. 29) recalls Moses' address to *I AM* as "the God who gives breath to all living things" (Num. 16:22). As for *they are created*, *I AM*, not a foreign deity, is always the agent of "to create," here a divine passive. W. H. Schmidt notes:

> Its object is always new and extraordinary: heaven & earth (Gen. 1:1); people (1:27); people of Israel (Isa. 43:1); wonders and novelties (Exod. 34:10; Num. 16:30; Isa. 48:6f; 65:17; Jer. 31:22; cf. Isa. 41:20; 45:8; Ps. 51:10; 104:30). . . . The determinative factor is not that there was 'nothing' prior to creation but that God's activity brings about something new, which (as such) did not exist before. . . . On its own, then, the verb does not describe a creation ex nihilo, but it refers precisely to that which other systems of thought . . . seek to ensure through discussion of creation

48. Ryken, Wilhoit, and Longman, *Dictionary of Biblical Imagery*, 260.
49. J. F. A. Sawyer, *TLOT*, 3:1100, s.v. *qbṣ*.
50. *HALOT*, 2:1198, s.v. *rûaḥ*, #1.
51. R. Albertz and C. Westermann, *TLOT*, 3:1203, s.v. *rûaḥ*.
52. *HALOT*, 1:184, s.v. *gwʿ*.

ex nihilo: God's extraordinary, sovereign, both effortless and fully free, unhindered creation.[53]

And you renew signifies to craft again as a new thing, in contrast to what is old or former and/or not yet in existence (see Ps. 103:5). *Face of the ground* refers to the surface[54] of the reddish-brown productive earth (humus) that produces and sustains vegetation, the basis of creatures with the breath of life.

Strophe G (Janus): Prayer That I AM's Glory and Joy Endure Forever 31–32

The final strophe, a quatrain, ends with petitions for *I AM's* glory and joy. The volitional mood segues into his concluding prayers that his meditation be pleasing to God and that sinners cease from the earth. The quatrain consists of the two petitions (v. 31) and a characterization of *I AM's* fearful sovereignty as seen in earthquakes and volcanoes (v. 32).

1. Prayer for *I AM's* Glory and Joy 31

Verse 31a pertains to *I AM's* glory forever and 31b to his joy in his works. The parallels suggest that *I AM's* glory is a metonymy for his works—that is to say, his creatures—and that "forever" is gapped in 31b. *May* expresses a prayer, not merely a wish. *The glory of* I AM denotes both a substantive aspect—his actual properties—and his action or disposition toward *his works* (v. 24), with which he renews the earth (30). Israel should declare this glory to the nations (Ps. 96:3). *Forever* (93:2) entails that God continue to renew the earth through his perpetual re-creation of the innumerable and various species (30). *May* I AM *rejoice* (see Pss. 96:11; 100:2) means "may he spontaneously dance for joy at each new creation." He rejoiced in his original creation, calling it "good." At that time, the angels sang for joy (Job 38:7), and Woman Wisdom was filled with delight (Prov. 8:30f.). He continues to do all things according to his pleasure (103:21). And so, as the Leviathan frolics in the sea (v. 26), *I AM* dances in heaven with him. *In his works* refers to all that was produced by his creative deeds, including predator and prey, the wild animals of the plains and of the forests (v. 13, 24), and the infinite variety of sea creatures, including the dragon.

53. W. H. Schmidt, *TLOT*, 1:255, s.v. *br'*.
54. A. S. van der Woude, *TLOT*, 2:1002, s.v. *pānîm*.

2. Sovereign Can Undo the Creation by a Look or a Touch 32

As the preceding quatrain combined *I AM*'s dispensing death (29) and life
(30), so the prayer combines *I AM*'s joy with his anger. Both give him glory.
The trembling earth (v. 32a) and the smoking mountains (32b) occur simultaneously, as when *I AM* descended on Mount Sinai in fire: "The smoke bil-
lowed up from it like smoke from a furnace, and the whole mountain trembled violently" (Exod. 19:18). But here he merely *looks at* (directs his eyes
upon) and *touches* them with his hands (cf. v. 28), so close is his relationship
to them. But this time, the earth trembles before the wrathful divine Warrior
at the prospect of divine judgment (Judg. 5:4; 1 Sam. 14:15; Pss. 18:7; 29:8; 77:18;
97:4). Earthquakes and fire symbolize the angry God's power and holiness;
they are weapons of holy war (Isa. 13:13; 29:6). *The mountains* (cf. vv. 6, 10),
though ancient and firm, now smoke as a consequence of his wrathful touch
(cf. Ps. 144:5–6).

This prayer functions as a janus to the concluding petition. It looks back
to the hymn's main body—the cause for praise—by celebrating *I AM*'s works
(v. 31) and characterizing his greatness with a relative clause ("who . . . "). It
looks ahead by shifting from the indicative to the volitional mood and shifting
the address to an imagined audience, not to God.

Stanza III: Conclusion

The hymn's conclusion consists of a contribution formula (vv. 33–34), a petition that sinners vanish from the earth (35a) and renewed calls to praise (35b).

Strophe A: Contribution Formula 33–34

Gunkel calls this final word a "contribution formula," with which the singer
lays his composition before the throne of God, praying *may my meditation*
(see n. 15) *be pleasing to him.*[55] His hope is couched in his resolves: *I will* (not
"shall") *sing* (see Ps. 96:1) *to* I AM *as long as I live* (v. 33a) and *as I rejoice* (see
v. 31) *in* I AM (v. 34b). *I* (emphatic) *will sing praise . . . as long as I am* signifies that he will be playing a musical instrument to produce the melody that
accompanies his sacred song (Pss. 33:2; 98:5a; 144:9; 147:7; see pp. 25, 107, 171).
He offers his song *to my God* (see 100:3).

55. Gunkel and Begrich, *Introduction to the Psalms*, 40.

Strophe B: Prayer That Sinners Vanish 35a

May sinners (103:10) *vanish from the earth* (see v. 32) *and the wicked be no more.* "Wicked" denotes a community that is guilty of sins of thought, word, and deed, betraying their inner hostility to God and his people.[56] They mar the creation and have no rightful place in it.

Strophe C: Calls to Praise 35b

1. To Self 35bα

Bless I AM, *my soul* (see v. 1).

2. To Others 35bβ

Praise I AM ("Hallelujah") denotes an interpersonal exchange in which one makes a favorable judgment of *I AM*'s person, expresses publicly their admiration of *I AM*, and asks the members of their audience—the form is plural—to join in bestowing honor on *I AM*.

PART III. VOICE OF THE CHURCH IN RESPONSE

God's providence, like God's praise, is profoundly deep in its meaning. God, in his love for mankind, has had the foresight to see what humans need for their preservation, growth, superintendence, and teleological orientation—for becoming the image and likeness of God. In the whole sweep of the cosmos and of human history, God has been expressing his kingship by acts of providence. As human horizons have expanded, both soteriologically by the incarnation and more recently through the developments of the human sciences, so our praise expands to ever new horizons.

But until the early seventeenth century, the Tudor zeitgeist was still influenced by astrology. In an excellent essay on the subject, C. S. Lewis observes,

56. K. Richards, "A Form and Traditio-Historical Study of *rš'* " (PhD diss., Claremont, CA, 1970; cf. *ZAW* 83 [1971]: 402). C. van Leeuwen (*TLOT*, 3:1262, s.v. *rš'*) says, "In contrast to the positive root *ṣdq*, *rš'* expresses negative behavior—evil thoughts, words and deeds—antisocial behavior that simultaneously betrays a person's inner disharmony and unrest (Isa 57:20)."

"We must never allow ourselves to think of astrology as something that belonged to the romantic or dreaming or quasi-mystical side of the mind. . . . Astrology was a hard-headed, stern, anti-idealistic affair; the creed of men who wanted a universe which admitted no incalculables."[57] Just as today we resist the principle of determinism, seeking free will, so did early-modern Christians. It was, then, an easy transition for the findings of astronomy in the seventeenth century, which gave more clarity to determinism, to give prominence to the theme of divine providence acting in concert with free will. At that time, Psalm 104 began to be interpreted as a celebration of this theological theme.

At the beginning of this change were latter Puritans in England, such as Matthew Henry (1662–1714), though later voices, like that of William Swan Plumer (1802–1880), also took up the theme.

I. Matthew Henry (1662–1714)

Matthew Henry was an influential commentator. He thought the same hand that had composed Psalm 103 followed with Psalm 104, like concave and convex perspectives. He divides it into seven themes: (a) the splendor of God's majesty in the upper celestial realm (vv. 1–4); (b) the creation of the sea and the earth (vv. 5–9); (c) the provision the Creator makes "for the maintenance of all his creatures according to their nature" (vv. 10–18, 27, 28); (d) the "regular course of the sun and the moon" (vv. 19–24); (e) the "furniture of the sea" (vv. 25–26); (f) "God's sovereign power over all creatures" (vv. 29–32); and (g) "a pleasant and firm resolution to continue praising God" (vv. 33–35).[58]

In the commentary that follows, Henry begins by saying that any service of worship begins with a summons "to stir up ourselves to take hold on God" in the worship (Isa. 64:7). With all our faculties, we cry out: "Bless *I AM*, my soul! . . . You are very great!" The psalm uses various symbols to express the sovereignty of God: his robes; his palaces in the heavens; the thick clouds that conceal his mystery yet act like chariots in which he rides strongly, swiftly, and with no opposition whatever; his retinue of angels—spiritual beings who are

---

57. C. S. Lewis, *Studies in Medieval and Renaissance Literature* (Cambridge: Cambridge University Press, 2007), 55–56.

58. Matthew Henry, *Commentary on the Whole Bible* (Chicago: Fleming H. Revell, n.d.), 626–27.

as a flame of fire (cf. Ezek. 1:14; Heb. 1:7) and like a flash of lightning. Yet "He is not so taken up with the glories of his court as to neglect even the remotest of his territories; no, not the sea and dry land."[59]

"He has founded the earth, v. 5. Though he has *hung it upon nothing* (Job 26:2) . . . as immovable as if it had been laid upon the surest foundations." God has "set bounds to the sea" (v. 6), which is also his. His mighty voice has strange effects of awe and fear (Ps. 77:16). For "he keeps it within bounds" (v. 9).[60]

"Having given glory to God as the powerful protector of this earth . . . [the psalmist] now comes to acknowledge him as its bountiful benefactor, who provides conveniences for all creatures": fresh water, from springs for their drink (vv. 10–11), food appropriate to man and beast (12–15), and protection. Our response is to be "humble and thankful," to delight in those gifts and to make our faces shine with joy.[61] God also takes care that all his creatures have suitable habitation, whether birds or animals (vv. 12–18).[62]

God's creatures teach us to praise and magnify him (vv. 19–30). There is no context where God's providence is not operative, so even the wide sea is provided for us as the sphere for shipping routes, and within it the mysterious sea monster Leviathan, "playing in the waters," and innumerable fish of all kinds have their habitat (25–26). All creatures are appropriately supplied within their seasons. But when God "hides his face," all are terrified, and when God's breath of life is withdrawn, they perish (28–29). For it is his Spirit that creates and sustains everything (30).[63]

"The psalmist concludes this meditation with speaking." We are to praise God (vv. 31–35). As a great God, his glory endures forever; as a gracious God, he rejoices in his works. Because he is a God of mighty power, the earth trembles at his look, and the hills smoke at his touch (31–32). Uniquely, it is man who sings and praises him; in joy he meditates upon God (vv. 33–34). But the wicked will vanish off the earth (35). Finally, for the first time in the psalm, "Hallelujah" ("praise *I AM*") is vocalized in climactic praise (cf. Rev. 19:1–10). [64]

---

59. Henry, *Commentary on the Whole Bible*, 627–28.
60. Henry, *Commentary on the Whole Bible*, 628.
61. Henry, *Commentary on the Whole Bible*, 629.
62. Henry, *Commentary on the Whole Bible*, 630.
63. Henry, *Commentary on the Whole Bible*, 630.
64. Henry, *Commentary on the Whole Bible*, 632.

II. William Swan Plumer (1802–1880)

William Swan Plumer lived in a very different age from that of Matthew Henry. Linguistics had taken a leap forward in interpreting Hebrew, Chaldean, Syriac, and other relevant languages that were largely closed to the Puritans but were open to Plumer's generation. A new generation of Commentaries on the Psalms was also available to him. Following biblical references closely in his commentary, Plumer is less focused on the phenomenal mysteries of the creation than he is on following the text grammatically and pursuing intertextual connections.[65]

Plumer interprets Psalm 104 as teaching and illustrating the great doctrine of providence: *I AM* will provide.

> 30. . . . If God cares for the *storks* and *conies* and all the myriads of living things in the air, earth and water, which is yet of comparatively little value, surely he will not forget his people.
>
> 31. If the human mind were not so besotted in guilt and enveloped in darkness, there never would be a doubt respecting the truths of natural religion; so abundantly are they declared and published in all the works of God.
>
> 32. No doubt this Psalm is fitly applied to the mediatorial reign of Christ, not only by the Apostle in Heb. i, but by pious men ever since. He made the world and it is his. He made the angels, and they are his. He made all nature and all nature obeys him. When on earth, the winds and the waves heard his voice and were hushed. He is the Lord of all.[66]

III. André Chouraqui (1917–2007)

We conclude with the contemporary French commentator André Chouraqui. A Jewish Christian, he combines his Hebraic scholarship with a Christian faith to deeply explore the text of Psalm 104.[67] He writes,

65. William S. Plumer, *Studies in the Book of Psalms* (Philadelphia: J. B. Lippincott & Co., 1866), 920–21.

66. Plumer, *Studies in the Book of Psalms*, 930.

67. I have consulted a Portuguese translation of Chouraqui's work: André Chouraqui, *A Biblia Livores, Salmos*, trans. Paulo Neves, vol. 2 (Rio de Janeiro: Imago, 1998), 193–94.

As a celebration of the light at the dawn of the day, so the psalm also celebrates the work of its Creator at the dawn of creation. Likewise, we see it celebrates the dawn of the new creation of the New Testament. As the Jewish scholar Kimchi observed, it celebrates the ability of the worshiper to sing. For the poet compares the dawn of day to a garment of light. As we know from the creation story, light is the first of God's creatures, while the universe is likened in ancient cosmogony to a building, whose roof retains the celestial waters (Gen. 1:6–7; Amos 9:6). Again, in alluding to ancient cosmogony in 6-7, the poet evokes the land as it was before the separation of the original waters and the two continents (Gen. 1:9–10), when the primordial sea existed.[68]

As we have insisted throughout our study of the Psalter, the poets may have used the worldview of their period of cultural history, but no forces are beyond the sovereign control of the Creator. God transcends all mythologies in all ages. This includes the new scientific hypotheses about the big bang or the electromagnetism of the stars or the gravitational pull of the planets. Without God at the center, as Psalm 104 celebrates, they are all variant forms of astrology!

PART IV. CONCLUSION

The theme of Psalm 104 is "*I AM*, my God, you are very great!" The psalm is a montage of images of Israel's God as Creator and Sustainer of all things. It begins with the radiant light and the splendor of the heavens that clothe the invisible God. Today, he is known through his Son, the Lord Jesus Christ, "who is before all things, and in him all things hold together" (Col. 1:17). He is "the Great Worker ever working."[69]

David describes *I AM*'s creation as seen with the naked eye, a very different perspective than scientific instruments can provide. The watery heavens above are separated from the earth below by a canopy that is translucent by day and star-studded at night. The flat earth is divided into dry land and the sea that is around and below it. The eyes of faith and reason see beyond immediate causes for the creation and its creatures to the ultimate Cause. When, in Psalm 139:13, David sings to *I AM*, the ultimate Cause, "You created my most

---

68. Chouraqui, *Salmos*, 193–94.

69. J. J. Stewart Perowne, *The Book of Psalms*, vol. 2 (Andover: Warren F. Draper, 1898), 225.

inward parts," he is not denying reproductive physiology, the immediate cause of David's development. David was unaware of evolution, but had he known of it, it would have been as inconsequential to him in Psalm 104 as sex was in Psalm 139. Secular man, however, prides himself on his insights into secondary causes, ignoring or denying the first Cause—the One who can be clearly seen (Rom. 1:19–20)—and so he stumbles to his destruction. A secularist is as foolish as a person who denies the existence of a magician because he discovers the trick. The faithful do not deny evolutionary creationism; rather, they marvel at the genius of the Creator who constructed a cell that could adapt to different habitats, becoming amazingly and gloriously complex. Evolution so understood is cause for praise, not unbelief.

I AM's sovereignty extends to all life, and there is majestic symmetry between all things. God should be praised for all, and that which threatens humankind should not be rashly exterminated. "Wildlife (10–12, 16–18)," notes K. Schaefer, "frames the domestic concern (13–15)."[70] And Zenger comments, "All creaturely life is received life."[71] What the apostle Paul says of mankind, "[God] himself gives everyone life and breath and everything else" (Acts 17:25), can be said of all creatures. People play only a supporting role in the cosmic drama (vv. 14–15, 23, 26). Thomas Gray's *Elegy Written in a Country Churchyard* eloquently expresses the disquiet of humankind apart from God. He writes,

> Full many a gem of purest ray serene,
> The dark, unfathom'd caves of ocean bear:
> Full many a flower is born to blush unseen,
> And waste its sweetness on the desert air.[72]

The faithful, however, realize every gem is seen by God and every flower is savored by God, and that makes all the difference.

From his heavenly temple, the Sovereign rides the storm clouds as a Warrior. As a Builder, he lays the foundations of the earth. As its Governor, he punished the earth once with a flood but will not do so again (vv. 6–9). In grace, he

---

70. Konrad Schaefer, *Psalms*, Berit Olam (Collegeville, MN: Liturgical Press, 2001), 257.

71. Karl Löning and Erich Zenger, *To Begin with, God Created. . .: Biblical Theologies of Creation*, trans. Omar Kast (Collegeville, MN: Liturgical Press, 2000), 43.

72. Thomas Gray, *Elegy Written in a Country Churchyard* (Boston: Estes and Lauriat, 1883).

not only tamed those seas and forced them to stay in one place, he transforms them into fountains to fructify the earth (10–12), and he adds the heavenly rain to sustain the vegetation that provides food for an innumerable and seemingly infinite variety of creatures. He does so with a largesse that staggers the imagination (13–15). The abundance of fertile seed since the creation makes the word "great" seem too small. At the same time, the Sovereign provides secure places of refuge for the exemplary stork and mountain goat (16–18).

He makes a time and place for everything. The moon marks off the nights, when the lion is lord; and sun provides the daylight, in which mankind is lord (vv. 19–22). But *I AM* is Lord of all. Ancient man feared the sea; the dragon epitomized his angst. But to *I AM*, the dragon is a rubber ducky floating in a tub.

The Sovereign is transcendent over creation yet immanent within it. He is intimately involved with each and every creature. He personally sends forth his own breath and creates each of them, and he feeds each as if with his own hands, as people feed their pets. He is dynamically turned toward, not away from his creatures. At the heart of the universe is a *joie de vivre*. *I AM* rejoices in his works, and the psalmist rejoices in him. *I AM* provides humankind with more than the water and the bread of the spring harvest; he adds the wine and oil of the fall harvest for their health and enjoyment. As the dragon frolics in the vast sea, *I AM* dances in heaven.

Nevertheless, this God must not be presumed upon. The psalm begins with the crash of thunder and with bolts of lightning and ends with the prayer that sinners vanish from the earth and that the wicked be no more. The closing scene of the cause for praise pictures *I AM* as merely looking at the earth, and it trembles; he touches its mountains, and they smoke. *I AM* who gives breath to "dust" also, in his anger, withdraws it, and creatures return to dust.

Here is a God worthy for the soul to bless and for people to shout, "Hallelujah!"

Glossary

Akkadian: an extinct Semitic language that was written in cuneiform and spoken in ancient Mesopotamia from the third millennium BCE until its replacement by Aramaic as the *lingua franca* in the mid-first millennium BCE.

anabasis: a figure for a writing, speech, or discourse, that ascends up step by step, each with an increase of emphasis or sense.

anadiplosis: a form of repetition in which the last word of one clause or sentence is repeated as the first word of the following clause or sentence.

anaphora: a literary device in which a word or phrase is repeated at the beginning of successive clauses for the sake of emphasis.

anthropomorphism: a figure of speech in which God is referred to as having human characteristics and/or functions.

antiphony: alternate or responsive singing by a choir in two divisions.

apodosis: the main clause of a conditional sentence. For example, "they will come" is the apodosis of "if you build it, they will come."

assonance: strictly speaking, the repetition of the sound or vowel in nonrhyming stressed syllables near enough to be recognizable. As used in this work it also includes repetition of consonants near enough to be recognizable.

bi-colon: the two halves of a colon.

Chaoskampf: a myth of cosmic war between nature deities.

cherub: a winged angel represented in ancient Middle Eastern art as a lion or bull with eagle's wings and a human face.

chiasm/chiastic: a rhetorical or literary figure in which words, grammatical constructions, or concepts are repeated in reverse order.

Cistercian order: a Benedictine reform movement established in 1098 by St. Robert of Molesme; the order emphasized solitude, recruitment of adult monks, and a return to manual labor.

clause: a unit of grammar consisting of a subject and a predicate.

colon: a line of Hebrew poetry; usually equivalent to a verse.

couplet: two verses united philologically and/or semantically.

covenant theology: a framework for interpreting Scripture wherein all the elect, both Jew and Gentile, participate in the covenants that God made with Adam and Eve, Noah, Abraham, Israel (the old being replaced by the new), and David. Since these all find fulfillment in Jesus Christ, the elect are unified by their faith in Christ.

desert fathers: early Christian hermits who, beginning in the third century, lived a life of asceticism in the Egyptian desert.

Donatism: named after their leader Donatus, this Christian movement in North Africa broke with the Roman church over the election of Caecilian as bishop of Carthage in 312. The Donatists opposed state interference in church life and possessed a strong ascetic discipline of penance and a willingness for martyrdom if necessary.

enjambment: a thought or sense, phrase or clause, in a line of poetry that does not come to an end at the line break but moves over to the next line.

form criticism: a method that seeks by common mood, grammar, and motifs to classify units of Scripture into literary categories. Normally, it then attempts to trace each type to its period of oral transmission; but that extension is not intended here.

hapax legomenon ("spoken once"): a word that appears only once in a defined corpus of literature.

hendiadys: two words that express a single thing or notion.

hymn: a song that praises God.

inclusio: a literary device used in Hebrew poetry in which key words or phrases are repeated at the beginning and end of a poem as a means of achieving closure.

Janus: a literary device deriving its name from a two-headed Roman god perched on a door and simultaneously looking forward and backward. In literature, it refers to a transitional passage that hearkens back to what precedes it as well as hearkening ahead to what follows, thus linking the passages together.

katabasis: a figure of a writing or discourse that descends step by step, each with a decrease of emphasis or sense.

lament (psalm): a song addressed to God that expresses the singer's feeling of being persecuted by enemies and abandoned by God and confidently petitions God for deliverance.

libretto: the text of an opera or other long vocal work.

litotes: a form of understatement in which something is affirmed by denying its opposite.

LXX (Septuagint): Roman numerals for "seventy," denoting the Septuagint, the oldest known Greek version of the Hebrew Bible, translated between the third and first centuries BCE in Alexandria. "Seventy" is a reference to the claims of the apocryphal *Letter of Aristeas* that 72 scribes took 72 days to complete the translation of the Torah; in common usage the term "LXX" has been extended to refer to the whole OT.

merism: from the Greek *merismos*, "distribution"; a literary device in which totality is expressed by referring to opposites or extremes; an example would be Genesis 1:1 where "heaven and earth" are used to represent the entire cosmos.

metonymy: a figure of speech in which some cause, effect, or circumstance pertaining to the subject is used for the subject itself.

Masoretic Text (MT): the authoritative text of the Hebrew Bible; in the seventh to tenth centuries CE, Jewish traditionalists (Masoretes) added vowel points, textual markers, and annotations in an attempt to preserve how the text was read; the oldest extant manuscript dates to c. 895 CE.

parallelism: the use in prose, but especially in a line of poetry, of balanced verbal constructions in grammar, sound, and/or meaning.

parataxis: the placing of clauses or phrases one after another without words to indicate coordination or subordination.

poetry: an elevated literary form in which special intensity is given to the expressions of feelings by terseness, concrete images, figures of speech, and some form of meter.

primeval: relating to the earth before it was made inhabitable.

prolepsis: the representation of something as existing before its existence.

prosopological: a representation of Christ from the perspectives of his humanity and deity.

protasis: the clause expressing some form of condition. For example, "if you build it" is the protasis of "if you build it, they will come."

pseudograph: a writing represented by an author other than the attributed author.

quatrain: a piece of poetry having four parts.

revia: one of the several disjunctive accents to indicate the syntax of a verse in the received Hebrew text.

rhetorical criticism: a study of how an author communicates meaning through various literary devices other than grammar, such as the structure of a literary composition.

scolia: grammatical, critical, and explanatory comments inserted in the texts used for teaching.

Second Temple period: the age from the construction of the Second Temple in c. 530 BCE to its destruction in 70 CE.

Sheol: the Hebrew term that denotes the grave and connotes the horror of death.

simile: a figure of speech involving the comparison of one thing with another thing of a different kind to make a description more emphatic or vivid.

stanza: the largest unit of a poem, unified by grammar and/or thought.

strophe: the largest unit of a stanza, unified by grammar and/or thought.

synecdoche: a figure of speech in which a part is made is to represent the whole or vice versa.

Syriac: the language of ancient Syria, a western dialect of Aramaic.

tautology: that unnecessary saying of the same thing twice.

Tetragrammaton (Greek, "four letters"): referring to God's name in Hebrew, YHWH, usually translated in English as "Lord," and in this commentary as "*I AM*."

type/antitype: a divinely intended exemplar by a person, place, or situation of a greater person, place, or situation.

typology: a unique species of promise and fulfillment. Whereas prophecy is concerned with prospective words and their fulfillment, typology is concerned with comparative historical events, persons, and institutions recorded in the Bible. Unlike allegory, which is a loose, literary device, typology is fixed by the biblical canon.

Ugaritic: an ancient Northwest Semitic language of Ugarit (in modern northern Syria), a small but powerful city-state that flourished between 1800 and 1200 BCE. Texts were unearthed at the site in 1928 by a French team of archaeologists and published in 1939. The deciphering of the language of these diverse texts (administrative, literary, and mythological) has helped clarify difficult Hebrew words and illumine parallels between Israelite customs and those of the surrounding cultures.

verset: a smaller part of a verse, unified by grammar and/or thought.

Vulgate (from the Latin *editio vulgata*, meaning "the common version"): this version of the Bible was translated primarily by Jerome, c. 383 CE. From the sixth century it became the accepted version of the Western church. In 1546, the Council of Trent decreed that it was the exclusive authority for the Bible.

zeugma: a figure of speech in which a word applies to two others in different senses. For example, "he *saw* the lightning and the *thunder.*"

INDEX OF AUTHORS

MODERN AUTHORS
(since the seventeenth century)

Index of Subjects

Aaron, 35, 242
Acedia, 23, 90
Akhenaten, Pharaoh, 295
Alexandrines, 3
Angels, 78n66, 83–85, 95, 237–38, 248, 280–81
Anger of God, 43–45, 47–49, 153–55, 157, 276–77, 286, 312–13, 315
Apotropaic psalms, 89
Arboreal imagery, 114–18, 306–7
Ark of the covenant, 15, 21, 77n63, 78, 179, 185, 195, 200, 236–38
Asaph, 34
Astrology, 316–17, 320
Augustine of Hippo: on confession, 157; on contemplation, 125, 263–64; on creation, 142, 156; on eternity, 57; on faith, 58; on forgiveness, 282–86; on God's judgment, 109n50; on God's reign, 287; on humility, 288; on incarnation, 224–25, 245–46; on justice, 246–47, 285–86; on love, 265; on praising God, 3–4, 124, 225, 264; on Sabbath, 121, 122, 124–25; on temptation, 90–91; *toto Christi* theme, 182
Authorship, 13–15, 34–36, 58–59, 67–68, 132, 146, 167, 190–91, 213, 233, 270, 295

Baal *versus* Yamm myth, 133–34
Beauty of God, 54–55, 86, 174
"Benefit of Christ Movement," 288
The Book of Common Prayer, 224

Bubonic plague, 77, 80–82
Builder, God as, 4, 137–38, 142, 150–51, 156, 160, 176, 208, 299–311, 320–22

Chaoskampf myths, 133, 136, 137, 143
Cherubim, 78n66, 237–38
Chiastic structure, 37, 44, 81, 82, 103, 113, 114, 119, 148, 150, 194, 218, 219, 227, 235, 237, 241, 255–56, 305
Christ. *See* Jesus Christ
Cistercians, 92–93
Civil millennialism, 206
Clothing, symbolism of, 299
Clouds: God speaking through pillar of, 243, 247; symbolism of, 195, 208, 210, 300–301
Contemplation, 58, 125, 247–48, 263
Creation: and destructive power of nature, 139, 197–98; God as creator, 4, 137–38, 142, 150–51, 156, 160, 176, 208, 299–311, 320–22; God praised by, 18–19, 177–78, 222–23, 227; God's power over, 139–40, 311–14, 318; and Sabbath, 120–23, 126–27

Darkness, symbolism of, 307–8
David: authorship of psalms, 13–15, 67–68, 132, 146, 167, 190–91, 213, 233, 270, 295; relocation of ark, 179
Death: certainty of, 40–43, 46–47, 278, 286; and God's breath of life, 312–14; as punishment for sin, 44–45

Grateful praise, 5, 101–2, 149–50, 162, 170,
191–92, 256–57
The Great Hymn to the Aten, 295

Hard-heartedness, 152–53, 157, 158–59,
160–61
Healing, 56–57, 274, 283–84, 285
Hexaemeron (Abelard), 126
Holiness of God, 141–42, 239, 245, 251–52
Honor and glory, 10, 19, 88, 168–69, 172,
174, 175, 186, 198–99, 314. *See also*
Righteousness
An Humble Attempt (Edwards), 206
Humility, 93, 142, 245, 287–88
Hymns, as genre, 5, 7, 135, 147, 168, 183,
191–92, 214, 233–34, 248–49, 270, 296
Hyperbole, 191

Idolatry, 11, 173, 199–200, 205, 209, 247
Image of God, 18, 96, 122, 156, 281
Inaugurated eschatology, 17–18
Instruments, musical, 181–82, 221–22,
225, 226

Jesus Christ: advent of, 206–7, 211; faith
in message of, 163; incarnation of, 95,
122, 224, 245–46; invulnerability of,
71–72; as judge, 187; and messianic
psalms, 70–72, 101–2; as name of God,
2–3, 260, 267; reign of God's kingdom,
61, 129–30, 205, 211, 229, 251–53; in rereading of psalms, 16–18; saving work
of, 71, 186, 224–26, 291; as shepherd,
151; temptation of, 90, 91, 95
John (apostle), 211
Joy, 7, 23, 107, 149, 156, 158, 177–78, 201,
207, 257–58, 259, 314
Judgment, 119–20, 178–79, 185, 187, 195,
210, 220, 224, 226, 240, 246, 275
Justification, doctrine of, 288

Kingdom of God: endurance of, 140–42;
established on earth, 9; under reign of
Christ, 61, 129–30, 205, 211, 229, 251–53
Kingship: as concept, 4; and enthronement festival, 19–22; of God, 132–33,

136–38, 151, 194, 201, 205, 210–11,
236–39, 279, 287, 299, 317–18; and
inaugurated eschatology, 17–18; and
protection, 74–75; and royal psalms,
68–70, 101–2

Lament, 31–32, 48–49, 59–60
Law, 140–41, 243–44, 285. *See also* Judg-
ment; Sin
Leviathan, 310–11
Life: brevity of, 40–43, 46–47, 49–50, 57,
278, 286; God's breath of, 312–14
Light, symbolism of, 203–4, 208, 299,
307–8
Lightning, symbolism of, 197–98,
300–301
Lions, symbolism of, 308–9
Longevity, as regal quality, 4
Love: faith working through, 58; for God,
86–87, 126, 202–3, 264–65; of God, 52,
122–23, 220, 261–62, 276–79
Lutes, 107
LXX (Septuagint), and Davidic author-
ship of psalms, 13–15, 67–68, 132, 146,
167, 190–91, 213, 233, 270, 295
Lyres, 181–82, 221–22

Majesty, as regal quality, 4. *See also*
Glory and honor
Masoretic Text (MT), and Davidic
authorship of psalms, 13, 270
Mercy and forgiveness, 51–52, 60, 231–
32n12, 244, 247, 252, 273–74, 276–79,
283–86, 291
Messianic psalms, 17, 70–72, 101–2
Miracles and signs, 153, 154, 163
Monks and monasticism, 90, 91, 92–93
Morality, 261. *See also* Sin
Mortality. *See* Life
Moses, 34–36, 58–59, 242
Mountains, symbolism of, 39, 198, 208,
305
Music: importance of musical psalmody,
180–82, 249–50; psalms as, 25–26;
used in praise, 106–7, 170–71, 213–14,
221–22, 225, 226

Index of Scripture References

354